T0333806

A Long Walk with Lord Conway

'It is life, after all, that is the greatest field of exploration.
We need not travel to remote places to find it.'[1]

Martin Conway

A Long Walk with Lord Conway

An Exploration of the Alps and an English Adventurer

Simon Thompson

Signal Books

First published in 2013 by
Signal Books Limited
36 Minster Road
Oxford
OX4 1LY
www.signalbooks.co.uk

A catalogue record for this book is available from the British Library.

ISBN 978-1-908493-80-4 Cloth

Production: Devdan Sen
Cover Design: Baseline Arts
Cover Illustrations: Portrait of Lord Conway of Allington by Augustus John
    (1930), The Samuel Courtauld Trust, The Courtauld Gallery, London;
    Simon Thompson
Front piece: 'Passage du Col de Burzil', from Ascensions et
    Explorations dans l'Himalaya (1894) (*Cambridge University Library*)
Maps: Sebastian Ballard
Printed in India

Contents

Acknowledgements and Sources

William Martin Conway, 1ˢᵗ Baron Conway of Allington, was born in 1856 and died in 1937. When his daughter, Agnes, died just 13 years later she left 14 packing cases of letters, manuscripts, papers and diaries to her friend and the executor of her will, Joan Evans. Evans sorted and catalogued the material and wrote *The Conways: A History of Three Generations* (1966), tracing the family history from the birth of Conway's father, William, in 1815, to the death of Agnes in 1950. After she completed the book, she gave those papers that she deemed to be of lasting interest to the Cambridge University Library. The papers contain a remarkable record of Conway's life, including an almost complete set of diaries from 1874 to 1935, over 2,000 letters to and from his parents, his first wife, his American parents-in-law, his daughter and several friends and acquaintances, as well as notebooks, articles, manuscripts, company prospectuses and press cuttings. I am grateful to the Cambridge University Library for allowing me access to these papers.

Joan Evans met Agnes in Rome in 1913 and they became close friends. Conway first recorded meeting Evans in 1918, when she visited Allington Castle in Kent. Her book, *The Conways*, was part of the inspiration for this book and an important source of reference for two reasons: it served as an invaluable cross-check as I tried to assemble a chronological record of Conway's life from his diaries, letters, articles, books and other sources; more importantly, it contains information and impressions that could only have come from someone who personally knew Conway, his first wife and particularly his daughter. *The Conways* contains some factual errors (as, no doubt, does this book) and reveals Evans' great affection for Agnes and her rather more ambivalent attitude to Conway, notwithstanding her assertion that she 'had, and have, an amused liking for Martin Conway; he was kind to me when I was a girl'.[2] However, without Evans' record of and insights into the lives of three generations of the Conway family, her personal knowledge of two of them, and her diligent sorting of the family papers, this book would not have been written.

I am also grateful to the Alpine Club, the Athenaeum Club, the Courtauld Institute, the Imperial War Museum, the National Portrait Gallery, Repton School, the Royal Geographical Society, the Savile Club, Seiler Hotels and Trinity College, Cambridge. I would particularly like to thank Romy Biner-Hauser, Louisa Dare, Jonathan Ford, Ruth Frendo, Prof. Lindy Grant, Tadeusz Hudowski, Glyn Hughes, Ruth Long, Julian Malone-Lee, Yvonne Oliver, Jamie Owen, Jennie de Protani, Jane Rosen, Peter Rowland, Jonathan Smith, Paul Stevens, Ian Thomas, Sir Robert Worcester and Edith Zweifel. Peter Hansen, Associate Professor at the Worcester Polytechnic Institute, Massachusetts, corrected several errors and provided numerous thought-provoking comments and new insights. Sebastian Ballard produced the excellent maps. Finally, I would like to thank Maggie Body and Brenda Stones, who helped to improve both style and content, and my publisher, James Ferguson, for his unflagging enthusiasm and support.

The spelling of numerous place names has changed over time and many towns and mountains in the Alps, particularly in the South Tyrol, have more than one name. In my text I have adopted the common English spelling (where it exists) or the name shown most prominently on the relevant national map. In the quotations, I have not altered the spelling adopted by Conway and others except in instances where the meaning is unclear.

THE ALPS

Chapter One
Departure

'We have secrets of our own, you and I – secrets that we never told
one another, even when we stood side by side together on the
mountain-top. But there was a thrill within each of us, was there
not? and each knew that with the other it was well.'[3]

The Alps, Martin Conway

On 26 August 1894, Martin Conway became the first man to walk the
Alps 'from end to end' when he completed a 1,000 mile journey
through Italy, France, Switzerland and Austria. On a midsummer's
morning, nearly 120 years later, I set out to follow in his footsteps.

Conway was born in 1856 and educated at Repton School and
Trinity College, Cambridge. After pursuing an American heiress across
Italy and marrying her in New York, he became the first Professor of Art
History in Britain at University College, Liverpool and later Slade
Professor of Fine Art at Cambridge. He was a pioneering explorer of the
Himalaya, Spitsbergen, the Andes and Patagonia, claimed the world altitude record in 1892 and was knighted for his 'remarkable work as a
traveller'[4] three years later. A newspaper article written in 1925 (one
year after Mallory and Irvine disappeared near the summit of Everest)
described him as 'perhaps the most famous of English mountaineers'.[5]
Conway discovered 'a great gold region, not improbably as rich and
important as the Rand'[6] and nearly cornered the Bolivian rubber
market with King Leopold II of Belgium. He was the founding director general of the Imperial War Museum, a Liberal and a Conservative
politician, and the first foreigner to see the crown jewels of Russia after
the revolution. He was also a prolific author and journalist, publishing
30 books and innumerable articles on art, architecture, climbing, crowd
psychology, exploration, skiing and travel. Shortly before he died he was
created 1st Baron Conway of Allington. Though largely forgotten today,
his name is still commemorated in the Conway Library in London,
Mount Conway in Canada, Conway Peak in New Zealand, Conway

Island in Antarctica and *Cochlearia Conwayi*, a small yellow flower native to Pakistan.

Conway was a clubbable man who 'knew everybody that was worth knowing'[7] and had a vast circle of friends and acquaintances in both England and America, drawn from the disparate worlds of art, literature, climbing, business and politics. Like most men of his class and generation, he was an imperialist, a racist and a snob. He was also a dreamer, a liar, a philanderer and a cheat. An adventurer in both the good and the bad sense of the word, Conway was a charming rogue who 'walked in sunshine all his life', according to contemporaries. But he was also a deeply discontented man, constantly searching for meaning and purpose in his life. And that search led him back, time and time again, to the Alps.

For most of history, the Alps were a remote and almost unknown region. Despite being at the heart of Europe, they were long regarded as peripheral: an ugly, unproductive and dangerous borderland that soldiers, merchants and pilgrims were obliged to cross as they travelled between northern Europe and the warm Italian south. Over time, the valley routes to the main passes became relatively well known, but the peasants who inhabited the stony pastures in amongst the highest peaks lived on the very margins of civilisation.

In the late eighteenth century, as industrialisation and urbanisation gathered pace on the northern European plains, this wasteland of rock and ice became the raw material from which poets and painters started to construct an imaginary idea. As science and technology enabled humankind to exercise ever greater control over their environment, the Alps came to be seen as a symbol of the savage majesty of 'unspoilt' Nature. Fear and abhorrence were gradually replaced by 'a sentiment of ecstatic wonder, not unallied to madness',[8] and the mountains were transformed into objects of beauty. Scientists turned the Alps into an outdoor laboratory where they developed and tested the emerging sciences of geology, botany and glaciology. Railways penetrated the region in the mid nineteenth century. Within a decade nearly all the highest peaks were climbed for the first time, most of them by English parties, and the Alps became 'the playground of Europe' – a ruggedly congenial meeting place for the English upper middle classes. As tourist infrastructure began to develop, remote and poverty-stricken mountain villages were transformed into popular holiday resorts for the rapidly expanding urban middle classes. Throughout this time, the imaginary construction of the Alps continued, as poets, scientists, painters, novelists, diarists, travel writers and guidebook editors added their emotional response to the mountain landscape. By the end of the nineteenth century, the Alps had become not so much a place as an idea – 'an appetite; a feeling and a love'[9] – and these vast inanimate folds and thrusts of rock, overlain by glaciers, forests and lakes, were shrouded in myths and memories.

In the early 1890s, Conway recognised that the Alps were sufficiently well mapped and described in guidebooks to 'devise a route, or rather a combination of climbs, the descent from each ending at the starting-point for the next, so that a climber might begin at one extremity of the snowy range and walk up and down through its midst to the other extremity over a continuous series of peaks and passes'.[10] He set out from the Col de Tende near the Italian port of Ventimiglia on 1 June 1894, arrived on the summit of the Ankogel near Salzburg in Austria 87 days later, and published an account of his journey the following year – *The Alps from End to End*.

Landscape is not just what you see; it is also how you look. Conway's book is both a record of his progress through a physical landscape of peaks and passes and a personal journey through culture, history and memory: an indirect account of the values, assumptions and beliefs – the 'what-goes-without-saying'[11] – of a late Victorian gentleman. I first read *The Alps from End to End* while researching a history of British climbing and it reawakened a long-standing ambition to make a long journey on foot through the Alps. As I read more of Conway's books, I began to recognise other parallels between his life and mine. Like Conway, I am the product of a middle-class upbringing, educated at one of England's old universities. As a young man I travelled widely in the Alps, the Himalaya, the Andes and Patagonia, unwittingly repeating many of Conway's climbing routes (all of them easy by modern standards). In later life I became a member of the Alpine Club, where Conway was President, the Royal Geographical Society, where he was Vice President, and the Athenaeum, which became his spiritual home in London. Like him, I have pursued a varied career, including working for a gold-mining company with interests in Bolivia and Peru – an industry that continues to attract its fair share of dreamers, liars and cheats – and trying my hand as a writer. As a result of these parallel experiences, many of Conway's descriptions of his life and travels were instantly recognisable to me, yet they were also strangely misshapen and deformed; familiar objects seen through the distorting lens of time.

The more I learned about Conway's life, the more I realised that, apart from the obvious limitation of being dead, he was the perfect companion for a long walk through the Alps: a man of wide and varied experience; a storyteller; and an acute observer of people and places. Here was someone who could point out not only the physical changes that have taken place in the landscape, but also how the English idea of the Alps has evolved over the past 120 years. So I decided to follow in his footsteps, and set out to explore both the mountains and the man. I read Conway's books, articles, lectures and public speeches, as well as his private diaries and personal letters. I visited the places where he was born, educated, lived and worked. And then I retraced his journey over the peaks, passes and glaciers of the Alps to discover how much of the world that Conway described still outcrops in the present, and how much lies buried beneath subsequent layers of history.

Chapter Two
Martin Conway 1856–94

How will it Affect my Eternal Destiny?

William Martin Conway, the only son of William Conway and his wife Elizabeth, was born in Rochester on 12 April 1856. He was preceded by two sisters: Elizabeth (Lizzie) and Martha (Minnie). During the course of his life, he was variously called Baby Brother, William, Will, Willie, Billy Boy, Josh and Herr von Konweg, but the name he used most often himself was Martin, and he later became Sir Martin and then Lord Conway.

Conway's grandfather was a prosperous wholesale grocer from Dorset. His first son inherited the business, while his second (Conway's father) was sent to Cambridge and entered the church. In due course, he became the vicar of a church in the Diocese of Rochester, England's second oldest cathedral, standing on the muddy banks of the River Medway in Kent. The family home stood on Boley Hill, the highest point in the centre of the small city. In an unfinished autobiography written around 1928 Conway remembered 'the great grim Castle to the left and the Cathedral to the right, with...a distant vision of the Brompton Downs surmounted by a countless row of windmills...All this comes back to me warmed with summer heat and enlivened by the sound of the Cathedral bells.' Charles Dickens, who also lived in Rochester at this time, painted a less bucolic picture of 'a monotonous silent city, deriving an earthy flavour throughout from its cathedral crypt'; a place of ragged street urchins, opium dens, and a cathedral close where tramps quickened their step 'that they may sooner get beyond the confines of its oppressive respectability'.[12]

Conway's father was a kindly, pious cleric, a member of the evangelical wing of the Church of England who, in return for being slightly looked down on in this world, anticipated significant preferment in the next. He expressed his philosophy of life in a letter to his son in 1875:

'This life is so short and uncertain, and eternity is so near and over-whelming, that our first thought in everything should be, how will it affect my eternal destiny?' During infrequent breaks from his religious work, his chief pleasure was to inspect new churches under construc-tion in the district, one of which, at Brompton near Chatham, he and his sister paid for and endowed with a good part of their inheritance when their aunt died. After her marriage, Conway's mother, Elizabeth, suppressed her natural gaiety, becoming 'dowdy in dress and prim in effect'[13] as befitted the wife of an evangelical clergyman. She took comfort in almost permanent ill health, requiring frequent visits to Folkestone, Bournemouth and other healthy resorts. Her husband wrote kind and affectionate letters to her, enquiring after her imaginary ail-ments, while his own health gradually failed.

In 1864, when Conway was seven, Lord Palmerston offered his father the Rectory of St. Margaret's, Westminster, with a canonry in the Abbey. It was a wholly unexpected preferment (the July 1864 edition of *The Churchman* described Canon Conway as 'unknown to fame and unheard of outside his own family'), reflecting the power struggle within the Church of England between High and Low Church. In his farewell address to the congregation at Rochester, Canon Conway observed that 'never was any appointment more...unlooked for' and confessed that he was 'more than ever impressed by the utter worth-lessness of worldly things compared with those which are spiritual and eternal'. Nevertheless, his new position carried an annual stipend of nearly £2,000 – a very large sum of money – and even when this was cut in half by legislation requiring that a higher proportion of the Abbey's income should be given to more needy beneficiaries than the senior clergy, Canon Conway's family remained very well provided for.

They lived at 17 Dean's Yard, adjacent to the Abbey, in a substan-tial London-brick Georgian house with a fan window above the front door. Canon Conway threw himself into his work, ministering to both the slum-dwellers of Westminster and the metropolitan elite. His appointment was designed to counterbalance the liberal views of the Dean of Westminster, Arthur Stanley, who was a prominent member of the 'Broad Church'. Educated at Rugby under Thomas Arnold, the influential headmaster, Dean Stanley, felt free to espouse his often controversial religious views because he held an unassailable position in society. He accompanied the Prince of Wales on a tour of Egypt in 1862 while his wife, Lady Augusta, the sister of Lord Elgin, often stayed with Queen Victoria, writing delightful little notes to her friends and acquaintances on royal stationery from Windsor Castle, Osborne House and Buckingham Palace. Meanwhile, young Conway roamed the precincts of the Abbey, taking a particular interest when Dean Stanley excavated some ancient tombs. In later life he claimed to have held the shrunken brain of King Richard II in his hand.

Conway's parents were torn between two competing notions of childhood: the first saw it as an age of charming innocence; the second as a time of depravity and barbarism. In general, the latter vision prevailed over the former, and their children were subjected to rigid discipline and expected to adopt adult standards of self-control from an early age. Like most Victorian members of the upper middle class, Conway's parents outsourced much of the rearing of their children, initially to nurses and servants and then to boarding schools. At the age of 10, Conway was dispatched to Holbrook Rectory preparatory school near Ipswich. After inspecting the establishment, his father wrote approvingly to his mother: 'I have seen the church...Sunday seems very well regulated. There appears everything here that is desirable.' Four years later, Conway went to public school. He wanted to go to Westminster School, but his father regarded it as insufficiently evangelical while his mother decided that he needed some fresh country air, so he was sent to Repton instead. Conway hated it: 'The discipline, the teaching, the games and the whole curriculum'.[14] But it was at Repton that Conway began to acquire the habit of taking and, in due course, giving orders: the essential self-confidence and authority that enabled a tiny English elite to rule over an Empire that spanned one quarter of the globe.

Outside school hours, Conway made regular forays into the countryside surrounding Repton, exploring churches and ruins, but his main interest was astronomy. He acquired a telescope, made a detailed record of sunspots, produced a star map and wrote a letter to his father asking whether it was permissible to study astronomy on the Sabbath. In common with other public schools of the day, Repton was more concerned with instilling a sense of Christian morality than providing an academic education. Like Thomas Arnold at Rugby, the school believed that 'what we must look for here is, first, religious and moral principle; secondly, gentlemanly conduct; thirdly, intellectual ability'.[15]

In 1872, at the age of 16, Conway caught his first glimpse of the Alps during a family holiday to Switzerland. In 1904[16] and again in 1920[17], he remembered it as a revelation: 'The sun rose in a sky perfectly clear. When I looked from my window across the green country over the deep-lying lake of Thun, I saw them – "suddenly – behold – beyond!" Jungfrau, Mönch, Eiger and the rest, not yet individuals for me…but all together a great white wall…a new revelation, unimaginable, indescribable…from that moment I also entered life.' His description deliberately echoed John Ruskin: 'At which open country of low undulation, far into blue…suddenly – behold – beyond. There was no thought in any of us for a moment of their being clouds. They were clear as crystal, sharp on the pure horizon sky, and already tinged rose by the sinking sun. Infinitely beyond all that we had ever thought or dreamed…It is not possible to imagine, in any time of the world, a more blessed entrance into life, for a child of such a temperament as mine.'[18] During the same holiday, Conway had his first experience of climbing a high alpine peak when he accompanied an older climber and his guide to the summit of the Breithorn above Zermatt. He did not return to the Alps for three years, but the high mountains had left an indelible impression.

Conway's parents expected him to follow in his father's footsteps, reading mathematics at Trinity College, Cambridge, before entering the church. He duly took the examination for a minor scholarship to Trinity in December 1873. Shortly afterwards Dr. Steuart Adolphus Pears, the headmaster of Repton, received a letter from the chief examiner: 'My colleagues in the Mathematical part of the examination, and myself (perfectly independently) detected Conway in several most clear cases of deliberately attempted deception. In three or four instances in each of the Mathematical Papers, a piece of Algebraical work which was totally wrong, became suddenly transformed in the last line and gave the right result which was exhibited in the printed paper…[A]fter utter confusion and a number of mistakes sheet 4 (so numbered) ends with the words "see next paper," and sheet 6 (so numbered) begins "From sheet

5 we have etc.," giving at once the result desired. This is the most deliberate falsehood I ever saw attempted in a paper...I feel that unless Conway is spoken to most seriously on the subject and induced to alter his ways, he stands a good chance of turning out thoroughly dishonest in other ways.'

Dr. Pears forwarded the letter to Conway's father and unfortunately also remembered that this was not the first time that Conway had been caught cheating. There had been similar deceptions with mathematical proofs in the past, and he had also been caught and punished for copying during a school examination. Utterly incapable of such deceit himself, Canon Conway was serenely certain of his son's innocence and wrote a letter to Pears, vigorously defending his son's actions. So far as the scholarship examination was concerned, young Conway maintained that he was dissatisfied with the work and so tore up the missing sheets before handing in the papers. That he had actually been caught in the act of copying during a school exam was harder to explain, but he rose to the task. His father's letter explained that 'he had in his pocket some drawings of Jupiter and some notes on his lessons. He affirms that the latter were not taken into the exam for the purposes of copying, but inadvertently; and that he did not copy from them. He says that in the course of the exam he amused himself by looking at his drawings...and on one occasion he drew from his pocket one of the papers containing the notes, but put it back as soon as he saw what it was.' His father continued: 'Let us suppose that this statement is untrue. Then one of two things must be inferred: either the boy must have had upon his conscience the burden of a persistent lie; or he must have cleared his conscience and be a confirmed hypocrite. The former can hardly be the case for he is a peculiarly light-hearted and joyous boy. Is the latter consistent with what you have subsequently known and said of him? Such sins rarely, if ever, go alone. Yet he has continually attended the Lord's Supper; he has been commended by you...; he has made close friendships with some of the best boys in the school (and boys are ordinarily the best judges of the truthfulness of their companions); and he has been trusted with the position of head of study and bedroom.'

It was to become a recurring theme of Conway's life that his popularity with his peers and position in society were called upon in mitigation of his often dubious behaviour. His father petitioned the Master of Trinity through a close family friend of undoubted probity and the matter was resolved in Conway's favour.

During his last year at Repton, Conway started the first of a series of diaries that form an almost unbroken record of his life from 1874 to 1935, two years before he died. Without third-party verification, it is impossible to tell how reliable large parts of them are, but I am inclined to think that they are fairly accurate. Apart from a few of his overseas trips, they were not obviously intended for publication, but rather form a private record of the people he met and places he visited. Conway's propensity to mould the truth to suit his purposes tended to increase in proportion to the size of the audience he was addressing: his diaries, in my judgement, are reasonably accurate; his letters less so; and his memoires clearly contain a number of deliberate inaccuracies and embellishments.

Conway's first diary records a home life dominated by religion, and as he grew older he found the pious propriety of family life increasingly intolerable: 'Every morning, at slow leisure...and even on the finest days, [father] gathered us into his room for Bible-reading and exposition, lasting often upwards of an hour. My impatience under this trial and the effort to hide it were almost unendurable. When at last the books were closed, I flung out into the open, hating Bibles and religion and bursting with desire for Nature.'[19] During school holidays in London he visited art exhibitions and attended the Children's Lectures at the Royal Institution, including several given by John Tyndall. Tyndall was both a distinguished scientist and a pioneer of alpine climbing, having made the first ascent of the Weisshorn in 1861. He was therefore a hero to Conway, who described his 1874 Belfast address to the British Association for the Advancement of Science as 'a glorious revelation'. Tyndall was a member of the influential X Club, whose purpose was 'devotion to science pure and free, untrammelled by religious dogma', and he used his 1874 address, in the heartland of Irish Protestantism, to argue for the superiority of science over religion. In the speech he claimed that science would provide a complete materialistic explanation of the physical world and its origins and advocated a rational and sceptical approach to religious dogma. His comments were sufficiently controversial to be reported on the front pages of newspapers in Britain and across Europe, and when the 18-year-old Conway read them 'the shackles fell off my spirit and a great sense of freedom came upon my mind...a gate was opened into a new world of thought'.[20]

After finishing school in the summer of 1874, Conway set off on a walking tour of the Peak District with two school friends from Repton. From Castleton, they 'walked up Cavedale which is splendidly romantic...Climbed to the top of Eldon Hill and had a grand view...Visited Peak Cavern and Blue John mines. Walked over moors to Chapel en le Frith for lunch at the Royal Oak...escaped from a man who said we were trespassing.' Back in London, he wrote up an account of his journey and 'got hold of a book called "Peaks, Passes and Glaciers" by members of the Alpine Club. Very much interested and took extracts.' He spent August in Ireland, staying with his schoolfriend George Scriven, who later captained the Irish rugby team, before joining his parents who were taking a cure at a spa resort in Belgium.

Conway moved into lodgings in Cambridge in October 1874, where he studied with private tutors. He retook the Cambridge entrance exams the following year and failed once again to win a scholarship, but was admitted to Trinity College in May 1875 and started university in the Michaelmas term of that year. Throughout his time at Cambridge he enjoyed an active social life: bicycling, canoeing, playing billiards and whist, going to lunch and dinner parties, attending the races at Newmarket and flirting with his friends' sisters during May Week. His parents wrote mildly reproving letters, to which Conway sent indignant responses: 'I don't know what has put it into everyone's head to write to me to tell me not to give up too much time to bicycling. I don't think that I have ever been out for more than two hours at a time.' However, his account of attending a promenade concert in Cambridge probably did little to allay his parents' fears: 'For about two hours there was a sort of bear fight going on in the hall. The concert was gone thro' with, but it was impossible to hear a note...In the scrimmage five men were collared by the police. About 11 o'clock at night the police station was attacked by the "Gown" and broken into but the police held their ground.' He also admitted that he had 'been forced into a great deal of society, sometimes considerably against my will', all of which left little time for the study of mathematics. As he noted in his diary: 'Cambridge life is so against early hours.'

As a young man, Conway had dark hair and a thick moustache. He shaved off the moustache when he was 46 but retained a full head of hair that gradually turned a silvery grey. By Victorian standards he was medium height – perhaps 5 feet 7 inches tall – and remained slim throughout his life (his shirt-maker's measurements, scribbled into his diary when he was 48 years old, were 'neck 15½; waist 27; chest 37'). He had a rather bulbous nose (later inherited by his daughter) and, as a result of undiagnosed short-sightedness in childhood, acquired the habit of staring intensely at objects and people even when they were quite close, a mannerism he did not altogether lose even when he started to wear glasses. Conway possessed great personal charm, and at Cambridge he was popular with academics and aristocrats alike. But despite having a wide circle of friends and acquaintances he regarded himself as an outsider, having neither the money to feel entirely comfortable in the company of carefree aristocrats nor the application required to become a true intellectual.

In the summer of 1875 Conway was invited to join a reading party travelling to Switzerland. He wisely told his father that they intended to study in Zurich, birthplace of the reformation in Switzerland. 'After much consternation and prayer for God's guidance', his father agreed to let him go, warning Conway that 'you will see the snow mountains some 40 miles off and it will be a tempting sight, but you must be satisfied with an excursion only now and then'. Immediately upon arrival, the party left Zurich and moved to Sterzing, in the devoutly Catholic Tyrol. Conway studied mathematics five and half days a week and explored the nearby Stubai Alps during the remaining day and a half, walking huge distances in an attempt to reach their summits. On the way back to England, he stopped off to visit art galleries in Munich, Dresden, Berlin and Hamburg.

Faith, Hope and Charity

On 21 March 1876 Canon Conway died, both liberating and abandoning his 19-year-old son. Conway continued with his normal round of lunch and dinner engagements in Cambridge before dashing back to Westminster, and then on to Rochester, to attend his father's funeral. A crowd of over 5,000 people gathered in Rochester as a mark of their respect for the gentle and hard-working cleric. The following Sunday there were memorial services at St. Margaret's and at Westminster Abbey, where Dean Stanley described Canon Conway as a saintly man: an adjective he rarely used. Conway's father left an estate of £10,202 to his mother, which provided an annual income of about £400, enough for a comfortable but not extravagant life. A rich uncle sent Conway £25 to cover his college expenses. That summer Conway went to the Alps for seven weeks, spending £50 on the holiday, £12 of it on guides. He climbed the Piz Morteratsch, the Piz Palü and the Piz Bernina, amongst others. The following year he sought and achieved election to the Alpine Club and began his climbing career in earnest, scrupulously recording each climb that he made between 1877 and 1887 in a special notebook. In later life Conway claimed that 'my main interest was not in climbing but in the scenery'.[21] but his diaries and notebooks from this period give a very different impression. Certainly the scenery is mentioned, but only as a backdrop to the wild exhilaration of climbing.

During the 'Golden Age' of alpine climbing from 1854 to 1865, 39 major alpine peaks were ascended for the first time, 31 of them by British parties. When Conway took up climbing, in 1876, the sport was still in its infancy and dominated by members of the London-based Alpine Club which, as the first of its kind in the world, did not feel the need to attach a prefix such as 'English'. There were many great alpine peaks still to be conquered, including La Meije (climbed by a Frenchman in 1877), the Dru (1878), the Charmoz (1880) and the Grépon (1881). However, all of these were considerably more difficult than the peaks climbed during the 'Golden Age'. Conway repeated most of the classic routes, put up a few relatively minor new routes, and climbed with many of the best alpinists and leading guides of the day; but he was never absolutely at the forefront of the sport in terms of technical difficulty, and always preferred snow and ice to rock climbing.

In 1877 he spent the entire summer in the Alps, from 28 June to 1 September, climbing mainly in the Pennine Alps with his Repton friend George Scriven. He also made his first attempt at writing for a wider audience, submitting an article on the 'Advancement of Learning' to *The Nineteenth Century*. There is a note in his diary, added in a later hand: 'My first essay at journalism'. Later in the year he sent an article to *The Cornhill* giving an account of his climbs in the Engadine the previous summer. Again, a later hand has added 'returned with thanks', but Conway became an expert at recycling old material and large parts of his Engadine essay appeared (some 26 years later) in the 1903 volume of the *Yorkshire Ramblers' Club Journal*. He also started to compile a climbing guide to the Zermatt district, estimating that it would take some two or three years to finish the work.

By 1878, Conway had resolved to abandon mathematics. He attended tutorials with two fellow students: J. J. Thomson, who later won the Nobel Prize and is credited with the discovery of the electron, isotopes, and the invention of the mass spectrometer; and Karl Pearson, one of the founders of mathematical statistics and an influential proponent of eugenics, whose speculations on relativity influenced the young Albert Einstein. Conway formed a lasting friendship with Pearson, but probably found mathematics tutorials in such company rather discouraging. Instead, he enjoyed reading Ruskin's mellifluous descriptions of 'Mountain Gloom and Mountain Glory' and through Ruskin discovered a growing love of art, architecture and history. His chief academic pursuit at Cambridge was to attend the lectures of Sidney Colvin, Slade Professor of Fine Art and Keeper of the Fitzwilliam Museum. Many years later, Conway recalled that 'we paid a guinea, in return for which we received an envelope full of photographic reproductions at each lecture'.[22] These photographs were the beginning of one of the great passions of his life. He also began to read widely and eclectically, studiously ticking off the Victorian 'canon' of good literature in his diary: Aristotle, Bede, Boswell's *Life of Johnson* ('very sticky stiff reading'), Burke, Chaucer, Defoe, Macaulay, Mills, Molière, Montaigne, Pepys, Plato and De Tocqueville.

Conway decided not to go up to Cambridge for the Easter term in 1878. Instead, he let his rooms and travelled to Paris, visiting Rouen, Beauvais, Versailles and Fontainebleau. He went to the Paris Exhibition, which celebrated France's recovery from the disastrous Franco-Prussian War of 1870, showcased a new invention called the telephone, and included a 'negro village' containing 400 (live) indigenous people from around the world. Conway thought the exhibition 'very stupid', but he was deeply moved by the churches and museums that he visited. In celebration of his new-found religious freedom, he attended High Mass most Sundays and often midweek as well. He also spent several weeks studying in the Louvre.

He described his daily routine in a letter to his mother: 'I have my coffee and bread and butter brought into my room at about 8, then I wake up, sit up in bed and read. [A]bout 10 or half past I get up partly and write and at 12 I go down to lunch. Then I go out to the Louvre to which I walk for the sake of exercise...I come back about 5 and have a cup of coffee at a cafe and watch the carriages in the Champs Elysées. At 6.30 we dine and afterwards I talk and read.' Almost to his surprise, he discovered that the more he studied a painting, the more he enjoyed it, and developed a particular interest in the Florentine School. Conway later added a note to his diary for this period: 'This was absolutely the commencement of my Art History studies and determined the course of my life! W. M. C. 1890'.

In July he travelled to the Alps with £50 borrowed from his mother, climbing mainly in the Pennine Alps with George Scriven and William Penhall, a daring young Cambridge medical student. They enjoyed a successful season including the first ascent of the Dom via the Domjoch which was 'exceedingly difficult in more than one place', according to Conway's entry in the guest book of the Monte Rosa Hotel. 'All the climbing swells have arrived...and so we poor young things have rather a hard competition however so far we have been more successful than anyone,' Conway boasted in a letter to his mother. He returned to Cambridge in October and took the History Tripos in December, obtaining a Third. Over Christmas and New Year he visited his mother and sisters, who now lived in Tunbridge Wells. He returned to Cambridge in January in order to satisfy the residency requirements for his degree and continued to read widely – Carlyle, Cervantes, Dryden, Racine and Shelley – before taking his BA on 18 April 1879. At the prompting of Professor Colvin, he also discovered a collection of early Netherlandish and German engravings at the Fitzwilliam Museum and some woodcuts of the same date at the University Library.

He was taken up by the University Librarian, Henry Bradshaw, an avuncular intellectual whose 'life was spent in quiet study and self-denying labour'.[23] Bradshaw was flattered by the interest shown by the young student: 'Here I have been for twenty-five years studying the early printed books of the Low Countries', he remarked, 'and during all that time not one single individual has taken the smallest interest in the subject.'[24] The history of art was an unusual, and not particularly well respected, area of knowledge – perhaps the equivalent of 'media studies' in Britain today – and the early printed books of the Low Countries represented a particularly esoteric branch of the subject. As Conway later observed: 'Art-history was not a University subject; it led to no tripos...If you were fool enough to take it up as a serious subject of study you shut yourself off to that extent from University honours...[The Slade Professor] was a luxury, and intended as such.'[25] However, Conway had stumbled upon an area of academia where he could easily establish a reputation as an authority, and one that appealed both to his developing sense of beauty and his instincts as a collector and a collator. In Bradshaw he had also found a mentor, an older man who took an interest in both his academic and personal development.

Conway began to 'pour out all my feelings' in his letters to Bradshaw, which varied from euphoric excitement to utter depression about his future prospects, often in the same letter. Bradshaw encouraged him – 'once begin to do what you have made up your mind to do, and half your difficulties and despondency will vanish' – and gently chided him for his dolefulness – 'three hours in the sunshine and fresh air made me feel a new man...which not even your letter could quite knock out of me'. Despite the intimacy of their correspondence, Conway continued to address Bradshaw with great formality until Karl Pearson wrote to him saying: 'By the bye, why always give B. and myself unlimited cause for amusement by addressing him as Dear Mr. B., why not Bradshaw or Brad or Braddie or what you will?' Thereafter, Conway addressed his letters 'Dear Bradshaw', explaining that his former reluctance to use this familiar style stemmed from the fact that he was not a King's College man, unlike Bradshaw and Pearson.

Having completed his degree at the age of 23, Conway had some difficult decisions to take about his future. He had no money of his own, stood to inherit little, and found it rather challenging to live cheaply. After presenting a particularly heavy college bill to his mother, at a time when she could ill afford to pay it, he tried to pre-empt the inevitable criticism of his extravagance by suggesting that she should pay for it out of the relatively modest amount of capital that she had available to support herself and her two unmarried daughters: 'I want you to face the matter and not try to get it out of income but regard it as capital sunk in my education', he insisted. Until the spring of 1879 he still intended to take orders and enter the church, but increasingly he found his evangelical upbringing in conflict with his growing appreci- ation of art and beauty: 'Beauty, in the opinion of my forebears and their friends was a dangerous thing, more likely to be a diabolic than a spir- itual agency...[B]y the aid of religion, Philistinism was imposed upon us and our possible nascent sense of beauty was intentionally atrophied.'[26] His diary entry for 12 April 1879 reads (probably in a later hand): 'It was at this time that, for about 3 days, I thought I had made up my mind to swallow all the dogmas and take orders...Ostensibly I returned to Camb to attend Theology lectures, but after a few weeks I ditched them and the whole ecclesiastical business with a sigh of relief.' In an unfinished autobiography written much later in life he reflected that 'I cannot remember a time when I did not live in fear of Hell and in almost equal fear of a heaven "where congregations ne'er break up and Sabbaths have no end".'

Conway was part of the generation that grew up in the midst of a crisis of faith in the Church of England, as scientific discoveries pro- gressively undermined a strict interpretation of religious texts. Religion was an all-pervasive part of early Victorian life and Conway's father, like the majority of his generation, believed in the absolute and literal truth of the Bible and in Bunyan's unforgiving God, who 'spareth none, neither knoweth he how to shew mercy to those that transgress his Law'.[27] The Church and the Bible represented the organising princi- ples that stood behind almost every aspect of Conway's childhood, defining the moral and ethical rules that governed human relations, marking the great rites of passage, and providing the context for many social interactions. It was a world of unambiguous authority and moral absolutism. When Conway's generation started to question their religious faith, they questioned almost everything that their parents stood for and believed in.

In later life, Conway became friends with Edmund Gosse who described the chasm of incomprehension that developed between the two generations as 'a struggle between two temperaments, two consciences and almost two epochs'.[28] When Gosse told his father of his religious doubts his father responded: 'If the written Word is not absolutely authoritative, what do we know of God?...What do we know of Eternity? Of our relations with God? Especially of the relations of a *sinner* to God?' Like Gosse's father, when Canon Conway was presented with a difficult question, he sought guidance in prayer. The answer, when it came, was invested not just with parental authority but also with the authority of God's will. When Canon Conway died, he spared his son the anguish of rejecting his father's Church, but Conway's strict religious upbringing remained a strong influence throughout his life. Just three years before he died, Conway recalled his undergraduate days at Cambridge: 'Our faith had been shaken by the arguments of Herbert Spencer and the discoveries of Darwin...The Catholic and Evangelical traditions failed to arouse any enthusiasm in our sceptical intelligences...One prop after another that had buttressed the religious structure of a previous generation was being knocked away, so that most of us could only take refuge in some sort of undefined agnosticism. Yet we were not irreligious – far from it.'[29]

It was not just at Cambridge that such issues were discussed. Membership of the Alpine Club consisted largely of young professionals, academics and clerics who were subject to similar doubts. Leslie Stephen, who was born some 20 years before Conway but had a similar evangelical upbringing, renounced his religious beliefs and left Holy Orders in order to become a man of letters in 1865, the same year that he became President of the Alpine Club. A 'man who substituted long walks for long prayers',[30] Stephen discovered in the mountains at least a partial substitute for the feelings of wonder, awe and exultation that had once been reserved for God. Describing his feelings about the Alps in *The Playground of Europe* (1871) he wrote: 'If I were to invent a new idolatry...I should prostrate myself, not before beast, or ocean, or sun, but before one of these gigantic masses to which, in spite of all reason, it is impossible not to attribute some shadowy personality.'[31] When Conway was elected to the Alpine Club in 1877, Stephen was still a significant intellectual presence and his views influenced many of the younger members of the club. In later life, Stephen invited Conway to join the 'Sunday Tramps', an informal group of climbers and intellectuals who went on long walks through the English countryside instead of going to church on the Sabbath.

Conway's decision to reject a career in the Church meant that he was now confronted with the necessity of earning a secular living. In order to allow him to continue his studies, Bradshaw applied on his behalf for a university research grant and in the meantime paid him £15 per quarter from his own pocket. This enabled Conway to spend several months studying the collections of engravings in the Bodleian and the British Museum. He wrote to his mother confiding that he planned to start a magazine dealing with art 'quite from the ethical point of view', from which he anticipated profits of £100 per year, noting that 'I have always regarded the priesthood of the pen to be just as real and noble a work as that of the visible church'. Fortunately for his mother's savings, the project never reached fruition.

With more borrowed money, Conway travelled to the Low Countries and Germany to continue his study of woodcuts, sometimes working as many as five hours a day in the library: 'I sit down to work...at 10 in the morning and feel sorry and surprised to find it 3 o'clock in the afternoon only five minutes afterwards as it seems.' Throughout this period he wrote regular begging letters to his mother, sometimes advancing the argument that by lending money to him now she would be saving future expense, and invariably reassuring her that he would soon be self-sufficient. He found it deeply frustrating that she failed to recognise the importance of his work but instead seemed to believe that, having completed an expensive education, he ought to be earning a living rather than spending her pension. From Hamburg he wrote: 'I am really bored to death in the matter of money...I find travelling by night to avoid hotel expenses, lunching at restaurants and calling it dinner, carrying my luggage through the streets...all this kind of economy I find is in the long run a mistake.' His mother visited Bradshaw in Cambridge to seek his advice. In a letter, he diplomatically told her that 'I cannot but feel convinced that if properly aided (I do not mean extravagantly) he will soon show how much he is worth.' Impressed by Bradshaw's apparent confidence in her son's work, she agreed to lend Conway more money. Bradshaw also increased his own allowance to £25 a quarter, which enabled Conway to continue his studies in 1880 in France, Holland and Belgium.

During this time Conway's youthful emotional response to beauty gradually evolved into a more mature appreciation of art. The influence of Ruskin – the 'scientific' observation of nature, the idea that great artists seek to express some underlying truth, and that art is the expression of the spirit of 'great men' – remained strong throughout his life. Sidney Colvin came from a very different background.[32] A classicist, who in later life was best known for his support of Robert Louis Stevenson and biographies of poets, Colvin was not himself an artist. Instead he attempted to apply a systematic approach to the study of art. In November 1879 Conway also came into contact with the German school of art historians while staying with Karl Pearson in Berlin. Unlike Britain, with its amateur tradition of antiquarianism and connoisseurship, there were seven full professors of art history at the University of Berlin, most of whom adopted a 'scientific', formalistic approach to the subject. Under these varying influences, Conway gradually acquired the habit of carefully observing and accurately describing what he saw, and what he felt, a habit that would serve him well in the study of art, and later in the description of landscapes in his travel writing.

In June 1880, with the help of Sidney Colvin, Conway was elected to the Savile, a gentlemen's club with 'a tradition of garrulity'[33] whose members included Edmund Gosse, Thomas Hardy, Rudyard Kipling, Robert Louis Stevenson and H. G. Wells. On 22 July 1880 at precisely 3.15 p.m. (according to his diary), Conway finished his first book, *The Woodcutters of the Netherlands*, a copy of which is still to be found in the Savile Club library. In the absence of any systematic approach to the study of art history in Britain, it was a ground-breaking piece of work. He took the manuscript to John Murray with a letter of commendation from Bradshaw and immediately set off for a holiday in Zermatt. Bradshaw, as always, wrote a letter giving him the reassurance that he sought: 'So far from having forgotten everything when you go back to your notebooks after a month's holiday...everything [will] have sorted itself beautifully and after a day's looking at things you [will] be able to sit down and write off in the forcible language you have so readily at your command a thoroughly valuable essay or series of essays on your subject.' In the event, John Murray rejected *The Woodcutters* as unsaleable and Conway spent the next year struggling to get three short articles published in an arts magazine.

The main purpose of his visit to the Alps in 1880 was to complete his research for the *Zermatt Pocket Book*. He had for some time been collecting and collating information on climbs in the Zermatt and Saas valleys, gathered from the *Alpine Journal* and other sources. In Zermatt he spoke to guides and climbers and checked the route descriptions that he had copied down. In keeping with his exploratory instincts, the guidebooks were originally intended to ensure that pioneering parties *avoided* routes that had previously been climbed. They were, of course, overwhelmingly used for exactly the opposite purpose. The *Zermatt Pocket Book* was the first practical guidebook for climbers ever written, and established a model that has been followed by thousands of imitators ever since, with its small format and terse descriptions of routes and times. The first slim volumes were published in 1881. They resembled pocket diaries, bound in black leather with a flap to keep the cover shut and a slot for a pencil. Conway borrowed £50 from Lord Ranfurly, a Cambridge friend, to finance their production ('the sales never repaid the cost') and sold them for half a crown (12.5p) each. A contemporary described them as the pemmican of alpine literature. When the first print run sold out some years later, Conway published a second edition in two volumes priced at half a crown each, 'divided at the Theodul Pass, the most inconvenient point possible, in order that Zermatt climbers might be obliged to buy both halves'.[34]

Before the advent of the sport of alpinism, only the most prominent mountains in the Alps were named. As the lesser peaks were progressively climbed during the 1870s and 80s it became necessary to name them too and, as guidebook writer, Conway was particularly active in this regard, adding numerous romantic names to the maps of Switzerland and France including the Wellenkuppe, the Windjoch and the Dent du Requin. As he observed: 'The secret of getting a name accepted is to put it about among the guides…as long as no one knows where the name originated no one will object.'[35]

Returning to London from the Alps, Conway was confronted with the stark necessity of earning a living. He reduced his outgoings by staying with friends and had three articles accepted by the *Magazine of Art* at £4 each, but the magazine decided to spread them (and the payments) over three years. He maintained a regular correspondence with Bradshaw and when he required a few facts to sprinkle over the opinions expressed in his art journalism he generally relied upon Bradshaw to supply them. 'It seems to me that no man has a chance in the literary world who has not plenty of cheek unless he is willing to do unlimited toadying and to fit his opinions to other men's grooves', he wrote disconsolately. He arranged to give eight lectures on early Flemish art in Tunbridge Wells, where his mother and sisters were living. Encouragingly, the first was attended by 23 people. His diary contains a clipping from a local newspaper describing the fifth in the series: 'Lastly, he came to the present day', it reported, 'and the question arose "What art have we?" This was not a day pre-eminent for musical composition. Could Wagner be placed on the same level as Beethoven? He thought not. It was not a day of painting, of architecture, of sculpture, or of drama. There remained however the novel, a species of literary art never handled before with the enthusiasm and success of today. In conclusion he referred to the lamented death of one who was so recently the greatest of living artists – George Eliot.' At the age of 24, Conway was acquiring the self-confidence, and the authority, to lecture on a wide range of subjects, many of them wholly unrelated to his rather narrow area of expertise. Encouraged by his success at Tunbridge Wells, he planned a series of lectures on Flemish fifteenth-century paintings at Folkestone, but gave up the project when only two tickets were sold.

At the end of 1880 Conway moved into Karl Pearson's chambers in the Inner Temple, and the two young men often set out together to dine at the Cheshire Cheese or the Cock Tavern on Fleet Street. Pearson was an extraordinary polymath who studied physics, philosophy, medieval German literature and Darwinism at the Universities of Heidelberg and Berlin after leaving Cambridge. When Conway moved into his chambers, he was studying law (he was called to the Bar in

1881) and deputising for the professor of mathematics at King's College London, while lecturing on philosophy, literature, socialism and women's rights in the evenings. Pearson was a scientific agnostic and a believer in social Darwinism and eugenics. He advocated war against 'inferior races' as a means of increasing the purity and efficiency of the race that maintained high civilisation (the English) and regarded it as a waste of money to try to improve the lives of people from poor stock. His letters are full of learning and irreverent undergraduate humour. He addressed Conway as 'Dear Moaner' and wrote a 'poem' mocking his new-found aesthetic sensibilities:

AE was an Aesthete with very long hair,
S was the Soap he never could bear,
T was the Twaddle he talked to his friend,
H was his Hope the time to amend,
E was the Error of bludgerdom's way,
T was the Twilight of high art decay,
I was the Idol of Self, his God.
    (Alas for the poet the letters were odd!)
C was the Comfort in which he dwelt,
D was the Dirt of which he s---t,
E was the Easel he never used,
V was the Vulgar he always abused,
I was the Ego who hated aesthetes,
L is the 'Locus' for such effetes.

In such company it was, perhaps, not surprising that Conway took a rather despondent view of his own progress and prospects in life. He was also in debt: he had no income, owed at least £130 to his mother, £50 to Lord Ranfurly and had other bills outstanding amounting to £25. A loose leaf of paper in his diary for 1881 reads: 'Without energy, without zeal, without power of...following a definite line of thought...floods of darkness...blotting out joy and labour-spirit, even blotting out the mere animal instinct of forward plodding, only now and then for a brief moment the faintest glimmer of a hope piercing the weltering gloom.' He took refuge in travel, going to Vienna and then to Germany to study and translate the literary works of Albrecht Dürer. He spent part of the summer of 1881 in Zermatt, but achieved relatively little that was new. Back in England, after staying with Lord Ranfurly in Ireland for some time, he continued his study of Dürer, writing an article on his engraving 'Melancholia', which shows humanity surrounded by the discarded tools of science, geometry and construction, contemplating the futility of existence. 'Very nervous, almost unable to work', he recorded in his diary.

In January 1882, he commenced a course of 12 weekly lectures in Brixton for the London Society for the Extension of University Teaching. A day later his diary proclaims: 'Killed Dürer!' He submitted the manuscript for publication in April and simultaneously applied for the Roscoe professorship of art at the newly founded University College in Liverpool (later Liverpool University), where an old university friend, Gerald Rendall, had been chosen as the first principal. Despite being an unpublished 26-year-old with a third class degree, Conway had high hopes of success after he met Rendall at a dinner in Cambridge, but in June he received a letter saying that no appointment would be made at present. Again he took refuge in travel, borrowing more money from his mother and journeying through France and Switzerland to Italy, where he visited art galleries in Milan and Florence and took Italian lessons. However, within a few weeks he wrote a letter to his mother explaining that 'a great weariness' had overtaken him that made 'books and pictures more than I can stand', so he travelled to Zermatt to recover his spirits.

That summer three of Conway's friends were killed in separate climbing accidents: William Penhall, Conway's climbing companion in 1878, died on the Wetterhorn; Frank Balfour, a brilliant young Cambridge biologist, was killed on the Aiguille Blanche de Peuterey; and W. E. Gabbett died on the Dent Blanche. 'Except as regards easy things my climbing days may be considered as over', Conway wrote to his mother. 'I cannot tell you the effect these accidents have had on me – it's not worthwhile...I have quite lost my nerve.' In response to the publicity surrounding the three deaths, Queen Victoria wrote to Gladstone asking whether she should speak out against mountaineering. Gladstone wisely counselled against it, but the summer of 1882 marked a turning point in Conway's climbing career. From that time on, the recreational, heroic motivation for climbing was replaced by the aesthetic and later almost mystical pleasure of exploring the mountain landscape.

The Rules of Engagement

Having abandoned climbing for the season, Conway turned his attention to Miss Rose Shakespear, who was holidaying in Zermatt with her family. Always scrupulous in noting his climbing routes and times, his diary records that he accompanied the Shakespears 'to the Riffel in the morning in the longest time on record'. His mother expected him to join her in Scotland in August but he declined. Instead he sent her his bills from the Monte Rosa hotel in Zermatt. Finally returning to London in October, Conway gave some University Extension lectures at Hampton Court and was invited, together with his mother, to stay at the Shakespears' house in Burnham. It was soon understood that the young couple were engaged to be married.

Meanwhile, in the world of publishing, his disappointments continued to mount. The Dürer book was rejected: 'What comes from the author himself is not very good. His reflections are not original and his style is disjointed and rough.'[36] But there was better news on The Woodcutters. Bradshaw persuaded the Cambridge University Press to take on the book and it was eventually published in 1884. However, as Bradshaw observed, the Cambridge University Press publishing department 'is so inferior that nothing but supreme merit will make a book sell'. The Press duly forgot to send out free copies of the book to experts in the field and as a consequence its publication was barely noticed. Just 25 copies of Conway's most scholarly work were sold; most of the remainder were burned.

The Literary Remains of Albrecht Dürer eventually appeared five years later. By that time Conway's style and approach to his subject had moved on substantially, but Dürer remains a rather disjointed book, showing his new-found faith in Karl Pearson's scientific agnosticism: 'Now speculation upon matters of science has been supplanted by experiment and the results of experiment are as universally accepted as once the dogmas of the Church. Science has won from the Church her boasted infallibility.'[37]

Conway spent the early part of 1883 courting Miss Shakespear, writing articles for the *Magazine of Art* and the *Alpine Journal*, and borrowing money from his mother. In March he travelled to Italy, meeting up with George Scriven, ostensibly to prepare University Extension lectures on classical and medieval mosaics, Raphael and Michelangelo. But when he arrived in Orvieto on 13 April, Conway saw a tall, graceful young woman with blue eyes and a mass of dark curly hair standing in front of the cathedral. Katrina Lambard was the only child of Charles Allen Lambard, one of the founders of the Chesapeake and Ohio Railroad, and Abigail Williams, both originally from Maine. They had lived in some style on Fifth Avenue, New York, until the Wall Street crash of 1873, when Lambard died of a heart attack. A close family friend, Manton Marble, helped Abigail to retrieve US$200,000 (about £40,000) of Lambard's considerable fortune and in 1879 they were married. Marble was the former owner and editor of the popular Democrat newspaper *The New York World* during the American Civil War (1861-5) and the years of reconstruction that followed. He sold the newspaper for a substantial sum in 1876. Marble had a somewhat ambiguous relationship with his beautiful stepdaughter Katrina. He flattered her, and she was utterly devoted to him: 'You see what I thrive on', she wrote, 'is first, to be loved to death; then flattered up to my eyes; and last of all to be spoiled as only you know how.' Throughout her life, Katrina signed many of her letters to her stepfather 'from your Big Girl'.

By good fortune, the Marbles and Katrina were staying at the same hotel as Conway, who contrived to sit next to Katrina at the *table d'hôte*. The next day the Marbles moved to Perugia and Conway followed. He spent the evening playing whist with them, discreetly borrowing some money from his aunt, Janet Guise, who happened to be on holiday in Italy. The following week he wrote a frantic note to his mother: 'I am almost pennyless please send me three £5 notes at once as Aunt Janet goes away tomorrow week and I shan't have her to borrow from for long.' His letters referred to the Marbles, but not specifically to Katrina: 'Some Americans named Marble I made great friends with. They are leading folk in New York and seem to know everybody of note who has visited America. They travel very slowly and will stop ½ hour before one picture and are utterly unamerican.'

George Scriven soon got bored with travelling very slowly and headed for home, but Conway stayed on, pursuing Katrina to Assisi. By this time, he was in the habit of guiding the Marbles around the art treasures of Italy during the day, and dining with them (at their expense) some four nights a week. The Marbles nicknamed him 'Herr von Konweg'. In Siena, Conway fell ill with fever. Katrina helped to nurse him back to health: '[The Marbles] brought me to their hotel to dinner every night all last week and sent me back with their manservant to put me to bed.' In view of his fever he asked his mother to send another £15 in case he should urgently need to return to England, but by the time the money arrived he felt sufficiently recovered to travel to Florence and Venice with the Marbles and Katrina. In Venice a spring fête was in progress: 'Gondola to Casa Foscolo where I took a room. Lunched with the Marbles...went with them to Academy, then to S. Zaccaria and a few other places in a gondola. Dined with them and sat out the evening on their balcony looking at the glorious fireworks and listening to the singing. Went to see S. Marco by moonlight.'

Katrina was beautiful, cultured and rich. Conway must have seemed like an unlikely combination of George and Cecil in *A Room with a View* – athletic alpinist and aesthetic art connoisseur rolled into one. It was a whirlwind romance conducted in the most romantic of settings. There was just one difficulty: Conway was engaged to Rose Shakespear, and no gentleman would ever break off an engagement.

Conway wrote to Rose's father explaining that increasing religious doubts had compelled him to abandon the Church of England and so he no longer considered that Rose had any obligation to him, but Rose refused to break off the engagement. He wrote to his mother, seeking to enlist her support: 'I have no intention of breaking off the engagement, tho' of course I am tremendously disappointed at finding...a gap widening between us...She has come out as a strongly practical matter of fact little woman.' Feeling ill with anxiety, Conway asked his mother to send him £10 so that he might spend a fortnight in the Dolomites to recover his health, and then set off with the Marbles and Katrina to visit Verona, Cortina, Merano, Chur and Basle. They finally parted company in Paris. Throughout this time his letters to his mother talked of the hard work he was doing in churches and art galleries, but made no mention of Katrina. Rose Shakespear was aware of Katrina's existence but not, apparently, her significance. In a letter to Karl Pearson she wrote: '[Conway] having as usual fallen on his legs, has met and made friends with charming Americans, Mr., Mrs. and Miss!'

Returning to England, the decision about the Roscoe professorship was deferred again, but Conway was invited to give a course of lectures in Liverpool on the history of painting in Tuscany. He was also invited to stay with the Shakespears, where he endeavoured to make himself disagreeable, but Rose continued to profess her love causing Conway to feel 'horribly ill and depressed'. His mother set out to reconcile the young couple: 'It appears that the whole affair would long ago have been ended had it not been for my mother, who has been bending the whole of her energies to accomplishing of what, six months ago, she seemed anxious to prevent.' Meanwhile, Katrina sent a long letter underlining the strength of her affection by renouncing all hope of further lovely French clothes: '[I] wish from my heart a long goodbye to any little Franck and Worth things, so long as I live, unless my having them were to make you happy...'

During October and November Conway commuted to Liverpool to deliver a lecture each Tuesday. As well as lecturing, he was expected to attend lunches and dinners with the great and good of the city, most of whom he regarded as hopelessly provincial. His diary contains a printed invitation from the Liverpool Art Club to a *Conversazione* where a selection of Turner etchings would be displayed, 'an opportunity of seeing which it is hoped that Members and their friends will avail themselves'. Conway underlined the sentence and added an exclamation mark. Meanwhile the situation with the Shakespears became even more vexing when it briefly appeared that Rose might be dying (slowly) from consumption, thereby introducing 'new and most damnable complications'. However, on Christmas Day, Rose finally wrote to Conway breaking off their engagement. She sent a second letter to Conway's mother ('full of misstatements', according to Conway) but, at last, he was a free man. He immediately wrote to Manton Marble asking permission to marry Katrina. Unfortunately, Rose had written a third letter to Katrina: 'I try to excuse you on the plea of your being an American, but still of whatever country, we should all endeavour to be true to ourselves and to those around us', it concluded. Katrina unwisely showed the letter to Marble, who wrote a long letter to Conway refusing to give his consent. Conway was shattered. But after a further exchange of letters, and the very obvious unhappiness of his beloved stepdaughter, Marble relented and invited Conway to visit them in New York.

Conway sailed on 3 May 1884, telling his mother that he was going to America at the suggestion of Lord Ranfurly to give a lecture on his ancestors, the Penns. It was his first long sea voyage and he proudly recorded that the S.S. *City of Rome* was the second largest liner in the world with a crew of 300, 150 saloon passengers and 850 Irish emigrants in steerage. He arrived in New York on 12 May. His diary is completely blank for two weeks until 1 June when he wrote, in triumph: 'MM gave his consent'. Ten days later, on 10 June, Conway and Katrina were married. In the page of Conway's diary there is a pressed lily of the valley and a cutting from a New York newspaper:

'The bride, apart from her intellectual powers, is endowed with personal charms above the average. High moral character, rare sweetness of disposition, a cultured mind and pure soul shine out from her luminous dark eyes and expressive face...The son of the former Canon of Westminster Abbey is...essentially English in type, more than common tall, with dark blue eyes...dark brown hair and a heavy mustache...Mr. and Mrs. Conway, both of whom have ample and independent fortunes, will pass their honeymoon in France and Italy.'

It seems that Conway might have been slightly economical with the truth about his financial position but, on a more happy note, the article noted that despite the short engagement Mrs. Conway had no need of a trousseau because she still had many unworn dresses and frocks from Worth following a recent visit to Paris.

Conway wrote to his mother explaining that he was now a married man and inviting her to join him and his wife in Paris. She refused. During July and August the young couple travelled in the Italian Alps. Conway hired a guide for a few days and climbed several peaks on the Monte Rosa, but most of the time they spent together. Conway was blissfully happy but Katrina, accustomed to staying in the best hotels in

Europe, found life in small mountain inns rather trying. They decided to spend a year living in Venice, scene of their courtship, while Conway wrote a book on Tintoretto, but the city was under quarantine because of an outbreak of cholera, so instead they returned to London, arriving at the beginning of September. Karl Pearson was the first of Conway's friends to dine with the newly married couple, but Katrina felt unwell and it soon became clear that, despite the precautions that she frankly discussed in her letters to her mother, she was pregnant. It was, in effect, the end of their romance, and for the remainder of their marriage Conway and Katrina led very separate lives.

The Desire for Possession

As a student, Conway had lived on about £120 a year, much of it borrowed. Katrina had a private income of US$1,200 (about £240) a year from a trust set up by her father, received a generous allowance from her stepfather, and stood to inherit a small fortune, so Conway immediately set about spending considerably more. The hard work and frugality that characterised much of middle-class life in the early part of Queen Victoria's reign was increasingly being replaced by leisure and profligacy. In Conway's case, the money came from his American parents-in-law, but a huge inter-generational transfer of wealth was also taking place in Britain, as the younger generation enjoyed the fruits of the great Empire their parents had built. In November 1884, the 28-year-old Conway and his young wife moved into 26 Park Street, Mayfair, just behind Park Lane (at a rent of £273 a year) and hired a charwoman, a cook and a parlour maid. Conway noted proudly in his diary that the house stood close to number 31 where Ruskin had lived while he was (briefly) married and where he had written *The Seven Lamps of Architecture* in 1849.

Katrina had been brought up to expect a life of idleness and comfort, her days filled with carriage rides, short walks, dainty meals, music, card games and the exchange of pleasantries with family and friends. She had almost no knowledge of how to run a household but she was imbued with the desire to create a beautiful and comfortable home and to support and encourage her husband in whatever career he chose to follow. In one of her earliest letters to Conway she had written: 'I wish to help you – to bring you courage and strength and desire to do each hour you live the worthiest things you are capable of.' Despite their increasingly separate lives, Katrina remained true to this ambition.

Having spent most of his life in evangelical boarding schools, ancient universities, foreign lodgings and rough mountain huts where 'the accommodation…is about equal to that of an English public house in a rural district', Conway was not particularly concerned with comfort. Instead he saw Katrina's money as a means of entering society. They dined out regularly with London's literary and artistic set. At one dinner, Katrina sat between Robert Browning and Henry James (one of Manton Marble's many friends), but she missed the comfort and indulgence of New York life and found English women dull. She invited Agnes Tracy, her closest friend from America, to stay in order to stave off her growing sense of isolation in London. Agnes arrived with a trunk full of gifts from the Marbles and wrote a letter to Katrina's mother observing that Conway 'does not believe in spending money on "living". His ideas are so unlike an American man's on all matters of luxury.' Agnes gave Katrina US$1,000 (£200) to pay the rent on Park Street and rapidly formed the view that Conway was both selfish and inconsiderate, while Conway decided that Agnes was a nuisance. He wrote to Manton Marble making clear his growing displeasure at her presence: 'Unsettled in mind and stomach – indigestion, liver, God knows what…I have not touched my lectures since Agnes arrived (don't think, by the bye, that she has been anything but perfect and sweet, or that I do anything but rejoice in her coming, or that I find her in the way…).'

When the Marbles heard that Katrina was pregnant they naturally assumed that she would have the baby in New York, in order to be close to her mother. Given the extremely short engagement, and Katrina's rather sudden pregnancy, perhaps they were also anxious to ensure that New York society saw that the baby was born 10 months after the wedding. Conway was horrified at the idea: 'Both by birth and education I am altogether against separating husband and wife AT ANY TIME FOR ANY REASON', he wrote to Marble. 'If I were to be in England and my wife in America English people would think terribly of it.' Part of his alarm appears to have arisen because there were rumours in Cambridge that Sidney Colvin intended to resign. Conway harboured dreams of replacing him as Slade Professor and feared the impact that any separation of husband and wife might have on his prospects of winning the professorship: 'Cambridge is the most touchy place in the world...my prospects there would be well-nigh ruined', he explained to Marble.

In the end, Katrina gave in to Conway's demands and remained in England. Marble knew that she was upset and so he gave her a brougham as consolation. 'Will you lend me your vocabulary just for one letter', Katrina wrote to her stepfather, 'because with the biggest words in mine I can only give you the faintest idea of what I felt on reading your letter...Your offer of the coupé simply takes my breath away!...Of course you know there is no pleasure in life to me, except music, comparable to that of having a carriage.' Hiring the brougham cost Marble £20 a month; more than the amount Conway had lived on before he was married.

Conway and Katrina travelled to Cambridge to launch his campaign for the Slade professorship, but Bradshaw was sceptical that Colvin would actually resign: 'I don't expect that kind of generosity from many people, certainly not from a Scotch man', he observed. In the end, Bradshaw was proved right: Colvin stood again and was re-elected unopposed. Instead of the glory of a Cambridge professorship, Conway was obliged to lecture at Liverpool and Croydon. But at least when he went to the British Museum or the National Gallery to prepare his notes, he could travel there in a brougham.

On 25 March 1885, shortly before his 29th birthday, Conway finally received a letter from Liverpool offering him the Roscoe professorship of art for five years at £400 a year. Manton Marble advised him to accept only if they reduced the residency requirement to the two winter terms, leaving him free to travel and study in Europe in the summer. The college authorities agreed to the condition and Conway started work preparing his lectures. Just a few weeks later, on 2 May, Katrina gave birth to a daughter, whom she named Agnes, after her dearest friend. The Marbles sailed from New York, arriving on 24 May. They took a suite in the Langham Hotel on Upper Regent Street and

Katrina immediately moved in with them. Conway sullenly remained in Park Street, looked after by the servants. After a visit to the Langham on 29 May his diary reads: 'TT ['Tommy Tinker' – Marble's nickname for his wife] upset, K upset, baby upset, I upset. A general upset today.' On 27 June, his diary reads: 'Abandoned!' After several blank days, the 7 July entry reads: 'This whole time has been a cruel waste...I have not had a moment that was not excruciating mental torture...tonight I would gladly leap into the sea and quit this unkind world – were it not that there are things for me and no other to do, TO DO.'

Conway was bitterly jealous of Katrina's relationship with her step-father and professed to find the shallowness and luxury of Marble's life offensive. Like most Englishmen of his class and generation, Conway believed that achievement could only be measured by the estimation of one's peers. Manton Marble, on the other hand, believed that success was measured in terms of money and celebrity. Conway tried to console himself that, despite his wealth, Marble's intellect was weak and shallow compared to his own, and it was true that Marble was not a great intellectual. However, he was a trusted adviser to President Cleveland, an authority on the arcane but at that time controversial subject of bimetallism (the use of both gold and silver to define the value of a monetary unit) and, above all, he was a highly successful newspaper man. As well as being rich, Marble was inquisitive, extrovert, worldly and commercially astute. Ironically, as the years went by, and his relationship with Marble matured, Conway's philosophy of life owed far more to Marble's American attitudes than to the world of Cambridge in the 1880s.

Conway, Katrina and baby Agnes were reconciled after the Marbles departed for New York; and Conway was perhaps busier at this time than at any other, preparing lectures for Liverpool, gaining a reputation as an arts correspondent and reviewer, and writing a short book on *The Artistic Development of Reynolds and Gainsborough*, which was published, to little acclaim, in 1886. Even Marble, normally a staunch supporter of his son-in-law, admitted to being disappointed: 'I do think the woodcuts give it a "cheap and nasty" look', he wrote. The book was dedicated 'to my Master, Sidney Colvin', whose position as Slade Professor Conway still hoped to usurp, and set out Conway's ambitions for the new field of art history: 'As an artist Reynolds has never yet been studied; no written life of him contains even an attempt to trace the origin and development of his style...What were his powers and his limitations? What is his relative greatness? Whence did he derive his powers? and what of them did he communicate to his successors?'[38] These, and 'a hundred similar questions', Conway set out to answer. As the first Professor of Art History (as opposed to art) in Britain, Conway had few precedents to follow and had to devise both the approach and content of his lectures and books from scratch – a far more challeng- ing task than that faced by modern art historians, who have a vast body of research to draw upon. It was also around this time that Conway stumbled, almost unwittingly, upon a big idea: that photography would transform the study of art. He was only dimly aware that in due course photography would also transform art itself.

Until the invention of photography, art critics had no easy means of comparing works of art located in different cities. The idea of build- ing a 'virtual museum' to educate the public, using photographs and casts of famous works of art, had been around since the mid nineteenth century, but Conway took the idea further, realising that by systemati- cally collecting and cataloguing photographs of works of art from around the world – from dealers, galleries, books, magazines and sales catalogues – he could compare and contrast different artists and trace the development of new ideas and techniques. Today, with thousands of glossy art books and the world's great art collections available at the ⋅ click of a mouse, this seems trivial. In the 1880s it was revolutionary. Even in 1904, Conway was still able to write: 'Photos are the engine of research now. People are only just beginning to find that out.' Conway became an obsessive collector of photographs. 'He would rather buy a photograph than get the most dainty meal Delmonico's could prepare', Agnes Tracy complained in a letter to Abigail Marble. His vast collec- tion of art photographs eventually formed the nucleus of the Conway Library in the Courtauld Institute, Britain's foremost college for the study of art history.

Conway exploited photography for the study of art, but failed to recognise that the very reproducibility of photographs threatened the aura of great works of art and, to some extent, of great landscapes. Conway instinctively felt that the journey to see a work of art or a landscape was part of a ritual that added to the value of the experience. He knew that rarity, freshness and remoteness are essential constituents of beauty, and recognised that 'the thing that makes the first sight... so incomparable and so irretrievable is that in it remoteness reverberates in its closest association with proximity'.[39] In *The Alps from End to End*, Conway described his reaction to a view of the Pennine Alps: 'The view, I suppose, is wonderful, but it did not move me...I was too familiar with every detail in it...Every object was swathed in reminiscences. There may be charm in this kind of retrospect, but it is not the charm of beauty...A country not one's own, should not be too well known. Its charm evaporates with its freshness.'[40] However, he failed to recognise that collections of photographs, like his own, would have a similar effect on art.

Over-exposure renders the beautiful banal. This is as true of great views as it is of great art. As early as 1861 a commentator noted that 'for an absurdly small sum, we may become familiar...with every famous locality in the world...The ubiquity of the photographer is something wonderful. All of us have seen the Alps and know Chamonix and the Mer de Glace by heart.'[41] Today, the Matterhorn is said to be the most photographed object in the world and every traveller to Zermatt knows exactly what they are going to see long before they arrive. Art sought an escape from the realism and ubiquity of photography in the concept of 'art for art's sake'; the idea that the viewer should look *at* the painting, not through it, as if it were a window on the world. A great landscape has no visual alternative to being a window on the world. As Susan Sontag noted: 'The image-surfeited are likely to find sunsets corny; they now look, alas, too much like photographs.'[42] In 1902, as Conway began the task of systematically filing his huge collection of photographs, Paul Cézanne wrote: 'If only we could see with the eyes of a new born child! Today our sight is a little weary, burdened by the memory of a thousand images...We no longer see nature; we see pictures over and over again.'[43] Thanks to photography, we can never reproduce the astonishment that Ruskin and Conway must have felt – 'suddenly – behold – beyond' – when first they caught sight of the Alps.

In August 1885, the Conway family went on holiday to Wales, staying in Llandudno with Conway's mother, Elizabeth, and his sister,

Minnie. Conway cycled, climbed Snowdon and took a boat to Liverpool to go house-hunting. In September they moved into 25 Prince's Avenue, Liverpool: a large, red-brick Victorian terraced house. Gradually Katrina was learning how to keep house and as time went by she even went shopping periodically. Conway wrote to Abigail Marble informing her that 'our household expenses are reduced about one third...The servants hate the change because they love their commissions from the shopkeepers.' Conway commenced two courses of lectures on Dürer and Egyptian art, which were poorly attended. His diary for 1886 also contains a flyer for a course of public lectures given by six different Liverpool professors at a cost of 10 shillings:

More's Utopia
On some of the more interesting forms of life dredged in Liverpool Bay
Imperial problems
Russia and its literature
The ideal of repose, as illustrated in Egyptian art [by Conway]
Some leading ideas of Thomas Carlyle's philosophy.

·He took part in the social and intellectual life of the city, regularly met friends from the climbing world, including Horace and Lucy Walker (the first woman to climb the Matterhorn), and cultivated the image of an irreverent young rebel. As an obituarist noted many years later: 'More puckish than donnish...[he] loved to give his real erudition an individual and provocative twist.'[44] Lucy Walker insisted that Conway's initials 'W. M.' stood for 'Wicked Man', because of his frequent 'leg-pulling'.[45] He became an active member of the Liverpool Art Club, fighting the Philistine Puritanism of the Liverpool city councillors and seeking to turn the gallery of the Liverpool Royal Institution into a public museum. In an effort to enlist his support for this campaign, he visited Ruskin at Brantwood, his home on the shores of Coniston Water in the Lake District.

In early 1886 the Slade professorship at Cambridge fell vacant when Colvin unexpectedly decided to retire. By a terrible coincidence, just a few days later, Henry Bradshaw, Conway's mentor and most influential supporter in Cambridge, died. John Henry Middleton was appointed Slade Professor, apparently on the recommendation of the Prince of Wales, and Conway was left disappointed. After completing his lectures at Liverpool, he disconsolately travelled to Germany to visit art galleries, churches and libraries.

The Marbles and Agnes Tracy were also planning a summer visit to Europe. Conscious of the strain that their relationship had been under during their last visit to London, Marble tried to prepare the ground by writing to Conway in advance: 'You have never referred with one effacing regret to the attitude of your disordered feelings in respect of Katrina joining us at the Langham...but I will assume...that you are beginning to realize that love is a progress and a daily conquest and not a bricks and mortar possession.' Marble proposed that they should all meet up in Zermatt, in effect on Conway's home ground. 'Bring along to Zermatt your youth, your wholesome nature, your unselfish and affectionate heart, your muddled head, your REGENERATE soul, and you and I shall have an immense sunshiny summer day.' Unfortunately, Marble's plans for a reconciliation went awry. Both Abigail and Agnes Tracy fell ill in Paris and Katrina rushed to France to nurse them, leaving Conway alone in Germany with baby Agnes and her nurse. His diary for 22 May reads: 'Berlin. Baby 33 inches long.' It is the first reference to his daughter since her birth. It was probably wishful thinking on Katrina's part when she wrote: 'I feel sure the little baby must be a comfort to you.' Bored with waiting, Conway decided to go to Zermatt alone 'with nurse holding baby on the final mule ride from Visp'. Abigail was confined to Paris suffering from rheumatism, and when Katrina finally joined Conway in Switzerland he handed over baby Agnes and immediately left with his climbing friend William Coolidge to carry out research for a new Climbers' Guide Book to the Lepontine Alps.

Agnes Tracy's husband had recently died of 'bodily disease brought on by extraordinary excesses'.[46] A newspaper article reported that he consumed three bottles of champagne for breakfast and went to sleep with a bottle of wine and another of brandy at his bedside in case he woke up during the night. His Will was being contested by his daughter from a previous marriage and Katrina decided that she must travel to America with Agnes, to provide moral support and to testify in the court case. Conway refused to give his consent to the journey and, when it became clear that Katrina still intended to go, he became petulant, failing to respond to telegrams and demanding money from Manton Marble for the expenses that he would allegedly incur because of Katrina's absence. In the end, Katrina travelled to America with Agnes Tracy, despite Conway's protests, while Conway returned alone to England at the end of the climbing season. He threw himself into Liverpool life, but fumed about Katrina's absence.

The Marbles, Agnes Tracy and Katrina all thought that it was Katrina's clear duty to support her closest friend and simply could not understand Conway's lack of consideration. At one point Conway wrote to Katrina threatening to resign his Liverpool professorship and follow her to America if she refused to come home immediately. Katrina's reply was uncompromising: 'I am always hoping that you will behave to me as a man and not as a spirited child. To say that you are "ruined and will resign your professorship" unless I return seems to me conduct hardly becoming of a husband to his wife who has been absent from him but a few weeks for the sake of doing a service to the best friend she has in the world at a time of great need…My dear child – do not let your thought of self blind you to the rights and happiness of the people to whom you are bound.' The notion of 'rights and happiness' was peculiarly American. In Victorian England, a woman gave up any right to independent happiness when she married. Katrina's determination resulted in a more respectful, but more emotionally distant, relationship with Conway.

In an effort to mollify him, Marble agreed to write off the substantial debts that Conway had already incurred since his marriage. He also agreed to increase Katrina's allowance to £900 a year ('including dresses and everything'), but he could not restrain himself from suggesting that the couple might try, for one year at least, to live within Conway's salary of £400 and Katrina's allowance. The conciliatory letter that Marble wrote to Conway marked a turning point in their relationship. The generous interpretation is that Conway recognised that he had been immature and selfish. Alternatively, he may simply have calculated that Marble would pay to keep Katrina happy. For whatever reason, from 1886 Conway's relationship with Manton Marble steadily improved and, as time went on, Marble gradually assumed the role of Conway's recently deceased Cambridge friend and mentor, Henry Bradshaw. From this time, too, the Marbles holidayed in Europe most summers, where they were invariably joined by Katrina and baby Agnes, leaving Conway free to do as he wished.

In January 1887 the designs were submitted for the new buildings of University College, Liverpool in the grand neo-Gothic style that gave rise to the expression 'red brick universities'. Conway again visited Ruskin, seeking his support for art education in the city. 'Went to Brantwood with K.', he recorded in his diary. 'Found Ruskin in most delightful state of mind. Had long and charming talk with him...K delighted.' Ruskin subsequently suggested that Conway should complete an article on 'Art' for *Chambers' Encyclopaedia*, after illness prevented him from doing so, an honour that made the Marbles (who were great admirers of Ruskin) 'prouder than peacocks'. However, a letter from Ruskin to the *Manchester Guardian*, pasted into Conway's diary, suggests that he was less enthusiastic about art education in the great industrial cities of the north: 'Here is my – not *opinion* – but very sure and stern knowledge. That it is impossible for Manchester, or any other towns the least like Manchester, to have schools of art in them at all. Art cannot be taught by fouling the skies over their heads and stealing their drink from other lands.' The editor of the *Manchester Guardian* noted that 'Mr. Ruskin's letter is quite in his playful little way', but Ruskin was absolutely serious, and he was not alone in his views. Even William Morris, a committed socialist, could not countenance the industrial north. In his utopian novel *News from Nowhere* (1890), London is transformed into a Garden City, but Manchester and the other northern industrial cities have simply disappeared.[47] Conway was increasingly conscious that, in order to succeed in his chosen career, he had to return to Cambridge or to London.

After completing his lectures in Liverpool, Conway and Katrina set off for Italy in April. Since Marble was unwilling to lend them more money, the young couple tried to persuade him that instead he should *invest* money in Italian art. Marble wrote to Conway acknowledging that 'after...protracted "coaxing" by Tommy Tinker [Abigail Marble] I have been overpersuaded to assent to your proposition for £50 for

Milanese rubbish to adorn the Liverpudlian shebang.' He enclosed a further £50 for Katrina's birthday present. And so began Conway's large, eclectic and ever-changing art collection, celebrated in his 1914 book *The Sport of Collecting*. It was a sport that involved Conway in 'borrowing' money from his father-in-law, dealing with shady art dealers, and frequently smuggling the works out of their country of origin. As the Cambridge examiners had predicted some years before, Conway was becoming 'thoroughly dishonest in other ways'. Moreover, despite his stepfather-in-law's generosity, which enabled Conway to live way beyond his means, he was inclined in later years to regret that he had not spent even more: 'I might have had a well-known Giotto for seventy pounds. Alas for the foolish economies and abnegations of an imprudently prudent youth!'[48]

Conway received encouragement in his new pursuit from Giovanni Morelli, an Italian art critic, whom he met in Milan in 1887. Morelli developed the technique of identifying artists' 'hands' by scrutinising the minor details in their paintings that were less likely to attract the attention of copyists and imitators. He told Conway that only by becoming a collector would he be able to test his knowledge of art, and bet him 20 francs that he could not find and buy a genuine Foppa painting in Milan. Conway needed little incentive to become a collector, for he was already someone for whom possession was a driving impulse: 'For...ownership is the very deepest relationship a person can have with things: not that they live inside him; it is he who lives in them.'[49] Conway collected works of art, as he collected alpine summits, as a means of defining himself: 'The first time I saw the snowy Alps...there arose within me an intense desire to be on them, to climb to the top, to look down from them and over the other side. I take this to have been a form of that general desire for possession which is so energetic a motive in most of us. We in a sense possess the places we have visited. We carry them away in our memories.'[50] After a protracted search through the shops and houses of the back-street art dealers of Milan, Conway finally tracked down a Foppa Madonna in nearby Brescia and claimed that he bought it for £4. He sold it 19 years later for £1,000.

From Milan, Conway and Katrina travelled through Lugano and Como to Saas Fee in Switzerland, but Conway climbed nothing of note.

'Attempted Nadelhorn...Was mountain sick on the final arête and could not get to the top. Swore off climbing.' By October he was back in Liverpool, lecturing on the Phoenicians. Just six people attended his evening lectures, so he cancelled the series.'How I have come to loathe lecturing', he wrote to Marble. Meanwhile his latest book, *Early Flemish Artists*, was published. Ruskin wrote a letter praising the book, but several other reviewers criticised it. Conway was thoroughly fed up with the academic world and with life in the provinces:'Our only object in staying [in Liverpool] is to gain something large enough to compensate for the death-in-life one lives here and we don't see any such compensation', he wrote to Marble. Within a few months he resigned his professorship (but continued to use the title 'Professor') and was succeeded by Bob Stevenson, Robert Louis Stevenson's cousin and fellow member of the Savile Club. Before leaving Liverpool, Conway resolved to organise an 'Arts Congress' in the hope that he would depart from the city 'in a blaze of glory'. But first he went on a walking tour of Shropshire, sending daily letters to Katrina with the injunction on the first that 'you must keep this letter (like your savings) with great care as it is my diary and will doubtless become of the greatest autobiographical value'.

The British Association for the Advancement of Science was at the height of its power and prestige at this time. In a striking reversal of the position set out in C. P. Snow's famous 1959 lecture on 'The Two Cultures',[51] Conway and many others believed that the arts and humanities were neither understood nor properly valued because of the intellectual dominance of science and technology in Victorian Britain. As Lord Clark, the art historian, later observed: 'One mustn't overrate the culture of what used to be called the "top people" before the wars. They had charming manners, but they were ignorant as swans. They did know something about literature, and a few had been to the opera. But they knew nothing about art and less than nothing about philosophy.'[52] Conway resolved to form a rival to the British Association for the Advancement of Science, which he called the National Association for the Advancement of Art and its Application to Industry. The Arts Congress in Liverpool was designed to further its aims.

The Association successfully played upon the *zeitgeist* of the late Victorian era and was Conway's rather minor contribution to the

Aesthetic Movement. It owed much to William Morris's belief that art and beauty should be an integral part of every aspect of life, including industrial and domestic design: the concept that you should 'have nothing in your houses that you do not know to be useful or believe to be beautiful'.[53] It also reflected a growing concern that Britain's future as the leading industrial nation in the world depended upon improving the attractiveness of its manufactured products, as its competitive advantage was progressively being eroded by low cost production from Germany and the emerging market of the United States of America.

In Liverpool, Conway found a fertile ground for his ideas. The port city was enjoying a cultural flowering in the 1880s, as the second and third generations of the rich mercantile families (many of whom had originally made their money from slavery) started to give their financial support to the development of art and education in the city. The Rathbone family were particularly generous patrons, while the Walker family endowed the art gallery in Liverpool that still bears their name. Conway, however, was not motivated solely by an altruistic desire to encourage the appreciation of art or to improve industrial design. He saw the Arts Congress as a means of extracting himself from the hated provincialism of Liverpool and re-launching his career in the artistic and intellectual world of London.

Released from the weekly grind of lecturing in Liverpool, he immediately travelled to London to discuss his plans with his friends Edmund Gosse, Rider Haggard and Henry James. He had lunch with Humphrey Ward, the influential art critic of *The Times*, dined with Sidney Colvin, accompanied Ruskin to an exhibition of watercolours, called on William Morris and Oscar Wilde, and persuaded the Duke of Westminster to lend his name to the cause, thereby firmly anchoring the new Association in London rather than Liverpool.

Sir Frederick Leighton, President of the Royal Academy and creator of exquisite paintings of languorous young women, agreed to become President. Lawrence Alma-Tadema, famous for his luxurious and decadent depictions of the Roman Empire, presided over Painting; Sidney Colvin took charge of Art History; and Walter Crane, the tile designer and illustrator of children's nursery rhymes, looked after

Applied Art. The inaugural meeting was held at Grosvenor House in London with the Duke of Westminster in the chair. William Morris proposed the founding resolution: 'That in view of the problems presented by the present conditions of art and industry in this country, it is advisable to form an association to be called the National Association for the Advancement of Art and its Application to Industry for the purpose of holding an annual congress in different parts of the country to discuss all questions of a practical nature connected with the furtherance of art.' The motion was seconded by Edmund Gosse. Oscar Wilde also spoke. Other than Morris, it is not clear that any manufacturers or industrial designers, who were essential if the Congress was to fulfil its stated purpose, were invited to the meeting.

In September, the Conways left their house in Liverpool and moved to 21 Clanricarde Gardens, a white stucco Victorian terraced house in Bayswater ('workmen came in and began to pull the furniture to pieces. Ambassadors of chaos.'). Since Conway had forfeited his £400 salary they were heavily in debt, but Agnes Tracy agreed to pay Katrina an allowance of £100 a year – about half the rental on their new home – as well as £100 to cover their moving expenses, and Marble paid the premium to purchase the lease. While Katrina set about making their new home comfortable, Conway continued his preparations for the Congress. The most contentious item on the agenda was the question of whether art galleries and museums should open on Sundays – the Liverpool contingent was fearful that the Orangemen of the city would start a riot – but the controversy was smoothed over and Conway returned in triumph to Liverpool in December for the opening ceremony. Sir Frederick Leighton gave the keynote address: 'Art has begun to receive a very great deal of lip worship in this country; pictures are widely bought and lavishly paid for; art schools swarm over the country; municipalities are liberal in forming fine museums...[but] with the great majority of Englishmen, the appreciation of art as art is blunt, is superficial, is desultory, is spasmodic...the aesthetic consciousness is not with them a living force, impelling them towards the beautiful, and rebelling against the unsightly.'[54] The artists and intellectuals present read papers and talked amongst themselves about the importance of industrial design and the need to improve the aesthetic quality of the nation's manufactured products. Whether any industrialists were present to heed their words is unclear.

Since the Conways could not afford to live in London on Katrina's income alone, the Marbles suggested that they should let their house and join them on a winter tour of Egypt. Conway and Katrina willingly agreed and as soon as the Arts Congress ended they left baby Agnes with Conway's mother and set sail with the Marbles for a six-month tour of Egypt and the eastern Mediterranean. In Cairo, Conway climbed the Great Pyramid, lunched 'with Zebehr Pasha in the Giseh Palace where he lives' and met Charles Moberly Bell, the Egyptian correspondent for *The Times*, who two years later became managing director of the paper. After exploring the mosques and Coptic churches of Cairo, they all set off on a two-month cruise up the Nile on a *dahabíyeh* – a boat with two large sails, a saloon and cabins below, and a flat open deck above, shaded with sail cloth and strewn with rugs and sofas. There was a crew of 22, including two cooks and two stewards, as well as Fritz, the Marbles' manservant, to look after the four passengers. Katrina soon fell into the normal rhythm of family life, going for gentle strolls, eating meals, playing whist, passing the time with gentle expressions of sentiment. Frustrated by the constant presence of his parents-in-law and the lack of wind, Conway hired horses and donkeys so that he could ride ahead of the boat and spend more time exploring the ruins of ancient Egypt.

It was Conway's first visit to the Orient and he was enraptured. His 1889 diary contains detailed descriptions and sketches of pyramids and temples, clearly intended for future publication, interposed with romantic descriptions of the landscape. At Luxor, the boatmen's cry as they hauled the sails was 'the sound of tortured souls, forced to labour a while upon a miserable earth...and all the while the river went rustling and rippling by and the breeze murmured softly about the boat...The sun was setting in glory and the hills were pale and violet.' On 14 February: 'A moonlit night on the Nile. Along the base of the hills lay like a soft bed the gathered wood smoke from distant village fires; the air sweet with its scent even at this late hour.' Conway bought antiquities pillaged from ancient tombs until his money was exhausted. Returning to Alexandria, they sailed up the coast to Greece, stopping at Port Said,

Jaffa, Beirut, Larnaca, Syria, Rhodes and Smyrna. In Athens he bought more antiquities with borrowed money, which he shipped, illegally, to England. Six months after leaving, they were back in London and Conway spent the rest of the year writing a book on Egyptian art. It was never published, although some chapters later appeared in *The Dawn of Art in the Ancient World* (1891), an ambitious work covering the history of art from the Stone Age to the Egyptian and Assyrian civilisations.

Throughout this time Conway's mother, Elizabeth, had been looking after Agnes. Illness and premature death were certainly more prevalent in Victorian times than they are today because the majority of the population had a poor diet and lived in insanitary and overcrowded conditions. Furthermore, when illness did strike, even those who could afford a doctor found that the medical profession had little to offer apart from a good bedside manner. Nevertheless, everybody in Conway and Katrina's family (apart from Canon Conway) lived to a very good age. Elizabeth Conway survived her saintly and devoted husband by 36 years despite suffering from constant ill health (according to her letters) and both the Conways and the Marbles had a tendency to treat illness as a medium of exchange: an opportunity to give and receive little acts of consideration, and a bargaining tool that enabled both sufferer and carer to negotiate some advantage. Elizabeth's care of Agnes, while her son and daughter-in-law enjoyed a prolonged holiday in Egypt, enabled her to write at regular intervals with vivid descriptions of her own ill health and the almost daily threats posed to the well-being of baby Agnes. Meanwhile Abigail Marble, who devoted her life to ensuring that her husband and her daughter were comfortable and free from anxiety, wrote soothing letters to Elizabeth, praising her stoicism: 'The very thought of Agnes being ill gives us all such an aching heart and would have killed Katrina, but for your extreme considerations. I blessed you a thousand times as I read your note – magnifying the charms of the dear child…belittling everything which could give K solicitude or vexation. I am very sensible of the torments you must have undergone.' After returning from Egypt, it was Katrina's turn to fall ill, and the return of Agnes was further postponed. Abigail once more set out to placate Elizabeth:'It is an immense comfort to me that you understand the requirements of a sick room – and that even a pleasurable excitement [i.e. the return of Agnes] may exhaust a patient.' She was also careful to point out the advantage to Conway in this arrangement: 'The "Herr" returned from Edinburgh Saturday morning and left the same evening for the Paris exhibition. We are all so glad that he can have that pleasure.'

Conway's trip to Edinburgh was to attend the second Arts Congress. He had persuaded the Marquis of Lorne to be its President, but compared to his triumph in Liverpool, the novelty had gone. Conway's diary for 1890 sets out his programme for the coming year: 'My work now is to produce the new edition of the Zermatt Pocket Book, to arrange the arts congress for this year (no place yet decided), and to write out my notes on our Eastern tour of last year.' He resumed his work as a journalist, writing pieces for *The Academy* and *The Art Journal*, including caustically funny reviews of any book that might compete with his own for the public's attention. After reading *Egyptian Sketches* by Jeremiah Lynch, Professor Conway observed that 'during the next few years we may look for plenty of bad books about Egypt...[but] *Egyptian Sketches*, like all amateur work, is not merely futile but noxious'.[55]

Conway was elected to the Committee of the Alpine Club and became active once more within the climbing community. He dined with and visited fellow climbers around the country including Charles Mathews, a member of a famous climbing family, close friend of Joseph Chamberlain and active member of Birmingham society. Conway persuaded Mathews to hold the third (and final) Arts Congress in Birmingham in November. He dined with Edward Whymper in London and stayed with Horace Walker in Liverpool, with fellow guests Cecil Slingsby and Katie Richardson, both outstanding alpinists. He also set about revising and updating the *Zermatt Pocket Book* with the help of William Coolidge. After this volume, his name continued to appear on the cover but, in characteristic style, Conway had lost interest in the project and all the work was done by Coolidge.

Coolidge was an American by birth who spent most of his life in Europe and 'ventured to include himself'[56] as an Englishman. His two great passions in life were studying the Alps and quarrelling with alpinists. His position as an authority on alpine history and geography was such that Captain Percy Farrar, the President of the Alpine Club, compared writing about the Alps without mentioning Coolidge to writing 'a Treatise on Theology without alluding to the Bible',[57] but Coolidge was even more famous for the long and bitter feuds that he entered into with almost all the leading climbers of the day. According to Arnold Lunn, 'Coolidge could do anything with a hatchet but bury it',[58] while Conway 'had the distinction of being the only eminent mountaineer with whom W. A. B. Coolidge found it impossible to pick a quarrel'.[59] Some of the correspondence between Coolidge and Conway still exists in the Alpine Club archives and the tone is remarkably cordial compared to the missives that Coolidge hurled at many other members of the club.

Having succeeded in befriending a notoriously difficult man, Conway set about turning the relationship to his advantage. Coolidge had edited Conway's first *Zermatt Pocket Book* and now the two 'jointly' wrote a series of *Climbers' Guides* to other regions of the Alps between 1881 and 1910. In practice, Coolidge did all the work, submitting long, pedantic, heavily annotated manuscripts, while Conway soothed the publisher after the ferocious attacks launched by Coolidge during the inevitable editing. In a letter to Coolidge, Conway gave some advice on how to manage T. Fisher Unwin, the long-suffering publisher of the guidebooks: 'Let TFU down lightly. Don't threaten him, but just send him your MS and he'll take it right, especially if you send him the short Lepontine Vol. first. Say you have borrowed a few pages from that to add to the other – as soon as he has put his money into a volume or two *we hold him*. Don't forewarn him of prospective troubles, and in case of a longer volume than usual, let him have the first part of the MS first and let that *be in type before he sees the last part* or knows how long it will be. It's only a question of management; if things get stiff I will ask TFU to lunch at the Savile, for election to which he is a candidate.'[60]

During the summer of 1890, Conway went climbing in the Alps while Katrina, still suffering from frail health, went on holiday with the Marbles in France and Switzerland. Young Agnes was bundled off to stay with Conway's mother, where she promptly fell ill. Concerned about Katrina's health, and determined not to allow her husband's holiday to be spoilt, Abigail Marble once again wrote to Elizabeth

Conway praising her virtue in nursing their sick granddaughter: 'I am unspeakably grateful...for your extreme considerations in withholding the temporary discomforts, disturbances and exasperations which form so large a part of our human experiences...my dear Mrs Conway, every letter from you to my dear child comes like a warm poultice to an aching spot.' Abigail skilfully countered Elizabeth's concerns about Agnes' health by underlining her own concerns about Katrina: 'Every hour here is a gain to K...To keep K away from London and its cares to the last moment is our most sincere desire.' However, her postscript rather undermined her carefully crafted image of suffering and ill health by noting that 'we live like "fighting cocks" so good is the table – there is no better one even in Paris'.

Meanwhile Katrina wrote to Conway encouraging him to travel to Italy after the Alps in search of antiques to 'bohemianise' their stolidly middle-class home in Bayswater. 'You realize, as no one else but I do, our zeal to make the house exquisitely lovely...we desperately want some incomparable chairs for the drawing room, a superb desk and a beautiful something for the window – this would free the two chests which are badly needed for the dining room...Then I want you to bring me a Michelangelo, Raphael, Titian and Leonardo for the hall where the rug hangs...But seriously dear Herr you can do the unheard of, with your knowledge and genius for ferreting out rare and lovely things.' When Conway obliged by buying a Foppa and several other paintings, Katrina was both delighted and slightly horrified by the extravagance: 'Of course you will never breathe the price of this picture to [Manton and Abigail Marble]...They would never understand.'

At 34, Conway's life consisted of an agreeable round of lunches, dinners and social calls. A day spent at home was a 'dressing gown day'; they were very rare. He continued to spend much of his time in London at the Savile Club with the literary group that circled around Edmund Gosse, Thomas Hardy and Rudyard Kipling, and he lunched with Robert Louis Stevenson on his last visit to the Club before he set sail for the South Seas. He dined frequently with the sculptor Edward Onslow Ford, whose work includes the Shelley memorial in University College, Oxford. Leslie Stephen invited him to join 'The Sunday Tramps' (motto: 'High Thinking and Plain Living') and during one of their long walks through the English countryside they stopped off for tea at the writer George Meredith's house in Leatherhead.

Conway gave occasional lectures, wrote occasional articles, and was elected a Fellow of the Society of Antiquaries. At the 1890 Annual Dinner of the Society of Authors (of which he later became chairman) Conway sat opposite Jerome K. Jerome. The toast to 'the chairman' was proposed by Oscar Wilde, while Professor Conway replied to the toast to 'Literature, Art and Science'. He dined with Henry Tate, the sugar magnate who had just offered pictures worth £90,000 (a vast fortune) to the nation, and wrote a letter to *The Times* supporting the idea of a National Gallery of English Art.[61] He attended a number of private viewings and art exhibitions but, despite his admiration for Ruskin, he had little enthusiasm for modern art: 'Went to see the new Burne-Jones "Briar Rose" cycle', he recorded in his diary. 'Pictures decorative and should be used as designs for tapestry – not properly PICTURES at all.' But above all, Conway was bored: he had no prospect of a proper career; after their first romance, his marriage was no longer very happy or fulfilling; and life seemed to be passing him by.

During the summer of 1890, a new vista opened up before him when he climbed Mont Blanc with Douglas Freshfield and then followed a variant of the High Level Route from Chamonix to Zermatt. In a letter to his mother he described it as 'the very cream of all my alpine experience...for the future I mean always to wander in the Alps and not to fix myself down at a centre as heretofore'. Some ten years older than Conway, Douglas Freshfield was the son of the managing partner of a large firm of London solicitors. He devoted his life to geography and mountain exploration, becoming President of the Alpine Club in 1893 and President of the Royal Geographical Society in 1914. Under Freshfield's influence, Conway resolved to become an explorer.

A Country Not One's Own

Explorers were the great celebrities of the Victorian era and Conway was inspired both by the sense of adventure and by the public esteem in which they were held. When David Livingstone set out to explore darkest Africa in 1852, the strange combination of missionary zeal, rational scientific inquiry and moral crusade against slavery turned him into a national hero.[62] His meeting with the opportunistic popular journalist Henry Morton Stanley in 1871 perhaps marked the end of the heroic age and the dawn of celebrity-seeking exploration. Three years later, in 1874, Livingstone was dead, racked by fever, dysentery, ulcers, haemorrhoids, depression and paranoia, while Stanley continued to win fame and fortune in the Congo. Conway, like many of his generation, was deeply moved by the death of the great explorer. His entry for the Repton School Poetry Prize in 1874 was entitled 'Livingstone':

T'is evening; on the hills the setting sun
Pours his lazy ray, his brilliant race is run
But e'er he sinks one living glance he throws
On Afric's land, which now responsive glows.

He sinks! Yet not as here but dimly bright,
But one unclouded orb of glowing light;
The tints of sunset climb the mountain's crest,
Whilst weary nature lays itself to rest.

But hark! What sound is this that strikes the ear?
A sorrowing group upon the slope appear;
A band of Afric's sons, with measured tread,
Bear the last relics of some loved one dead.

And so on, for 124 lines.

London was the capital of the world's greatest empire and the undisputed centre of world exploration. Explorers set sail down the Thames from the Port of London as they had done for centuries: 'From Sir Francis Drake to Sir John Franklin...the great knights-errant of the sea...Hunters for gold or pursuers of fame...What greatness has not floated on the ebb of that river into the mystery of an unknown earth.'[63] But by the 1890s, the unknown earth was shrinking fast. The great mountain chains of Asia and South America were amongst the few remaining remnants of unexplored terrain outside the Polar regions. As Conway later observed in a paper delivered to the Royal Geographical Society: 'The abodes of snow, polar and mountainous, alone stand forth to challenge exploration. It is not in the nature of man to decline that challenge.'[64]

The Royal Geographical Society was the great clearing house for exploratory endeavours around the world and activities 'in the field' were often less important than politics within the RGS, where patrons, editors and other opinion-formers largely determined the public reputation of explorers and the sponsorship they received. Douglas Freshfield was one of the prime movers within the Society and he introduced Conway in 1890. The original aim of the RGS was 'the promotion and diffusion of that most important and entertaining branch of knowledge, Geography'.[65] The subject occupied a sort of no-man's-land between art and science, and while many geographers certainly aspired to scientific respectability, entertainment – derring-do and good storytelling – still formed an important part of its appeal. Geography was also ripe for commercial exploitation, as Edward Stanford, publisher and purveyor of maps to generations of explorers, astutely identified when he opened the world's first specialist map shop in London.

Conway had alighted upon an activity that played to many of his strengths: he was an outstanding social networker, a proficient climber, a competent journalist and lecturer, and a keen observer of landscapes. Moreover, he had an unfulfilling marriage and, through the anticipated generosity of his stepfather-in-law, the means to pay for an extended separation from his wife while he mounted an expedition to some remote corner of the earth. The 1893 edition of *Hints for Travellers, Scientific and General*,[66] the explorer's handbook published by the RGS (and edited by Douglas Freshfield), identified Tibet and the native states on the northern frontier of India as areas demanding the attention of English explorers, so Conway resolved to mount an expedition to the Himalaya. When he wrote to Marble outlining his plans, Marble replied with remarkable prescience: 'It is not quite relevant to your art career to be climbing mountains, but I perceive that alpine, Caucasian or Himalayan supereminence may be the cornerstone of artistic eminence. Events are often perfectly logical like that.'

In early 1891, Conway published *The Dawn of Art in the Ancient World*, but following the death of his Cambridge friend and mentor

Henry Bradshaw, and his repeated failure to win the Slade professorship, his interest in art had waned. His main preoccupation now was the organisation of the expedition. He read numerous books on exploration, including Stanley's *Through the Dark Continent*, Burton's *Pilgrimage to Al-Medinah and Meccah*, Hooker's *Himalayan Journals* and Nansen's *First Crossing of Greenland*. He also called on Rudyard Kipling's father, who was director of the Lahore Museum, while he was on leave in London, in order to pick up tips on Indian travel.

At Freshfield's suggestion, he initially intended to explore Sikkim and even thought of climbing Kangchenjunga, the third highest mountain in the world. Freshfield later made the first circuit of the mountain in 1899, which was a considerable mountaineering achievement in itself. It was not climbed until 1955, when Joe Brown and George Band reached the summit. After calling on Francis Younghusband, Conway shifted his attention from Sikkim to the Karakoram. Younghusband was an Indian army officer, who was elected the youngest Fellow of the Royal Geographical Society and awarded the Founders' Medal after travelling from Peking through Manchuria and across the Gobi Desert to Kashgar, before making the first crossing of the Mustagh Pass near K2 to reach Baltistan in present-day Pakistan. Younghusband gave Conway advice on flower presses, barometers and the temperament of the local Baltis, and later wrote to him from India after Conway had returned to England emphasising the importance of exploration rather than mountaineering: 'Mere climbing of peaks just for the sake of saying one has been up them I don't much care about, but what I shall look forward to with special interest is yr. observations on these glaciers.'

Having largely abandoned hard alpine climbing after the death of his three friends nearly a decade earlier in 1882, Conway set out his new philosophy of mountain exploration in a paper entitled *Centrists and Excentrists*, which he presented to the Alpine Club in 1891: 'Just as a man is a better and finer creature in proportion as his sympathies and interests are large and numerous, so is mountaineering...of a high type in proportion as it gives play to the largest number of dignified human tastes, and awakens the largest number of fine human emotions', he opined. In order to achieve mountaineering of this 'high type', Conway believed that the climber 'must alternate between high and low, difficult and easy, between ice and woodland, meadow and rock, snowfield, valley and lake'.[67] The ideal climber, according to Conway, was a mountain explorer, concerned with both beauty and scientific research, capable of climbing the highest mountains but equally interested in valleys and passes. In fact, the ideal climber bore a striking resemblance to Conway.

Conway's paper, which dismissed the younger and more technically competent members of the Alpine Club as mere 'gymnasts', and implied that they lacked intelligence, antagonised a good part of his audience and resulted in a lively debate. Conway was delighted. In his diary he wrote: 'Went to AC meeting where my "Centrist" papers were attacked. A pleasant evening.' His dogmatic approach was later explained by C. Wilson, his obituarist in the *Alpine Journal*: 'His life was essentially religious and mountaineering...being a part of his religion, he held, as many zealots do, that having the true faith it was his duty...to belabour the unorthodox.'[68] Wilson went on to observe that while in his youth Conway 'was looked upon as what used to be called "a very superior person" and...was not readily approachable by his juniors...Later in life [he] became a very good "mixer"...he knew everybody that was worth knowing.'

In June 1891, with the support of Freshfield, Conway was voted £500 by the Royal Geographical Society and £100 by the Royal Society. Conway confidently predicted that he would make a profit of at least £1,000 from the expedition, but in the meantime found it necessary to borrow £500 from Marble. Adopting the same technique that he had used with his mother, he assured Marble that 'I ask it as the capital with which I am to go into business'. Although he would never have admitted it, Conway had, in effect, decided to become a 'professional' mountaineer, and was now subject to all the commercial pressures that beset that profession. The life blood of the professional climber is publicity: without it, he or she cannot sell the books and lectures that provide their income. Unfortunately, outside a small circle of dedicated climbers, the British public has rather unsophisticated tastes when it comes to mountaineering. They either like very high mountains that they have heard of, even if they are relatively easy (Mont Blanc in Conway's day; Everest today); or slightly lower mountains with a reputation for killing lots of people (the Matterhorn in Conway's day; K2 today). Conway had no intention of competing with the young 'gymnasts' on technical difficulty; he therefore had to climb a very high mountain (preferably the highest then climbed), and imply that it was extremely dangerous to do so, whilst retaining sufficient scientific respectability to satisfy his sponsors.

The Royal Geographical Society arranged instruction in surveying, mapping, geology, botany and photography for aspiring British explorers at a cost of 2s. 6d (12.5p) per hour. Conway dutifully visited Kew Gardens to study Himalayan botany and discussed surveying with Colonel Henry Godwin-Austen, an experienced member of the Indian Survey, responsible for mapping large parts of the Astor, Gilgit and Skardu districts in present-day Pakistan. Conway later dismissed Godwin-Austen's maps as 'all rot',[69] but his own maps were not immune from criticism. As one user later noted: 'I was trying to reconcile nature with Conway's map; and my difficulties were scarcely less than those which disturbed the peace of Victorian theologians.'[70]

Conway corresponded with Albert Frederick Mummery, the greatest climber of his day, about the expedition. In one letter Mummery, whose apparent indifference to vertical drops was widely attributed to his acute short-sightedness, asked Conway: 'Are you good at selecting routes? I don't think I am.' When they climbed together in the Alps in July, Conway soon realised that Mummery's route selection tended to involve climbing at a standard that was at the absolute limit of his ability. The most spectacular climbing photograph of himself that Conway could find for an 'illustrated interview' that appeared in the *Strand Magazine* in 1897 shows him climbing on the Grivola in the summer of 1891, looking distinctly uncomfortable on a very tight rope held by Mummery. Conway also climbed with Mummery's companion, Miss Lily Bristow, who two years later made the first traverse of the Grépon, then considered the most difficult climb in the Alps, with Mummery and Cecil Slingsby.

Conway and Mummery continued to correspond about the Himalaya after their return from the Alps, but agreed that their objectives were incompatible. 'I have come to the conclusion that the party has no chance of ascending any of the great Himalayan peaks', Mummery wrote. 'It is neither strong enough nor fast enough to grapple with such long and probably steep ascents. As this is the only part of the expedition which truly excites me I have made up my mind not to go.' Nevertheless, Mummery was amongst the first to congratulate Conway on his achievements when he returned, and Conway later described Mummery as 'the greatest climber of this or any other generation', although he noted that 'he loved danger for its own sake'.[71] Mummery died four years later on Nanga Parbat, making the first attempt to climb an 8,000 m peak.

During his summer in the Alps, Conway met Edward Fitzgerald, a young climber from Trinity College, Cambridge, who was unable to go to the Himalaya but later accompanied Conway on his walk through the Alps. He also discussed his plans with Harold Topham, an outstanding climber and three times winner on the Cresta Run. Topham pulled out after spending a few days climbing with Conway in the Graian Alps. Rapidly running out of possible companions, Conway invited Oscar Eckenstein to join him in the Karakoram. He was an odd choice of companion. A Jew of German ancestry, famous for doing one arm pull-ups, Eckenstein was described as having the 'beard and build of our first ancestry'.[72] His father was a prominent socialist who fled Germany in 1848 and moved to England, where Eckenstein was born and grew up. He inherited many of his father's rebellious tendencies, conducting a long and bitter feud with members of the Alpine Club, who regarded him as 'an insufferably arrogant engineer'. Katrina was sceptical about Conway's choice of companion: 'I...tremble in my shoes a little, remembering as I do how much he was disliked in Zermatt and what a cad he was held to be', but Conway had previously collaborated with Eckenstein's sister, Lina, who translated some of Dürer's papers in the British Museum, and Eckenstein was probably the world's leading expert on modern ice climbing equipment. Conway was convinced that he would be useful, and so he befriended him.

While Conway climbed in the Alps, Katrina went with Agnes and the Marbles to the Dutch seaside resort of Scheveningen. As Katrina and Conway led their increasingly separate lives, she returned to Scheveningen with the Marbles each year from 1893 to 1898. As always during their periods of separation, she wrote regular letters to Conway, but there was little to tell: 'You know that this is not the place of great news – sky, sea, wind, sleep and food – with music, talk and cards filling the hours from dress to bed time.'

Back in London, Conway continued his lessons at the Royal Geographical Society and was introduced to Lieutenant Charles Bruce of the 5th Gurkha Rifles, who agreed to accompany him on his expedition. Charlie 'Bruiser' Bruce was the fourteenth child of Lord Aberdare, the great South Wales coal magnate, former Home Secretary and President of the Royal Geographical Society. Bruce had a distinguished career as a soldier and mountaineer, later commanding the 1st Battalion of Gurkhas at Gallipoli in the First World War and leading the 1922 Everest expedition. He was liked and respected by his troops and fellow climbers for his constant good humour, prowess at drinking and wrestling, and ability to swear and tell bawdy stories in English and several local dialects. As the mountain historian Kenneth Mason observed: 'Bruce's laughter was a tonic throughout the Himalaya.'[73] At Eckenstein's suggestion, they also recruited Mattias Zurbriggen, an outstanding alpine guide. Zurbriggen insisted on 'testing the powers' of Bruce, whom he had not previously met, before he agreed to join the expedition. The two climbed together in the winter of 1891 and Zurbriggen soon decided that Bruce was 'a first-rate mountaineer as well as a good and kind-hearted man'.[74] Bruce also brought four Gurkha soldiers on the expedition, two of whom later accompanied Conway on his walk through the Alps.

During the winter, Conway continued his planning and sought the advice of Edward Whymper, conqueror of the Matterhorn in 1865, who was regarded as the world's leading expert on high altitude exploration after his 1879–80 expedition to the Andes. The 1893 edition of *Hints for Travellers* listed Whymper's 'South American Outfit' as a guide for future mountain explorers. It included four ordinary woollen suits of various weights, one dress suit, 12 flannel shirts, two white shirts, three neck ties, six shirt collars and 26 pocket handkerchiefs amongst his personal effects. *Hints for Travellers* also provided a list of essential scientific equipment, including a prismatic compass, hypsometrical apparatus (to measure the boiling point of water), barometer, sextant, artificial horizon, theodolite, tachometer and plane table. 'The nature and extent of his battery will be matters for the traveller himself to decide', the book noted, but added that 'revolvers are more useful for the moral effect they produce than any actual service they render'.[75] Despite all this equipment, many experts were sceptical about the scientific value of mountaineering expeditions. When Conway wrote to Kew Gardens to inform them that he intended to follow Whymper's example, they immediately wrote back saying: 'I am afraid that if you take Whymper for your model you will do nothing in Botany.'

Conway went on a short walking holiday in Wales with Bruce, during which he was introduced to Lord Aberdare, who helped to enlist the support of the authorities in India. Lord Lansdowne, the Viceroy, wrote to Bruce advising him to delete the term 'mountaineering party' from the expedition prospectus and substitute 'a party of exploration', because 'mountaineering is a sport and couldn't be taken official notice of, at least in my case'. The official letter from the Royal Geographical Society to the Viceroy referred to the expedition 'paying particular attention to any point that the Indian Government may desire to have elucidated', a phrase that was inserted at Bruce's suggestion to indicate that they would investigate any passes that might have military significance, as the British Raj worried about the threat posed by Russian expansion to the north.

Conway was determined that the expedition should make his reputation both as a scientific explorer and as a popular travel writer. Before the dawn of expedition photography, he recruited the painter A. D. McCormick to record their travels in watercolours that could be used to illustrate a book. Conway agreed to meet McCormick's expenses (in fact they were paid by Henry Willett, a wealthy brewer and patron of the arts who lived in Brighton) on the basis that they would divide McCormick's pictures, taking alternate picks. Five years after the expedition, some of McCormick's paintings were also used to illustrate a book entitled *The Kafirs of the Hindu-Kush* by Sir George Scott Robertson KCSI, the British Agent in Gilgit. Lieutenant Colonel Lloyd-Dickin, part hunter, part naturalist, agreed to undertake scientific work and Heywood Roudebush, an American relation of Agnes Tracy, also joined the party and shared the expenses.

By February all was ready and they set sail for Karachi. Conway wrote a letter to Freshfield from the ship: 'My men do not quarrel amongst themselves and Eckenstein is thus far an admirable companion.' The other members of the expedition had already agreed not to publish anything until Conway had read a paper at the Royal Geographical Society. On the ship, they finalised the other business arrangements for the expedition: 'Whatever other profits may come to us directly from the expedition (such as profits on the sale of natural history specimens after the Royal Society has received its due share, mining rights, valuable acquisitions of whatever kind excepting always such antiquities and works of art as any of us may purchase or otherwise acquire) are divided 10 p.c. to Zurbriggen, 30 p.c. to Eckenstein, 60 p.c. between Bruce and me.' This is the first reference to mining rights in Conway's diaries. In later life they became something of an obsession.

Conway was smitten with the romance of India, especially Kashmir, and recorded his impressions in Ruskinian prose: 'The whole effect was like a tangled skein of many-coloured silks. All was pageantry; people, sheep, mosques, palaces, tombs. No-one and nothing beheld belonged to my world, or to an ugly world. All floated in a romantic atmosphere in which the impossible might become true and from which the normal was banished.'[76] From Srinagar they travelled to Gilgit and spent nearly two months exploring the valleys around Rakaposhi. They passed through the small but troublesome kingdom of Hunza, which had been at war with Kashmir until December 1891 when an expeditionary force under the command of Colonel A. G. Durand was sent 'to bring the Hunza people to their senses'. Conway described it as 'a very sporting little campaign which had left no ill-feeling behind it'[77] and noted that when his expedition arrived six months later they enjoyed 'an extremely friendly and delightful welcome'. Conway was so enamoured of the place that he wrote to Katrina suggesting that they move to Hunza for two years. Fortunately for Katrina, the enthusiasm passed.

As they climbed up into the mountains, the tone of Conway's diary and book changed. No longer a sightseeing tour, this was now a scientific expedition. He made studious observations of the weather, geology and botany, recorded times and distances, and produced a detailed map. He also collected specimens: 'Over 300 different kinds of flowers, over 200 geological specimens...some 40 butterflies, not many beetles, two human skulls which we risked our lives to pilfer from the Nagyr graveyard, native musical instruments, and all manner of odd stuff.' All these were subjected to detailed scientific examination back in England, including the skulls, which were measured and described in great detail by W. L. H. Duckworth, scholar of Jesus College, Cambridge.[78]

Conway's party was not an entirely happy one. Lloyd-Dickin left after Hunza, suffering from ill health. Roudebush also left early, and so too did Eckenstein after a furious row with Conway. Eckenstein's friend Aleister Crowley, the occultist whose obituary described him as the 'wickedest man in the world', recorded that Eckenstein 'had quitted the party...principally on account of his disgust with its mismanagement'.[79] Conway's account of his departure was more succinct. In a letter to Abigail Marble he stated simply: 'Eckenstein turned out a blackguard.' Conway immediately notified Douglas Freshfield who wrote to the press, in his capacity as Honorary Secretary of the Royal Geographical Society, advising them that any communication about the expedition offered to them, except by Conway, would be 'unauthentic and unlawful and might give occasion for legal proceedings'. Conway later received a letter from Eckenstein's lawyer demanding £200 for breach of contract and £12 for expenses, which he ignored. A decade later Eckenstein and Crowley organised their own expedition to the Karakoram. Upon his arrival in India, Eckenstein was arrested for spying and imprisoned. It was widely believed that the authorities had been tipped off by Conway, who was President of the Alpine Club at the time. Eckenstein was only released after the personal intervention of the Viceroy.

Conway also argued with Bruce, after demanding that he contribute £300 to the expedition. Bruce had already agreed to meet all of his own expenses, but flatly refused to pay anything more. Katrina, as always, was sympathetic to her husband's plight: 'To have had two traitors in your small camp – one in money and the other in allegiance – seems to me too cruel', she wrote. Fortunately Marble agreed to make up the shortfall in the budget and Bruce, in his normal good-humoured way, ignored the dispute and stayed with the expedition. Conway saw to it that his argument with Eckenstein became public knowledge, thanking everyone except Eckenstein in his articles about the expedition, but he never disclosed his disagreement with the Hon. Charles

Bruce, who was both popular and well connected.

The party journeyed up the Hispar glacier over the Hispar Pass and down the Biafo glacier to Askole, where they were briefly joined by Mr. Churcher of the 87th Fusiliers who was on a hunting expedition in the district and brought with him a banjo, to which they sang:

'We love you all,
Petites or tall
Whate'er your beauty or your grade is,
Coy or coquettes
Blondes or brunettes
We love you all, bewitching ladies'

while noting that 'a mental reservation had certainly to be made with respect to the hags of Askole – a most ill-looking lot, so far as we could judge'.[80] From Askole they walked up the Baltoro glacier, mapped the position of K2, Gasherbrum and Masherbrum, and climbed a subsidiary summit of Baltoro Kangri, which Conway named Pioneer Peak. Conway recorded that his barometer gave a height of 22,600 ft (6,900 m), which he rounded up to 23,000 ft (over 7,000 m), thereby claiming a new world record for altitude – a crucial element in obtaining publicity for his exploits. Unfortunately Pioneer Peak has since been measured at just 21,322 ft (6,500 m), nearly 1,000 ft lower than the previous record. In an interview with the *Pall Mall Gazette* following his return, Conway explained that 'as he could not climb Mount Everest, which is politically inaccessible, he transferred his attentions to the highest peak available, which he called Pioneer Peak'.[81] He failed to mention that in order to reach the foot of Pioneer Peak he had walked past four 8,000 m peaks including K2, the second highest peak in the world, which towers nearly 7,000 ft (2,100 m) above Pioneer Peak, but is incomparably more difficult to climb.

On the journey home, Conway bargained for rugs and silver but was frustrated by the lack of opportunity to buy antiques. As he later observed: 'India is not a very good country for hunting antiquities. One cannot carry away a Jain temple.'[82] Nevertheless he did succeed in stealing some Tibetan manuscripts from the library of a monastery and also removed a large Gandhāra carved relief from a Hindu temple after slapping and then bribing the guardian. He finally arrived back in London on 20 December, 10 months after leaving, and immediately went to an Alpine Club dinner to deliver a triumphant speech.

Conway's was the first major mountaineering expedition to the Himalaya. It made some advances in planning and logistics for extended travel over glaciers, as well as mapping some 5,000 square kilometres of difficult mountain terrain. Conway named numerous peaks in the Karakoram, including Hidden Peak (Gasherbrum I or K5), Broad Peak (K3) and the Ogre, first climbed by Doug Scott and Chris Bonington in 1977. He also named the glacier leading to the foot of K2 the Godwin-Austen glacier and the place where it merges with the main Baltoro glacier 'Concordia', after a similar junction on the Aletsch glacier in Switzerland. *The Times* wrote a leader on the expedition on 27 September 1892 and when Conway got back to England he immediately started work on *Climbing and Exploration in the Karakoram-Himalayas,* which was published in 1894. The French translation, published in 1898, was entitled *Ascensions et Explorations à Sept Mille Mètres dans l'Himalaya*, a somewhat misleading title since the highest point reached by the expedition was in fact 6,500 m.

In keeping with his ambition to be taken seriously as a scientific explorer, *Climbing and Exploration in the Karakoram-Himalayas* is a rather stilted book. A kindly reviewer noted that he 'tells his tale most clearly and pleasantly...[and] avoids the fault, not unknown among writers on Alpine travel, of mild facetiousness...Mr. Conway does not...think that a love of the mountains is best demonstrated by a contempt for science.'[83] As well as being an example of scientific exploration, it was also an emphatically imperial project. In the introduction Conway recorded with gratitude the fellow countrymen whom he met on the frontiers of India: 'Men who are there maintaining and extending so worthily the prestige of England's imperial power and the honour of her name.'[84] The last line of Charles Bruce's 1937 obituary of Conway states that 'it was Conway's expedition which brought the Himalaya to Europe'. Did he mean that Conway popularised the Himalaya in Europe, or that Conway's mapping of the Karakoram literally appropriated the region for England?

. With the forthrightness characteristic of his countrymen, A. P. Harper, a leading New Zealand climber in the 1890s, gave his views on the guiding force behind the expedition in the *Alpine Journal*: 'It was the opinion of the chiefs of the A. C. world in 1893 that the success of Conway's expedition was largely due to "young Bruce". Knowing Bruce in later years and seeing his ability as a leader...I have no doubt that opinion was correct.'[85] With his army experience, Bruce certainly managed most of the logistics and planning for the expedition in India. In a letter to his sister, he also claimed to have carried Conway on his back after Conway refused to wade across a glacial river. Halfway across, Bruce lost his footing and both men ended up in the freezing water. However, it was Conway who wrote the official account of the expedition and enjoyed the public acclaim in England, giving 10 lectures in 1893, 21 in 1894 and 24 in 1895. While Bruce returned to his regiment, Conway was made a Vice President of the Alpine Club and, in due course, received a knighthood 'for his remarkable work as a traveller'.

No one would claim that Aleister Crowley was a reliable witness. Nevertheless, when he and Eckenstein made their expedition to K2, some ten years after Conway, they employed several porters from the earlier expedition, some of whom claimed that Conway never actually reached the summit of Pioneer Peak: 'I was very disgusted at the bad taste of some of the coolies who had been with him in saying that he had never been on the mountain at all, but turned back at the foot of the ice fall', Crowley noted. 'How could such common creatures presume to decide a delicate scientific question of this sort?'[86] In 1934, Bruce wrote an account of the expedition in which he gave most of the credit to Zurbriggen: 'The only first class mountaineer...that is, [someone] capable of personally leading and carrying out great attempts on a great Himalayan peak...was Mathias Zurbriggen.'[87] Unusually, we also have Zurbriggen's record of the expedition, written in 1899.[88] From his account, it appears that he and Bruce did the greater part of the route-finding, while Conway was primarily engaged in mapping. In contrast to Conway's dramatic account of scaling Pioneer Peak, Zurbriggen recorded that he sat on the summit, drank a little cognac and smoked a good cigar while admiring the view. However, Zurbriggen was careful not to antagonise any of his 'patrons', and it appears that the text of the English translation of his book was carefully vetted by Conway before publication.[89]

Radical Tendencies

Conway's diary for 1893 is missing. He spent much of the year working on his map and the book while Katrina fell dangerously ill with appendicitis. In order to speed her recovery, Conway wrote to Manton Marble advising him that he had 'determined not to see her again until she is really stronger', so the Marbles came over from New York to nurse her. When she was through the worst, they took her to Scheveningen to convalesce. Meanwhile Conway, who was possibly suffering from malaria, went for a month-long cure at Marienbad, where he was joined by several friends ('The English are few in number and select so we all knew one another'). He wrote to Manton Marble, asking him to recommend 'a few fairly clean French novels of recognised merit' and dreamt up a scheme for 'Haussmannizing London'. By the autumn, both Katrina and Conway were recovered and Conway renewed his efforts to be elected as Slade Professor at Cambridge, only to be disappointed a third time. Instead, he took over the editorship of the *Alpine Journal* and plotted with his artistic and journalistic friends to oust John Henry Middleton, the incumbent Professor.

Having secured some reputation within geographical and mountaineering circles, Conway craved a position in public life. After attending a meeting held to establish an Imperial-Liberal Committee in support of Lord Rosebery, he resolved to become a member of parliament and wrote to Edward Marjoribanks, the Liberal Chief Whip. He confided that 'I have at one time or another had beliefs and principles enough to stock all three parties, but I have come down now to a simple willingness to fight in line with one party; and, on the whole, I prefer the Radicals – not that I believe in their entire creed and all its possible developments, but that I find myself able to go, in a broadly consistent fashion, with all the Radical tendencies as far as they are yet revealed. I should, of course, give the party I joined the same kind of loyal support that I should give my own side in a game of football.' Apparently satisfied by this statement of Conway's commitment to the

Liberal cause, Marjoribanks recommended that he should stand as parliamentary candidate for Bath. Since Bath returned two members of parliament at that time, Conway set out to find a second candidate 'who must be rich enough to pay the bulk of the expenses and not too able to throw me into the shade'. He failed to find the perfect running-mate, but fortunately Marble agreed to meet the costs of his election campaign. Marble also paid their rent in both London and Bath, since Conway was once again heavily in debt and could not afford to do so himself. A few weeks later, Conway and Katrina travelled to Bath to attend the adoption meeting. In his memoirs, Conway recalled that 'Katrina was entirely new to British politics but was ready to throw herself into the fray as she most efficiently did...As the train slowed down in [Bath] station, "By the by," she asked "what are our politics?" before I had time to answer we were in the station and she was canvassing the porter!'[90]

On hearing of his decision to stand for parliament, Douglas Freshfield wrote an Epitaph to Conway's career as a climber and art critic:

> Here lies – all politicians do –
> One born to play a different part
> Who to his better self untrue
> Lapsed from the High Alps and High Art
>
> Our sleeping-bagger is no more
> He dallies down the Primrose Path!
> Upon the carpet-bagger's door
> We chalk in sadness –'Gone to Bath'
>
> The Lord have mercy on his soul!
> And may Bath voters – how he'll bore 'em! -
> Plant at the bottom of the poll
> The party from the Karakoram!

Conway replied:

> As lies the snow on Himalay

All politicians lie, you say;
The difference, if you wish to know,
Is snow lies high and we lie low.
Than candid snow far whiter we,
As quickly I will make you see;
For who, in any mortal state,
Candider than a Candidate?

Conway persuaded the managers of the Liberal party in Bath to lobby Lord Rosebery (who had recently succeeded Gladstone as prime minister) to give him a knighthood in order to improve his chances of success in the next election. When they agreed to try, he wrote to Marble in triumph: 'Now, perhaps, you will see the inwardness of my candidature. If I can score that advantage this summer, I shall be to the good whatever the result of the election!' However, for Katrina it was a revelation to meet the Liberal section of the Bath electorate. It was her first real exposure to poor people and she started to see politics as more than just a means of securing a knighthood for her husband. 'Her heart went out to the poor of Bath – she saw in them a career and they LOVED her', Conway told Marble. Conway's attitude to poverty was somewhat different. He believed that 'the poor you will always have with you, but you will not always have me'.[91] Like many rich Victorians, he ascribed poverty to a combination of inferior breeding and fecklessness and hardly noticed the people of the abyss and the nether world that they inhabited. On one occasion Conway attended an 'at home' at a friend's house and became vaguely conscious that some of the servants seemed rather friendly towards him. It was only when he returned to his own house that Katrina informed him that she had lent their servants to the hostess for the day. 'I never know them by sight', Conway happily confided in a letter to Marble. If he did recognise that there might be a few 'deserving poor' he never acknowledged the fact except, perhaps, as a spur to fight even harder in the 'struggle for existence in human society'. Later in life, Conway came to admire the writing of St. Francis of Assisi, and delivered a lecture on 'Francis of Assisi and the Popular Revolution',[92] but even St. Francis sought only to sanctify poverty, not to eradicate it, and Conway was primarily interested in the 'great man's' influence on art, rather than his social ideals.

After his long journey through the picturesque poverty of the East, Conway was keen to resume his interrupted social life in England. He attended a number of dinners and receptions in Liverpool and hosted a 'smoker' for his friends at home, where he supplied good cigars, whisky and anecdotes. Dining societies formed an important part of his social life and he was invited to join three new ones: the Kinsmen was an Anglo-American club, frequented by actors; the Cosmopolitan was formed to continue the excellent entertainment once provided by the French ambassador to London, after the ambassador was recalled to Paris; while the Dilettanti was said to be the oldest dining club in London, founded by Sir Joshua Reynolds and friends. There were also numerous dining clubs linked to other societies, such as the Royal Academy, the Royal Society, the Alpine Club and the Royal Geographical Society, where groups of friends met before or after society functions. Conway's diaries contain menus from some of these occasions, which typically consisted of ten or more courses, accompanied by an equal number of wines, toasts and replies. Conway, who was evidently a good public speaker, was frequently called upon to propose or reply to a toast. Some of the menus have a few scribbled prompts on the back to remind him of an apposite anecdote.

With little prospect of an early election to propel him into parliament, Conway soon got bored with constituency work in Bath and began to plan another expedition. After the hardships of the Himalaya and the months of work that had followed preparing his book and map, Conway wanted to undertake a journey that, whilst newsworthy and capable of being turned into a book, did not involve anything too lengthy or arduous. In the end, he set out to demonstrate the truth of his *excentrist* creed by undertaking a journey of exploration through the entire length of the Alps. It was an idea that had first occurred to him in the Himalaya, where he had discussed it with Zurbriggen. By the middle of 1894 he had completed his research and devised 'a route, or rather a combination of climbs, the descent from each ending at the starting-point for the next, so that a climber might begin at one extremity of the snowy range and walk up and down through its midst to the other extremity over a continuous series of peaks and passes'.[93] He had also settled on a title for the book: *The Alps from End to End*. On 30

May he took the train to Turin, at the start of a three-month journey. Meanwhile, the Marbles sailed from New York to collect Katrina and Agnes and take them to Scheveningen.

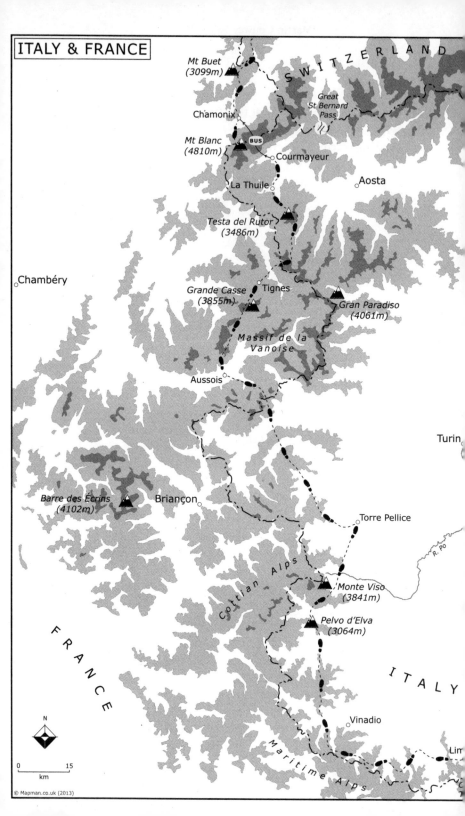

Chapter Three
Through Italy and France

The Excitements of Frontier Travel

Today, we think of the Alps as a prosperous and peaceful region where the crest of the mountain range forms a natural frontier, with Italy holding the southern slopes, France to the west and Switzerland and Austria to the north. But peaceful cohabitation of this mountainous region represents the exception, rather than the rule. The Roman Emperor Augustus, and Charlemagne, King of the Franks, both succeeded in uniting the entire alpine region under one ruler for a period of time, but for most of history it has formed a fiercely contested borderland between different ethnic, linguistic, religious and national groups. The oldest inhabitant of the Alps of whom we have detailed knowledge was 'Ötzi', a 5,000-year-old man, found frozen in the Similaun glacier on the border of Austria and Italy in 1991. He was about 5 feet tall, dark-haired, brown-eyed and had charcoal tattoos. He was wearing well-made deerskin shoes, a bearskin hat, goat-hide clothes and carried a primitive rucksack made from grass matting. He also had a stone arrowhead in his body and at least one other person's blood on his clothes. Given this long history of violent conflict in the alpine region, it probably seemed quite natural to Conway that the Alps should be inhabited by warring neighbours, and not particularly surprising that he should be prevented from commencing his walk 'from end to end' at his intended starting point because of the tense military situation on the Italian–French border.

Conway arrived in Limone at the foot of the Col de Tende on 1 June 1894. He travelled from London to Turin by train and steamer, with two soldiers from the 5th Gurkha Rifles, Amar Sing Thapa and Karbir Bura Thoki, both of whom had accompanied him on his Himalayan expedition. They were 'lent' to him for his European travels by Charles Bruce (now a Major), in order that they might learn the craft of climbing snow mountains under first-rate European guides. In Conway's account of the journey, Amar Sing and Karbir play a somewhat similar role to 'Modestine' in Robert Louis Stevenson's *Travels with a Donkey in the Cévennes*, providing comic relief while acting as 'good weight-carriers'.[94] Conway was joined in Turin by his young Trinity friend, Edward Fitzgerald, now 23, who had left Cambridge after failing to be selected as cox of the Varsity boat. Fitzgerald arrived with his manservant, James, whose job it would be to accompany their luggage from hotel to hotel, while the rest of the party climbed.

Conway invited Mattias Zurbriggen, the outstanding mountain guide who had accompanied him to the Karakoram, while Fitzgerald had two guides, J. B. Aymonod and Louis Carrel, who had accompanied Whymper to the Andes in 1879. The party therefore consisted of eight people, who assembled in Conway's hotel room in Turin, 'surrounded by a chaos of unpacked baggage consisting largely, as usual, of unnecessary things'.[95]

The party that set out to follow in his footsteps some 120 years later consisted of me and a large rucksack, containing absolutely nothing unnecessary. I had planned to travel from London to the Col de Tende by air to Nice and then by train to Limone. However, the traditional summer strike by French air traffic controllers meant that all flights to France were cancelled. Instead, I caught a plane to Turin, flying over the Alps on a cloudless day with the summit of Mont Blanc clearly visible below. In Turin, the Airport Express train drivers were also on strike, so I took a local bus to the city centre, caught a train from Porta Nuova to Lingotto, then another to Cuneo, and finally a bus to Limone, arriving some 20 hours after leaving home. It was not an auspicious start.

The Col de Tende lies about 40 km north of the Mediterranean coast. It was designated as the western end of the Alps by John Ball, one of the founding fathers of British alpinism, who decided, for reasons that are not entirely clear, that it marks the point of separation between the Alps and the Apennines. Its status was confirmed by Conway's friend William Coolidge, the leading Victorian authority on the history and geography of the Alps. Conway consulted Coolidge on his route through the Alps, and Coolidge contributed a rather dull chapter to

The Alps from End to End suggesting other possible itineraries. Coolidge no doubt recommended that the walk should start at the Col de Tende, but the decision to end it at the Ankogel, just to the east of the Grossglockner, was almost certainly taken by Conway. The Hochalmspitze lies further to the east, has a large glacier, and is some 100 m higher than the Ankogel, but Conway dismissed it as 'a mere buttress point' and claimed that the Ankogel is the 'last of the snowy alps'.[96] Today most people would probably acknowledge that the eastern 'end' of the Alps is in Slovenia, not Austria.

Conway and his party travelled from Turin to the Col de Tende by the same route as I did, taking the newly constructed railway via Cuneo to Limone. From Limone, they walked up the pass to inspect the railway tunnel that was being blasted through the mountain below the Col, which would ultimately link Turin by rail to Ventimiglia and Nice. It was their first day in the mountains and young Fitzgerald set the pace up the hillside: 'His habit is to carry no knapsack but to fill his large pockets with things. It takes him some time to get up momentum; when that is accomplished all he has to do is keep pace with his pockets.'[97] As they walked through the tunnel the Gurkhas tested the acoustics by singing 'Ta-ra-ra-boom-de-ay', a song they had been taught by Roudebush in Kashmir. Emerging at the far end of the tunnel, and still in Italian territory, they asked permission from the border guards to climb the Roche de l'Abisse, and were refused, because their chosen route would have taken them close to six forts on the southern side of the pass, defending the approaches from France. As Conway observed: 'Fortunate people who live in islands or without bellicose neighbours have no idea of the excitements of frontier travel in Central Europe.'[98]

The forts were just the latest manifestation of thousands of years of conflict in the region. Some 2,000 years ago the area around the Col de Tende was inhabited by Celtic tribes, who were defeated by the Romans as they progressively took over the entire alpine region. Roman power diminished in the fifth century and the First Kingdom of Burgundy established control over the western flanks of the Alps. After the Burgundians were conquered by the Franks in the sixth century, the region became part of the Holy Roman Empire founded by Charlemagne in AD 800. Following Charlemagne's death, various duchies and principalities became established inland, while the coast was dominated by Saracens, who made periodic incursions into the mountains. Saracen pirates crossed the Col de Tende in AD 906 and sacked the monastery of Pedona, near present-day Borgo San Dalmazzo. They also briefly gained control of the Mont Cenis pass, far to the north, where they massacred English pilgrims travelling to Rome in AD 921 and again in 923.[99]

In AD 843 Charlemagne's empire was divided into three and the Second Kingdom of Burgundy was established. As this kingdom declined in power in the eleventh century, several powerful counties and duchies emerged, notably the Duchy of Savoy, which became the longest-surviving royal house in Europe. By the beginning of the fifteenth century, the duchy stretched across the Alps from its capital in Chambéry, north to Geneva and east to Aosta. The Dukes of Savoy gained Nice from the Counts of Provence in 1388 and Piedmont in 1419. In 1559 Duke Emmanuel-Philibert transferred his capital from Chambéry to Turin.

The Dauphins of the Viennois also came to prominence at about the same time as Savoy, establishing control over Grenoble and Briançon as well as land on the eastern slopes of the Alps including Monte Viso, to the north of the Col de Tende. During the thirteenth century, the Dauphins added several new territories to the north, including the Chamonix valley. The Dauphiné was sold to Charles V of France by Humbert II, the last Dauphin, in 1349. Given the long and convoluted border between Dauphiné (later France) and Savoy, it was inevitable that the two powers would come into conflict. At first they attempted to adjust their borders by land swaps, progressively moving, either wittingly or unwittingly, towards a situation where the main crest of the Alps formed the boundary between the two, with the Dukes of Savoy holding the land to the east and France holding the western slopes. In 1355 France exchanged the area around Chamonix for land north of Grenoble. In the Treaty of Utrecht (1713), Savoy exchanged Barcelonnette for the land around Monte Viso formerly held by the Dauphins. When Conway visited in 1894, both French and Occitan, the language spoken in large parts of southern France before it was systematically suppressed, were still widely spoken in this region of Italy.

The Duchy of Savoy also gained the crown of Sicily under the Treaty of Utrecht, which it exchanged with the Austrians for Sardinia in 1720, thereby making Savoy part of the Kingdom of Piedmont–Sardinia. Following the Revolution, France attacked Savoy, gaining control of Nice in 1793 and Piedmont in 1802. After the defeat of Napoleon the territory was restored to the Kingdom of Piedmont–Sardinia at the Congress of Vienna in 1815. Within Conway's lifetime, as part of the unification of Italy, a deal was done between King Victor Emmanuel of Piedmont–Sardinia and Napoleon III of France, whereby the King agreed to cede Savoy and the County of Nice to France in exchange for French military support against the Austrians, who held Lombardy and Venetia in northern Italy. The treaty was subsequently put to a plebiscite in which 99.8% voted in favour of annexation to France, amid widespread allegations of vote-rigging.

Most of Italy was unified in 1860 when the Piedmont army, moving south through the peninsula, met up with Garibaldi, leading his army of volunteers north from Sicily. Victor Emmanuel was excommunicated for attacking the Papal States, forcing the Pope to retreat to the Vatican, but nevertheless emerged as the first King of Italy, although he continued to style himself Victor Emmanuel II (of Piedmont–Sardinia). Ironically, the great 'Italian' patriot Garibaldi was born in Nice, which Victor Emmanuel had just handed to France, and many people in the royal court could barely speak Italian. The House of Savoy continued as the royal family of Italy until the abdication of King Umberto II in 1946.

The boundary established in 1860 between France and Italy did not follow the crest of the Alps in a number of places, including the Col de Tende, because large parts of the Maritime Alps were the personal hunting ground of Victor Emmanuel, who insisted that they remain part of his kingdom. This remained the situation when Conway visited the region in 1894. Although Italy was theoretically unified in 1860, the country continued to be deeply divided. In the years immediately prior to Conway's visit, the Italian prime minister, Francesco Crispi, plotted with Bismarck of Germany to wage war on France, partly in the hope that a war might unite the fractious Italians against a common enemy. When Sicily appeared to be on the brink of revolution again in 1894, the year of Conway's journey, Crispi accused the French of being in conspiracy with the rioters and sent troops to the border, thereby preventing Conway from starting his walk at the Col de Tende.

In keeping with this long history of mobile frontiers, the secret fortifications that the Italians were so anxious to hide from Conway now lie inside France. The border was adjusted to run through the summit of the Col after the Second World War in 1947. As a result, while Conway was forced to take the train back to Borgo San Dalmazzo and a stagecoach to Entracque, I was able to stand on the new international border at the top of the Col de Tende and look down into France before walking back through Italy to Entracque.

The Maritime Alps

Conway started his journey on 1 June 1894, but realised almost immediately that he had made a mistake: spring snow lay deep on the summits and extended well down into the valleys. He recommended that future travellers should delay their start until at least 21 June. When I set out on 25 June, there was still a lot of snow on the peaks, and patchy snow down to about 1,800 m, but the valleys were vibrant with wild flowers, buzzing insects and contented cows standing knee-deep in sunny pastures.

My first day's walk took me from the Col de Tende to Trinità, on the outskirts of Entracque, over two low cols and through cool deciduous woods with groves of laburnum trees, bright with yellow blossom. There is nothing like the feeling of setting out on a long walk, casting off the clutter of urban life and carrying all that you really need on your back. As a 14-year-old, on my first long independent walk, I remember the warden of Steps Bridge Youth Hostel, near Dartmoor, sniffing the crisp morning air and saying: 'You could walk a 100 miles on a day like today.' Despite the passage of time, that feeling has never deserted me. As I set out to walk the Alps from end to end, 'I felt that life had little better to offer than to march day after day in unknown country to an unattainable goal.'[100]

Trinità is a small farming community in a wooded valley, with trim vegetable gardens and fields filled with poppies. Conway followed a mule track up the Valle de Rovina into the heart of the Maritime Alps and camped beside a dark lake in a rocky cirque. Today, his mule track is a road, so I walked up the neighbouring valley, beside the powerful torrent of the Gesso della Barra, and crossed the Colle di Fenestrelle, descending a snowfield to reach the head of the Rovina valley. As I passed through a deserted campsite a large American regaled me: 'Do you speak English?' he shouted. 'You sure look English!' Looking down at my white winter legs, baggy shorts, khaki shirt and Berghaus rucksack, I had to admit that I was unmistakably English. He informed me that the mountain huts were all empty because 'the Italians hate snow, and there's one helluva lot of snow up there!'

Conway's rocky cirque has been dammed, creating the artificial but beautiful Bacino del Chiotas. In this early part of the season, the lake was surrounded by snow-covered peaks while the lower slopes were bright with fresh green shoots and blood-red blooms of alpenrose. Both Conway and I laboured up the scree slopes of the Colle del Chiapous beneath a baking sun and looked up at Argentera, the highest peak in the Maritime Alps at 3,297 m, happily dismissing its ascent on account of the accumulation of soft spring snow.

In contrast to my earlier wild enthusiasm, I felt increasingly like Pliable in *The Pilgrim's Progress* as I plodded up the slope and began to wonder: 'If we have such ill speed at our first setting out, What may we expect 'twixt this and our Journey's end?'[101] Descending the northern side of the col, I found out. Sinking through deep soft snow into a gap between two hidden boulders, my bare leg came into sharp contact with a rock, just above the ankle. The combined weight of my body and my rucksack then forced me downwards into an apparently bottomless pit. When I eventually managed to extricate myself, a 5-inch-long strip of skin hung from a single point of attachment just below my knee, like a piece of *tagliatelle*. I sat down on my rucksack and watched awestruck as blood gushed from the wound. The Rifugio Morelli-Buzzi was not far away, so I slid down the slope to the hut leaving a trail of blood in the snow. The guardian produced a huge first aid kit, doused the wound with disinfectant, and eventually staunched the flow. He then wrapped my leg in a large surgical dressing. He did all this with great skill and kindness, and entirely free of charge. Next day, I hobbled down the mountain to the Terme di Valdieri.

It was a cool, clear midsummer morning, promising a hot day ahead, and the path meandered lazily through larch forest and rocky meadows filled with wild flowers. If you are going to slice your leg open at the start of a long alpine walk, this is a great place to do it. It was once the private hunting ground of the Dukes of Savoy, who constructed beautifully engineered mountain paths, just as the British once did in the Scottish Highlands. Whether they did this as a form of self-aggrandisement, out of a desire to 'improve nature', or simply to provide work for impoverished locals, I do not know, but I was grateful. The hot baths at Valdieri seemed little changed from Conway's day. Just as in 1894, the Grand Hotel was shuttered for the winter, but a nearby *albergo* was open, so I bought a cappuccino and examined the bloody dressing on my leg. I decided that if the flies were particularly attracted to it, I should start to worry.

From the hot springs I walked up the Valle di Valasco to King Victor Emmanuel's Reale Casa di Cassia, a surprisingly humble hunting lodge with two turreted towers, surrounded by scattered trees and boulders in a flat meadow of glossy spring grass. Victor Emmanuel was an arch-conservative, a small, bluff man with a passion for the army, hunting and women. During a visit to England, Queen Victoria ascribed his brusque manner and coarse sexual remarks to 'the low level of morality'[102] in Italy, while his subjects joked about him being 'the father of the nation'. Rosa Vercellana, the semi-illiterate daughter of an army officer, became his mistress when she was 14 and the King was often seen driving to and from her house dressed in rough outdoor clothes with his two hunting dogs. When his prime minister impugned his masculinity by suggesting that Rosa also engaged in orgies with other men, King Victor Emmanuel challenged him to a duel. His prime minister wisely backed down from a no-win situation.

Writing in 1904, Conway was enraptured by the romance of the Valle di Valasco: 'Planted amidst umbrageous copses and beside laughing waters...No ogres, we may be sure, lurk in the fastnesses of these hills, but only the most delicate fairies, glittering with dew.'[103] Geoffrey Winthrop Young – poet, mountaineer and 'athletic aesthete' – was an admirer of Conway's prose: 'We can climb our storied heights with him without fear of bumping our heads against the low ceiling of last century emotional repressionism.'[104] The Valasco valley is certainly beautiful, but there were no fairies that I could see; just a group of Italian schoolchildren picnicking by a waterfall. Conway's guides were astonished by the number of chamois and bouquetins that they saw in the valley. They were protected in 1894 in order that the King of Italy might more easily shoot them. Today the valley is a nature reserve, and their numbers have presumably increased. There were marmots too in the high meadows. Writing in the 1930s, George Mallory's teacher, R. L. G. Irving, described them as 'jolly little fellows in thick fur coats...The official advice given in a marmot nursery is the opposite of that given to small boys: "little Marmots should be heard but not seen".'[105] Unlike Italian schoolchildren, little marmots still heed the advice given to them by their elders.

At this point, just four days into his journey, Conway got lost. He intended to head up the valley and cross a pass to Vinadio, but instead he crossed an intermediate spur, and came back down a parallel valley almost to his starting point. His book makes light of the incident: 'The compass indicated north unexpectedly far to the right...still the map is in many places so inaccurate that this did not concern us.' His diary is more forthright: 'Blundered...into the Val Miana and crossed a pass into the head of the Val Rossa...descended to King's hunting box at the head of the Val di Valasco and so returned to the Baths.' It is harder to get lost these days. There are good maps of the entire region, and all the major valleys and cols, and many of the peaks, have clear paths. Like Conway, I relied on map and compass, dismissing the use of a GPS as cheating, but on several days I hardly opened my map, simply following the well-signposted paths. This is surely a loss. Not knowing exactly where you are adds to the feeling of solitude that is such an important part of being in the mountains. Way-marked paths reduce the feeling. Explanatory boards, pointing out objects of interest, completely destroy it. As Roger Deakin observed: 'More and more places and things are signposted, labelled and officially "interpreted". There is something about all this that is turning the reality of things into virtual reality.'[106]

After this unfortunate incident, Conway was at pains to point out his prowess at map reading and gradually gained the respect of his guides. By the time they reached the Tyrol, Aymonod admitted that 'I have come to the conclusion that all young men who want to be guides should learn the use of map and compass'. But he immediately added the caveat: 'We are too old to learn, of course.'[107] Maps no longer hold the same mystique. One of my favourite books as a young child was the Ladybird book, *Understanding Maps*. On the cover there were three rural scenes and three corresponding Ordnance Survey 1-inch maps. The pictures could have come straight out of Hoskins' *The Making of the English Landscape*, with rolling fields, orchards, rivers and an ancient stone bridge. I soon discovered that maps show not only the present, but also the past; that you can peel away the motorways, trunk roads, railways and canals to reveal a landscape of Roman roads, hill forts and burial mounds. There may be children who plot imaginary journeys through towns and cities, but for me it was the north-west of Scotland, with its deeply incised coastline, mountains, lakes and beguiling empty spaces, where I imagined myself tramping day after day.

It was only later that I realised that maps are also instruments of power and that the Ordnance Survey was originally established in order to facilitate the subjugation of Scotland. By virtue of his ability to read a map, Conway knew more about the Alps than the people who lived there. Whereas their knowledge was local, acquired from direct experience or handed down from generation to generation, Conway had access to knowledge of the entire region. When they found themselves back at their starting point, Conway 'was minded to be annoyed, till a moment's reflection convinced me that the day had been delightful; and that one expedition was as just as good as another'.[108] This, of course, was nonsense: Conway was definitely annoyed. At this early stage in the journey, his authority as an enlightened, educated Englishman had been undermined. Instead of trying again, he invented a rule: 'One of the rules of our journey being never to attempt any expedition twice, we had to travel round by the valleys to our next climb.'[109] This useful new rule entitled Conway to miss out all the mountains between Valdieri and the Màira valley. He hired a carriage to take himself and Fitzgerald to Borgo S. Dalmazzo (while the guides and Gurkhas walked, perhaps as a punishment for having witnessed Conway's embarrassment). From there, they took a train back to Cuneo, a steam tram to Dronero and a stagecoach to S. Damiano. The following day they took another carriage to just below the village of Stroppo in the Màira valley. This was, of course, a very clear example of cheating by Conway, so I decided to walk to Stroppo since I planned to cheat in other ways later on. It took me three days.

Hints for Travellers

Conway made up the 'rules' that applied to his journey as he went along, and so did I. Neither of us adopted a particularly pure ethical approach to the task. Conway appears to have defined a 'peak' as any mountain over about 10,000 ft (3,000 m). On this basis he claimed 21 peaks, although in fact he only reached the summit of 19, stopping just short on two others. He also claimed to have crossed 39 passes, but his definition of a 'pass' is less clear. He clearly intended to climb more peaks and fewer passes when he set out, but as he later observed: 'To climb a peak is to make an expedition, but to cross a pass is to travel.'[110]

Conway started the journey with seven companions and never had fewer than two other people with him when he climbed. For about half of my journey, I travelled alone. Bad weather prevented both of us from climbing some peaks; and where Conway indicated that he had intended to climb a particular peak but was prevented from doing so by bad weather, I tried to climb the peak if the weather was good. This compensated for peaks that Conway climbed but I did not, for the same reason. In the end I climbed 22 peaks, got close to the summit of one other, and crossed about 40 passes.

Throughout his journey, Conway was accompanied by the two Gurkhas, Amir Sing and Karbir, who carried all his equipment. Although he does not specifically say so, I suspect that Conway carried nothing more than a light knapsack. As C. Wilson noted in his obituary of Conway in the *Alpine Journal*: 'He told the guides where to go, while they did what work there was to do – and they "carried" – for he liked to go light.'[111] In contrast, I 'carried' for myself, but warm and rainproof clothing is dramatically lighter today than it was in Conway's day. In addition to weight-carrying, the Gurkhas also acted as manservants. Conway's description of the tasks they performed in the Gonella hut on Mont Blanc gives some idea of their role: '[Karbir] began cutting up wood at once. He lit the fire, fetched snow in pans and put it to melt...He unpacked our things and gave each what he at the moment was on the point of wanting...he kept sweeping the floor so that the snow brought in on boots had no time to melt. He washed every pot, pan, cup, knife, or spoon...stirred up the straw in our beds; and all the time kept the fire burning and lent a hand to the cook when it was needed.' Meanwhile, Conway 'sat outside the little hut and studied its wonderful and interesting surroundings'.[112]

Conway does not state how much his 'outfit' weighed, but it must have been a lot. His *Zermatt Pocket Book*[113] contains a checklist of essential alpine equipment including:

A wine tin to hold 3 or 4 bottles

A pocket wine-bag or flask (ebonite gourds are sold by Silver and Co., Leadenhall Street, they are much recommended)

A soft hat, knitted climbing-cap, knitted waistcoat, strong gaiters, comforter, slippers, water-proof gloves lined with wool (Bax, 62, Piccadilly)

Pocket knife, which should contain an instrument for opening tins and a corkscrew (Hills in the Haymarket)

Pencils and painting materials

Smoking materials and a large tobacco pouch, pipe cleaners

Opera glasses, aneroid, compass

He also provided some useful hints on lightweight camping in the mountains: 'A camp should consist of two tents – one of them for guides or porters. The traveller's tent should be solid, and should possess a double roof or fly. It should be so firmly planted that no gale can overthrow it. Its furniture should be sufficient for comfort...Keep a man with you to fetch water and do the rough cooking.'[114] Another advantage that Conway enjoyed was that Fitzgerald's manservant, James, transported the baggage not required on the mountain from valley to valley. As a result, when Conway and Fitzgerald arrived at a hotel they were immediately able to appear properly attired for dinner. In contrast, I typically spent the first half hour or so after arrival doing laundry.

Conway states that he 'traversed on foot about 1,000 miles'.[115] This is not strictly true. He used trains, steam trams, stagecoaches, carriages, hay carts and horses to reach his destination, and missed out large sections of the walk through the Maritime and Cottian Alps altogether. I calculate that Conway used transport to cover over 200 miles, or about one fifth of his journey. I walked the sections where Conway used transport, but also cheated by using three cable cars, two trains, a mountain tram and a bus, for reasons that will become clear. I recorded how many hours I walked and approximately how many metres I climbed each day. In total I climbed about 260,000 ft (80,000 m) – nine times the height of Mount Everest – and calculate that I must have walked about 1,000 miles (1,600 km), including zigzags.

Perhaps the biggest difference between our two journeys was that Conway completed his walk in a single summer, whereas I spread it over two. Conway acknowledged that 'busy persons whose annual holiday must be short [could not] experience...the charms, excitements, and delights which reward the explorer of distant and unknown regions of the earth',[116] but he apparently thought that a three-month summer holiday in the Alps was within the grasp of any reader. By juggling work and other commitments I managed to take just over twelve weeks of holiday spread over two summers, and considered myself very lucky. Conway completed the journey in 87 days, whereas I took 94. He took 22 rest days and claimed that he was 'on the march' for the remaining 65, but in fact during 12 of these he used transport rather than walking. I had 14 rest days and walked during the remaining 80 days.

Which of us faced the greatest challenge on the journey? The answer is unquestionably Amir Sing and Karbir, the two Gurkhas, who spent three months in an unfamiliar country, eating foreign food, often sleeping rough or in the least comfortable accommodation, climbing each day with very heavy packs, frequently cutting steps, and doing all the work in the hut or camp. By comparison, Conway and I had it easy.

My first stop en route to Stroppo was the Rifugio Questa at the head of the Valasco valley. The hut was perched on a rocky spur above a frozen lake surrounded by snow-covered peaks. At first I appeared to be the only person staying. The guardian was Italian but, to my surprise, the assistant guardian was Nepalese. Like me, he spoke little Italian, but good English so I told him that I was retracing the footsteps of two Gurkhas who were the first Nepalese explorers of the Alps in 1894. The idea was clearly so ridiculous that he pretended not to understand. Or perhaps as a Buddhist from Khumbu he was not prepared to concede precedence to Hindu Gurkhas in relation to Nepalese exploration of the Alps. Soon we were joined by two Frenchmen from Annecy who proudly informed me that this was their first time outside France. They had crossed over the border that morning, intended to return the following day, and resolutely refused to speak anything but French while they were away. This cast me in the unlikely role of polyglot, since the guardian did not admit to speaking any French. As a result I spoke schoolboy French, phrase-book Italian and threw in a few random words of Portuguese (my default foreign language after living in Brazil), which confused everybody.

Unlike Conway, I do not speak Italian, so before arriving in Italy I had invested in a Lonely Planet Italian phrase book. I used to like LP guides. They were written by hippies for hippies and always contained interesting information about local drugs legislation. How things have changed. Under 'Chat' my LP phrase book suggested: '*Lavoro nel campo delle relazioni pubbliche*' ('I work in public relations'). The plaintive '*Ho perso il mio gruppo. Ha visto un gruppo di australiani?*' ('I have lost my group. Have you seen a group of Australians?') also suggested a rather different target audience these days. The largest section in the book was entitled 'Shopping'. The hippies have grown up, and look at them now. Meanwhile my French companions were explaining to me why they never left France: '*La France a les plus belles montagnes du monde*', one of them stated. '*Les Alpes...*', an expansive gesture suggested the extent of French territorial possessions in the region, '*...le Jura, les Pyrénées...*' There was a brief hesitation, but his companion soon took up the running with '*La Corse.*' '*Mais oui*', the first agreed, '*la Corse!*' I nodded my head in agreement. This was good stuff. I could cope with this kind of conversation.

From the Rifugio Questa I followed another well-engineered path passing through rocky cirques dotted with translucent icy pools and ruined barracks to the Colle di Vascura. On the north side there was a continuous snow slope, rather than the zigzag path shown on the map, and I rather gingerly glissaded down to Lago Malinvern, a blue-green tarn in a jagged bowl of yellow lichenous rocks. At the Rifugio Malinvern the young female guardian was sunbathing. I averted my eyes while she dressed, and ordered a *tè al limone*, wondering how Conway would have reacted in similar circumstances. Beneath the Colle d'Orgials flowery meadows sparkled with water springing down the mountainside on its way to Venice and the warm Adriatic. Near the Colle della Lombarda I crossed briefly into France. Here too, the frontier was adjusted after the Second World War. Every few hundred metres there was a border stone marked 'F 1947' placed about 10 m below the crest of the ridge on the Italian side, to prevent the perfidious Italians from sneaking up and looking down into La France.

By late afternoon thunder clouds were gathering and the hot air became charged and leaden. Just before reaching the pilgrims' town of Sant'Anna di Vinadio the storm broke and huge drops of rain exploded like bullets on the dusty track. I took a room in the sanctuary and visited the church. It was filled with pictures, many hand-drawn, of car wrecks and industrial accidents, giving thanks for deliverance. Back in my room, I tried to have a shower without getting the dressing on my leg wet. This involved pushing my leg through a small gap between the sliding doors and balancing my foot on top of the lavatory, so that water would not run down it. It was not an elegant position, nor very stable, but it proved to be reasonably effective under Sant'Anna's protective gaze.

Next day I walked to Sambuco in the Stura valley. Yesterday's rain had fallen as hail in the mountains and piles of icy stones glistened like jewels in the forest shadows. On the seventh day after setting out from the Col de Tende I rested in Sambuco and took a bus down to Vinadio (Conway's objective on his ill-fated walk from Valdieri) to buy a new bandage for my leg. My phrase book contained the word for 'Band-Aid', so I went into a *farmacia* and asked for a *grande cerotti*, pointing to the grubby, blood-stained, 9-inch surgical dressing on my leg. I came out with a 'sterile tampon' and something that resembled the knee-length stockings that old women used to wear beneath long skirts, except that mine was a stretchy white fishnet design.

I felt oddly light-headed without boots and rucksack to anchor me to the earth, as if gravity had been turned down for the day. After a cappuccino, I bought some bread and local cheese, and floated around the enormous walls and fortifications that surround Vinadio. In Conway's day, the route over the Colle della Maddalena from Barcelonnette to Vinadio was one of only three carriageable passes over the Alps between the Mediterranean and the Mont Cenis tunnel. In Valdieri, some friendly *carabinieri* had promised Conway that if he reached Vinadio he would surely be arrested,[117] and they were probably right. Murray's 1892 *Handbook for Travellers in the Alps of Savoy and Piedmont* (edited, of course, by Coolidge) noted that 'any traveller who sketches in this neighbourhood will be called on for his passport, and liable to detention until he can prove he is not French'.[118] I arrived back in Sambuco in time for dinner, where I was seated with two elderly Italian gentlemen at one end of a large *osteria*. After just six days of walking, good food and wine already tasted unbelievably delicious and I happily exchanged grunts and nods of approval with my fellow solitary diners.

The Cottian Alps

Next day I walked over the Colle del Mulo. It was a perfect morning and the path wound comfortably up through a rocky, wooded gorge to high open country sprinkled with gentians and alive with insects. After my first rest day I had settled into a rhythm where I was almost unconscious of the effort of walking, able to enjoy the scenery or simply let my mind wander. On a day walk, during a busy working week, you inevitably spend time planning what you need to do when the walk has ended. On a long walk, the walk is the end, and you live life simply in the present: 'The keen enjoyment of mere animal existence', as the explorer Richard Burton described it. During the afternoon, storm clouds began to build over the Italian plains, but the mountains were bathed in sunlight. I spent the night in a fashionable *locanda* in Vernetti. Rustic implements were artfully scattered around the stone-flagged courtyard and Teutonic mountain bikers posed beside their steeds like knights in black lycra.

Dropping down to the Màira valley the following day, I finally got back onto the trail of Conway. The path to Stroppo and Elva was recognisably the one that he described in his book, but the human landscape was transformed. When Conway and his party passed this way the peasants stopped work and stared at the exotic party of travellers passing through their land. Following his Himalayan expedition, Conway invariably climbed in a turban, which he believed provided the best protection against both heat and cold. No doubt it also tended to lead conversations with strangers in a direction that was likely to do him credit. Fitzgerald wore his Norfolk jacket with its famously capacious pockets. The three guides were all from Italy, but the Gurkhas must have caused a sensation and were probably the first coloured people that the locals had ever seen. The peasants greeted this strange party of travellers with long salutations: 'It was not merely "good-day!" but "we wish you an enjoyable walk and fine weather" or something even more elaborate.'[119]

Now the hillsides are silent. The population of Elva was 1,319 in 1901; today it is just 114. Near Stroppo, a maze of terraces and faint overgrown paths lead to abandoned fields and orchards. When Conway was here, Italy had barely started to industrialise and the vast majority of the population still lived on the land. Samuel Butler, who explored Piedmont on foot in the 1880s,[120] described some small cottage industries, spinning wool or weaving linen on hand looms, but most people survived by farming. Many high villages now lie abandoned. A few houses have been converted into weekend homes, but the fields are gradually reverting to rough woodland. The peasants have long since left the land to work in the factories of Turin and Milan, or crossed the Atlantic to America. Are they better off? Of course they are. They are better fed, better housed, better educated and better able to fulfil whatever potential they may have. But walking through these deserted fields and orchards it is hard not to feel nostalgic for a lost way of life. In one apparently abandoned hamlet of rough stone-built houses, a solitary old woman stepped out of her front door as I passed and greeted me. When I reached the end of the village I turned around. She was still standing alone in the middle of the stony track, as if listening to a distant echo of songs and laughter from her childhood.

Both Conway and I stayed at the inn at Elva. The weather had settled into a stable pattern of cool, clear mornings and thundery afternoons, and the storm broke soon after I arrived. I sat in the bar with a glass of wine, wrote my diary and consulted my maps. The proprietor looked over my shoulder and pronounced my map '*antica*'. When the skies cleared a little I wandered round the small village. A large fifteenth-century church was decorated with striking wall paintings. Conway did not mention the church, but he did commend the excellence of the coffee in the inn. The inn has certainly been rebuilt since 1894, but the room where I slept did not appear to have been cleaned. Murray's 1892 *Handbook for Travellers in the Alps of Savoy and Piedmont* noted that 'the traveller must not expect, in remote villages, or at houses frequented chiefly by Italians, the cleanliness and comfort to which he is accustomed in similar cases in Switzerland'.[121] It remains a strange fact that in Switzerland the hotel rooms are invariably clean and smell faintly of disinfectant, and so does the food. In Italy, on the other hand, the rooms may not be spotlessly clean, but the food can sometimes be about as close as a middle-aged man on a solitary walk is likely to get to ecstasy. At the inn in Elva, the pasta was very good indeed and after the meat course the proprietor/chef did a lap of honour round the dining room, while the locals rightly applauded his efforts. Cheese and delicious *dolce* followed. I gratefully thanked the proprietor for a memorable meal and attempted to pay, but he waved me aside. I pointed out that I needed to leave very early the next morning, but still he refused to take payment that night. The following morning it was his wife, of course, who got up early to accept my money and see me off, fortified with caffè latte, fresh warm bread and local honey.

The church clock chimed six on Sunday morning as I set out, brushing dewy flowers aside as I walked along the undulating grassy ridge towards Pelvo d'Elva, Conway's first 'peak'. I dumped my heavy rucksack at the Colle della Bicocca and walked up to the foot of the rocks. Conway described a rocky *couloir* which had a difficult move about halfway up, while Fitzgerald climbed the arête directly to the summit. I felt relief, tinged with slight regret, when I found a simple scrambling route to the summit, which stands just a little above 3,000 m. Until Pelvo, I had no real measure of what Conway regarded as 'difficult'. To the south I could see much of the route I had followed over the previous week, while to the north lay Chiesa, my destination for the night, nestled in a green wooded valley with the snow and rock pyramid of Monte Viso rising behind it like a child's drawing of a mountain. Conway noted that Coolidge had made the first British ascent of Pelvo d'Elva in 1890,[122] while John Ball made the first (recorded) crossing of the Colle della Bicocca in 1860. Today, Ball's col has become a car park and Coolidge's peak is a Sunday morning stroll.

Like many Victorian travellers, Conway had a profound fear of heatstroke. A section entitled 'Diet and Precautions for Health' in the 1892 *Handbook for Travellers in Switzerland* advised that 'you may drink of cold springs, when heated, on condition that you do not sit down afterwards'.[123] After descending to the inn at Casteldelfino, Conway ignored this sage advice, drank a litre of cold milk and promptly fell ill with a chill. His diary entry for the next day reads: 'In bed all day. A dog who goes to the baker...and waits for a roll [is] the chief amusement of the place.' Here he wrote the first of ten articles for the *Pall Mall Gazette* (a forerunner of today's *Evening Standard*), which had paid £100 for a serialised description of the journey. Conway also appears to have sold the story to the *Contemporary Review*, which published the articles under the title of 'An Alpine Journal'.

Until 1713, when it became part of Savoy, Casteldelfino was known by its French name Château Dauphin, after the fourteenth-century castle built there to protect the route over the Colle dell'Agnello from Briançon and the Queyras, which was once the main route connecting western Dauphiné with its possessions on the eastern slopes of the Alps. Now the castle is in ruins and the inn has gone, so I stayed in Chiesa, a nearby village of stone houses with sturdy timbers supporting huge flag-stone roof tiles.

After recovering from his chill, Conway set out to climb Monte Viso (3,841 m), staying in a small hut that must have been close to the present-day Bivouac Andreotti. The view from Pelvo had convinced me that Viso was carrying too much snow from the afternoon thunder-storms and I decided that I was not prepared to climb it alone. So while Conway battled up the mountain and descended in a storm, I skirted around it, going up the Vallanta valley, climbing a zigzag track through pine forest and meadows, and crossing two rocky cols. Between the cols the mist came down and the path meandered around frozen lakes and patchy snow. Through wispy cloud I walked through an eerie forest of cairns in a barren rocky valley. After crossing a huge boulder field, I reached the Lago Grande di Viso, where the ice was stained red with algae. The Viso hut was vast and empty. One of the dormitories was named 'William Mathews', after the brother of Conway's Birmingham friend Charles Mathews, who made the first ascent of Monte Viso in 1861. An English guide and two clients eventually arrived, the first English people I had met since setting out from the Col de Tende. They had taken eight hours to reach the summit of Viso, and almost as long to get back down, floundering through deep, unconsolidated snow.

Next day was supposed to be a short walk down to Crissolo in the Po valley, but I took a clever shortcut and so ended up wandering randomly through meadows, forests and farmyards before blundering onto a track that miraculously took me to the right place. I spent the afternoon washing, shopping, eating and drinking. The next day was also easy, in theory, up to the grassy Colle di Porte and gently down through forests to Torre Pellice. Once again, Conway met numerous peasants on the way, including 'a mewling idiot boy, buttoned up the back into his clothes. He jauped and whooped like an animal, and was as hard to pass as a frightened goat.'[124] I did not see a single soul. In dense mist, I probably crossed the wrong col and descended about 200 m down a boulder- and snow-filled gully before arriving on a rocky plateau. Eventually I found a track and followed it down through forests near a quarry producing the crystalline slabby paving stones that are so characteristic of the region. Conway also commented on the quarries, though they must have been much smaller then. After walking along a road for a while, a good path dropped down to Torre Pellice through chestnut and beech wood. I crossed the Pellice River and entered a rundown warehouse district. Conway described Torre Pellice as 'a new railway town'. It is no longer new, but it still sits at the end of the railway line to Turin.

A Parting of the Ways

'It would hardly interest the reader to know how we went from Torre Pellice to Modane', Conway wrote in his book. 'There are various routes leading through hilly though hardly mountainous country, and we took one of them, in bad weather.' From this description, the reader might suppose that Conway travelled through hilly country, in bad weather, on foot, but they would be mistaken. In fact, as his diary (but not his book) makes clear, what Conway did was to take a train from Torre Pellice to Turin, where he paid off Zurbriggen. From Turin he travelled to Bardonecchia by train and then on to Modane. In other words, once again, Conway cheated, so I walked from Torre Pellice to Modane. It took me six days, going at a leisurely pace.

Conway was probably persuaded to go to Turin by Fitzgerald, 'the greatest dilettante of the mountain world',[125] according to mountain historian Walt Unsworth. Bertrand Russell, who knew Fitzgerald at Cambridge and climbed with him in the Alps, described some of his accomplishments: 'He was lazy and lackadaisical but had remarkable ability...notably in mathematics. He could tell the year of any reputable wine or cigar. He could eat a spoonful of mixed mustard and Cayenne pepper. He was intimate with Continental brothels. His knowledge of literature was extensive, and while an undergraduate at Cambridge, he acquired a fine library of first editions.'[126] Fitzgerald was clearly a man of many talents and he inherited a substantial fortune, but he found it hard to concentrate. In later years he mounted expensive climbing expeditions to New Zealand and the Andes, but he was beaten to the first ascent of Mount Cook by a New Zealand party and failed to reach the top of Aconcagua (at that time, the highest mountain ever climbed) even though Zurbriggen, who accompanied him on the trip, reached the summit quite easily. Conway and Coolidge cultivated Fitzgerald in the hope that the younger man would take on some of the burden of checking the Climbers' Guides to the Alps, but Fitzgerald could not be bothered. He died quite young, in 1931. In his obituary, Conway described him as a 'solitary and reserved young man...full of ambition to accomplish something, but he did not know what'. Recalling their journey together through the Alps, Conway wrote:'He would stay with me for a few days...then he would fly away to London or Paris for an interval of comfort and good food...He would not stick to his job.'[127] Conway also complained to Katrina about Fitzgerald's unreliability. In one of her letters she asked:'Was Fitzgerald frightened, or tired, or bored, or what, that he has such frequent and imperative calls to take him away from you?' Conway's reply is missing, but it is fair to assume that he failed to mention that, in Torre Pellice, he too succumbed to temptation, and hurried off to the fleshpots of Turin.

My route to Modane took me across the Pellice, Germanasca and Chisone valleys, which still contain communities of Waldensians, a Christian sect originating in Lyon in the twelfth century, who were declared heretics by the Pope in 1194 and eventually merged with the Reformed Protestant church in the sixteenth century. The Waldensians suffered long periods of persecution, culminating in 1685 when Louis XIV revoked the Edict of Nantes, which granted religious freedom to Protestants in France. Victor Amadeus II, the Duke of Savoy, who was Louis' cousin, followed his lead and French and Piedmont troops invaded the valleys of Pellice and Chisone, laying them waste. Many Waldensians sought refuge in the Calvinist city of Geneva, but in 1689 a group of about 1,000, with financial support from King William III of England and the Low Countries, defied France and Savoy and marched back from Geneva to their homes in the Pellice valley, skirmishing with French troops and destroying the Catholic images that had been installed in their chapels as they went. For much of the way, my walk followed, in reverse, the route that they had taken.

From the Pellice valley I climbed laboriously up to the Colle Giulian on a dull, muggy day to find a large party of Italian walkers on the summit. Two young women indulged in rather exhibitionist stretching exercises, while the men gawped and joked. Dropping down into the Germanasca valley I discovered that a new village had sprung up around a chairlift since my map was made. A huge crowd of enthusiasts had gathered for a mountain biking festival, the contestants clad in protective suits and helmets, like miniature American footballers. The village of Ghigo was animated with crowds of weekend revellers from Turin, which lies just 75 km away, but as dusk fell the humans were replaced by cows ambling gently through the main square on their way to be milked. Despite the large number of visitors in the valley, the mountain paths were less distinct and more overgrown than hitherto. As Conway said, the scenery was hilly rather than mountainous, but the colour and variety of wild flowers was breathtaking, and the warm breeze was fecund with drifting seeds and pollen. From the Massello valley I followed a mule track through ruined villages to a high alp where a grizzled old shepherd and his son were tending a flock of long-eared sheep. Crossing the Colle dell'Alberglan, I dropped down to the Chisone valley and the well-kept village of Usseaux, with its stone houses and flagstone streets. Next morning the owner of the B&B provided a feast of ham, cheese, yoghurt, fruit and lemon cake, and then pressed me to take bread and plums for my lunch.

My route took me along the front line of a nineteenth-century war zone. Before the unification of Italy, Piedmont was a buffer state between France and the Austrian territories of Venetia and Lombardy in northern Italy. During the 1840s more than half of government spending went on defence and Piedmont's large army of 150,000 men played a decisive role in the unification of Italy in 1860. In this part of the Alps, every major valley is heavily fortified and almost every feasible pass has at least a small barracks. From Usseaux, the huge fortress at Fenestrelle is clearly visible in the valley below, and on the ridge above the town the Via dei Forti connects a line of fortifications overlooking the Susa valley. When I reached the summit of the Testa dell'Assieta a vast war memorial materialised from the mist. On the way down, mountain bikers emerged noiselessly out of the clouds and swooped past me as I descended the track towards the Rifugio Daniele Arlaud.

In the Arlaud hut, the assistant guardian was a tall, thin African, perhaps an Ethiopian or Eritrean refugee from Mussolini's 'place in the sun', who put a spectacular amount of sugar into a very small, extremely strong espresso. The powerful combination of sugar and caffeine would have jolted Frankenstein into life without the need for electricity. It was near here that Horace Walpole's Prince Charles spaniel, Tory, was eaten by a wolf in 1739, causing Walpole's companion, the poet Thomas Gray, to observe that Mont Cenis 'carries the permission mountains have of being frightful rather too far'. Distant relatives of the wolf that snacked on Tory apparently still live in the wilder parts of the Gran Bosco di Salbertrand, but on the path that I followed down to the valley an area of the forest had died. Parasites clung to skeletal trees and toadstools warted from rotting trunks. Whether this patch of wilderness had been poisoned by the distant belching of industrial plants or by more natural causes was impossible to tell.

After many days away from busy roads it was a shock to descend into a valley containing a motorway, a main road and a railway. Cars and lorries roared past in a continuous torrent of hot metal, leaving eddies of dust and diesel fumes. I hurried across and scrambled back into the sanctuary of the hills, rejoining the route of the Waldensian refugees through sunny overgrown terraces and abandoned villages. With their heavy flagstone roofs, the houses in this region have a limited life. When the roof timbers rot, the houses implode. The fashion for restoring them has come just in time; a few more decades and there would be nothing left but hollow shells, like bomb craters.

After staying overnight at the Rifugio Levi Molinari, the final day of my walk to rejoin Conway took me back into real mountain country. A path through a magnificent rocky cirque led to the border on the Col d'Ambin (2,899 m). On the French side, a snow slope led easily down to a perfect mountain tarn. Hundreds of tiny flowers – purple pinheads in a dense green pincushion – clung to the ice-polished rocks. Boulder and snow slopes led steeply down to a larger lake, still partially frozen, and a small refuge where I stopped for a *jus de pomme*. A long hot slog followed, along the dusty track to Bramans. I took shortcuts between the final zigzags into the valley, wading through deep waves of summer grass while crickets frothed around my knees. At Aussois, I finally caught up with Conway. Ignoring rest days, it had taken me 18 days to walk from the Col de Tende to Aussois, whereas Conway had taken just nine. But on the other hand, Conway left out most of the route.

Through the Vanoise

Today, crossing borders within the European Union is easy. In 1894, with Italy and France close to a state of war, Conway had to register his party's passports with the police at Modane, and submit his intended onward route for approval. But then, as now, the currency was the same on both sides of the border. In the late nineteenth century the gold and silver coins in circulation in France, Italy, Switzerland, Belgium and Greece were accepted in all five countries. And while today the British pound remains resolutely outside the Euro zone, in Conway's day English sovereigns were accepted almost everywhere in Europe.

Conway caught the 2 o'clock diligence from Modane along the right bank of the valley as far as Avrieux and then hired a drunken porter to carry his bags up to Aussois. When they arrived, the town was apparently deserted. At the inn they found out why: the entire population was 'flattening their noses against the windows to catch a glimpse of the Gurkhas'.[128] They pressed on, and spent the night in a chalet at Plan Sec, while I stayed in Aussois. The town has expanded since Conway's time. There are a couple of ski lifts, and new apartment blocks cluster around the old village, but on the whole the developments blend in and it still retains a village atmosphere. Next morning I bought fresh bread at the *boulangerie* and *tomme de Savoie fermière* at the *fromagerie*, and then climbed up a good track through warm forest scented with pine resin. At Les Balmes a low-slung, stone-built house of prayer seemed to have grown organically out of a little alp like a toadstool. Higher up, the path markings changed from red dashes to the *tricolore*, indicating that I had joined the *Grande Randonnée 5*, a long-distance footpath that passes through five countries on its way from the Hook of Holland to Nice. The path contoured along the side of la Dent Parrachée, with distant views of the snowy white Dauphiné Alps and red paragliders slicing through the clear blue sky.

In his review of *The Alps from End to End* in the *Alpine Journal*, Coolidge perpetuated the myth of the heroic English explorer commanding the undying loyalty of his men, when he talked of the trust that Conway placed in his comrades being 'deservedly met by their unwavering confidence in their leader'.[129] Conway records a conversation near Modane that suggests that their confidence did occasionally waver just a little, despite their increasing respect for his map-reading ability:

'There,' I said to Aymonod, 'is our pass.'
'Perhaps,' he answered.
'And that is the Dent Parrachée.'
'Part of it perhaps; we shall see; the peak may be behind.'[130]

I have skied in the Vanoise many times, at Courchevel, Méribel, Tignes and Val d'Isère, but never walked or climbed there. In summer, the country has a wide, open feel to it, with big skies, broad rocky slopes and few trees. I spent the night at the Refuge de l'Arpont, a crowded way-station on the GR5, then continued north towards Tignes. As I set out, the peaks were clear, but a latticework of morning mist obscured the valley, with denser clouds periodically making bold incursions up the mountainside. At the Lac des Lozières two shallow pools almost choked with reeds glinted in the morning sun. The path dropped down a grassy hillside to the Torrent de la Leisse where the GR5, the GR55 and the Via Alpina all converge. 'More utter desolation and dreariness than now surrounded us cannot be imagined', Conway wrote of the valley of the Leisse. But he was toiling through heavy wet snow, whereas I walked along a good path in the sunshine, with marmots whistling from the grassy slopes beneath the ochre and grey limestone buttress of la Grande Casse and the dark shaley mass of la Grande Motte.

Apart from transient walkers and skiers, there are fewer people in these mountains than in Conway's day, but the population was draining away even then. Conway bought some milk from an old woman who told him that she had 15 children but not one of them still lived in the village. Instead they had gone to Paris and Canada, seeking an easier life. While the people have largely gone, there are still sheep on the hillsides and the *patou* dogs[131] that protect them from predators. Typically powerful Pyrenean mountain dogs, a *patou* is separated from its parents and siblings at about eight weeks and brought up with the flock, where the young puppies bond with the lambs. At four months they are introduced into the flock full-time. A single dog can protect a huge herd of sheep provided they flock together rather than spreading out over the hillside. Walking along the path I was conscious of being stalked by a *patou* long before I was aware of the sheep. The dog eyed me up and down for a while, and then escorted me through the scattered sheep. As soon as he was satisfied that I did not pose a threat he ran back into the middle of the flock and nuzzled a sheep. These remarkable guard dogs operate quite independently of humans, whereas normal sheepdogs, which are used to round up sheep and to drive them from one place to another, live with humans and respond to their commands.

Conway intended to climb La Grande Motte, but the weather was poor and the south face was still plastered with snow in mid June. I, like thousands of other skiers, have taken the cable car to within 200 metres of the summit on the other side of the mountain, and felt no desire to go again. Instead, over a lazy lunch of bread and cheese leaning comfortably against a sunny rock splashed with neon-green lichen, I idly plotted my way up the crumbling cliff. The valley path continued past a couple of mirror-still lakes to a rocky col where there were distant views of les Grandes Jorasses with la Dent du Géant perched on its left shoulder, but it was the view of the valley as it unfolded that marked the greatest contrast with what had passed before. Conway described 'a pleasant walk to the borders of the charming Tignes lake, where there were chalets and cows by the water's edge...soft air played over the lake and bore towards us the lowing of the kine, the clang of their bells, and the ceaseless song of water falling far away'.[132] Today Tignes is a major resort at the centre of a huge ski domain, the first that I had passed through on my walk through the Alps.

A ski resort without snow is nearly always a depressing place, but Val Claret, which forms part of the 'Station de Tignes', is a particularly dispiriting sight. This is tourism on an industrial scale: a vast dormitory complex from which thousands of packaged tourists emerge each morning, their bellies filled and their pockets emptied, to be mechanically conveyed to the mountain tops. The overwhelming impression is of vast expanses of discoloured concrete and steel. There is absolutely no concession to the local environment, local materials or the vernacular architecture of the region. Around the resort, bare bulldozed slopes, ski lifts, cables, pylons, water cannons, plastic pipes and other ski detritus lie scattered across 'le plus bel espace de ski du monde'.

Conway was present at the birth of winter tourism, promoting the attractions of skiing as a sport for English gentlemen, when 'the ordinary tourist is absent; the crowd of loungers and trippers is away at home at its business and the whole country and all the mountains and hillsides are free to those active-bodied and minded people for whom the mountains are the finest playground in the whole world'.[133] Today, skiing has been transformed into a massive industry. Over 50 million winter sports enthusiasts are drawn to the Alps each year where they spend an estimated US$100 billion.

The word 'nostalgia' was originally coined to describe the feelings of Swiss peasants towards their mountains when they were forced by circumstances to live on the plains.[134] For the British too, appreciation of landscape tends to be nostalgic. For many, particularly ex pats, the word automatically evokes images of unspoilt countryside, while the magnificent view of London from Hampstead Heath only becomes a landscape if you insert the word 'urban'. The British still live under the influence of the Romantic movement, longing for an imaginary rural idyll and fearing the incipient destruction of the countryside. John Jackson, a modern American landscape writer, takes a more optimistic view: 'We are not spectators; the human landscape is not a work of art...[it is] made by a group of people who modify the national environment to survive, to create order, and to produce a just and lasting society.'[135] Like most Victorians, Conway was also inclined to view the future with optimism: 'It is not likely, much though we may desire it, that in our time the tide of touristdom will abandon the Alps...But with the advance of civilisation perhaps its manners and tastes will improve, and may, at some far distant time, come to demand a kind of housing that will not utterly destroy the very beauty which it blindly travels to seek.'[136] Looking at the Station de Tignes, it is hard to share such optimism.

The place where Conway camped beside the Lac de Tignes is now a golf course, built in an apparently futile attempt to lure unsuspecting summer tourists to this hideous resort. Across the lake is a huge shabby crescent-shaped block of 1960s flats. I walked through a ghost town of barred and shuttered shops and down a deserted road to Les Boisses. The village is situated beside the barrage of the Lac du Chevril, which in 1952 inundated the old village of Tignes, once perched beside the Isère river. Conway would not have mourned its passing: 'The path to Tignes by no means descends into the lap of luxury. I doubt whether all the Alps hold a fouler inn than the Grand Hôtel des Touristes. Cows are stalled in the kitchen...There is not a chair in the house...No cheesemaker's chalet that ever I entered compared for filth with this loathsome den. And the food is equal to the accommodation.'[137] I was more fortunate, staying in a slightly eccentric *hôtel de charme* specialising in Savoyard cuisine. The old woman who sold milk to Conway in the Vanoise told him that milk has four children – 'cream, cheese, sérac, and pigs' – and these remain the principal ingredients of Savoyard cooking. Two of the greatest recipes from Savoy are *tartiflette* and *croziflette*. *Tartiflette* is a baked dish made out of onion, cream, cheese, bacon and potato. *Croziflette*, on the other hand, is a baked dish made out of onion, cream, cheese, bacon and pasta. Both are delicious after a long day's walk, washed down with a *pichet* of rough red wine.

Conway was so appalled by the hotel at Tignes that he decided to walk up the valley to Val d'Isère in search of better accommodation. There he found a single inn whose keeper greeted him with the words: 'You are English. You know Mr. Coolidge... You don't like the inn at Tignes. Tell that to Mr. Coolidge; he will laugh like this – he! he! he!'[138] My father visited Val d'Isère in 1947, almost exactly midway between Conway's visit and mine, and bought a black and white postcard of a tiny hamlet, apparently little changed from Conway's day. When he arrived, the French army and police were trying to clear out a stubborn group of French 'resistance fighters' who had decided that a life of casual banditry was preferable to eking out an existence by farming in a hard land. My father and his group of English climbers, several of them recently released from military service, were greeted by the remaining villagers like conquering heroes. Today there are dozens of inns to choose from in Val d'Isère, but you are unlikely to receive such a welcome.

The Graian Alps and Mont Blanc

Next day I followed a narrow path up through scattered pine trees and traversed a grassy hillside high above the flinty expanse of Lac du Chevril. A rough road led to the Lac de la Sassière. The lake existed in Conway's day – he said that it mirrored Lac de Tignes – but its size has since been expanded by a dam. Across the valley of the Isère, Tignes looked less obtrusive at a distance, beneath the snow-covered northern slopes of la Grande Motte and la Grande Casse. A track beside the Lac de la Sassière led to the foot of the Glacier de Rhêmes, which was easily climbed to the Colle della Goletta (3,117 m). After a brief spell in France, I was back in Italy.

Conway's preference for Italy over France reflected a wider English fascination with Italians and prejudice against the French. As Conway observed: 'Fancy the horror (if it were a possibility) of being mistaken for a Frenchman';[139] but it was even less likely that an English gentleman would be mistaken for an Italian. Like Ruskin and the Pre-Raphaelites, Conway studied the art and architecture of Italy, learned the language, and was both attracted and slightly appalled by the emotionality of the people. Conway regarded the Italians as passionate, lazy and luxurious, whereas the English were a warrior race: strong, courageous and manly. He acknowledged that there were also some artistic Englishmen, but he regarded them as racially distinct: 'The fighting and governing Englishman, who has founded a world empire, is in a general way recognised as the inheritor (doubtless from a mixed ancestry) of Teutonic characteristics; the artistic English are often described as Celtic, which in modern use only means not Teuton.'[140] But whether of Teutonic or Celtic extraction, Conway was in no doubt that an Englishman was superior to the southern European races.

A glacier descent and scramble over loose scree and rubble brought me to the Col Bassac Déré, with a glimpse of Monte Rosa in the distance and the Gran Paradiso closer at hand. Conway climbed the Aiguille de la Sassière up a heavily corniced ridge of hard snow before descending to the hamlet of Fornet in the Valgrisenche. Today the snow on the Sassière has gone, revealing the crumbling grey shale beneath, and Fornet has simply disappeared from the map, possibly flooded beneath the artificial Lago di Beauregard. I descended to the Rifugio Mario Bezzi and a splendid dinner of minestrone, pasta, pork, cheese and cinnamon ice cream. One might think from these descriptions of endless gluttony that I was gaining weight, but in fact I was losing it at an alarming rate. My clothes hung off me like a scarecrow, and I was running out of holes to tighten my belt.

I woke to the sound of rain drumming on the roof of the refuge. Dawdling down the Valgrisenche, past miserable wet cows, I arrived at the Albergo Perret in Bonne at about 10.30, had a coffee, and decided to stay the night. Conway was granted permission by the Italian army to stay in a military refuge near the Lago di S. Grato, above the village, and we both set out early the following morning to climb the Testa del Rutor (3,486 m). 'Never did day open less promisingly,' Conway recorded in his book, 'but we were determined to reach La Thuile somehow.'[141] I had similar thoughts as I set out on a damp, grey morning, with a wind that threatened worse to come. Following a good path towards the Rifugio degli Angeli al Morion, I entered dense cloud at about 2,000 m and it got markedly colder. The hut was closed, but I sheltered in the winter room and put on an extra layer of clothing. Descending slightly, I passed two small murky lakes in dense mist and climbed over loose piles of mud and moraine. There were no cairns and no signs of a path, so I simply continued uphill, climbing polished slabs of schist streaming with meltwater to the bottom of the glacier. On the map, the col appeared to be due north, but with visibility down to a few metres, and still no sign of cairns, finding it was going to be difficult. Strapping on crampons, I made a rising traverse across the glacier towards the north and decided to climb an obvious snow-filled couloir. Peering blindly up into the murk, I hoped that it did not end in a vertical rock wall. I kicked up steep firm snow in the gully and skittered over some mixed ground, conscious of an ever-increasing drop, made more precipitous in my imagination by its invisibility. The snow band narrowed to nothing and I was forced onto a rocky rib on the left that led to the ridge. Visibility on the far side was, if anything, worse. I could just make out a boulder slope leading down, presumably, to the Glacier del Rutor below. Turning left, I walked easily along the crest of the ridge to the Testa del Rutor and searched for the spectral white statue of the Madonna that stands on the rocky summit.

The climb up to the ridge was probably no harder than Scottish grade II, but it was an adventure because the outcome was uncertain, and that is the big difference between climbing today and climbing in Conway's day. Most modern climbers, most of the time, follow well-known routes that they *know* they can climb before they set out. Conway knew the Alps better than most people – he had written the only climbing guides that then existed and he was a close friend of Coolidge, who was a walking alpine encyclopaedia – but almost every climb that Conway did on his walk through the Alps was an adventure like the Testa del Rutor, because he did not know for sure that it was feasible.

Dropping down onto the glacier from the summit of the Testa del

Rutor, I tried to follow the bottom of the rocky ridge as it curved away to the north, but the dense cloud and the flat snow-covered glacier merged into one, creating a complete white-out. All directions – left, right, up and down – looked identical. I followed a compass bearing and occasional reassuring glimpses of rocks to my right, putting each foot down tentatively, uncertain when and where it would land and hoping that there were no hidden crevasses. Eventually the glacier steepened slightly and visibility improved. Scrambling down moraine, I rejoined the glacier lower down, before leaving it on the right bank just above the snout, where a short scree slope led to the path over the Passo di Planaval. I finally emerged from the clouds near Lago Verde. The path dropped steeply over ledges and shelves of rock, past the Rifugio Deffreyes, to the shrunken Lago del Ghiacciaio, sitting in a bowling green meadow. Below, the first trees appeared and a signpost directed me to a spectacular waterfall, roaring over a rocky ledge and shuddering into the misty depths. Conway also stopped to admire this fall, and insisted upon his companions doing the same. Views began to appear down the Rutor valley, with occasional glimpses of les Grandes Jorasses behind a veil of mist. At La Joux the wooded path passed another cascade and joined the road to La Thuile, where I arrived some 30 minutes later.

La Thuile lies at the foot of the Little St. Bernard Pass, the route used by Caesar on his return from the conquest of Gaul in 49 BC. Today the roads leading to La Thuile are lined with huge 'chalet-style' condominiums. For weeks I had walked through the Italian Maritime and Cottian Alps passing abandoned villages where there was virtually no new development, apart from a few renovations of old farmhouses, but such is the magnetic pull of Mont Blanc that in La Thuile developers jostle with each other to build on every vacant plot. I stopped at the first hotel that I came to in the centre of town, which was run by a friendly family whose chief joy in life was to shout Italian at foreigners. In the restaurant, a rather meek Englishman at a nearby table made the mistake of praising the *entrecôte* and was warmly embraced by the proprietor. I decided to play down my enjoyment of the meal and got away with a two-handed handshake and a torrent of Italian. Meanwhile a group of Germans, dressed in black leathers, were hammering out the finer details of the best motorbike rides in the Alps. They were well into their fourth litre of wine when I left and there was no sign of them at breakfast.

From La Thuile, Conway took a carriage down to Courmayeur and stayed at the Hôtel Royal ('the best, very good and comfortable'[142]). I walked down the road, passing through the tunnel above Pré St. Didier with its sudden and dramatic view of les Grandes Jorasses, and then followed minor roads through Verrand and the chalet suburbs of Courmayeur. The Aosta valley was ruled from the other side of the great alpine chain and retained French as its language for most of its history. Part of Savoy since 1025, the valley was the last fragment of the Duchy's great Burgundian dominions to survive after 1860, when nearly all its other French-speaking possessions passed to France.

Conway travelled from Courmayeur to Chamonix via the summit of Mont Blanc (4,810 m). He walked up the Miage glacier and stayed at the new Italian Alpine Club hut, opened in 1891, which was then called the Bionnassay hut and is now called the Gonella hut. Next day he climbed up the Dôme glacier to the summit of Le Dôme du Goûter. Conway took a ¼ plate Luzo camera with him on his walk through the Alps and used lantern slides to illustrate his subsequent lectures. Most of the slides have broken or faded over the years but a few still survive in the Royal Geographical Society archives, and one shows the view from Le Dôme du Goûter looking back towards the Aiguille de Bionnassay. From the Dôme they walked along the ridge to the summit of Mont Blanc and then descended to Chamonix via Les Grands Mulets.

I had intended to follow the same route. However, the Gonella hut was shut, apparently because rockfall has undermined its foundations. The Dôme glacier is the only feasible route up Mont Blanc from the Italian side for someone of my climbing ability, and I was not equipped for a bivouac at high altitude, so I decided to catch the bus to Chamonix and climb the mountain from the French side. The Mont Blanc tunnel goes directly under the crest of the Alps, connecting northern and southern Europe. As you emerge on the Chamonix side, there is a distinct change in the landscape, but it is hard to pinpoint exactly why. In the Alps, the north-facing side of the valley (the *ubac*) is typically rockier and more densely forested than the sunnier and more fertile south-facing slope (the *adret*). From Courmayeur, Mont Blanc towers above the sunny *adret*, whereas from Chamonix it sits atop the shady *ubac* slope. With the eye inevitably drawn to the highest peak in the Alps, perhaps this accounts for the slightly more sombre atmosphere of the Chamonix valley.

The ownership of Mont Blanc reflects the complex history of the region. The southern slope is Italian because the House of Savoy ruled the Aosta valley from the eleventh century. The north slope (Chamonix) became part of the Dauphiné in 1268, was sold to France in 1349 and given to Savoy in 1355 in exchange for land elsewhere. France conquered it in 1792, lost it in 1815, and finally gained control within Conway's lifetime in 1860. The Swiss also hold a small portion of the north-eastern slope of the Mont Blanc massif. Originally part of the Bishopric of Sion, it was conquered by Savoy in the thirteenth century but recovered by Sion in 1475. It became part of Valais in 1798 and finally Swiss when Valais joined the Federation in 1815.

In keeping with this long history of disputed borders, ownership of the actual summit of Mont Blanc is still in doubt. In 1796 Napoleon decreed that the border passed along the highest ridge of the mountain seen from Courmayeur, and from the actual town of Courmayeur (as opposed to the administrative district) the summit is obscured by a slightly lower intermediate peak. A demarcation agreement signed by both nations in 1861, after the annexation of Savoy, shows the border between France and Piedmont passing through the actual summit. Since subsequent redefinitions of the French–Italian border in 1947 and in 1963 did not address the summit of Mont Blanc, the 1861 treaty probably still stands. However, French cartographers prefer Napoleonic decrees to bilateral treaties, and so they show the international boundary passing over the subsidiary summit of Mont Blanc de Courmayeur, thereby giving France sole ownership of the highest physical (if not moral) ground in Europe. Italian maps, on the other hand, show the border passing through the main summit, so while the French may claim Mont Blanc as their own, the Italians claim joint ownership of Monte Bianco.

When I arrived, the town centre of Chamonix was heaving. I went to the Club Alpin Français office and tried to book the Grands Mulets hut, but a guide advised against the route because of the risk of icefall. That left the Goûter (which joins the route taken by Conway fairly close to the summit), but the hut was fully booked. The guardian told me that if I called back at 8 o'clock the following morning I might get a place in three days' time. The following morning the line was permanently engaged, so I decided to press on with my journey and return to Chamonix at the end of the season, when Mont Blanc might be slightly less congested.

As a consequence, it was late September before I returned to Chamonix with my wife, Fiona, to climb Mont Blanc. There was a chilly *fin de saison* feel to the town. The crowds of holidaymakers had drained away and the population had reduced from its summer peak of about 110,000 to its low-season level of about 30,000. I like Chamonix. It is big and ugly, but unlike Zermatt or Grindelwald, the two other traditional alpine centres, it still feels like a real town rather than a group of expensive boutiques set in an alpine theme park. Chamonix is built on tourism, but tourists are not the main preoccupation for many of the people who live and work there. Hesitate for a moment while you are ordering a drink in a pavement café and your young waiter's eyes will drift upwards to the beckoning peaks. It is a relaxed sort of place, lazy but active, with a sense of community, despite the constant turnover of tourists. Out of season, friends greet the bar staff as they cycle past, steering their bicycles with one hand and eating pizza with the other. Dogs go to sleep at the edge of the road, and car drivers avoid them, instead of aiming at them as they would in August. Chamonix is a cosmopolitan place and increasingly the lingua franca in the bars and restaurants is English.

The forecast was good, and to my amazement we managed to book a place in the Goûter hut for the following night, so we went to the Bar National for a celebratory beer. In the 1960s and 70s, this was the favourite hangout for British climbers in Chamonix. As a visiting American climber once observed: 'Basically in Chamonix the scene centres round two bars: the "Nash", or Bar National, and Le Drug Store. Only the English hang out in the Nash. At Le Drug Store you find all nationalities. That's where the English go when they're looking for a fight.'[143] Such behaviour would have shocked Conway, for whom climbing was a gentleman's sport. High jinks were tolerated, but not bad manners. John Ryan, an Anglo-Irish landowner and perhaps the finest British alpinist before the First World War, was blackballed by the Alpine Club for showing 'incivility to some older members'.[144]

Conway lived in a profoundly unequal society. One quarter of England and Wales was owned by just 710 individuals, and 92% of the nation's wealth was owned by just 10% of the population. With such great disparities between rich and poor, the small upper and middle classes lived in constant fear of insurrection and anarchy, and anti-social behaviour of any kind was severely punished. In 1912 a quarter of males aged 16 to 21 who were imprisoned in London were serving seven-day sentences for offences such as drunkenness, 'playing games in the street', riding a bicycle without lights, gaming, obscene language and sleeping rough. Despite this, the prison population was far lower than it is today. If Edwardian standards of crime and punishment were applied today, half the population of Britain would be permanently locked up in gaol.[145]

Next morning we rose at a leisurely hour, ambled to the station and caught the train to Les Houches, where we went into the Office de Tourisme to check that the lifts were still working. The whole of the French public sector had been on strike the previous week in protest at the government's decision to raise the retirement age to 62 and the young man in charge appeared to be continuing some sort of unofficial action. Unable to obtain any useful information in either French or English, we agreed that after being unhelpful to tourists for up to 35 hours a week, he certainly ought to retire no later than 60. As a consequence of this helpful discussion, we just missed the cable car and had to wait 20 minutes for the next. At the top we discovered that we had also missed the tram, and the next did not leave for an hour. Our friend in the tourist office had also omitted to mention that the tram no longer runs all the way to the Nid d'Aigle, at the start of the path to the Goûter hut, because a large accumulation of water beneath the glacier threatens to wash away the line in a flash flood. Furthermore, despite the excellent forecast, the weather was looking distinctly unsettled. All in all, our leisurely start was beginning to look rather ill-judged.

With the cloud closing in, we sprinted up a bouldery zigzag path from Mont Lachat, over a col, across the shallow bowl of the Désert de Pierre Ronde and up the ridge to the Tête Rousse. It was after 16:00 when we crossed the little snowfield above the Tête Rousse hut and started to climb up the ridge to the Goûter hut. The ridge was an icy but easy scramble, like a Scottish Munro with altitude. Numerous cables installed to make the climb easier added immeasurably to the difficulty, because it is almost impossible to resist the temptation to haul oneself up them, hand over hand, like a comic book commando. We were soon climbing in dense cloud and steady snowfall. We were also completely alone, which was disconcerting since the hut takes well over 100 people. At one point a guide appeared out of the swirling clouds above us, dangling two clients on short ropes. He was on his way down and said the hut was absolutely packed. When we eventually arrived just before 18:30, people were standing elbow to elbow in the boot room, with a huge mound of rucksacks in one corner. I pushed my way through the crowd to the Reception, fully expecting a fearful row, to be greeted with 'we were wondering where you were', a meal ticket and two places for dinner. Perhaps being called Thompson helps. When I lived in France in the 1970s there was a popular French movie called *Les Carnets du Major Thompson* (based on the novel by Pierre Daninos) about a crusty old English officer living in Paris. French people of a certain age still assume that all middle-aged Englishmen called Thompson must be like Major Thompson. Perhaps Frenchmen called Clouseau experience something similar in England.

After a good-humoured supper with a crowd of Dutch climbers, washed down with litres of water to rehydrate, we went to bed at 20:00 and about half an hour later inevitably had to get up and stagger into the freezing darkness in search of the latrines. All the other occupants of the crowded dormitory did the same thing, at roughly 10-minute intervals, throughout the short night. On my wife's expedition, she enjoyed a conversation with a charming Englishman, standing next to her in the queue, about the worst hut latrine. He made a compelling case for a particularly revolting specimen in the Spanish Pyrenees, while she advocated the Konkordia hut in Switzerland where, in addition to the normal discomforts, you have to contend with piped Swiss pop songs from the 1980s. Sadly, the day of the really spectacular long drop has passed. I remember one, I think it was near Arolla, where you could look down through the lavatory seat and see nothing but air for hundreds of feet, like a vertigo-inducing version of the opening scene from Danny Boyle's film *Trainspotting*. Of course, there is no mention of latrines in Conway's articles for the *Pall Mall Gazette*. As Virginia Woolf, the daughter of Conway's friend Leslie Stephen, observed in 1923: 'That you couldn't have done ten years ago – written quite openly about water-closets in a respectable weekly.'[146]

At 02:30 the sleepers' alarms started to go off and the normal chaos of an alpine start in an overcrowded hut continued for an hour, until suddenly we were out into the cold, cold night. We walked steadily upwards in the darkness for about two hours, following the line of torches snaking up the dark bulk of the mountain ahead. A thousand stars sparkled in a vast moonless sky and the beams from our headlamps illuminated dancing fragments of ice in the chill night air. There was hardly any wind and it was completely silent apart from the slow, rhythmic crunch and groan of crampons in snow. Like Conway, we sheltered briefly beside 'Monsieur Vallot's hut' to put on extra clothes, but while Conway 'had no predecessors' tracks to abbreviate our toil'[147] we followed a deep trench in the snow. As we reached Le Dôme du Goûter a brilliant band of yellow appeared in the east, punctured by the jagged outline of the Pennine Alps, and slowly spread along the horizon until a rainbow-coloured halo seemed to encircle the earth. When dawn broke a rose-pink sundrift crept slowly down the snow and ice of the surrounding peaks. To the east, the lights of Chamonix were still visible in the dark shadow of the valley. To the west, rocky ridges soared above a lilac-grey sea of morning mist.

There must have been at least a hundred other climbers on Mont Blanc that day, but the extreme cold did not encourage them to linger on the summit. The highest point is a gently curving ridge on a vast dome of snow. In Conway's day there was a hut on the summit and 'man has rooted the evidence of his activity deep into the icy mass and strewed its surface with shavings and paper, so frozen down that the storms of the whole year have not sufficed to remove them'.[148] Perhaps we have global warming to thank for defrosting and removing this debris. Without rocks to add interest to the foreground, or other peaks of comparable height to give scale to the middle distance, the view from Mont Blanc is grand rather than beautiful. Conway scribbled a note to Agnes on the summit to say that he was 'in the sunshine, looking all over Italy' and I too gazed south along the route that we had both followed through the Maritime and Cottian Alps, and then east to the Bernese Oberland and Austria beyond.

While Conway and his party had the summit to themselves, we were soon joined by other climbers, grateful for the well-trodden track, but anxious to create the illusion of solitude in their summit photographs. We tumbled back down the mountain to the hut in less than two hours and carried on down the ridge on rocks slippery with yesterday's snow. We finally removed our crampons just above the station at Mont Lachat, where we gratefully caught the tram back to Bellevue, the cable car to Les Houches, and the train to Chamonix. Conway descended via the Grands Mulets hut and stayed at Couttet's Hotel in Chamonix ('comfortable, frequented by English and Swiss climbers'[149]), where Whymper died on 16 September 1911, but which no longer exists. We stayed in Les Praz, and drank a glass of wine on a terrace looking up at Mont Blanc, smug in the knowledge that we had been standing on the summit just 10 hours earlier.

In the restaurant, there was a large and noisy group of middle-aged Englishmen. They appeared to be lawyers or accountants from the north of England, on a golfing holiday, and they all had nicknames. They took it in turns to tell stories about past holidays where 'Wally' was totally wrecked and 'Moose' got so pissed that he fell downstairs. They were without their good wives, and so in good spirits, and they were obviously sharing rooms because there were regular accusations of snoring and counter-accusations of somnambulant sexual advances. They were big, beery men, the backbone of England, and conservative to the core; exactly the sort of people that Conway would have despised for 'vulgarising' the Alps. As Conway observed of the Palace Hotel in Montana, in a letter to Marble written in 1909: 'It's pretty promiscuous, being full of golfers, who are a freemasonry of a peculiar sort. They are a very ugly lot to look at.'

Meanwhile, back in the middle of the summer, having deferred Mont Blanc to the end of the season, I left Chamonix and continued on my way to Switzerland. After the ascent of Mont Blanc, Fitzgerald found himself urgently called to Florence on business. His mother, who was corresponding with Katrina, assumed that he was still with Conway and appealed for news of their progress. This left Katrina in a quandary: 'I can't continue to write as if giving her the news she longs for from her son', she wrote in a letter to Conway. 'Why did he leave you and why doesn't he return?' But after their long day on Mont Blanc, even Conway decided to have two rest days in Chamonix before continuing his journey.

The view of the Mont Blanc range from the Brévent or Flégère above Chamonix is rightly regarded as one of the finest in the Alps: 'Perhaps the most vulgarised but certainly one of the very loveliest low points of view in the mountains of Europe',[150] according to Conway. He returned to Flégère in June 1930, when he was feeling old and depressed, and recorded in his diary that he immediately felt 'greatly improved in health, spirits and strength'. When I reached Flégère, a bulbous lenticular cloud had settled on the very top of Mont Blanc, but the snowfields below sparkled with morning light. To the left of the huge snowy dome of Mont Blanc stands the Aiguille du Midi, with an icy ridge leading to the rocky spires of l'Aiguille de Blaitière, l'Aiguille du Grépon and the Grands et Petits Charmoz. Further left, and set back, framed by the sinuous valley of the Mer de Glace, is the shadowy north face of les Grandes Jorasses with just a few east-facing angles on the Walker Spur picked out in the early morning light. Left again, l'Aiguille du Dru and l'Aiguille Verte were silhouetted against a diamond sky. To Conway, almost all of these mountains had a personal association. The Charmoz and the Grépon were first climbed by Albert Mummery in 1880 and '81. The two highest points on les Grandes Jorasses were reached by Edward Whymper and Horace Walker in 1865 and 1868 respectively. Whymper also made the first ascent of l'Aiguille Verte in 1865, while the Dru was climbed in 1878 by Clinton Dent, who had seconded Conway's application for membership of the Alpine Club two years earlier. Almost every major peak within view (except Mont Blanc itself) was first climbed by a member of the Alpine Club, and Conway and his fellow English climbers looked upon these mountains with almost proprietorial pride.

For modern climbers, too, these peaks are shrouded in myths and memories. Wildly exaggerated stories of heroic triumphs and epic failures are handed down from generation to generation until they become an accepted part of climbing lore, and the mountains themselves seem to assume a shadowy, sometimes friendly, sometimes malign, personality. But the real beauty of the view from the Aiguilles Rouges is not so much the distant piles of rock and ice as the magnificent contrast with a foreground of bright alpine meadows, fir trees and sunny rocks. As Conway observed: 'Nine-tenths, or even more, of the interest of scenery, and most of its beauty, resides in the foreground and the middle distance.'[151]

I followed the Tour de Mont Blanc path along a high belvedere before dropping down to the road that leads over the Col de la Forclaz to Switzerland. A forest track led past waterfalls to the Refuge de la Pierre à Bérard, a small building tucked under a huge boulder as protection against avalanches. Next day, as I climbed the rocky slopes of Mont Buet (the '*Mont Blanc des Dames*'), the real Mont Blanc gradually appeared behind the ridge line of the Aiguilles Rouges. A rounded shoulder of slatey rubble led easily to the summit (3,099 m) and continued northwards, with views of bedded limestone cliffs and soft wooded valleys to the west. Further on, the ridge narrowed and steepened to give an exposed scramble down some rotten rocks where I was grateful for an abundance of cables. Two chamois nonchalantly ambled along a narrow rubble-strewn ledge above a vertical drop as I descended. Conway insisted on a rope at this spot and I am not surprised; it looks daunting from above, although it is actually quite straightforward.

After scree-running down from the side of the ridge, I slogged across moraine to the Col du Vieux, climbed easily to the summit of Le Cheval Blanc, and so entered Switzerland. The great slag heap of Le Cheval Blanc looks down onto two reservoirs. The Lac du Vieux Emosson, the higher of the two, was a 'desert of small stones', according to Conway, before it was flooded. Today the artificial lake adds interest to a desolate hollow of broken rock and patchy grass. The valley of the bigger and lower Lac d'Emosson, with its rocky shore dotted with pine trees, was once productive cow pasture. The route to the Vieux Emosson led past slabs of sandstone, dipping at about 30 degrees, on which ripple marks and footprints of ancient dinosaurs are clearly visible. There is no mention of this in Conway's account, so I presume that they were discovered after his time. I spent my first night in Switzerland in the subterranean dormitory of a restaurant, in a fine position overlooking the barrage of Lac d'Emosson.

Chapter Four
Sir Martin Conway 1895–1918

The Hunt for Reputation

The Alps from End to End was published one year after Conway's journey, in 1895, and was generally well received. A reviewer in the *Geographical Journal* noted that the 'book abounds in adventure and incident of the usual type, told with a cheery heartiness which strikes one pleasantly like a mountain breeze';[152] while a hard-bitten Scottish climber, writing in the *Scottish Mountaineering Club Journal*, correctly surmised that 'the author's aim was the production of a popular work rather than one of any intrinsic mountaineering merit'.[153] Like all the best travel writing, *The Alps from End to End* brings a real sense of freshness and wonder to a subject that was, even then, pretty well known. Conway wrote the book in haste during the journey, and it was originally published in serial form in the *Pall Mall Gazette*. Some of the original manuscripts, written in pencil on small scraps of paper, still exist in the Cambridge University Library. They differ remarkably little from the published version. When Conway revised his drafts, his prose tended to become mannered rather than polished. He was far better at extemporising. *The Alps from End to End* is his best book because it is light and almost lyrical, like a long anecdote told to a group of friends after a good dinner.

Pleased with the reviews, Conway wondered what he should do next. Until an election was called, little was required of him in his capacity as Liberal party candidate for Bath, but he was anxious to capitalise on the publicity generated by his two travel books. In a letter to Marble he wrote: 'Just now my reputation is on the tremble – that is my feeling – and the nails must be rightly knocked in.' The Slade professorship was falling vacant and Conway once again put his name forward. His artistic friends, led by Onslow Ford, got up a testimonial, and so too did Colvin. Conway's former colleagues at Liverpool University also lobbied on his behalf, but Conway himself was becoming increasingly disillusioned with the process: 'The hunt for reputation is not a beautiful thing; and the nearer one approaches to the attainment of even a small one, the less beautiful does humanity appear from the newly attained standpoint.' In February Conway was elected Chairman of the Society of Authors. Both he and Marble felt encouraged by this success, but just a few weeks later he learned that he had failed once more to win the professorship at Cambridge. 'The result sickens me of art', he wrote to Marble.

In March Conway went to Oxford to give a talk to the University Alpine Club and dined with Arthur Evans, the Keeper of the Ashmolean Museum. Evans had earlier sounded out Conway on whether he wished to stand for the Slade professorship at Oxford, but Conway had equivocated, preferring his alma mater. Now that Cambridge had rejected him, he tried to rekindle the interest of Oxford, but to no avail. Charles Moberly Bell, whom he had first met in Cairo, also approached him to see whether he would go to Kashmir as correspondent of *The Times* to cover the military campaign in Chitral, but Conway hesitated and Bell offered the assignment to Francis Younghusband instead. Younghusband's account of the siege and relief of Chitral, strongly endorsed by *The Times*, sold 3,000 copies in the first two weeks after publication, impressing the young Winston Churchill amongst others. But despite these setbacks, Conway did receive one good piece of news: he was awarded a knighthood in the Queen's birthday honours.

Conway's knighthood was recommended by Lord Rosebery, the Liberal prime minister, theoretically 'in recognition of your remarkable work as a traveller so remarkably embodied in your monumental book', but actually because Conway's lobbying in Bath had paid off. The local Liberal party had convinced Rosebery that a knighthood might just help Conway to win the marginal seat. As a young man, Archibald Philip Primrose, 5th Earl of Rosebery, stated that he had just three ambitions in life: to marry an heiress; to win the Derby; and to become prime minister. He married Hannah de Rothschild, the greatest heiress of her day, in 1874; 20 years later his horse 'Ladas' won the Epsom Derby; and he became prime minister. Rosebery was reputed to pep up his political speeches by taking a small sniff of cocaine. He took, perhaps, a somewhat larger snort before deciding to recommend Conway for a knighthood. Explorers, alpinists, art historians, journalists and authors were united in their astonishment, but all rushed to congratulate the new knight. Coolidge maintained that Conway's knighthood 'was a BITTER pill'[154] to Douglas Freshfield in particular, but Coolidge was engaged in a vendetta with Freshfield at the time and was never a reliable judge of character. Conway himself confessed to being mildly disappointed. He had lobbied to be made a Knight Commander of the Indian Empire but 'the number for the year was made up without me and I was offered an ordinary knighthood as a stop-gap'.[155] Nevertheless, as he acknowledged in a letter to his mother: 'We are all very pleased, as this kind of thing has for an author a distinct money value.'

With a general election now looming, Conway was required to campaign in Bath, but having been awarded a knighthood, his main objective had been achieved, and he found it rather hard to raise much enthusiasm for the task. Politics in the 1890s was a kind of performance art, a combination of the pulpit and the stage, and famous political speakers, such as David Lloyd George, attracted huge partisan crowds and frequent brawls. Both political parties typically used public houses as committee rooms during elections, which did little to encourage calm and rational debate[156] and many voters regarded election-day handouts and bribes as a basic civil right.

Conway spoke at numerous political meetings in Bath, addressing the major issues of the day: the opposition of the Tory majority in the House of Lords to the budget measures passed by the Liberal government in the House of Commons; Irish home rule; disestablishment of the Welsh Church; and a proposal to address the British propensity to consume excessive quantities of alcohol by shutting down a large number of public houses. His speeches were greeted with numerous 'hear hears', cheering and prolonged applause, according to the Liberal press, while a Tory-leaning journalist stated that 'whatever he was in London, down here in Bath he has been unconscionably dull'.[157] Conway spoke frequently about the importance of the Empire, a subject on which he felt particularly well qualified as a traveller. He observed that 'it was well at such a time that their affairs were in the hands of a statesman so calm, so sober and so strong as the present Prime Minister. (Cheers.) Mr. Balfour (hisses), speaking at the recent horticultural anniversary of the Tories (laughter), or rather of the squabbling alliance nicknamed "Unionist", arrogated to his own party...the sole right to be called the party of the British Empire. Never was any claim more preposterous. (Hear, hear.) The true Imperial party must be the party that would make the Empire healthy and strong (cheers)...',[158] and so on, and so on.

'We are getting on well enough', Conway wrote to Manton Marble. 'We keep Katrina driving around in a carriage all the afternoon, up and down the streets. It's not hard work and it pays very well...only one man has come wanting to be bribed so far.' He relied upon his celebrity as a mountain climber to carry the day: his campaign poster featured Big Ben standing above a snow-capped mountain. The election cost Manton Marble £434 and the results were announced on 15 July. Conway was soundly beaten by the Tory candidate, by 3,445 votes to 2,917. His diary entry for 16 July reads: 'All awoke with headaches – I with an intense feeling of relief. Returned to London by 6 pm train.' In his 1932 memoir, *Episodes in a Varied Life*, Conway claimed that he had specifically asked to fight a seat that he could not possibly win, simply in order to practise his public speaking.[159] Two days after losing the election he travelled to Windsor Castle to be knighted: '[Queen Victoria] gazed in a manner that might imply that she saw everything in an utterly unmoved and wholly observant fashion, or that she was simply vacuous and saw nothing; the latter I expect was the truth.'

Conway might now be a knight of the realm, but at 39 he still had no career and no income. The winter was taken up with lecturing and odd jobs for the Liberal party. He dined with Lord Rosebery at 10 Downing Street, and stayed with him at Mentmore Towers, a neo-Renaissance Rothschild palace in Buckinghamshire, and at Dalmeny Park, a neo-Gothic castle and home of the Earls of Rosebery in Scotland. There he met Herbert Asquith, the future Liberal prime minister, whom he described to Marble as being 'a small man, the image of the salesman at Stanford's map shop', and his wife Margot, who was 'not a bit pretty but...a good talker...They say she used to set her cap at Lord R.' Margot Asquith maintained her reputation as 'a good talker' throughout her life: when the actress Jean Harlow mispronounced her Christian name, Margot pointed out that the 't' was silent, 'as in Harlow'.

Conway too was an entertaining guest, but the Liberal party offered him only 'dreary work' as a hack political writer. At Lord Rosebery's request, he started work on an *Apologia* for the Liberal administration, but the work was never published and Conway's thoughts were soon turning back to exploration. For a time he planned to travel with Katrina in India for a year or more, studying the art and architecture of the country, but later dropped the idea.

In 1895 Agnes was 10, and growing up fast. Her German nurse recorded that 'she has grown so tall I have nearly to stand on tiptoe when I want to wash her face or do her hair...she is less rough and more sensitive...I am sure she will grow up an uncommon clever woman'. In later life, Agnes said that her only regret about her childhood was that Katrina insisted on dressing her in strange 'artistic' garments that made her feel conspicuous. With their growing daughter and new-found social status, Sir Martin and Lady Conway decided that they must move from their incurably middle-class home in Bayswater. After viewing several possibilities, Katrina set her heart on the Red House on Campden Hill, near Holland Park. Built in 1835, the house was set in a large garden with stables and greenhouses. It was demolished in 1965 to make way for the Kensington and Chelsea Civic Centre. The lease was owned by William Kemp-Welch, who had reputedly spent £9,000 restoring the house before going bankrupt. Katrina immediately set about persuading her stepfather to 'lend' them the money to purchase the lease. She wrote a long letter to Marble explaining how they would be able to afford it, if they had just a little help, in which she speculated on the health of Conway's mother, from whom they expected to inherit an income of £400 a year: 'She − poor old lady − is ill with what the Dr thinks a clot on the brain. Everyone speaks of the change in her and that in their opinion her days are numbered. Still, she is alive now.' To Katrina's disappointment, Elizabeth Conway remained alive for another 16 years.

When Katrina wanted something, she typically wrote to her step-father in the style of a young girl. She initially asked for just £200 extra a year, but once Marble had agreed in principle, her demands steadily escalated. As the negotiations proceeded she even sent a 'budget' to Marble, which unquestionably understated their expenditure, but nevertheless pointed to a much larger deficit than £200 a year:

Food, groceries, oil, soap, domestic requisites	£300
Servants' wages	£120
Agnes' education	£50
Fuel	£30
Rent on the Red House	£425
Margin for extra and unforeseen expenses	£500
Total	£1,425

At this time, the Conways' guaranteed income consisted of Katrina's trust fund, which produced about £240 a year. Agnes Tracy paid an 'allowance' to Katrina of £100 per year, while Conway's highly uncertain earnings as a writer, journalist and lecturer amounted to perhaps £500 in a good year. For the balance, they relied on Marble. In the end he agreed to pay the full rent of £425 per year, plus taxes of £75, plus a premium of £400 to acquire the lease. However, Agnes Tracy was so shocked by Katrina's extravagance that she cut her allowance of £100 per year and so, despite Marble's generosity, the Conways were soon in debt once again.

They moved into their new home in February 1896 and two months later celebrated Conway's 40th birthday. With her eye for dramatic colours and lighting, Katrina set about making the house beautiful, with potted palms, rugs from Constantinople, silks from China and oil paintings from Italy. During the winter season of 1896 they entertained 76 guests to dinner. Now that her domestic arrangements more closely approximated those she was accustomed to in New York, Katrina began to feel more self-confident in London society, establishing some close friendships, particularly with professional musicians such as Katharine Goodson, one of the leading female pianists of the time (whom Conway always called 'Squizzle'), and Annette Hullah. Squizzle lived with the Conways for a time at the Red House before she married the composer Arthur Hinton (whom Conway called 'Moccles'). Conway tolerated this growing domesticity because his plans to escape from it were already well advanced.

At first Conway thought of going back to the Karakoram to establish himself as an expert on the region, but having visited the Himalaya once, and lectured on it 55 times, he was thoroughly bored with the subject. The vogue for polar exploration was reaching its peak at about this time and Conway recognised the commercial potential of a book and series of lectures based on Arctic exploration. Following his Karakoram adventure he also had a better understanding of the economics of expeditioning. He had been paid a very good advance of £1,000 for the expedition book (which had taken well over a year to write) and earned about £10 plus expenses for each lecture, but the total income arising from the expedition had barely covered the cost, never mind his living expenses in London. If an expedition to the Arctic was going to pay for itself, it would have to be cheap.

In the end he decided to go to Spitsbergen (Svalbard) where he intended to make 'the first crossing of the island'. Warmed by the Gulf Stream, Spitsbergen was easily accessible by boat from Britain and had been well-known to whalers and fur trappers for generations, but in his expedition prospectus Conway described the interior as unexplored. The British obsession with Arctic exploration was such that there were no less than three separate expeditions to this 'unexplored' island in the summer of 1896 alone, as well as numerous English sportsmen attracted by the walrus shooting. Any sense of Arctic isolation was further undermined during the summer months by the appearance of a weekly boat from Norway bringing tourists and mail to the island. A photograph in *The Bath Herald* showed one of Conway's companions reading an earlier edition of the newspaper during the expedition, and Conway felt compelled to write a letter to *The Times*[160] refuting the suggestion that Spitsbergen was 'overrun' with tourists and that there was a comfortable hotel on the island. However, never one to turn down a journalistic opportunity, Conway later contributed an article to *Travel*[161] magazine entitled 'Spitzbergen as a Summer Resort'.[162]

Despite the burgeoning popularity of Spitsbergen, Conway's celebrity status as an explorer was sufficient to secure a small grant from the Royal Geographical Society. Initially they offered £100, which Conway instantly rejected, telling them 'to spend the money on sweetmeats and distribute it among the Fellows'. After lunch with Sir Clements Markham, the President of the RGS, the sum was increased to £300. Conway also asked Marble for a loan of £400, but for once

Marble declined, because of the very considerable claims that had recently been made on his generosity by Katrina. As a result, Conway was obliged to borrow the money from the bank. The party consisted of J. W. Gregory, a well-known African explorer and author of *The Great Rift Valley of East Africa*, who later drowned in a whirlpool on the Amazon; A. Trevor-Battye, Arctic explorer and author of *Ice-bound on Kolguev*; E. J. Garwood, a capable mountaineer and geologist who later travelled to Kangchenjunga with Douglas Freshfield; and Conway's cousin, H. E. Conway, who had pretensions to being an artist.

The journey across Spitsbergen was unpleasant, rather than difficult – 'one of the most laborious and one of the least interesting expeditions I have ever made'[163] – and achieved very little. Conway hated the cold, wet slog across the boggy tundra of the interior, but enjoyed steaming around the island in their small ship, observing the ever-changing colours of the sky reflected on ice floes and glaciers. Returning to civilisation in Norway, Conway took what he described as a Turkish bath (presumably a sauna): 'For six weeks I never had my clothes off', he wrote to Katrina. 'You may imagine I needed the bath.' He also met Fridtjof Nansen, recently returned from the *Fram* Arctic expedition during which he had reached a record latitude of 86°13' north. 'He talked to me almost all the time', Conway proudly reported to Katrina, '[and] introduced me to his wife of whom he seems very fond...They say she has presented him with two children in his absence, having consoled herself with a Christiana physician.' Nansen later sent Conway a stuffed walrus head, which Conway mounted and hung in the hall of the Red House.

Despite his rather modest achievements compared to Nansen, Conway was satisfied with his expedition. 'My journey has really been very successful', he wrote to Katrina, 'and I think I can make it appear a really greater success than it was.' The following year he published a rather dull book entitled *The First Crossing of Spitsbergen*. It did not sell well. The publisher, J. M. Dent, wrote to Conway stating that 'the book has to my astonishment gone absolutely dead'. He cited Nansen's rather more exciting book *Farthest North* as a contributory factor, and it cannot have escaped his attention that Conway's title bore a striking resemblance to Nansen's earlier book, *The First Crossing of Greenland*.

Determined to establish himself as an expert this time, Conway went back to Spitsbergen the following year, in 1897, for a second trip that achieved even less than the first, although he did experiment with travel by ski. In his account of the expedition he noted that a man engaged in toilsome physical exertion 'is incapable of analysing [the scenery] or noticing its more delicate and evanescent qualities'.[164] Despite this drawback, he wrote a second book, *With Ski and Sledge over Arctic Glaciers*, which appeared in 1898 but achieved no greater success than its predecessor.

Conway returned from his second trip to Spitsbergen with no clear plans for the future. There were new enthusiasms for cycle touring, golf and Turkish baths, but after failing to win the Slade professorship for the fourth time he had largely given up on art and architecture. On 15 June 1897 he 'gave a "smoker" – about 150 men came – it went on till 2 a.m. Chinese lanterns and small band of music in the garden'. He called on the Duke and Duchess of Bedford, who intended to visit Spitsbergen, and attended Gladstone's funeral. He spent part of the winter of 1898 in Grindelwald, where Coolidge now lived, skating, tobogganing and taking long walks through the pristine winter landscape. He rode in a motor cab for the first time: 'It vibrates more than a horse carriage but is more nimble at getting thro' traffic.' He was elected to the Hakluyt Society, the explorers' club, and to the Athenaeum, an intellectual club. Conway put his name forward for membership of the Athenaeum in 1881, one year after he was elected to the Savile, but had to wait 17 years to achieve his ambition. He was proposed by two fellow Cambridge men: the writer and alpinist Oscar Browning and Sir Frederick Pollock, graduate of Trinity College, Cambridge and Professor of Jurisprudence at Oxford. He received four blackballs, but Pollock attributed this to 'the normal activity of the member who blackballs everybody on principle'. Shortly after his election he invited Aleister Crowley, the self-styled 'Great Beast 666', to lunch at the Athenaeum to discuss the Karakoram and even agreed to support his application for membership of the Alpine Club. Crowley was just beginning to establish his reputation as a dabbler in the black arts, which later led a newspaper to accuse him of 'orgies, blasphemy, obscenity, indecency, stealing, cannibalism, kidnapping, blackmail, murder, and unspeakable crimes'.[165] Crowley's name mysteriously disappeared from the Alpine Club ballot shortly before the election took place, suggesting that Conway had had second thoughts. In his *Confessions*, Crowley simply observed that 'Sir Martin Conway had been kind enough to second me; but the record of climbs which I put in to qualify for admission was much too good...it is an outrage to the spirit of the club to do anything original.'[166]

Conway also had lunch with Edward Fitzgerald, whose expedition had reached the summit of Aconcagua in Argentina one year earlier in 1897. Fitzgerald himself turned back about 1,500 ft (500 m) below the summit but Mattias Zurbriggen pressed on alone, thereby establishing a new altitude record of 22,841 ft (6,962 m). With his interest in the Himalaya and the Arctic now exhausted, Conway decided it was time to visit the Andes.

After suffering losses on his two Spitsbergen expeditions, Conway badly needed the financial support of Manton Marble to launch an expedition to the Andes. Before asking him for a loan, Conway decided to set up a committee to promote cordial relations between England and the United States, which he knew would appeal to Marble's interest in Anglo-American affairs. Just as the institutions of donor-dependent African states gradually alter their behaviour to maximise aid rather than real economic activity, so Conway was becoming increasingly dependent upon handouts and patronage from the rich and powerful. He persuaded James Bryce (later Viscount Bryce), a distinguished alpinist who was elected President of the Alpine Club in 1899, to chair the committee. Bryce had been President of the Board of Trade under Lord Rosebery and later became British Ambassador to the United States. Herbert Asquith and Joseph Chamberlain (the latter possibly through the intervention of Charles Mathews) also joined, but many other leading politicians, including Rosebery, declined, probably because Conway was getting a reputation as an unreliable outsider; a dilettante who lacked commitment to the cause. Even Charles Moberly Bell, managing director of *The Times*, whom Conway had first met in Cairo and who had helped Conway to obtain a steady stream of lucrative journalistic commissions, began to wonder if Conway was really serious about his political career. He sent a poem to Conway in February 1898:

One week we watch in wonder, how you stroll
Plane-tabling on the peaks of Himalay,
The next we cheer you struggling at the poll.
Bath, Alps, Spitsbergen, where are you today?
At home, or off on some new expedition
Professor, critic, climber, politician?

Bell's opinion was important, since his leaders in *The Times* could
determine the fate of politicians. As the *Dictionary of National Biography*
noted, 'Bell's overflowing energies prompted him to utilise the resources
of *The Times* for many enterprises that were strictly beyond the bounds
of journalism'.[167] But the committee served its purpose, giving Conway
the confidence to ask Marble (who had now moved to Brighton, so
that he and Abigail might be closer to Katrina and to their friend Henry
James, who lived in Rye) for money to finance his expedition. He confidently predicted that it would cost less than £600 and that 'the profits
on it ought therefore to be not less than £1,000'. The Royal Society
voted him £100, the *Daily Chronicle* agreed to pay £150 for a series of
articles, and he borrowed a further £250 from his faithful friend and
benefactor Henry Willett, the Brighton art collector.

Conway wrote to Edward Whymper to ask him for advice on the
best season for climbing in Bolivia: 'I'm afraid if some Englishman does
not bag Bolivia soon it will be collared by a foreigner', he wrote. His
letter betrayed his envy of and rivalry with Fitzgerald: 'If you and I had
£5,000 a year a piece to spend on mountain exploration we might have
rolled the whole lot out flat by now!' With remarkably little knowledge of the Andes and no particular objective in mind, Conway set sail
for Peru on 13 July 1898.

He took with him two Swiss guides, Pellissier and Maquignaz, but
could not find an English companion willing to accompany him on
the trip. Expeditions inevitably place a strain on personal relationships,
but in many cases the shared experience of hardship and danger forms
the foundation of lifelong friendships. While Conway generally
remained on cordial terms with his companions, he rarely climbed with
the same person for more than one season, probably because he simply

got bored with their company. Conversely, despite not being a particularly good sailor, he thoroughly enjoyed long sea voyages because of the opportunity they afforded for socialising with a large number of fresh and interesting acquaintances. His diaries contain numerous postcards of sleek liners, the earlier ones with both masts and funnels, together with the list of first class passengers. Conway ticked off the names of the people that he had befriended during the voyage, in some cases adding short comments, such as 'pro-Boer' or 'senile'.

On the journey to Peru, the ship stopped first in the West Indies, before passing through the Panama Canal. 'The talk was of...the sugar industry...of fruit-growing, and the need of swift steamers to pour the oranges and bananas and mangoes of Jamaica into the London market, the need for retrenchment in public expenditure; of the negro and labor [sic] questions...Such talk with a number of men...is the best preparation for viewing their country. A week or two so spent expands life.'[168] In Barbados 'the ways simply abounded in niggers; their bits of cottages were everywhere; their babies swarmed like flies in Egypt'.[169] He took refuge in The Club, 'among a group of captains and shipping agents, the local personification of that old and most respectable company, the Royal Mail, which seems to hold the West Indies in the hollow of its hand'.[170] The next stop was Haiti, which in 1804 had become the first Black-led republic in the world: 'Its bays, its beautiful hills...its incomparably fertile soil, its wealth of water, should combine to make it the very garden of the earth; but it is a garden inhabited by people sinking back into savagery and for whom there will be no salvation till the white man has shouldered them again as part of his burden. The day that the United States, having brought prosperity and order to Cuba and Porto Rico, adds Hayti...to its growing empire, will be the most fortunate that has ever dawned on those unhappy regions since Columbus discovered the island of Hispaniola.' Conway observed that 'however well self-government may suit some few white races, it is poison to blacks, and the man who takes it away from them will be their greatest benefactor'.[171]

Arriving in Peru, he went by rail to Lake Titicaca, by steamer to Chililaya, and by cart to La Paz. From La Paz he set off, with mules to carry supplies, to climb Illimani (6,438 m), which is visible from the city. When the mules could go no further he tried to recruit local Indians to act as porters. As a reviewer of his account of the climb noted: 'The Indians...seem to be rather more worthless than the coolies of the Karakoram-Himalayas, and may be aggressive.'[172] Conway's party was soon reduced to himself and his two Swiss guides, who led to the summit and then stepped aside so that Conway might enjoy his moment of triumph. His telegram to the *Daily Chronicle* described the view from the summit as 'astounding',[173] while a rather more considered account in the *Alpine Journal* some months later conceded that 'the view, of course, ought to have been magnificent. As a matter of fact, clouds enveloped the greater part of the horizon.'[174]

The successful ascent of Illimani gave Conway the confidence to try Mount Sorata, then thought to be the highest mountain in Bolivia. Impatient with recalcitrant porters, Conway tried to use a sledge to haul supplies over the glacier, as he had done on Spitsbergen, which no doubt impeded their progress. With the climbing season drawing to a close, they were forced back by bad weather and abandoned the attempt. Katrina sought to console him in defeat: 'Words fail me to tell you how magnificent I think your achievement and how lofty the spirit in which you relate it. Your bravest deed of all was the turning back from Sorata, and the one of which in every sense I am most proud.'

Once again, Conway demonstrated his propensity to exaggerate the altitude attained on his expeditions. A telegram to the *Daily Chronicle* stated that the highest point he had reached on Mount Sorata was 'well over 23,000 ft and probably as much as 24,000 ft'.[175] Had this been true, it would have represented a new altitude record, beating Fitzgerald's recent ascent of Aconcagua (22,841 ft). Unfortunately, when Mount Sorata was climbed six years later by Miss Annie Smith Peck, a 54-year-old American mountaineer, it proved to be just 20,892 ft high, and Conway turned back well below the summit. He repeated the claim that he had reached 'somewhere about 24,000 ft'[176] in an interview with the *St. James's Gazette* after his return to London, despite the fact that even his own map, published by the Royal Geographical Society, gave a surveyed height of 21,490 ft for the summit.

Meanwhile, Conway continued to make some pretence of serious scientific exploration. He collected mineral specimens and attempted to survey an area of Bolivia near Lake Titicaca, but his latest obsession was mining. The 1880s and 1890s saw numerous gold rushes around the world, including the Witwatersrand in South Africa (which ultimately led to the Boer War) and Kalgoorlie in Australia. Conway was by no means alone in getting caught up in the excitement. Lloyd George, the rising star of the Liberal party and future prime minister, actively promoted the Welsh Patagonian Gold Fields Syndicate in 1893, which never produced any gold, and numerous other public figures were involved in more or less honest attempts to cash in on the gold fever that gripped the City of London. In Bolivia, Conway visited several mines and was impressed by the opportunity mining gave 'to young fellow-countrymen to display, on the margins of South American civilisation, the self-same qualities which have made the British Empire'.[177]

Before leaving the country, Conway called on the President of Bolivia, General José Manuel Pando, to whom he dedicated his account of the journey. According to Conway, the President spontaneously offered him a concession to exploit all the natural resources found within the Acre Territory, 'a vast swampy region, I believe about the size of France, profusely watered by a group of the highest tributaries of the Amazon...the main source of supply of what was called Para Rubber'.[178] What the President apparently failed to tell Conway was that the Acre Territory was claimed by (and today forms part of) Brazil. General José Manuel Pando probably hoped that Sir Martin Conway was a man of higher social standing and greater substance than the typical British opportunists and adventurers who visited his country, and that British investment in Acre, via Bolivia rather than Brazil, might strengthen his claim to the Territory.

Had Conway succeeded in climbing Mount Sorata, he would probably have returned to England immediately, but having failed he decided to go on to Chile to attempt to climb Aconcagua and so at least equal the world record for altitude set by Fitzgerald's expedition (which he must have known still stood, despite his exaggerated claims about Sorata). He travelled by train to Antofagasta, by ship to Valparaiso, and then by mule to Baños del Inca at the foot of the mountain, writing a letter to Manton Marble en route in which he calmly informed him that he had spent £576 to date and would need a further loan of £350 to complete his travels. Both Conway and his guides were well acclimatised after their extended stay on the *altiplano* of Bolivia and made the ascent of Aconcagua in a week. In his account of the climb, Conway stated that he turned back just below the summit. His explanation was that 'when Vines ascended Aconcagua, [he] made a record for altitude, and I thought it likely that, if I reached his peak, I should be accused of mere jealousy, whereas if, after overcoming all the difficulties of the mountain and being within ten minutes of, and at the very outside 50 ft below, the highest point, I turned back, I could not be so accused'.[179]

It is a curious explanation. According to Fitzgerald's account,[180] Stuart Vines, the expedition geologist, and Nicola Lanti, an Italian porter, made the second ascent of Aconcagua a month after Mattias Zurbriggen had made the first. It was common practice to give the credit for an ascent to the English climber, even if he was led to the summit by a foreign guide or porter; but to completely ignore the first, solo, ascent by Mattias Zurbriggen was most unusual. Perhaps Conway preferred to highlight Vines' second ascent because he thought that Zurbriggen's success on both Pioneer Peak in the Karakoram and Aconcagua in the Andes might detract from his own role in the former. More importantly, it is almost inconceivable that Conway would have turned back just 50 ft below the summit of Aconcagua having travelled so far to climb it.

The reason for this tale appears to be that Fitzgerald, lacking self-discipline as usual, had failed to deliver the manuscript describing the first ascent of Aconcagua to his publisher on time. When Conway published his newspaper articles about the ascents of Illimani, Sorata and Aconcagua in the *Daily Chronicle*, he dramatically (and probably quite deliberately) reduced the public interest in Fitzgerald's forthcoming book while increasing the interest in his own by (erroneously) claiming a new altitude record on Mount Sorata. As Fitzgerald's publisher wrote: 'As it is, it can hardly be held that Mr. Fitzgerald's expedition has accomplished a "record" climb...The interesting articles which you contributed to the Daily Chronicle are naturally fresh in the memory of all who are interested in mountaineering exploits, and we have received substantial evidence from several quarters that Mr. Fitzgerald's forthcoming book has lost a considerable part of its value by its postponement.' Perhaps fearing the criticism of his peers in the Alpine Club and the Royal Geographical Society when his deceit about the height of Sorata was revealed, Conway made up a story about 'doing the decent thing' on Aconcagua.

Unlike Conway's expeditions to both the Himalaya and the Andes, Fitzgerald's expedition probably did accomplish a 'record' climb (there is an earlier disputed claim relating to an ascent of Kabru in the Himalayas), and while Aconcagua is a straightforward mountain in good weather conditions, involving nothing more than a long and boring trudge up scree-covered slopes, it is nevertheless the highest peak outside the Himalayas. Conway's 1920 memoir hints that some, at least, of his peers both recognised and strongly disapproved of his deliberate attempt to discredit Fitzgerald's achievement: 'I have regretted my action since,' he wrote. 'It did not accomplish all the result intended.'[181]

Emboldened by the ease with which he had climbed Aconcagua, Conway continued south to Patagonia, travelling by ship to 'Sandy Point' (Punta Arenas) where he arrived on Christmas Day and was invited to dinner by the manager of the English Bank. Conway noted that 'perhaps the greatest danger run by a young Englishman who goes in search of fortune to remote foreign cities is the utter loss of the traditions of home life. Many a young man whom I have encountered has lamented to me the fact that, perhaps for years, he had been entirely cut off from the society of ladies of his own class...The tendency thus created to adopt lower standards...is a great danger.'[182] Conway also recorded a story about a young Englishman who had established a sheep station in Patagonia, five days' hard riding from Punta Arenas, who had travelled into town before Christmas and purchased a copy of *With Kitchener in Khartoum*. Conway commented that 'the battle of Omdurman was fought on the 2nd of September 1898, and before the 2nd of January 1899, the full story of the campaign had been written in the Soudan, printed, bound, and published in London, exported to Magellan Strait, and carried up to the remotest point in Patagonia – a remarkable instance of the shrinking of the world in our own days'.[183]

The Chilean navy lent Conway a steamer to take him through the Straits of Magellan to Tierra del Fuego, where he attempted to climb Mount Sarmiento with Maquignaz and two Chilean sailors, but was driven back by the notoriously bad weather of the region. The peak was finally ascended in 1956 by a very strong Italian party. Conway had by this stage formed a rather low opinion of the indigenous population of South America, and cheerfully applied some of Karl Pearson's contemporary thinking on eugenics. He described the Alaculof Indians that inhabited the southern part of Chile near the Magellan Straits as 'a pestiferous nuisance to the pioneers of civilisation' noting that 'as they cannot fit themselves into the fabric of the civilised world they have become a rapidly diminishing and doomed race. Only anthropologists will regret them...Yet it is impossible not to extend pity towards these unfortunates, while wishing them swift euthanasia.'[184]

Grand Schemes

Conway's South American journey was his last as an explorer and a mountaineer. '[The mountains] had called me as things of beauty and of wonder, things terrible and sublime, and instead of glorying in their splendour here I was spending months in outlining the vagrant plan of them on a piece of paper.'[185] He published an account of his journey in two volumes: *Climbing and Exploration in the Bolivian Andes* appeared in 1901 and *Aconcagua and Tierra del Fuego: A Book of Climbing, Travel and Exploration* in 1902. The first maintained some pretence that the journey had involved serious exploration. In the 'Industry and Commerce' section of *Hints for Travellers, Scientific and General*, the Royal Geographical Society encouraged British explorers to examine the commercial potential of a country's resources, what products might find a market there, accessibility for trade, and suitability for immigration and colonisation. Accordingly, Conway set out a detailed, and highly optimistic, account of the potential to develop rubber, coffee and cocoa industries on the eastern slopes of the Cordillera Real of Bolivia. He described the forest area east of Sorata as 'a great gold region, not improbably as rich and important as the Rand',[186] and confidently predicted a gold rush, leading to an agricultural boom. 'When the people come, the wealth they may take out of the ground is almost limitless',[187] he mused. The second book, describing his travels in Chile, is more discursive, with descriptions of people met along the way and observations about life in general. He had ceased to be an explorer and had become merely an adventurous traveller. Conway, I suspect, would have identified with Bruce Chatwin, another great populariser of travel in Patagonia. They shared a love of wild places, beautiful objects and amusing anecdotes. Conway would have enjoyed Chatwin's nomadic assertion that 'Man's real home is not a house, but the Road',[188] but he would also have known that it was absolute nonsense. Both men would have found life intolerable without delicious gossip in fashionable houses.

Conway arrived back in London on 7 February 1899. He wrote a series of articles about his travels for *Harper's Magazine*, the *Alpine Journal* and the *Journal of the Royal Geographical Society* and read a paper at the Linnean Society. He also resumed his active social life, attending meetings of the Camera Club and sitting next to Samuel Clemens (Mark Twain) at a dinner party: 'Found him most entertaining and interesting but with a clearly marked bohemian background. His lecture tour reminiscences were delightful. Billiards till 2 a.m.' Twain passed the winter of 1899/1900 in London, working to pay off his creditors in America, and the two men met several times, presumably sharing reminiscences about travel, writing and debt.

On 2 May 1899, Agnes celebrated her fourteenth birthday at the Red House. Both her parents were out for the day but she had a pleasant party, inviting five girls her own age to tea, supervised by Conway's sister Minnie, with Annette Hullah, one of Katrina's musical protégées, to entertain them. While playing hide and seek, Agnes climbed onto the roof of the conservatory and fell through a skylight, fracturing her skull and severing a nerve that paralysed half her facial muscles. After the accident, she was unable to close her right eye and the right side of her mouth drooped open. Agnes coped with this trauma with remarkable stoicism, but her mother was utterly devastated. For Katrina, beauty was the highest accomplishment for a woman and she found her daughter's disfigurement unbearable. She grew increasingly nervous and thin, rarely left the house, and spent her days obsessively practising the piano. As Conway sadly wrote to Abigail Marble: 'The sight of Agnes is killing K.'

In July 1900, after Agnes had recovered from her initial injuries and returned to school for a time, she was taken by Katrina to a clinic in

Sweden for treatment of the nerve. Agnes made some progress, but Katrina found that she could not cope with the sight of so much suffering: 'There are women from all countries...and suffering from all diseases', she wrote to Conway. '[Agnes] makes friends with everybody and the ugly side of the people and the life here – which to me is like a perpetual BLISTER – leaves her quite untouched.' Katrina decided to leave Agnes at the clinic and return home to London. Annette Hullah, who had agreed to accompany them to Sweden, stayed on for a while but she too had to return to England in December. Agnes wrote a letter to 'Grannie [Elizabeth Conway], Aunt Minnie and Aunt Lizzie' (who still lived with their mother at home) thanking them for their letters but regretting that she had no news because 'unfortunately you are the only people who write nice and often and tell me news and nearly everything I know is from you'. On 31 December 1900, Agnes celebrated the start of the twentieth century alone and completely penniless in her Swedish clinic, because both her parents had forgotten to send her any pocket money.

Conway was preoccupied with how best to exploit the Acre concession and spent many days consulting Manton Marble and drafting up a prospectus. With his growing reputation he was at last being offered numerous opportunities in politics, exploration and the academic world, but he felt restless and unable to commit to any one of them. His diary entry for 27 August 1899 reads:

'Over the last days and weeks I have been offered and refused:
To be parliamentary candidate for Lincoln
Ditto for Plymouth
Principal of University College, Liverpool
Leader of the Antarctic expedition
Leader of the expedition sent by British Museum to make scientific exploration of Patagonia.'

With respect to the Antarctic expedition he added: 'I am too old now and besides do not feel inclined to leave K and Agnes again for a long journey of exploration.' But just a few weeks later his diary reads: 'Feel all agog today to go and climb Mustagh Ata.' Better sense soon prevailed and he abandoned the plan. As Conway later reflected: 'For all of us there are many kinds of joy as yet unexperienced, many activities untried, many fields of knowledge unexplored. We must not spend too large a fraction of life over one, or the rest will escape us. It is life, after all, that is the greatest field of exploration. We need not travel to remote places to find it.'[189] Conway finally resolved to stand as Liberal party candidate for South Wolverhampton and was adopted by the constituency in November 1899, but within a few months he had changed his mind and decided to return to Bolivia instead.

He spent the winter lecturing on the Andes and *The Alps from End to End* and, like the rest of the country, became increasingly preoccupied with the Boer War. His entry for 16 December reads: 'Went to Savile and Athenaeum Clubs. Everyone depressed and silent, brooding over the bad news from S. Africa.' A relation, Frank Conway, enlisted and died of typhoid in Pretoria. Conway wrote to the War Office suggesting that a company of Gurkha 'mountaineer-scouts' be sent to South Africa under the command of Major Charles Bruce, his companion in the Karakoram. The scheme was approved by the War Office, but the India Office refused to release Bruce. Given the Gurkhas' extensive experience of guerrilla warfare on the North West Frontier of India, it was probably not a bad suggestion. Part of the objection by the India Office was, perhaps, the use of coloured soldiers to fight (and possibly defeat) white men, particularly when the British army had so far failed to do so.

Negotiations for the formation of the 'Bolivian Acre Chartered Company' continued sporadically. Conway took the scheme to various City financiers including the Rothschilds, who rejected it, while Manton Marble kept them financially afloat: 'No words can tell you the Heaven that your gorgeous cheque has brought us,' Katrina wrote to him, 'for in spite of the hundreds of millions floating in the air around us...just for the moment, in spite of it all, we are counting each little silver sixpence!' Conway discovered that a consortium led by Athole Reader held a similar rubber concession in Peru and the two men decided to join forces. Eventually they succeeded in raising £24,000 of capital, of which Conway (or rather Marble) contributed £2,000. It was decided that Conway and Reader should travel to Peru and Bolivia to carry out the first inspection of the land whose prospects they had so assiduously sold to their investors. Conway recorded in his diary that Reader was 'a rather sharp operator', which proved to be a very accurate assessment. He later married Ella Rawle, a former Wall Street stenographer who became a highly successful mining entrepreneur, nicknamed 'the Copper Queen'. An American journalist described her as 'a woman of fine presence with a genius for talking magnates into venturesome promotions'.[190] In 1907 Reader was charged with 16 counts of perjury relating to the sale of the Cerro de Pasco mine in Peru, but was stylishly and successfully defended in court by his wife.

With the fare borrowed from Marble, Conway set sail for Peru, via New York, and briefly became embroiled in a violent revolution in Panama, where he was obliged to take refuge in the British Consulate, and then spent two days on HMS *Leander*, which happened to be anchored offshore, until the fighting subsided. Naturally, he wrote an account of this excitement for *The Times*, entitled 'The Great Central American Game'.[191]

In Peru, Conway and Reader set out to visit their rubber concession: 'Hear news today of dangerous Indians in our forest, of difficulties of transport ahead etc.', Conway recorded in his diary. Two days later they discovered that the forest was in fact in Bolivia, not Peru, and that Bolivia had granted the concession to an entirely different company. Undaunted, they continued to La Paz where they indulged in an orgy of deal-making, involving rubber concessions, gold mines and railways. Conway wrote to Katrina to describe the progress they were making: 'The bare fact is that we are likely to be multimillionaires in a few months' time. I have secured a third stake not merely in a gold mine but in a great gold district as big and apparently rich as the Klondyke...India-rubber pails [sic] into insignificance alongside of this, but I have got plenty of that too...Tomorrow I have an important interview with the President, when I hope to secure the contract for building all the railroads of Bolivia...it is a vast new career that opens out now...After all I have not been such a fool as people think.' It made wonderful reading, but Conway was a dreamer not a businessman. The 'great gold district' was acquired on a whim, with little or no information on its geological prospectivity. The scheme for the formation of 'The Bolivian Railroad Development Co.' was dreamt up in Conway's hotel room and presented to the President the following day. At the end of this frantic period of activity, Conway's diary records that various agreements and concessions were duly signed, but in a later hand Conway has added a quote from *The Rubáiyát of Omar Khayyám*:

'The moving finger writes, and having writ
Moves on, nor all your piety nor wit
Can lure it back to cancel half a line,
Nor all your tears wash out a word of it.'

The return trip from La Paz to London took 43 days. Finally back in England, Conway and Marble 'sat late talking gold mines and dreams'. Just as his relationship with Bradshaw had fuelled his interest in art, and his friendship with Freshfield had influenced his decision to become an explorer, now his American stepfather-in-law mentored him as he sought to enter the world of business. A few weeks later, with letters of introduction from Marble, Conway sailed for New York intent on raising capital for his new ventures. When a Wall Street banker cabled for a reference, a London bank replied: 'Social position first rate. Reputation excellent. Chairman of Society of Authors. Probably next President Alpine Club.' Prospective investors in gold mines, rubber plantations and railways probably found this summary of his background and experience rather less than persuasive. In New York Conway dined with Mark Twain and other friends and relations, and visited numerous financiers to discuss Bolivia. While his daughter sat alone and penniless in a Swedish clinic, the end of the old century saw Conway walking down Fifth Avenue in New York, buoyed up by dreams of the vast fortune that awaited him in the new.

While he was in America, Conway wrote 'A Letter to a Friend', which appeared in *Harper's Weekly* on 31 December 1900, describing his feelings upon finding himself in New York at the start of the twentieth century (unlike the millennium, the twentieth century was generally agreed to start on 1 January 1901). Conway was a remarkably international man for his time. He had travelled widely and spent long periods in Paris, Berlin, Vienna, Florence and The Hague. He spoke good French, translated works from German and Dutch into English, and could get by in Italian and Spanish. As a young man he had fallen in love with Italy, seeing the country through the medium of its art: 'It was not like entering a foreign land, but rather as though at last coming home...Nothing was unexpected. The painters had told the truth, but the reality was more entrancing than any pictures.'[192] But the romance of Italy faded with his interest in art. In middle age, Conway became obsessed by celebrity and money, and nowhere suited his acquisitive mood better than New York. At the beginning of the new century, Conway claimed that he always aspired to remain an outsider in continental Europe – a visible and obvious foreigner – but in New York he wanted to be an insider. Of course, he had an American wife, but it was largely through the increasing influence of his stepfather-in-law, Manton Marble, that Conway became 'Americanised'. He saw New York as a younger, brasher, more self-confident version of England: 'The English-speaking world runs everywhere upon the same lines...It engulfs the other races, and either moulds them into its own type (in the case of most Teutons) or reduces them to servitude, and makes them sweep streets, black boots, cook food, and perform the like menial offices.' He described Anglo Saxons as 'the large, red, conquering race...bringing with him those atrocious despotisms law and order, truth-telling and cold baths'. And yet one of the attractions of New York, in Conway's mind, was that law and order and truth-telling were not held in quite such high esteem as in England: 'If the choice must lie between red tape and corruption, I for one, with New York before me as an object lesson, will choose corruption every time...The inhabitants of New York will stand corruption, but they won't stand for inefficiency.' The article ended on a wistful note: '[New York] cast off the nineteenth century some time ago and the twentieth century finds it ready...What a capital for the British Empire it would have been, but for the short-sighted and...parochial ideas of our forefathers.'

When Queen Victoria died just 22 days later, Conway was in Washington. His almost exact (fictional) contemporary, Soames Forsyte, gave a sober assessment of the changes that had occurred in English society during her long reign: 'Morals had changed, manners had changed, men had become monkeys twice-removed. God had become Mammon – Mammon so respectable as to deceive himself...An era which had canonised hypocrisy, so that to seem respectable was to be.'[193] He might have been describing Conway.

By the beginning of February, Conway was back in London and was offered the Presidency of the Alpine Club by James Bryce. However, as the Victorian era ended, his other dreams were collapsing one by one. More experienced and ruthless operators, mainly from America, had entered the competition for Bolivia's natural resources. In his absence, one of his rubber syndicates had failed to secure its concession and was later dissolved. Negotiations to raise capital for the development of Acre continued but made slow progress; and there was almost no activity in relation to his mining rights. Although he continued to dream, in his heart Conway probably knew that he was not cut out to be a successful businessman. During a chance encounter with Cecil Rhodes in 1895, the great empire-builder had told Conway that 'grand schemes are rot unless you can boil them down to business details', and that is precisely what Conway failed to do.

In the absence of anything better to do, Conway started writing a history of Spitsbergen and formed a dangerous liaison with Mrs Kemp-Welch, the wife of the former owner of the Red House, who 'helped him with his writing'. Conway spent several mornings, afternoons and evenings each week at her house, apparently unaware of the distress he was causing at home. On 20 April 1901 Katrina, already deeply depressed after Agnes' accident, locked herself in her bedroom and attempted to commit suicide by taking an overdose of opium. Conway climbed up the outside of the house, smashed the window and broke into her room. She recovered, physically unharmed, but increasingly susceptible to depression and ill health. A few days later Conway recorded in his diary that he had taken delivery of a peacock which 'arrived from the Zoological Gardens and promptly left over the wall'. He terminated his relationship with Mrs Kemp-Welch in disgust some weeks later, when he discovered that he was not the only man upon whom she lavished her affections.[194]

Conway dined at the Savoy with Captain Scott, who had been chosen to lead the Antarctic expedition in his place. He had no regrets: 'I have done with exploration now, and the days of my youth are at an end. If they were happy, it is to the mountains that I owe the happiness.'[195] He was awarded the Gold Medal for Mountain Surveying at the Paris Exhibition in 1900, but it was in recognition of his work in the Karakoram, now nearly a decade earlier. His political career was also at an end. The Liberal party had finally lost patience with him, and Conway had, in any case, lost·interest in politics.

At the age of 44, it seemed that the future had little in store for Conway, but on 13 May he received a letter from the Vice Chancellor of Cambridge University inviting him to become Slade Professor of Fine Art. Amongst his old friends there were still some who remembered the promise of his earlier years, before he set out to become a celebrity.

History, Theory and Practice

Conway was elated that his old university had finally recognised him, despite his rather undistinguished career as a student. He was required to deliver just 12 lectures each year on the 'History, Theory, and Practice of the Fine Arts', for which he was paid £340 a year – his first regular salary for over 12 years. It was as if the clock had been turned back on Conway's life. In August he set off for Zermatt, where he found several of his old climbing friends, including Charles Mathews. He took Agnes, Katharine Goodson ('Squizzle') and Arthur Hinton ('Moccles') to the summit of the Breithorn. Agnes was 16, exactly the same age as Conway when he made his first ascent of the mountain. He and Agnes then travelled together through the Italian lakes to Milan, Monza, Florence, Perugia, Assisi, Siena, Pisa, Padua and Venice, visiting churches, art galleries and museums. For both of them, it was a very happy summer and one that probably influenced the future course of Agnes' life.

According to Conway's 1932 memoirs, he first met Robert Witt in Siena, while travelling with Agnes, and discovered that he too had amassed a large collection of art photographs.[196] However, there is no mention of this in his diary and, in reality, the meeting probably took place in less romantic surroundings. Wherever they first met, the two men apparently agreed that Witt would concentrate on collecting photographs of pictorial art from the Renaissance onwards, while Conway would collect everything else. Until this time, Conway's photographic collection had grown in a somewhat haphazard manner in response to his immediate needs as a writer and lecturer, and his instincts as a collector. From about the time of his appointment as Slade Professor, and particularly following his decision to revise and update his book *Early Flemish Artists*, he set about arranging the entire collection into chronological order. Each photograph was mounted on a standard-sized sheet of pale beige card, and if the photograph was too large it was cut in half. As the historian Lindy Grant observed, he took pictures 'from learned journals, catalogues and books, many of which were rare and valuable, in acts of biblio-barbarism that should have shamed Attila the Hun',[197] but the approach of grouping all items of a similar age together provided Conway with fresh ideas and insights into his subject. Many of the cards have handwritten notes and cross references, displaying an extraordinarily wide-ranging knowledge of the subject. The objects that particularly captured his attention were often obscure and unshowy, and much of the work that he did to identify their age and provenance was painstaking, unrewarding antiquarianism, demonstrating a genuine passion for his subject.

While Conway and Agnes were travelling in Italy, Katrina had been in Munich and Paris with the Marbles. All of them returned to England in October in time for the start of the university term. Conway began his first lecture as Slade Professor with commendable honesty: 'It is exactly ten years since the study of Art-history ceased to be the main preoccupation of my life...I cannot therefore stand before you, clothed in the panoply of complete knowledge of the latest discoveries in Art-history or the finest *nuances* of recent Art-criticism; but Art is wide as Life itself and whoso has once given himself to her, never escapes her sweet enthrallment.'[198] As he went on to recount various anecdotes from his travels in the Himalaya, the Andes and Egypt, his audience might have wondered whether he had ever possessed any knowledge of art history, but in due course his central thesis emerged: 'The most perfect artist is he who, with the most unerring certainty, selects from the infinite complex of Nature what for him are the elements of beauty, and depicts them and them only with strict veracity and least expenditure of means...a Work of Art is...an incarnation of beauty in flight from soul to soul.'[199] For his inaugural lecture as Slade Professor he had returned to the ideas of Ruskin, the first Slade Professor of Fine Art at Oxford.

Conway's relationship with Marble had matured to such an extent that he sent him drafts of his lectures for approval. However, when Marble criticised one of them for being poorly thought through, Conway reverted to his petulant younger self, threatening to give up the work and resign the professorship. In the end, wiser counsel prevailed, and he simply ignored Marble's advice and submitted the lectures for publication without amendment. He was delighted to be given rooms in his old college, but in other respects he did not find Cambridge life as agreeable as he had anticipated. The Fellows of Trinity College treated him courteously but showed scant regard for his worldly achievements. As Conway observed in a letter to Marble: 'Camb...cares so little about what office a man fills and judges him mainly by what he is in College Halls and Combination rooms.' When his first term of office came to an end in 1904, Conway decided not to seek re-election. His lectures were published in two books, the discursive *Domain of Art* (1901) and *Early Tuscan Art* (1902), a somewhat anecdotal account of the development of art from the twelfth to the fifteenth centuries, emphasising the role of 'great men'.

Despite his academic duties, Conway had not altogether forgotten his Bolivian dreams, but now they were couched in artistic terms: 'We are waiting day after day for news from Bolivia, and are very hard up the while. This reminds me of Hogarth's picture of the poor poet in his garret with a map of the mines of Peru hanging on his walls.' After fulfilling his lecturing commitments until the autumn, he sailed for New York in February 1902 to renew his efforts to raise finance for the Acre concession. His fellow passengers included Gerald Duckworth, the publisher and stepson of Leslie Stephen, Sir Philip Burne Jones, son of Edward Burne Jones and himself an artist, and Joseph Duveen, the art dealer, with whom Conway established a long and slightly murky relationship. After protracted negotiations Conway succeeded in selling a 50% interest in the Acre rubber concession for US$25,000 (approximately £5,000). He cabled £1,000 to Katrina to pay off their most pressing debts and even repaid £400 to Marble. He had dinner with President Theodore Roosevelt, visited a shipyard to enquire about the cost of 'stern wheelers' capable of navigating the Amazon, called on

John Pierpont Morgan, who declined to invest in the project, and wrote a notice of an exhibition of Philip Burne Jones' paintings for *The Herald* to earn some pocket money.

Meanwhile, through Lord Curzon, the Viceroy of India, Conway was introduced to some potential German investors in the project. Immediately after arriving back in Liverpool from New York, he set off for Berlin, where he met Baron Oswald von Richthofen, the German Foreign Minister, on 3 June 1902. Two weeks later Conway's diary reads: 'Brazil issued an ultimatum that unless Bolivia revokes the Acre concession, Brazil will cause a revolution in Acre and will cut that country off from the Atlantic. Gave a garden party for the Alpine Club and had a fine afternoon – the first for weeks it seems. About 180 people came...The peacock died.' Conway called on King Leopold II of Belgium on 24 July: 'He said that Belgium would take 1/3 if anything, must have guarantees as to position on directorate...Asked after Stanley.' One of the King's company officials, who had been involved in the establishment of the Belgian Congo, joked with Conway about the difficulty of getting 110,000 rounds of ammunition on board a ship bound for Zanzibar for one of their early missions.

Even by Conway's business standards, the next few months are rather hard to unravel. He travelled to Germany to promote Playa de Oro, a gold mine in Ecuador, discussed building a railway line between Tocantins and Araguaia in Brazil, and attended several board meetings of the Art Reproduction Company, which he had established to produce prints of great works of art. On 26 September the Central News Service carried a story that Conway, the US Rubber Co. and King Leopold II of Belgium were 'forming a large combine to control the Bolivian supply of rubber'. The next day Katrina engaged a footman, so presumably she believed the story to be true. In October an expedition arranged by Conway left London to carry out a detailed survey of the Acre concession while Conway returned to Berlin to seek finance from Deutsche Bank. On 1 November, having run out of money, he was obliged to borrow £100 from his old friend and long-term creditor Henry Willett, the Brighton art collector. Finally, on 13 November 1902 Bolivian troops in Acre capitulated to the Brazilians, leading to international recognition that the Acre territory was in fact part of Brazil, not Bolivia.

Conway's hopes of untold wealth were dashed. The footman was dismissed and Katrina wrote a letter to her stepfather recalling 'the chains of pearls and diamonds reaching to my feet, the palaces in every country of Europe with their orchestras playing at my bidding, the museum of photographs of all the art of the world since the pre-historic age' and gave 'a little sigh over the dreams of the past as contrasted with the realities of the present'.

Conway's diary for 1903 opens with a page setting out his rather more prosaic ambitions for the New Year:

1. Complete and publish Spitsbergen History
2. Finish Egyptian lectures
3. Get "Art Gallery" publication started
4. Obtain materials for new ed. of Flemish Artists and give lectures on them at Camb
5. Write my views on the origin of Anc. Egyptian style of architecture
6. Get all my photo collection in order

His entry for 2 January reads: 'K says we owe £1,200', but by 19 January Marble had raised her allowance and 'put them back on their feet'. In March 1903, Brazil paid US$575,000 (approximately £110,000) compensation to the Acre concessionaires. From Conway's rather confusing account of the various interests that he had sold in the concession, it is hard to disentangle exactly how much of this compensation he was entitled to. He was in the USA when the payment was made and appears to have received a relatively small amount: about £4,000 was paid directly to him, with a further £7,500 paid to Marble. Conway cabled £500 to Katrina 'as a personal present' and invested the balance in the Florida Oil and Mining Co. and the Manufacturers Commercial Company, where he also became a director.

In public, Conway always maintained the pretence that he had made a fortune in Bolivia. In his 1932 memoirs he gave a rather flattering account of his part in the Acre negotiations and then wrote: 'No doubt my diaries contain some account of them, but I am writing these Episodes entirely from memory, as likely thus to be easier to read than if they were weighed with...unimportant minutiae...I am telling the truth exactly as I remember it.'[200] Rather ungenerously, Conway even chose to ignore Henry Willett's frequent financial assistance, noting only that the Brighton art collector 'would have done much for me, if I had given him the chance'[201] – a wonderfully crafted Conway sentence which is not quite untrue. The reality is that the proceeds from his Acre adventure probably did little more than clear his debts leaving a small surplus for investment, while the rest of his 'fortune' was provided by his wife's stepfather.

While he was still in the USA, Conway dined with Morgan ('J. P. was quite agreeable in a rough fashion') and later visited his home with Joseph Duveen to view his remarkable art collection. Duveen famously observed that Europe had a great deal of art, while America had a great deal of money. He made his fortune by persuading self-made American industrialists and financiers that a collection of fine art would automatically confer upper-class status upon its owner. Duveen cultivated friendships with impecunious European aristocrats, nouveau riche Americans, and with art experts, such as Conway, who might introduce him to lucrative deals, or make useful attributions of paintings. It was not long before the Slade Professor of Fine Art was receiving commissions from Duveen for various undisclosed services. As Joan Evans, author of *The Conways* and herself an art historian, observed with obvious distaste: 'Martin found Jews congenial and for a long time made his closest friends among them. He passed (though few people knew it) into the category of crypto-dealers.'[202] At one point Conway wrote to Marble about negotiations to sell a family collection of pictures from which he expected to 'clear £5,000...as my share'. However, the deal either never materialised or, if it did, perhaps Duveen took all the profit.

As Slade Professor, Conway also formed friendships with many artists and art critics, including Roger Fry, an influential member of the Bloomsbury Group credited with introducing modern art to Britain. Fry sought Conway's assistance in 1903 for the launch of the *Burlington Magazine* and J. P. Morgan eventually financed the venture, possibly following an introduction from Conway. Conway also established and became chairman of a society for publishing photographs of 'great works of art difficult of access', later named 'The Arundel Club'.

Back in England, and feeling unusually debt-free, the Conways went on a spending spree. They acquired a gramophone, had electric lighting and a telephone installed in the Red House, and bought a 7 h.p. Panhard motor car. Conway engaged a man named Mitchell as chauffeur, joined the (soon to be Royal) Automobile Club, and both he and Katrina ordered motoring clothes from their tailors. Mitchell was subsequently demoted from chauffeur to under-gardener after a series of misadventures including 'unlawfully driving a motor car at greater speed than 10 mph' (fined 30 shillings), being 'caught in a police trap near Lewisham travelling at 26 2/3 mph' (fined £3) and being arrested while 'drunk when in charge of a car' (fined £2). However, before this demotion, Mitchell took the Conways on a series of motoring tours, visiting stately homes and cathedrals across southern England, and they also had the car hoisted onto the deck of a ship so that they could travel through France. It was Katrina's first summer holiday with Conway for years and she enjoyed it immensely. After endless holidays staying in grand hotels with her parents, the car gave Katrina a liberating sense of freedom, allowing her to travel where and when she chose.

Conway wrote an article for *Country Life* describing the novel idea of 'motor touring'. Rudyard Kipling was a fellow enthusiast: 'Lunched...at Athenaeum and talked cars with Rud. Kipling...he recited to me his newly written Shakespearean, Wordsworthian and other parodies on the car'. Conway's new hobby proved to be rather expensive. His diary for 3 February 1904 noted that after just 10 months 'repairs and new tyres have cost us up till now £150' (plus his chauffeur's wages of £65 per year). However, their new-found access to unfrequented parts provided an unexpected bonus. During their motor tour of France they chanced upon an antique shop where Conway spotted two Venetian Renaissance paintings – 'The Finding of Paris' and 'Paris Given to Nurse' – that he later convinced himself were early Giorgiones. However, his diary reveals that 'my first cry when I saw them...was "Carpaccio" and his name is written on the back'. He purchased both for £8. Neither Roger Fry nor Bernard Berensen, the great Renaissance art expert and close associate of Joseph Duveen, initially accepted them as Giorgiones (although Fry revised his opinion), but Conway later wrote a book entitled *Giorgione as a Landscape Painter*

(1929) seeking to justify his attribution. Conway also bought a Flemish triptych for £44. Notwithstanding their Acre windfall in March, by the summer of 1903 the Conways were once more in debt, so he decided to sell the triptych to his friend and benefactor Henry Willett for £100: 'I should gladly have kept it but the profit will prove handy just now', he noted in a letter to Marble. Unfortunately, Willett did not like the painting and asked for his money back. As Conway observed, this was 'rather a blow' since it was in fact worth considerably less than £100.

In July 1903 Agnes was accepted to read history at Newnham College and in October she went up to Cambridge. Initially she studied history, like her father, but later switched to archaeology. Agnes was both intelligent and, perhaps because of her rather unconventional upbringing and facial disfigurement, very determined. Katrina proudly took her to Cambridge and they wandered around the town together admiring the colleges. 'In her little heart [she] bewails, I think, that she is not a man', Katrina wrote to Marble, 'with a seat in the Hall of Trinity and Gothic window from which she could look out upon stately courts and cloisters. Newnham alas! has none of these.' Conway was delighted that Agnes was going to his old university and encouraged her growing love of art and history. The two met often during Conway's last two terms as Slade Professor and Agnes also invited Katrina to stay with her at Newnham. Katrina never forgot the hardness of the bed, nor the rabbit pie that she was served for dinner, but she was ambitious for her daughter. When one of Agnes' tutors predicted a brilliant first, Katrina wrote to Marble: 'I hope so, for there are few things her parents would value so much.' Agnes, she wrote, was 'already on fire with a hundred different interests but (if I know her) will lack the concentrated effort to make her distinguished in any one. She has her father's love of variety and change.'

In March 1904 Conway delivered his final lecture and retired from academic life. During the course of the year he published three books. His first thought was of the mountains. He travelled to Grindelwald to visit Coolidge and finished writing *The Alps*, which was illustrated with watercolours by his old Karakoram companion, McCormick. The book contains romantic descriptions of the high mountains, tinged with a certain sadness that he could no longer aspire to reach their summits:

'The peaks have become inaccessible once more. They again belong to another world, the world of the past. The ghosts of our dead friends people them, and the ghosts of our dead selves...old passionate hopes and strivings, the old disappointments and regrets, the old rivalries, and the old triumphs, vaguely mingling in a faint regret.'[203] When Conway wrote this he was just 47, yet they sound like the words of a lonely man whose active life is drawing to a close. Building on the research that he had done at the time of his Arctic explorations he also published *Early Dutch and English Voyages to Spitsbergen* as well as *The Great Masters*, comprising 'reproductions in photogravure from the works of the most famous painters'.

A few days after his last lecture as Slade Professor, Conway received a cable from his agent in Bolivia informing him that a rich deposit of gold had been discovered on the Kaka River within one of his concessions. The river formed part of the 'great gold district' in which Conway had bought a one-third stake in 1900. Conway and his associates financed a scientific expedition to explore and map the concession in 1901 which returned to England and reported its findings in 1902. The following year the syndicate hired a mining engineer named Beard to assess the feasibility of developing a gold mine, and it was his cable that Conway received on 7 April 1904. With his academic career at Cambridge behind him, the cable reignited his enthusiasm for business and he immediately resumed his activities as a promoter of mining and rubber stocks. Within a matter of months he was appointed President of the Newfoundland Exploration Syndicate, with a salary of $1,000 (about £200), and a director of the Black Hart Mine in California. He also became a director of Potentia, an international agency established to compete with Reuters and Associated Press with the rather unusual selling proposition, for a news service, of guaranteeing 'absolute reliability (even if late)'. The agency failed to attract any business, but not before it had provided Conway with several all-expenses-paid trips to France and Germany.

The Newfoundland syndicate succeeded in raising $25,000 of financing through an American mining entrepreneur called Verner de Guise. Less encouragingly, Beard, Conway's agent in Bolivia, drew bills totalling £1,400 to pay expenses relating to the Kaka River deposit, which Conway was unable to pay. There were also disquieting reports that Beard had been seen frequenting the bars of La Paz and Lima. Conway summoned Beard to New York for a meeting where he summarily sacked him. The following day Beard served a summons on Conway for breach of contract. Following the advice of de Guise and his other associates, Conway contracted a mining engineer called Armas to take over the management of Kaka and de Guise sent his son, Anselm, to work with him in Bolivia.

Back in England, Conway invited his old Cambridge friend Lord Ranfurly to become a director of the Kaka Mining Company, an invitation that Ranfurly accepted with alacrity, even claiming to have a detailed knowledge of gold dredging operations. Conway also did some corporate entertaining. As the arms race with Germany gathered pace, he went with a group of city financiers and potential investors to watch the launch of the first Dreadnought in February 1906. 'We stood close to the King', he recorded proudly in his diary.

With his academic commitments at an end, Conway resumed a full social life. He sat next to Edward Elgar (a fellow member of the Savile Club) at a dinner and then went with him to catch the last hour of *Die Meistersinger* at the Opera House. He attended Stanley's funeral at Westminster Abbey. He travelled to the United States, called on President Roosevelt (who invited him to go for a walk next time he was in Washington) and proposed the President's health at the 4th July dinner of the American Society, praising him for his 'courage, manliness and strength of will'. Early next year, Conway went to the Royal Geographical Society to hear his old friend, now Sir Francis Younghusband, present a paper describing his brutal 1904 invasion of Tibet. The following month Conway was awarded the Founder's Medal of the Royal Geographical Society by Sir Clements Markham. It was a long-overdue honour, in Conway's opinion. Some 13 years earlier he had sent a letter from the Karakoram to his mother informing her that 'I am working all I can to win a Geographical Society medal', but as Conway told Marble: 'Their policy now is to make the medal a closing incident in a traveller's career.'

In August 1905, Conway wrote a letter to *The Times* warning of the despoliation of the Alps and proposed the formation of an English

League for the Preservation of the Beauty of Switzerland: 'With the railways have come the "trippers"...These people, of course, have as much right to visit the "playground of Europe" as more leisurely and appreciative travellers...[but] some mountain resorts in Switzerland could be named where persons of taste and cultivation were accustomed to spend weeks, but where, under the changed conditions of the present time, no visitor of that class willingly prolongs his stay beyond a day or two.'[204] Conway also became interested in crowd psychology, writing a series of articles for *The Nineteenth Century* entitled 'Is Parliament a mere Crowd?', 'The Individual versus the Crowd' and 'Suffragists, Peers and the Crowd', in which he bemoaned the decline of individualism, and railed against the despotism of the masses, manipulated by unscrupulous politicians. Marble disapproved of the articles and Conway tried to get them published anonymously. When he failed, he consoled Marble by informing him: 'No one ever pays any attention to what I write...I have no faculty of attracting public attention. Moreover I don't expect any further political activity to come my way...and I no longer want any office or appointment, but to work quietly at my photos till I die.'

An Englishman's Home

Having abandoned climbing, exploration, politics, art and academia, but still convinced that unimaginable riches awaited him from his mining speculations, Conway sought a new diversion as he approached the age of 50 and decided to become a country gentleman. On 15 May 1905 he placed an advert in *The Times*: 'Wanted to purchase, old manor-house or abbey, built in the sixteenth century or earlier, with old garden, not much land, no sporting facilities, preferably five miles or more from a railway station.'[205] He received two responses to the advert and a few months later purchased Allington Castle in Kent from Lord Romney for £4,800. He also acquired a further 20 acres of adjacent land for £3,300, on which there were some unsightly industrial buildings, which he demolished. Conway claimed in his memoirs that he paid for Allington with profits earned from the Acre concession.[206] In reality, he had just £1,200 in readily marketable investments to make the purchase. Manton Marble provided the balance, but insisted on a mortgage over the property. The purchase price was, however, just the start of the expenses.

Conway first mooted the idea of buying a castle as early as 1888 when he resigned his professorship at Liverpool and visited Stokesay Castle near Ludlow during a walking tour of Shropshire: 'I should like to buy the place and do it up and live in it. No doubt it could be bought very cheap but the doing up would be very expensive.' It was a prediction that proved to be entirely correct in the case of Allington. By 1933 he claimed to have spent £80,000 on the restoration, although this was almost certainly an exaggeration, since he was trying to let the castle at the time. Allington Castle was the jewel in the crown of Conway's collection of antiquities. Soon after making the purchase Katrina wrote to Marble describing Conway's plans for the castle: 'Herr has been wonderful...Every window, door, fireplace and even the cupboards have now been placed in the most perfect positions. The beauty and convenience of it all are perfection. Only one little detail of the entire scheme is lacking – the millions to carry it out!'

Ruskin would have been horrified as Conway ignored his dictum that an ancient building should be conserved, but never restored, in order to preserve the accumulation of history represented by its decay. His first step was to strip the ivy from the partially ruined walls of the castle, which were repaired and rebuilt to their original height, complete with battlements. Rooms were restored, the moat was cleared and extended and a new driveway constructed. Conway identified Roman walls, a Saxon moat and a Norman tower. Agnes, who actively researched the castle's history, established that it was built in 1281 and remodelled into a mansion in 1492. Conway was convinced that there had once been a long gallery dividing the two inner courtyards and set about rebuilding it. Joan Evans, the medievalist, cast doubt on whether this ever formed part of the original plan of the castle, but it soon became 'the earliest Long Gallery in England' in Conway's account of the castle's history. It took over five years to complete the initial 'restoration' work and he continued to undertake major building projects until 1932. In the 1970s the castle was used to film the outdoor scenes in the television series 'Colditz'.

In order to pay for this massive building programme, more money-making schemes were embarked upon. To the great disappointment of Agnes and particularly Katrina, who missed the social life of London and felt lonely and isolated in rural Kent, Conway sold the lease of the Red House for £1,500 to Herbert Hoover, the future president of the United States. He smuggled into the United States the Foppa Madonna that he had bought for £4 in Brescia in 1887, and sold it for $5,000 (£1,000), proudly boasting in his memoirs that he had defrauded US Customs.[207] He sold his investment in the Manufacturers Commercial Co. at a profit of £2,335 and continued to earn commissions from Duveen for various unspecified tasks. But on 5 January 1907 – 'a dull-minded day of sorrow and regrets' – he suffered a major blow. Verner de Guise, who was acting as Conway's agent in New York, confessed that he had lost £6,500 'playing ducks and drakes' with Conway's investments.

Despite this setback, Conway continued to promote his mining interests in South America. Armas, the new manager of the Kaka gold deposit, also obtained the rights to the Ocavi tin mine in Bolivia. Conway succeeded in raising £16,000 of capital from a syndicate of investors, including £3,500 from Marble, and ordered equipment for the mine. He then tried to float the company on the stock exchange, but failed. Facing an imminent cashflow crisis, Armas wrote to Conway demanding a further £8,000 of working capital, which Conway was unable to raise. The operation appears to have been mothballed until about 1912, when Conway finally managed to raise an additional £5,000, including a further £1,000 from Marble. 'This time I pray heaven we may turn his money into big profit', Conway wrote to Katrina. Ocavi limped on until 1916 when all mention of the mine ceases.

Conway became chairman of Inambari Para-Rubber Estates Limited, which was floated in February 1907, but three-quarters of the offering was left with the underwriters. He was also struggling to attract investment for the gold dredging operation on the Kaka River, which flowed through the Inambari concession. Kaka briefly turned into a platinum deposit until tests demonstrated that the sand contained no osmiridium, whereupon it reverted to being a gold deposit. After various complex related-party transactions, for which Conway received shares (probably illegally) as commission, Inambari Rubber took a 25% interest in a company called Incahuara, which was formed to exploit the Kaka gold deposit. In December 1908 Lord Ranfurly, now chairman of Incahuara, wrote to Conway stating that the company must go into liquidation the next day unless Conway could raise £15,000. Miraculously, Conway succeeded. Inambari Rubber staggered on for several more years, never making any money, with Conway presiding at 'stormy annual meetings', while Incahuara Gold went through a succession of financial crises and reconstructions before finally going bankrupt.

Verner de Guise's son, Anselm, wrote a book in 1922 entitled *Six Years in Bolivia: The Adventures of a Mining Engineer*, which gave an account of his work at both the Ocavi tin mine and the Kaka River deposit before the First World War. The gold dredge at Kaka consisted of a vast wooden raft which excavated sand and gravel from the river bed and passed it through a trommel to separate the dense but tiny flecks of gold from the lighter river sediment. Components to construct the dredge, and most of the consumables, had to be shipped to Lima, transported to La Paz by rail, steamer and cart, and then carried to site by mules, along narrow trails cut through the dense forest. Had they found any gold, it would have been exported the same way – by no means a straightforward proposition bearing in mind that numerous outlaws, including Robert Leroy Parker ('Butch Cassidy') and Harry Longabaugh (the 'Sundance Kid'), were active in Bolivia at this time. However, this particular problem never arose, because almost no gold was found: 'The hopes that had been placed in the...claim were, one after another, wiped out. High mounds of tailings from the gold dredge arose in the river, but the gold recovered from the sluice-boxes during the weekly "clean-up" was lamentably small in amount. At last, I received instructions to lay the dredge up, pending a decision to be arrived at by the directors in regard to which course they would follow.'[208] On 13 January 1911 Conway recorded in his diary that 'the situation is simply damnable'. The company was liquidated in 1912. Conway's 'great gold region, not improbably as rich and important as the Rand' had proved to be an illusion.

It was a similar story with the Papua Lands rubber syndicate and the Motor Mail Van Co., in both of which Conway was an investor and a director. Conway attended the first board meeting of Papua Lands in 1907. The flotation was postponed in 1909 and the subscription was reported to be 'not going as well as we could wish' in February 1910. Conway last mentions the company in 1914. Meanwhile, an initial capital-raising for the Motor Mail Van Co. was under-subscribed and the company went into liquidation. Conway was subpoenaed to give evidence in a court case brought by one of the creditors, but the directors were exonerated of any wrongdoing.

Throughout this time, the costs of restoring Allington Castle continued to escalate. In December 1907, when Conway's business affairs were at a particularly low ebb, he asked his mother for a second mortgage on the castle, which she refused. In 1908 he attempted to get his hands on part of her inheritance, but other members of the Conway family intervened and prevented him from doing so. Conway's diary entry for 30 September 1908 is typical of this period: 'Corben [the builder restoring Allington Castle] came up with a bigger bill than I expected. I owe him £1,110. Incahuara needs £20,000. Ocavi is in a bad way. Thus we are not very happy just now.' He consoled himself by writing an article entitled 'How a Great Gold Field was Discovered'. It was never published.

In the midst of this chaos, Conway celebrated his 50th birthday, had operations for piles and gallstones (at home, at a cost of £350), and published *No Man's Land, a History of Spitsbergen from its discovery in 1596 to the beginning of the Scientific Exploration of the Country* (1906). Agnes obtained a Class II degree in the History Tripos, Charles Bruce and Douglas Freshfield tried to persuade Conway to take part in an expedition to Everest, and Katrina 'had a nerve storm'.

Although Conway's diaries for this period are packed full of meetings with financiers and fellow directors, it is hard to determine his state of mind. His chaotic business affairs and preoccupation with restoring Allington seem to have squeezed out his normally active social life. After writing 20 books during the 22-year period from 1884 to 1906, he published nothing from 1906 until 1914, although he continued to contribute articles on art and travel to various newspapers and magazines. He received a letter from Karl Pearson, still a professor at London University, 'spending all my energies on work, enjoying my life thoroughly...Income precisely what it was 21 years ago.' Pearson's letter mentioned a few old Cambridge friends, but their names do not appear in Conway's diaries, suggesting that he had lost contact with most of them. 'You can feel the bonds of old friendships and meet men on the old terms', Pearson wrote in his letter, 'but...the things that draw men together, the common hopes, the common ideals, the common problems and inspirations have all gone with the years and you feel that...they do not understand you.' Conway called on Pearson at University College, London. 'He is very little changed – thinner and of a sweeter expression than of old – just the same old chap.' But while Pearson had changed little, Conway had changed a great deal and he found that he had little in common with one of his oldest friends. While Pearson refused both an OBE and a knighthood because of his socialist ideals, Conway renewed his quest for money and celebrity.

With most of his business ventures in liquidation or with insufficient funds to do any real harm, Conway's life calmed down a little in 1909. He was invited to Switzerland by Henry Lunn, a religious figure and founder of the travel agent Lunn Poly, who did much to popularise skiing as a winter sport for gentlemen. During the visit Conway learned to play auction bridge and Lunn was rewarded, as he expected, with an article in the *Pall Mall Magazine* extolling the virtues of alpine winter sports. He also continued work on his photographic collection, which now occupied a good part of the long gallery at Allington. After graduating from Cambridge in 1906, Agnes lived at Allington and Conway decided that she should help him with collating his art photographs. During this period, Agnes wrote *A Children's Book of Art* (1909), which was well reviewed, while Katrina succumbed to almost permanent ill health and depression. For over a year, she never left the castle.

In March 1909, Abigail Marble died quite suddenly, causing Katrina even more distress. Manton Marble moved in with them at Allington, together with his faithful manservant Fritz, and an atmosphere of mourning descended upon the castle. Since Marble now lived at Allington, it seemed quite natural that he should pay all the household expenses and builder's bills (which in June 1909 alone amounted to £3,300) and provide them with a new £700 car. Conway's diary for 22 April reads: 'I am utterly idle these days except for the buildings.' For the next few years, Conway had almost no income, because his various business ventures were too strapped for cash to pay his directors' fees. He relied on Marble to waive the mortgage payments due on the castle and to pay his living expenses, as well as meeting various cash calls to prevent his companies from sliding into bankruptcy. After sending a particularly long list of outstanding bills to Marble for payment, Conway wrote: 'I'm always in hopes of being able to fill the pit but each month the chance seems further off fulfilment.' He signed the letter: 'Your devoted and expensive Billy Boy'. Nevertheless, Conway was outraged by Lloyd George's proposal to introduce state pensions for the poor and felt compelled to write a letter to *The Times* 'which they may fear to print':

'[Parliament] has penalised the fitter classes of society in the interests of the less fit. The least fit class in the country is the old people who have failed to provide any savings against their old age, and that large class of cheats who manage to pretend that they are in that case...All so-called social legislation tends to act in the same way. The birth rate of the fitter class is diminishing year by year, and we calmly sit by and watch the consequent degeneration of our race with idle hands. We take the human rubbish that emerges and give it compulsory education, housing acts, inspections of all sorts and at all seasons, all at the expense of the fitter class.'[209]

His preoccupation with the degeneration of the English race reflected a renewed interest in eugenics, possibly following his meeting with Pearson. Later in the year Conway presided at the Eugenics Society, where Sir Edward Brabrook, a noted anthropologist, read a paper on 'Eugenics and Pauperism'. On a more congenial note, Conway was invited to become the first president of the Alpine Ski Club, formed by Sir Henry Lunn to encourage fit young gentlemen to pursue the sport of ski mountaineering (and to occupy the rooms in his alpine hotels during the slack winter season). Ernest Shackleton was guest speaker at the inaugural dinner.

In 1910, with the first phase of the building works at Allington nearing completion, Conway took his first long summer holiday for several years, making a nostalgic journey through the Bernese Oberland and the Pennine Alps to the Italian Lakes. He stayed in a hotel 'just as all Swiss inns were in the '80s...There is no-one here – only the names in the book of all my old dead climbing friends – Horace Walker and the rest. [The hotel] has the old books in it and the old chess board and the old piano and is generally equipped for folks who don't exist anymore...People come up here now by train for lunch but not over the mountains – for the old race of wandering climbers exists no more.'

Back in London, Conway visited the exhibition of Manet and the post-Impressionists arranged by Roger Fry in November 1910, which included works by Gauguin, Matisse and Van Gogh. Virginia Woolf, the daughter of Conway's old friend Leslie Stephen, wrote that 'on or about December 1910 human character changed', but the exhibition left Conway unmoved. His imagination still roamed the world of Ruskin. Ten years later, in a letter to *The Times*, he wrote: 'Bolshevism and post-impressionism may be different faces of the one thing...It is easy to pour scorn on post-impressionist art. Personally I can find no pleasure in it...I love the past and find small delight in what the future seems to be offer-ing.'[210]

By 1911, life in his nearly complete castle was becoming humdrum, and Conway's thoughts turned once more to mountains and other infatuations. The front of his diary for the year contains a quote from the Arabian warrior poet Labid ibn Rabi'ah: 'The mountains remain after us, And the strong towers when we are gone.' Early the following year Conway renewed his acquaintance with Mrs Kemp-Welch while Katrina was in Switzerland with Agnes, now 26, who was having another painful, but this time partially successful, operation on her damaged facial nerve. Conway was soon spending as much time with Mrs Kemp-Welch as he had a decade earlier, simultaneously writing guilty, sentimental letters to Katrina, professing his undying love: 'I love you on another plane from all others whatsoever – a much higher plane – and I worship you as the Queen of the Heaven of Heavens. My dear sweet angel of goodness and mercy...Your loving Herr.' Upon receipt of these reassuring words, Katrina suffered a complete nervous breakdown. From the clinic near Geneva she wrote a short and moving letter to Conway: 'It is strange, dearest, but the more sublime the mountains are, the more sad I feel. They seem to belong to you, not to me. Wherever one looks the beauty is divine but I feel as if I would like to gaze just once more and then go to sleep. What a wonderful thing life is – and the poor human heart.' After attending a concert, Katrina was reminded of 'those young days at The Red House, before the shadows began to fall'. Looking back over her marriage, she felt increasingly despondent: 'All those 28 years come back to me, ever since the morning when I left my mother to follow you across the seas. God alone knows how during these last many, many, many years I have striven through illness, discouragement, adversity, financial troubles, to help you all I could...but since the coming of this "Anno nuovo" every peak of your mountains – from Alps to Jura – has day and night screamed out to me "failure – failure – failure" until in their full chorus I hardly hear the sound of my own child's voice.'

Marble, feeling old and isolated in Allington, responded to this cry for help from his beloved stepdaughter in the only way he could: 'I think you should feel flush in your trouser pockets this year, because that's GOOD for you to feel so – good like medicine when you are run down, dispirited – so I proclaim to you, to Dandy Girl, that you are flush beyond all doubt. Nobody is busted and nobody is going to be; and I will cash all your expenses, without help from your allowance...This is my little pill for the Dandy Girl's health now administered.'

In the midst of this crisis Elizabeth Conway died at the age of 83. Conway had largely ignored her for decades but, as all children do when their parents die, he must have wondered whether there was something he should have said or done while she was still alive. In a letter to Katrina he concluded that 'there's nothing to regret...Once she failed to help me when I thought she should – that's about all.' As he tidied up her affairs, he was astonished to discover that his two long neglected and still unmarried sisters, Lizzie and Minnie, who had spent their entire adult lives nursing his mother, hated her and each other with almost equal vehemence. After Elizabeth's funeral, Conway travelled to Switzerland. On the advice of the doctor who had been treating Agnes, they moved Katrina to a sanatorium at Mont Pélerin, near Vevey. Her condition steadily improved after Conway's arrival, but she became nervous whenever he was out of her sight. Nevertheless, Conway soon got bored and decided to visit Coolidge in Grindelwald.

Conway and Katrina returned to England, but Agnes was dispatched to Rome (together with the Roman section of Conway's photographic collection), in order to give Katrina more peace and quiet. It seems not to have occurred to Conway that, after spending the whole of her life in New York and London, the unremitting peace and quiet of an empty castle in rural Kent may have contributed to Katrina's depression. Conway filled the long hours writing articles for the *Burlington Magazine* and *Country Life*, rehashing old material on Dürer, Florentine art and art photography, but also writing new pieces on subjects as diverse as Roman sculpture, Persian carpets, Saxon crosses and birdcages. Much of this was pure journalism, designed to earn a few pounds, but some of his articles were truly scholarly, reflecting insights and ideas that arose as Conway continued to sort and catalogue his immense photographic collection. Since the filing system was chronological, in the absence of other evidence, Conway often had to estimate the age of items in his collection based solely on detailed observation of the object itself. In an article on a bowl in the Treasury of S. Mark's in Venice, Conway wrote with obvious delight: 'Its secret, then, must be wrested from the vase itself; we have no exterior aids.'[211]

In the spring of 1913, Conway went on a motor tour of England and Wales, where he met George Bernard Shaw 'swaggering through the main street at Llangollen'. During the summer Katrina and Conway travelled to Italy to restore Katrina's health. With the castle buildings now complete, Conway started work on the grounds, planting 4,000 trees in 1913 and writing a number of articles for *Country Life* describing the restoration. At the invitation of Henry Lunn, Conway and Katrina celebrated the start of 1914 in Switzerland, staying in Wengen and Mürren. Katrina judged the costumes at the fancy dress ball while Conway rewarded his patron with an article in *Country Life* describing the 'Joy of Winter Sports': 'The middle-aged and the young-old can renew their youth in the most surprising fashion...The pains and anxieties of home life drop away from him. The past is as though it had never been, the future as though it was never coming.'[212] A press cutting in Conway's diary reported that 'Mürren has come very much to the fore in recent years...a large number of society people have gone there this year.'

In March 1914 Conway had false teeth fitted. In May he discovered that he was suffering from gout, and took a rest cure at Contrexéville. He returned to Allington for the summer. His diary entry for 2 August 1914 reads: 'We hear that Germany has declared war. Our magnolia has come into blossom for the first time.' A magnificent magnolia tree, now a century old, still stands in the second courtyard of Allington Castle.

The Spoils of War

The quantity of Conway's journalistic output remained high during the early years of the war, but quality sometimes suffered. The August 1914 'Holiday Number' of *The Quiver* included an article by Conway entitled 'Tragedies and Heroisms among the Mountains', sandwiched between a short story entitled 'The Pretty Girl' ('Her wide, eager glance seemed to leap from peak to peak, as if she were already treading their infinite solitudes...') and a full-page advert for Fry's delicious chocolates. In the article, Conway described a situation where it might be necessary to sacrifice the life of one climber by cutting the rope, in order to save the lives of the rest of the party. 'Such cases have happened and have been recorded, but we are proud to say that up till now no Englishman has been involved in so disgraceful a salvation.'

Despite the war, life initially went on much as normal. At the weekend they entertained guests at Allington. During the week, Conway left Katrina in the empty, silent castle and drove to London, where he lunched or dined at the Athenaeum, attended society and board meetings and wrote occasional articles. With travel and building work at the castle curtailed by the war, he also published a book he had been planning for eight years. *The Sport of Collecting* tells various more or less credible stories about his art collection. In Conway's mind, it was more in the nature of a prospectus than a book, because 'if we ever want to sell our pictures it will add to their value'.

Agnes did voluntary work finding accommodation for Belgian refugees (for which she was awarded an MBE and the Médaille de la Reine Elisabeth of Belgium in 1918). Conway supported the war effort in his own manner, writing an article for *Country Life* in which he recalled that when, in the fifth century, 'the Huns swept over the still glorious lands, which had blossomed in the pride and splendour of the Roman Empire, burning and destroying in mere lust of rage...they made for themselves a name of disgrace which will be theirs to the end of time. Now', he continued, 'the new Huns, ghastlier than the old...with the destruction of Rheims Cathedral, have finally crowned themselves with that immortal crown of shame which no future repentance will avail to remove from their brow, low in the dust though it shall presently be laid.'[213]

Conway's diary for 1915 is missing. Perhaps there was little to record. He wrote *The Crowd in Peace and War*, a renewed attack on the crowd – 'its silly sentimentality, its fickleness, its lack of restraint, its noisy clamour about matters often of small moment, its yet more annoying indifference to others of vital importance, its susceptibility to the wiles of demagogues, its admiration of itself'[214] – and a spirited defence of individualism against the encroachments of socialism: 'it is always the superior individual whom the crowd sacrifices, and always the inferior whom it fosters'.[215] According to Arnold Lunn, Conway regarded it as his best book. Written in the midst of the war, it contrasts the British love of individualism and diversity with 'the rigid uniformity of Prussian discipline'[216] and contains a brave, though somewhat muted, defence of conscientious objectors, where Conway was clearly torn between his belief in individualism and his conception of 'manliness'. The book also attacked what we might now call the 'nanny state', including the proposal by Lloyd George to limit the opening hours of licensed premises in order to increase productivity in munitions factories: 'Could anything be more absurd?' Conway asked. 'Lest a gunmaker or shipbuilder in Glasgow drink too much, Mr. Asquith must not take a glass of sherry with his lunch at the Athenaeum.'[217] It was, perhaps, an unfortunate example to choose, since the prime minister's well-known fondness for drink gave rise to the expression 'squiffy' and probably did more than any drunken Glaswegian to hinder the war effort.

Conway also returned to the serious study of art history, writing a lengthy academic paper on 'The Abbey of St. Denis and its Ancient Treasures', which is still quoted today. In May, the spas on the continent being unavailable, he went to Llandrindod Wells for a rest cure, where he was ordered to drink saline and sulphur water before breakfast, lunch and afternoon tea, and complained about the unenlisted young men whom he saw in the town who 'ought to have been at war'. In July Conway and Katrina went on a motor tour to the Cotswolds, Liverpool, the Lake District and Scotland. The only hint of the bitter struggle taking place was the sight of 'countless ships of war of all sizes and kinds lying at anchor, far as the eye could see' at Rosyth.

On 12 April 1916 Conway celebrated his 60th birthday. It was a fairly typical day: 'Breakfast at the Athenaeum. Read at Burlington Fine Art Club. Lunch at the Palace Hotel Grill Room. Visited Agnes. 4:10 train home.' He lobbied, unsuccessfully, to be made a trustee of the National Gallery, but was elected to the Council of the Society of Antiquaries and appointed a trustee of the Wallace Collection. However, both posts were largely honorary and Conway soon became bored with them. Back at Allington, Manton Marble's health was deteriorating and Conway missed their long conversations together.

Around this time, Conway also completed his part in the revision of one of his first books, *Early Flemish Artists*. It was a subject on which he had first lectured in Tunbridge Wells, soon after he graduated in 1881, and returned to during his time as Roscoe Professor in Liverpool, towards the end of which, in 1887, he published the book. He started work on a revised edition after attending an exhibition of Flemish pictures in Bruges in 1902, when he became aware of the vast amount of new research that had taken place while he was focused on exploration. By 1917 he realised that he would never complete the work and, following an introduction from Roger Fry, he enlisted the help of Professor Tancred Borenius to edit and complete the manuscript. It was finally published as *The Van Eycks and their Followers* in 1921. Unlike the original version, which Ruskin praised but which generally received rather poor reviews, the revised edition was recognised as the first work to 'seriously tackle the task of writing about early Netherlandish painting in [a] connected sequence'.[218]

On 11 January 1917, Conway went with Katrina to the Guildhall to hear Lloyd George speak: 'I was disappointed...K thought he looked underbred, shifty and unreliable.' Nevertheless, he felt moved to write a letter to Alfred Mond, the First Commissioner of Works, pointing out the need for better organisation of Lloyd George's Liberal supporters. By coincidence, Mond happened to be looking for someone to act as director general of a proposed War Museum. Two months later Conway was appointed: 'Lloyd George decided for me – said I was the man for the job and congratulated Mond on his wise choice!' The post did not carry a salary ('which means that I'll be made a KCB in due course'), but Conway was given a room in the Office of Works and a secretary. Agnes was soon co-opted as Honorary Secretary of the Woman's Work section of the new museum, occupied the office next to Conway's, and did most of the hard work.

Initially Conway approached the task with enthusiasm, particularly when he thought that the museum might be housed in the Tower of London, and imagined that it would include an official residence for the director general. However, the work did not prove to be as agreeable as he had hoped. While many aspects of Conway's life and career may have lacked consistency, the one ideal to which he had remained reasonably faithful was a belief in the redeeming power of beauty. He was now required to attend endless committee meetings, and to persuade army officers and bureaucrats, all of whom had far more pressing tasks, to help him to collect war trophies. As an article in *The Times* observed: 'Looked at from one angle of vision, nothing more grim and terrible than the Imperial War Museum has ever been got together.'[219] The conflict between his ideals and his job became acute when it was proposed that the War Museum should be built in Hyde Park on the banks of the Serpentine. Conway opposed the choice of site on the grounds that it would 'involve the destruction of too many fine trees and too pretty a place', but his opposition did little to endear him to the bureaucrats. With Katrina still ill, and Manton Marble fading, Conway felt increasingly isolated and depressed: 'I am bitterly gloomy...pressed by memories. All the glory has gone out of life...I would gladly lay the burden down', he recorded in his diary on 30 June 1917.

In his capacity as director general of the museum, Conway travelled to the front line in France three times in 1917, visiting Arras, Amiens and Verdun and climbing up to Vimy Ridge to view the German lines. Soon after his first visit, in July 1917, Manton Marble died. He was 83. The competition for the affections of Katrina that had characterised their early relationship had long since been forgotten and the two men had become close friends and confidants. Conway desperately missed Marble's company and remained depressed for many months: 'A horrible sad and lonely day – misery invading me like an hourly rising flood', he wrote in his diary in December. In 1918 he made his final journey to the front, visiting the Chemin des Dames, scene of the Second Battle of the Aisne in which the French suffered 40,000 casualties in the first day of combat.

During his first visit to the front, before Marble died, Conway felt almost euphoric, caught up in the idea of being present at a defining moment in history: 'Everyone today feeling dignified by the great events around us', he wrote to Katrina. 'Exultation of mind seems to be inescapable in this atmosphere. It is impossible to be happier than I am...every man I meet knows more than I shall ever learn. Each day is like a year at Varsity.' On subsequent visits, the horror of what he was witnessing began to sink in, and Conway became increasingly stupefied by the scale of the destruction: 'One cannot spend day after day examining ruined towns and villages with fresh interest. There is a sameness about them, and one forgets each in turn in a fog of remembrance of destruction...a sense that reparation is impossible, and then a blind desire for mere vengeance.'[220] His account contains strangely anomalous passages giving detailed descriptions of the landscape or undamaged ancient churches behind the lines, as if seeking reassurance that there was still some beauty left in the world: 'Gun flashes illuminated the eastern horizon like summer-lightening and as soundless. Six great searchlights...reared their huge shafts into the air, and intersected almost overhead. A faint thin bed of mist made islands of phosphorescent light where the beams penetrated it. Stars spangled the sky.' He fell back on art to try to make sense of the scenes that he witnessed: 'In the depths of the cavern were horses calmly feeding...men cooking at improvised wood fires, others resting. It was a scene most romantic and picturesque, made for Salvator Rosa...we skidded out again and once more passed a row of corpses awaiting burial by the roadside.'

Conway was impressed by the senior officers that he met, describing Field Marshall Sir Douglas Haig as 'a tall and fine looking man, with great attractiveness, a charming smile, and expression full of sympathy and much lambent play',[221] but he was almost indifferent to the fate of ordinary soldiers. While the damage to Amiens Cathedral moved Conway deeply, he expressed no emotion as he watched 'shells bursting over the German lines and ours. Walking wounded passed us coming up from the front. Burial parties with stretchers...collecting the dead.'[222] The sheer scale of the suffering dehumanised the 'Tommies' in his eyes. 'I suppose the answer is that...the upper and lower classes belong in fact to different races', he mused at one point. The experience also undermined any vestigial belief that he might have had in a beneficent God, and gave him a horror of life everlasting: 'I cannot imagine the millions of unfortunate men who fell in the...war, standing in serried ranks...waiting to begin a new life...in which war...again awaits them.'[223]

Unable to travel to the Alps, Conway sought solace in mountain memories, writing an article for the *Alpine Journal* in 1917 entitled 'Some Reminiscences and Reflections of an Old Stager'. With the *Journal* bereft of news after three years of war, Conway recalled past triumphs and reflected on what the mountains meant to him now: 'There is beauty wherever nature reigns...a man need not travel far to find it, but...the power to behold it must be once kindled in the heart...by a divine inspiration. Then beauty will meet him everywhere and will dwell with him and increase its dominion over him till he himself fades away into that kingdom of mystery whence all beauty emanates and where it eternally abides.'[224] He became increasingly convinced that a museum filled with inanimate guns, tanks and shells could never convey the human desolation of war, and believed that only great art could do justice to the valour and endurance he had witnessed.

Meanwhile, a lack of servants was making life intolerable at Allington Castle: '[Katrina] heard of two [housemaids] desiring a country place together – hurried after them but found that they had been snapped up...There are no housemaids to be had!' Conway and Katrina were forced to shut up the castle and moved into a furnished flat in London. Conway had his boxes of art photographs transferred from the long gallery at Allington to the Office of Works. His diary records that he spent many of his working hours at the War Museum office sorting through old photographs, admiring the beauty of ancient Burgundian buckles.

Banished from his castle, lonely and bored at the age of 63, with no previous parliamentary experience, Conway decided that the time had come to enter politics. He pursued his goal with characteristic disregard for ethics. His diary for 7 August 1918 reads: 'Called Central Conservative Office and discussed question of a constituency at next election with Sir John Boraston.' Eight days later his diary reads: 'Called at Coalition Liberal Whip – Captain Guest – to discuss question of being a liberal candidate at next election.' He also lobbied his cousin Professor R. S. Conway at Manchester University and through his mediation was invited to attend a Committee of Selection for the Conservative candidate for the newly created seats for the Combined Universities of Birmingham, Bristol, Durham, Leeds, Liverpool, Manchester, Reading and Sheffield. He was interviewed and adopted on 29 August. By custom, a University candidate did not address meetings or make speeches, but Conway hired a political agent to campaign on his behalf. Various exhibitions of War Museum material providentially held at Manchester, Liverpool and Leeds also enabled him to re-establish contact with members of the universities. His diary for 23 September records that he 'drove to [Leeds] Town Hall to be the guest of the Lord Mayor who was an old schoolfellow of mine at Holbrook and Repton...Got some political propaganda going.'

On 11 November 1918, while Conway was on his way to the dentist, he 'heard explosions and beheld folk expectant on pavements and windows...bugle boys sounding the "all clear" as after a raid. In the Mall met great wave of a huge crowd coursing towards Buckingham Palace. Big Ben once more striking. Cheers sporadically everywhere...Nothing like as rowdy as Mafeking, but very joyous.'

Six weeks later, on 23 December 1918, in the 'Khaki election' called by Lloyd George to capitalise on the victory celebrations, Conway became the Conservative member of parliament for the Combined English Universities.

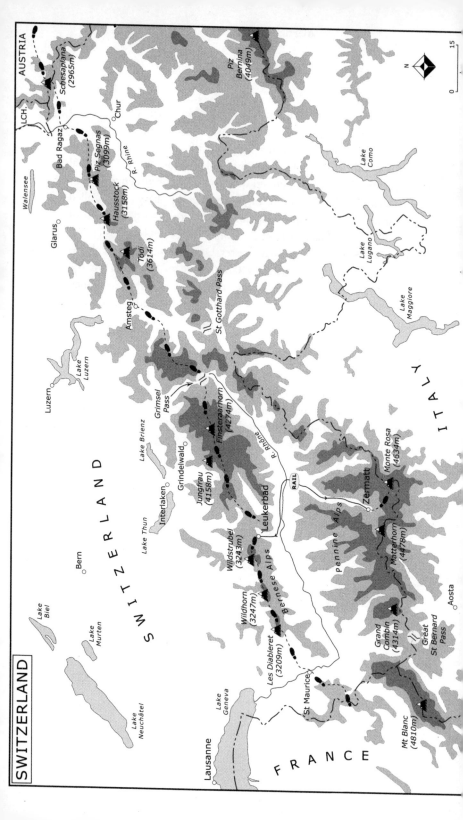

SWITZERLAND

AUSTRIA

LCH.

Schesaplana
(2965m)

Bad Ragaz

Piz Segnas
(3099m)

Chur

Hausstock
(3158m)

R. Rhine

Piz
Bernina
(4049m)

Glarus

Tödi
(3614m)

Walensee

Lake Como

Lake Lugano

Amsteg

St Gotthard Pass

Lake Maggiore

Luzern

Lake Luzern

Grimsel Pass

Finsteraarhorn
(4274m)

Grindelwald

Jungfrau
(4158m)

R. Rhône

ITALY

Lake Brienz

Interlaken

Lake Thun

Leukerbad

Wildstrubel
(3243m)

Bern

RAIL

Zermatt

Monte Rosa
(4634m)

Pennine Alps

Wildhorn
(3247m)

Bernese Alps

Matterhorn
(4478m)

SWITZERLAND

Les Diableret
(3209m)

Grand Combin
(4314m)

Great St Bernard Pass

Aosta

Lake Biel

Lake Murten

St Maurice

Lake Neuchâtel

Lake Geneva

Mt Blanc
(4810m)

Lausanne

FRANCE

N

0   15

Chapter Five
Through Switzerland

Across the Valley of the Rhône

Orson Welles was apparently responsible for the famous summary of Switzerland's achievements in the film version of Graham Greene's *The Third Man*:

'In Italy, for thirty years under the Borgias, they had warfare, terror, murder and bloodshed, but they produced Michelangelo, Leonardo da Vinci and the Renaissance. In Switzerland, they had brotherly love, they had five hundred years of democracy and peace – and what did that produce? The cuckoo clock.'

Sadly for Switzerland, this account is wrong on two counts: the cuckoo clock was invented in Bavaria; and the Swiss did not have 500 years of brotherly love, democracy and peace. In fact, just a decade before Conway was born, in the mid 1840s, Switzerland was on the brink of civil war and the Austrian Chancellor, Prince Metternich, described what we would probably now call a 'failed state': 'Switzerland presents the most perfect image of a state in the process of social disintegration...[It] serves troublemakers of every sort as a free haven...the Confederation staggers from evils into upheavals and represents...an inexhaustible spring of unrest and disturbance.'[225]

The Swiss Confederation was formed in the late thirteenth century in response to the threat posed by the Habsburgs. By the fifteenth century, Switzerland was a regional superpower, defeating the Burgundians at Nancy in 1477 and the French at Novara in 1513. The unusual combination of a diet rich in protein, a hard life in the mountains and strong discipline made the Swiss peasantry formidable soldiers. However, after a crushing defeat by the French in 1515, internal differences within the Confederation undermined its authority and the centralisation of power that progressively took place in neighbouring countries never occurred in Switzerland. Unable to build a consensus at home, the Confederation declared its neutrality and the Swiss took no further part in foreign wars. However, they continued to fight each other at regular intervals, and Swiss mercenaries were prized by France, Spain and Naples until the nineteenth century, and continue to act as bodyguards to the Pope to the present day.

Religious conflict raged intermittently within Switzerland from the fifteenth to the nineteenth century. The Swiss Reformation had its origins in the city state of Zurich and spread rapidly to the other northern cities, but many of the more southern, rural and conservative parts of the country remained resolutely Catholic. After a series of wars and local skirmishes, the Catholics finally lost their commanding position within the Confederation in 1712. While French revolutionary armies swept away petty kingdoms, duchies and other vestiges of feudalism across most of Europe, in Switzerland Napoleon effectively preserved them. After overrunning Switzerland in 1798, the French initially set up the rational, highly centralised Helvetic Republic, with equality before the law and a uniform code of justice. But the Swiss populace, accustomed to their local rights and privileges, rebelled and social unrest followed. Napoleon could not afford to have the approaches to the strategically important alpine passes disrupted by civil disorder and conceded the Act of Mediation in 1803, which established a loose Federation of 19 semi-autonomous cantons from the feudal patchwork of forest cantons, subject territories, prince-bishoprics, princely abbeys, counties and city states that formed the Swiss Confederation.

Schiller's romantic *Wilhelm Tell* (1804), with its mythical portrayal of hardy alpine individualism, refusal to offer obeisance to anybody, and appeal to an older, more traditional sense of order, helped to frame a growing sense of Swiss national identity. Despite being divided by language, religion, culture and tradition, Switzerland survived the nineteenth-century wave of nationalism intact. The German-speaking Swiss remained loyal to the Federation during the unification of Germany. Perhaps more surprising, the Italian-speaking Ticino, which lies south of the main alpine chain and is geographically part of Italy, also remained loyal during the unification of Italy, despite the fact that the Ticino had

1. Bivouac at Festi
Rocks:
(Left to right)
Adolph
Andermatten,
Conway, a porter,
George Scriven,
Franz Andermatten
(1881)
(*Alpine Club*)

THE DAILY GRAPHIC, THURSDAY, NOVEMBER 3, 1892.

MR. CONWAY'S TRAVELS IN THE HIMALAYAS: THE FIRST SIGHT OF "THE WATCH TOWER OF INDIA"

2. 'The First Sight of the
Watch Tower of India', The
Daily Graphic, 3 Nov 1892
(*Cambridge University
Library*)

3. 'Palabre à Dirran'.
Illustration from Ascensions et
Explorations dans l'Himalaya
(1894)
(*Cambridge University Library*)

4. 'Au Sommet du
Pic des Pioniers'.
Illustration from
Ascensions et
Explorations dans
l'Himalaya (1894)
(*Cambridge University
Library*)

5. Martin Conway (c1895)
(*Royal Geographical Society*)

6. The Gurkhas, Amar Sing and Karbir, leaving the Hannover Hut on the Ankogel on the last day of the walk through the Alps from End to End (1894)
(*Royal Geographical Society*)

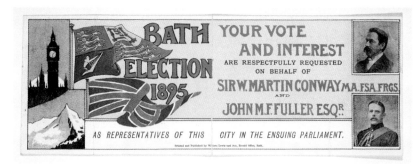

7. Bath election poster 1895
(*Cambridge University Library*)

8. Martin Conway in 1895
(*National Portrait Gallery*)

9. Allington Castle seen from the River Medway c1895
(*Maidstone Museum*)

10. Allington Castle, the crown jewel of Conway's collection of antiquities, after the restoration c1930
(*Maidstone Museum*)

11. War Museum Committee 1917–18: Conway (second from the left) with Sir Alfred Mond on his left.
(*Imperial War Museum*)

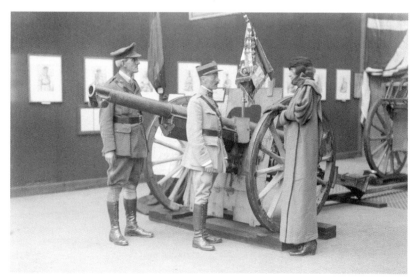

12. Katrina, Lady Conway, at the Imperial War Museum Galleries at the Crystal Palace (c1922)
(*Imperial War Museum*)

13. The Athenaeum Club: Conway's spiritual home in London from 1898-1937
(*Athenaeum Club*)

14. Conway in 1920
(*National Portrait Gallery,
London*)

7

PLAYING BRIDGE AT MÜRREN : SIR MARTIN CONWAY, M.P.

15. (Left)
Sir Martin Conway MP 'with a bad hand' at Mürren (1922)
(*Cambridge University Library*)

16. (Bottom left)
Cartoon from The Graphic,
1 August 1925
(*Cambridge University Library*)

17. (Bottom right)
'The Climber' (1931)
(*Cambridge University Library*)

SIR MARTIN CONWAY

THE CLIMBER.
" Fearless minds climb some day unto crowns."—SHAKESPEARE (*modified*).
SIR MARTIN CONWAY.

been a 'subject territory' ruled by corrupt German-speaking Swiss for centuries.

During the early nineteenth century there were revolutions in numerous cantons and cities as the prevailing semi-feudal laws and customs were progressively replaced by more liberal, democratic constitutions. Religious conflict also flared up as liberal anti-clericalism clashed with religious fundamentalism. Furthermore, Switzerland frequently gave refuge to would-be revolutionaries from neighbouring countries, adding to the chaotic state of affairs described by Prince Metternich. By 1847, Switzerland was close to civil war, with a real possibility that the Austrians, Prussians or French might intervene and divide the country. However, a lightning attack by the Protestants, led by General Dufour, split the Catholic forces and a new constitution, approved by referendum, established a system of local democracy that underpinned a period of peace and stability lasting until the end of the First World War. Anti-Catholic sentiment persisted amongst the Protestant population, however, and Jesuits were banned from the country until 1973.

During the First World War, the Swiss army, which was modelled on Prussia's, sympathised and covertly cooperated with the Germans, creating a major rift between the French- and German-speaking parts of the country. Simultaneously, Switzerland became home to many of the world's most active revolutionaries, as Lenin, Trotsky and others sought asylum in the country. A general strike by urban workers in 1918 was actively opposed by the conservative rural peasantry and crushed by the army, but the introduction of proportional representation in 1919 strengthened the position of the socialist party in the country. During the Depression, the typically high quality, high value goods produced by Swiss industry suffered disproportionately, leading to mass unemployment, but the dramatic rise of Fascism in both Italy and Germany persuaded the Swiss socialist party to move from class conflict to social partnership. An agreement signed in 1937, and extended at five-year intervals, virtually eliminated strike action in favour of negotiation and arbitration.

After the invasion of France in 1940, Switzerland was totally surrounded by Germany and its allies. Despite significant pro-Nazi leanings amongst the German-speaking majority, the country mobilised and prepared to defend itself. Today Switzerland is once again surrounded, this time by the European Union. The decision to remain outside the EU represents just the latest example of the Swiss rejecting the centralising aspirations of feudal lords, foreign conquerors, politicians and European bureaucrats. Switzerland is a profoundly divided country united by shared values – of hardy individualism, conservative localism and a willingness to compromise – rather than a common identity. The conservatism, in particular, is deeply ingrained. Public opinion in Switzerland often seems to lag many decades behind liberal European thought. Women were only enfranchised in 1971 and a recent vote banned the construction of minarets in the country. Despite the sophistication of the economy, the social attitudes of many modern Swiss still resemble those of the sturdy, independent peasants that Conway met on his travels.

Conway's chosen route through Switzerland deviated from the main alpine chain, heading north into the Bernese Alps, thereby missing out the whole of the Pennine Alps apart from a short side trip, by stagecoach and train, to Zermatt. It continued north of the main ridge, passing through the Tödi range, ignoring the higher Bernina Group to the south, before crossing into Austria. The route was designed, so far as possible, to pass through country that was new to Conway, but a further consideration appears to have been that at fairly regular intervals it passed through towns that contained first-class hotels frequented by English tourists.

My first full day's walk in Switzerland started in a dark tunnel driven through rocks on the eastern side of Lac d'Emosson. I sang 'Ta-ra-ra-boom-de-ay' in deference to Conway's Gurkha companions as I passed through. It was a day of light but persistent drizzle, with a cool wind chasing wispy clouds across the wet grey rocks and patchy snow of the Tour Sallière. Leaving the lakeside, I climbed up about 500 m to the windswept Col de Barbarine and dropped down into the upper Emaney valley, unchanged since I last visited it as a schoolboy nearly 40 years ago. A broad grassy rake led easily to the Col d'Emaney where a break in the clouds gave a glimpse into the mist-filled basin of the Lac de Salanfe, with the remnant glaciers and massive limestone buttresses of les Dents du Midi looming up behind. After dropping down to the lake in torrential rain, and a short climb to the Col du Jorat, the path descended 1,600 m through rocky alps, fir, birch and finally chestnut woods to Evionnaz in the Rhône valley.

Conway described a fertile valley full of vines. Today there is a BASF factory and, nearby, an expensive new fire station donated by the company, suggesting that their products are either highly inflammable or explosive. Conway hitched a ride on a hay cart, while I followed the Via Francigena, the old pilgrims' route to Rome, through fields, villages and woods. When Conway arrived in St. Maurice, he felt too lazy for tourism, and I too managed to resist the temptation to visit the Fairies' Grotto, a cave first opened to tourists in 1863. But St. Maurice is a pleasant town, with a pedestrianised main street, an eleventh-century abbey and a chateau protecting a bridge over the Rhône. The abbey marks the site of the tombs of the Roman legionnaire Maurice and his men, who were massacred for failing to persecute the local Christians with sufficient enthusiasm. The tomb became a place of pilgrimage after the Edict of Milan in AD 313, which allowed Christian worship throughout the Roman Empire. The abbey itself was founded by King Sigismund of Burgundy in AD 515 and the Treasury contains relics said to date from the reign of Charlemagne. It was sacked by Saracens in AD 940, rebuilt in the eleventh century, and in the Middle Ages became one of the holy places of Christendom, visited by pilgrims travelling over the Great St. Bernard Pass on their way to Rome.

In 1894 Conway was either unaware or simply uninterested in the history of the abbey, but in 1912 he wrote an article on 'The Shrine of the Theban Legion' in the *Burlington Magazine*. He admitted that 'when the youngsters of my day hurried past S. Maurice, it was not of treasuries and relics we were thinking, but the "treasuries of the snow"',[226] and went on to explain the successful business model adopted by the Abbey of St. Maurice: 'Where the Abbey scored was in its vast capital of relics. Other shrines with the body of a considerable saint would obtain the favour of a great man, or barter for some other sacred relic, by parting with a finger bone...But the Abbey of S. Maurice could and did go into business on a larger scale. They were universally believed to possess the skeletons of upwards of six thousand authentic martyrs [the legionnaires allegedly massacred along with S. Maurice]...[and] were able and willing to trade off not merely a single bone, but a full-sized legionary for suitable consideration.'

Conway had a rest day in St. Maurice, but instead of visiting the abbey he travelled by steam train to Vevey in search of English tobacco, for Vevey was a place 'where all things English are to be had'.[227] Today the grand Victorian hotels, built to accommodate English tourists attracted to the Clarens shore of Lake Geneva by Rousseau, Byron and Shelley, have an elegant, majestic air to them. In the nineteenth century, they must have looked garish and new. But for Conway, bereft of English company after the departure of Fitzgerald from Chamonix, it was a sanctuary. He filled his pouch and pockets with English tobacco and made up bundles which he posted to himself at intervals along the route. He bought fresh fruit in the market and an English paper to read in a café overlooking the lake. That night he returned by steam train to St. Maurice.

Since transport was available for the next leg of his journey to Gryon, Conway naturally took it. He hired a coach for himself and the baggage, while the guides and Gurkhas walked. 'Chestnut and walnut trees reached down their heavy arms so low that I could raise my hand and feel the coldness of their unripe fruit as we zigzagged up amongst the vineyards',[228] he recorded. Leaving St. Maurice in the late afternoon by the bridge below the chateau, I climbed up through overgrown fortifications constructed by General Dufour on the opposite bank of the Rhône and walked through peaceful rolling vineyards and scattered farmhouses to Bex. Towards Lake Geneva distant factories and chimneys bore witness to the fact that the wide U-shaped valley of the Rhône provides one of the few places suitable for modern industrial development in this part of Switzerland. Bex grew rich on its salt mines, which were first worked in 1544, and as I followed the track beside the Avançon river I passed other relics of the early industrial revolution in the form of numerous stone-built watermills hunched up over the fast-flowing river: the remains of the 'endless waterwheels' referred to in Conway's account.

The industrialisation of Switzerland followed a very different pattern from Britain. Cloth, wool and linen manufacturing started to develop in Switzerland during the fifteenth century, and the country rapidly gained a reputation for the quality of its products. In the late seventeenth century, Huguenot refugees fleeing religious persecution in France brought their skills as goldsmiths, watch-makers and printers. By the late eighteenth century, large parts of Switzerland started to industrialise with perhaps 100,000 weavers and spinners. However, with few natural resources other than water-power, and a strong tradition of peasant smallholdings, these enterprises remained scattered and small scale; more akin to small Pennine mill towns than the vast coal-fired conurbations that sprang up during Britain's industrial revolution.

Above the valley floor, this was still recognisably the same country that Conway travelled through, with steep vineyard tracks, tidy chalets, shady maple woods and sunny meadows. Only the distant whine of high-powered motorbikes, accelerating around hairpin bends, reminded me that I was travelling in the twenty-first century. Arriving in Gryon as dusk began to fall, I looked back across the valley of the Rhône to the grey pyramid of les Dents du Midi, framed by the dark shadows of ash trees and silhouetted against a smoky rose sky, and felt amazed to be alive.

Not far from Gryon lies the village of Leysin, home of the International School of Mountaineering where some of the best British climbers of the 1960s and 70s, including Dougal Haston, Don Whillans and Peter Boardman, taught a succession of young students and travellers how to climb in the mountains and how to drink at the Club Vagabond. Leysin was also the subject of a detailed study by the Reverend Thomas Malthus, the great demographic doomsayer, at the end of the eighteenth century. Contrary to Malthus' general prophecy that the human population would always grow to the point where it was checked by famine or disease, and 'kept equal to the means of subsistence, by misery and vice', in Leysin he found a village inhabited by a healthy and apparently happy population. Throughout the high valleys of the Alps, before the dramatic economic changes that occurred from the 1850s onwards, social practices had evolved to maintain the fragile balance between the human population and the scarce natural resources of the mountains.[229] Around many high villages, like Leysin, cultivable land represents less than 10% of the available land area. Before the development of alternative sources of income, villagers relied on a combination of crops and hay cultivated in fields around the village, and pastoralism on the high meadows – an agro-pastoral system called *Alpwirtschaft*. In spring the animals were taken to successively higher meadows as the snows melted; and in the autumn the process was reversed. The animals over-wintered in byres in the village, fed on hay gathered during the summer months. It was a simple question of energy: on high pastures, cattle yield more calories for human consumption than crops. Each family was permitted to own only as many cows as they could over-winter with hay from their fields around the village. This ensured that the high pastures were not over-grazed in summer. Because of the acute shortage of labour in the busy summer months (in contrast to the surplus during the long winters), the villagers had to cooperate with each other, with common herds of cattle and communal maintenance of paths and huts on the high pastures. Inward migration was strongly discouraged by the system of land ownership, and each individual village could almost be regarded as a self-sufficient ecosystem. Marriage was deliberately restricted or delayed by social practice to reduce fertility. Inheritance systems were designed to avoid partition of farms, so that each family maintained ownership of viable parcels of crop- and hay-growing land. Men did not marry before they inherited sufficient land to support a family, and those that did not inherit either remained celibate or migrated. The high mountain villages were often healthier places than equivalent peasant communities on the plains, with relatively low levels of child mortality, probably because of easy access to clean water and a diet rich in milk and cheese, but it remained a precarious existence. In the seventeenth century the population in many high valleys declined dramatically when the climate cooled with the onset of the 'Little Ice Age', and only started to recover when potatoes were introduced during the eighteenth century.

From the mid nineteenth century onwards, this traditional pattern began to break down as villages ceased to be 'closed corporations' and progressively opened up to cottage industries, trade and tourism. Conway saw the Alps in the early stages of this transition. In 1904, he observed that 'the life now being lived by the peasantry was in all essentials the same life that had been lived by their ancestors for hundreds of years, ancestors bearing the same names and owning the same properties that are still borne and owned by their living descendants'.[230] Increasing knowledge of the long history of human occupation provided Conway with a new understanding of the landscape: 'Its picturesqueness became involved in a tangle of human memories, accumulated activities, monumental accomplishments of successive bygone generations.'[231] As he grew older, he became just as interested in the fertile valleys as he was in the austere landscape of rock and ice above the snowline, and increasingly fearful of the impact of tourism on the rural economy: 'The great charm and recreative power of mountain-wandering arose from the fact that the climber cut himself off from the life of the Cities and Plain and exchanged it for the life of the hillside. He came into communication with another set of men, with other habits, other ideals. Each year that passes in the Alps makes that change less considerable and by so much less the salutary.'[232] When Conway walked through the Alps, Leysin was a tiny hamlet with a single small *pension*, but Murray's *Handbook* of 1892 noted that 'this place is beginning to be frequented in winter [and] a large *Kurhaus* is in course of construction'.[233] In later years it grew into a vast sanatorium and today the town remains almost entirely dependent on service industries, particularly tourism, with a tiny proportion of the population engaged in agriculture.

The Bernese Alps

The path that Conway took from Gryon, through sun-dappled woods and flowery meadows, has been paved with asphalt. The 200 cows that he found in the green amphitheatre of Solalex have been replaced by 200 cars, and the cheese-makers' chalet is now an expensive restaurant. Refugees from Geneva and Lausanne crowd into this once remote valley seeking Sunday asylum in the sublime. Both Conway and I stayed at Anzeindaz, a small cluster of chalets surrounded by high summer pastures, with the steep scree slope of Les Diablerets to the north and the craggy Grand Muveran to the south. During the day a four-wheel-drive taxi takes lazy tourists from Solalex to Anzeindaz, spewing out diesel fumes and shattering the silence of the hills. But later, after the crowds have gone, it is still a pretty place to sit and drink a glass of wine in the evening sun. I went to bed at 9 o'clock but was almost immediately awakened by a cacophony of firecrackers from a nearby chalet celebrating a summer fête. The percussion of fireworks was accompanied by frenzied bell-ringing as a herd of cows in a neighbouring field went berserk. Finally silence returned to the mountains, allowing moos and men to sleep in peace.

The route that Conway followed to the summit of Les Diablerets (3,209 m) was horrible. A steep scree-filled gully meandered its way through contorted strata of unconsolidated rock to a col. Above, steeper and marginally more consolidated rocks led to the summit. Victorian alpinists hated rock climbing, yet they were prepared to climb on choss like this. It may have been only *Facile*, but I would have felt happier climbing a route several grades harder on solid rock. The view from the summit compensated for the effort. Above a broken layer of fluffy cumulus, Mont Blanc, le Grand Combin, the Pennine Alps and the Bernese Oberland glistened on the hazy blue horizon. Between the mountain ridges, the deep trench of the Rhône valley runs almost straight from its glacier source to Martigny, then abruptly turns through 90 degrees and flows into Lake Geneva. To the north and west lie gentler lands: the scattered village of Les Diablerets in a verdant hollow of dark woods and lustrous meadows dappled with the shadows of drifting clouds. And in the distance, ridge upon rocky ridge faded into the sepia plains of northern Europe. The view from an elevated position is routinely called 'imperious', for reasons that I fail to understand. Perhaps a Wall Street banker observing street-life 30 storeys down, with a 'panoptic god-like'[234] view, feels imperious, but if gods or devils reposed up here, in this pure air and piercing sunlight, I suspect that they would watch the rise and fall of human empires in the valleys below with complete indifference.

Sadly, so-called civilisation is closer than it looks. Walk down from the rocky summit, across a small snowfield, and a bulldozed rubble ridge leads you to the high altitude funfair of 'Glacier 3000'. There is a snow bus to transport the punters across the glacier to the Tour St. Martin, husky sledge rides, and an 'alpine coaster' – the highest roller coaster in Europe. Actually, it's good fun – and very frightening if you can resist the temptation to use the brakes – but it would be more at home in Alton Towers. It is just a desperate attempt to wring the last few Swiss francs out of the mountain before the glacier melts.

The Tsanfleuron glacier, so proudly proclaimed in the 'Glacier 3000' literature, is very low and very vulnerable to climate change. It has shrunk dramatically since Conway's time, revealing a vast area of 'lapis' – a corrugated, pale grey limestone pavement, riddled with micro caves and canyons. Beneath the soggy glacier, the rock is worn smooth by ice. Further down the mountainside, the runnels and caverns become increasingly pronounced as acid rain progressively etches the surface of the rock. Near the bottom, bright clusters of flowers burst out of dark crevices like fireworks exploding in a night sky. I scrambled through this limestone labyrinth to the road and followed it south to the Sanetsch Hotel. The hotel was brand new when Conway stayed here in 1894. It has since been expanded and refurbished to serve crowds of weekend holidaymakers, but the view is largely unchanged, across the Valais to the Val d'Hérens, with la Dent Blanche and the Matterhorn in the distance, wreathed in afternoon clouds. Only the dam at the end of Lac des Dix is obviously modern. According to legend, the Val d'Hérens was settled by Saracens in the eighth century and the residents of the valley are still said to be dark-skinned and dark-eyed, with a particularly guttural patois. The Allalinhorn, which stands between Zermatt and the Saas valley to the east, may have derived its strange name from Allah.

Conway's long journey through the Alps did not entirely insulate him from financial concerns. Letters from Katrina mentioned small amounts received and large bills to be paid, but she congratulated him on his economy in the Alps. 'The cheapness with which you are managing this climbing expedition seems to me nothing short of sublime', she wrote at the end of June. Conway left the Sanetsch inn 'regretfully...though regret was tempered with some resentment at the proportions of the bill'.[235] I experienced a similar sentiment. In Italy, I ate like a lord and never begrudged the bill. At the Sanetsch Hotel the *demi-pension* consisted of cheese fondue, dry bread and a single scoop of ice cream for dinner, followed by a breakfast consisting of the same ingredients, without the ice cream. The cost was at least twice as much as a four-course feast and a generous breakfast in an Italian mountain inn.

In Conway's day, Switzerland was relatively cheap. As the main beneficiaries of the industrial revolution, English middle-class travellers
enjoyed massive purchasing power in the less developed parts of Europe.
While many Swiss towns and cities were already quite wealthy by the
1890s, in the mountainous regions a peasant economy prevailed.
Contemporary accounts talk of barefoot sellers of milk, fruit, crystals
and wild flowers, chasing stagecoaches and swarming around groups of
tourists like flies. But the peasants in Switzerland were free men, who
carried arms, and demanded 'honour' even from noblemen, and the
Alpwirtschaft system of cultivation demanded a high level of social cohe-
sion.

Swiss neutrality, effectively established in the sixteenth century and
confirmed by treaty in 1815, played a crucial part in the development
of the economy. As early as 1797 a French aristocrat bemoaned the fact
that the Swiss 'enrich themselves by the misfortunes of others and found
a bank on human calamities'.[236] As tourism started to grow in the mid
nineteenth century, the banking system became increasingly sophisti-
cated, providing long-term finance for major tourist projects, such as
hotels and railways. During the Second World War, the German
Reichsbank deposited over SFr 1.6bn in gold in the Swiss National
Bank[237] and Swiss industrialists grew rich supplying precision instruments to the German armaments industry. In the immediate post-war
years, the Swiss made vast fortunes supplying manufactured goods to
war-torn Europe and the banks' highly profitable 'wealth management'
business has continued to thrive, not least because of the Swiss willingness to take money from anybody, without enquiring too diligently
about its provenance. It has always seemed strange that a country that
does not permit its own citizens to mow their lawns on a Sunday (lest
they disturb the peace) should be happy to look after the money of
tyrants, murderers and drug dealers; but morality in Switzerland is a
curiously parochial affair. A strong tradition of local democracy has produced something that, to British eyes, looks remarkably intolerant: a
local tyranny of the conservative majority, concerned only with their
own well-being. Perhaps it has something to do with the Calvinist tradition of predestination – the idea that some people are elected to salvation, while others are condemned to eternal damnation, and there is

absolutely nothing that they can do about it. Certainly there is nothing that the British tourist can do about the cost of travel in Switzerland. If you want to enjoy the Swiss Alps, you simply have to pay.

From the Sanetsch Hotel I wandered back up the road to the top of the pass and turned east, climbing an undulating, narrow ridge of black shale. The four great rivers that flow out of the Alps – the Po, the Rhône, the Rhine and the Danube – have shaped the history of Europe. I had already crossed the valleys of the Po and the Rhône, and this narrow ridge marked the watershed of the Rhine. A drop of water landing on the south side would flow to the Mediterranean; one landing on the north would end up in the North Sea. From the top there was a good view back towards Les Diablerets and the lapis below. Conway likened the white limestone karst scenery to a glacier. Over the past hundred years much of it has been colonised by plants, but the resemblance is still there.

Beyond the col, I entered a barren rocky valley and dropped down to the bleak, muddy moraine lakes at Gouilles. Conway climbed the Wildhorn (3,247 m) from the west, via the Col du Brochet. I went up the north-east flank (out of sequence, with Fiona, as acclimatisation for Mont Blanc), climbing easily up the Ténéhet glacier, a low-angled ramp of ice down which sheets of melt water flowed, creating a kaleidoscope of bubbles and ripples on the water-ice below. When Conway stood on the summit, 'the highest point was of snow and looked down on the rock-peak where the surveyor's signal stands'.[238] Now a metal cross stands on a rocky summit. The cloud came down as we climbed and the view was partially obscured by shifting mists, which added to the lonely atmosphere of the peak. Conway had a clearer view and admired a 'wooded and grassy plateau decked with several little lakes'[239] perched above the valley of the Rhône. He later discovered that just a few weeks earlier a hotel had been opened in the tiny hamlet of Montana. Conway returned in 1909 and stayed at the Palace Hotel at Montana, which by then boasted an 18-hole golf course. Today Montana and the neighbouring hamlet of Crans have fused together into a sprawling golf and ski resort.

From Lac de Ténéhet, a sombre lake set beneath dark crumbling cliffs, I followed a slippery track over limestone ridges and sink holes, before crossing onto easier sandstone terrain near the Rawilpass. In the mountains the fat of the land is cut away to reveal the stony skeleton beneath. Faults, folds and geological boundaries are all laid bare. Less obviously, I had also crossed a linguistic boundary. For somewhere between Lac de Ténéhet and the Rawilpass, French gives way to German. On this barren mountain pass lies the fault line between the two great languages and cultures of northern continental Europe, and there is absolutely nothing to signify the change.

Swiss French is fairly pure, albeit accented, but Swiss German or *Schwyzerdütsch* is an unwritten collection of local dialects which, like English, are a strange jumble of languages. When I paid for my first coffee on the German side of the linguistic boundary I said '*danke schön*' to which the waitress replied '*merci viel mal*'. In most countries, as education improves people stop speaking in dialect, but the German-speaking Swiss are proud that they can still identify each other's home regions from their accents and vocabulary, and many feel uncomfortable speaking 'high German'. Like every other country, Switzerland is becoming increasingly globalised and international in its outlook. French-speaking Swiss probably look to Paris, as much as Geneva, as the centre of their language and culture, but the older generation of *Schwyzerdütsch*-speakers still look to their home village, underlining the strange parochialism of Switzerland. Conway would be delighted, for as he noted: 'It would be a poor result of education if it planed away dialects.'[240]

Conway spent the night in a dirty cow shed near the Rawilpass. When the peasants returned with their cows they brought clouds of flies with them, and he passed an uncomfortable night. I attempted to sleep at the squeaky-clean Wildstrubelhütte, but cleanliness is no cure for snoring. I can tolerate constant, repetitive snoring, but everybody in the Wildstrubelhütte that night, apart from me, appeared to be suffering from Cheyne-Stokes syndrome – an endlessly repeated cycle, characteristic of poorly acclimatised sleepers, where an unpredictable number of shallow breaths are followed by two or three enormous nasal gulps of air, after which the breathing almost ceases completely for a few seconds, before the cycle repeats itself.

Another vexing problem in mountain huts is window etiquette.

The British traditionally like to sleep with the window open in all but the most extreme conditions, in order to allow the fetid fug of a crowded dormitory to disperse. Germans, on the other hand, detest fresh air and will instantly shut any window they find ajar, with a stern Teutonic glare at the offending Brit. It is interesting to note that even in Conway's day, the German aversion to fresh air was widely acknowledged (at least by the British). In his book, he noted that 'the night was so unusually warm that a foreign gentleman, whose nationality the reader must divine, was compelled to get out of bed and open his window – such at any rate was the almost incredible tale he related to his horrified compatriots at the early breakfast table!'[241]

Next day, Conway intended to climb the Wildstrubel (3,243 m), but instead he got distracted by the Plaine Morte, a large flat glacier, and wrote one of the most memorable passages of his book. I too crossed the Plaine Morte on a muggy, misty day. The snow was soft and the air felt exhausted and used up. I navigated across 3 miles of disorientingly flat glacier by compass and miraculously arrived at the foot of the Wildstrubel almost exactly where an indistinct path struck up through boulders and scree to the summit. Towards the top, the passage of many feet had created myriad paths all zigzagging up a slope of patchy snow and loose rock. There was almost no view from the summit and it was, without doubt, one of the least memorable mountain days I have ever experienced.

Conway, on the other hand, was ecstatic. 'The whole white area was before us, doubtless one of the most remarkable sights in the Alps. It is so large, so simple, so secluded. It seems like a portion of some strange world…Beautiful too it was, with the beauty of all great snowfields; its large undulations, its rippled surface, glinting under the touch of the low risen sun. To add to its mystery, there came over the sky a veil of mist…Here a man might come and, setting up his tent for a week, learn what it is to be alone. He might wander safely in any direction and, climbing the wall at any point, look out upon the world of hotels and tourists; then returning to his lone abode, he might kindle his solitary lamp and cook for himself the cup of contemplation.'[242]

Here was a landscape, largely unchanged since Conway's time (provided you ignored the encroaching ski lifts from Crans Montana to the south), where we fundamentally disagreed on its merits. Appreciation of landscape is, of course, acquired, not innate. Children do not 'appreciate' landscape; they gradually absorb ideas about what constitutes beauty and ugliness as they grow up. For Conway, and for me, the landscape of the Plaine Morte was a construct of our imagination, projected onto snow, rock and ice. We looked at essentially the same physical environment, and we saw something completely different. Part of the difference arose because I was exhausted after a sleepless night during which I had come close to committing mass murder in a crowded dormitory, and 'nature always wears the colors of the spirit',[243] but there was more to it than that. Like most of my generation of climbers, I find plodding across flat snowfields boring. Like most of his generation, Conway found doing the same thing fascinating. Today, we see the desolation of polar snowfields and glaciers (sometimes calving into the sea in spectacular fashion) almost daily on television. In Conway's day, the two Poles were *terra incognita*; a land of fable and fascination. Conway had fallen prey to the national obsession with vast, empty, icy spaces and the beauty of untrodden snow, and when he walked across the Plaine Morte he was enchanted because he imagined himself following in the footsteps of Parry, Franklin and Ross. It was an obsession that would later take him to Spitsbergen and the suggestion that he might lead an expedition to Antarctica.

Both Conway and I felt that we had earned a rest day in Leukerbad. Founded by the Romans, the hot baths have a pleasant setting in a steep-sided valley nestled beneath the Gemmi (probably a corruption of 'Chemin') Pass, which was once the main route between the Bernese Oberland and the Valais. Even in Conway's day, Leukerbad was a major tourist resort with a permanent population of about 600. Today the tourist brochure for the town proudly boasts that Conway's friend Mark Twain stayed here in 1880. However, it fails to give his account of Leukerbad in *A Tramp Abroad*, where Twain described how he 'entered the narrow alleys of the outskirts and waded towards the centre of the town through liquid "fertiliser"'. As Twain observed: 'They ought to either pave that village or organise a ferry.'[244]

With 1,500 permanent inhabitants, and beds for 8,500 visitors, Leukerbad advertises itself as the centre of '*wellness globale*', but most of the visitors that I saw did not resemble the slim, tanned models in the brochure. Both Twain and Conway stayed at the Hôtel des Alpes ('the best, electric light',[245] according to Murray's 1892 *Handbook for Travellers*), which stands on a grassy mound overlooking the town. It must once have been a fine Victorian hotel, but it has been spoilt by an ugly extension. Conway's trunk had been sent ahead, so that when he arrived he was immediately able to wash and go down to dinner wearing glossy evening dress, as convention required. In the years before and after the First World War, Conway frequently visited Switzerland as a guest of Sir Henry Lunn. In one of his many books, Henry Lunn's son, Arnold, described the consequences of not being properly attired for dinner in a Swiss hotel: 'It would have been unthinkable for an Englishman not to dress for dinner...I remember one miserable outcast whose registered luggage did not arrive for a week. Everybody was kind to him, but he lost caste. He was slipping. He knew it. We knew it. The head waiter knew it. And then the cloud lifted. His luggage arrived. I shall never forget the expression on his face when he appeared for the first time in evening dress. He looked like a man who had been cleared by court martial of a disgraceful charge.'[246] Standards of dress have since relaxed, but even today the Hôtel des Alpes in Leukerbad would probably have looked askance at the evening clothes that I had in my rucksack, so I settled for more modest accommodation on the outskirts of the old town, now paved and cleared of 'fertiliser'.

The Pennine Alps

At this point in his journey, Conway set off on a jaunt. He had originally intended to walk to Ried in the Lötschental but a letter from Fitzgerald, waiting for him at Leukerbad, persuaded him to change his plans and he travelled to Zermatt instead. 'Fitzgerald has deserted me the last ten days', Conway wrote to Manton Marble, 'but I hope to meet him again to-night. He halves my costs and is very precious.' As a result of Fitzgerald's absence, Conway had spent nearly two weeks in the company of the two Italian guides and the two Gurkhas. Conway enjoyed the company of the Gurkhas; he found them amusing. Major Charles Bruce was also proud of his troops. He wrote to Conway periodically during his walk, checking up that 'the Gurks' were 'bucking up and doing proper work' and asking Conway to 'give the boys a hug for me'. As Conway observed in an article for the *National Observer*: 'Being, as we doubtless are, one of the leading races in the world, and distinctly the first of the governing and compelling races, the number of peoples who we care or are able to range ourselves beside is smaller than the number of those to which we feel ourselves superior and on whom we frankly look down. Within the confines of the Indian Empire there is only one stock with which the typical Anglo Saxon is in entire sympathy. It is that of the Gurkhas...Quainter looking creatures cannot be imagined. They are short and broad...They chatter everlastingly with their high pitched voices, their bodies jiggering and quivering with fun. Of course they never cringe to you...They are brave...these men, beautifully brave, and they scorn all coward races...Nowhere will you find a more sporting lot than the Gurkhas; they love every form of sport, but they love those best in which a man can get hurt.' In short, the Gurkhas were ideal imperial subjects: 'Companionable, readily disciplined [and] full of *esprit de corps*'.[247]

Unlike the Gurkhas (who had volunteered to serve in the Indian army), Conway's Italian guides were not imperial subjects and so did not always know their place. As Conway observed: 'Climbers have often expressed astonishment at the success with which guides...follow, over long distances, a faintly marked trail. They usually refer the power of doing this to some special intelligence, whereas it is really due to absence of intelligence. If a man's mind is nearly a blank, he can keep his attention fixed on the dull minutiae of the stones in the way.' In contradistinction, Conway, as an enlightened Englishman, concentrated on the 'larger and more important observations, which are the chief preoccupation of the explorer',[248] and so, periodically, he got lost.

Conway's profound sense of the superiority of his race was, of course, backed up by the indisputable fact of the largest Empire the world has ever known. And while the British did not actually occupy the Alps by military force, they nevertheless invaded almost every aspect of the mountains – aesthetic, scholarly, economic, religious and sporting – and made them their own. Through their literature and poetry, scientific and geographic research, sporting activities and insistence upon tea, English food and Anglican church services, the British used their economic power to impose their cultural norms – their canons of good taste and behaviour – on the Alps in general and Switzerland in particular. Murray's 1892 *Handbook for Travellers in Switzerland* informed its readers that 'the wants, tastes, and habits of the English are more carefully and successfully studied in the Swiss hotels than those of any other part of Europe' and reassured visitors that 'guests of other nationalities are ejected from the public sitting-room [on Sundays] while English service is performed'.[249] In 1914 there were no fewer than 52 English churches in Switzerland and over 100 hotels offered Anglican church services each Sunday.[250] As Tolstoy observed: 'An Englishman is self-assured, as being a citizen of the best-organized state in the world, and therefore as an Englishman always knows what he should do and knows that all he does as an Englishman is undoubtedly correct.'[251]

Conway probably expected to meet some English acquaintances at the Hôtel des Alpes in Leukerbad. In their absence, the temptation to travel to Zermatt, where he would certainly find some fellow members of the Alpine Club, proved too great. Conway was a clubbable man. The scope and breadth of the clubs, societies and other voluntary associations that he joined is extraordinary, giving a lie to the traditional image of the 'idle rich'. Amongst his interests he was a member of:

The 1920 Club
The Alpine Club (president)
The Alpine Dining Club
The Alpine Exploration Club
The Alpine Skiing Club (president)
The American Society
The Ancient Monuments Society (chairman)
The Anglo American League (committee member)
The Appalachian Club (hon. member)
The Arundel Club (chairman)
The Association of Academies of All Nations
The Athenaeum (committee member)
The Authors' Society (chairman)
The Automobile Club

The Auto Cycle Club

The British Fine Arts Club

The Burlington Fine Arts Club

The Camera Club

The Central Asiatic Society (council member)

The Cosmopolitan Club

The Cyclists' Touring Club

The Dilettanti Society

The Eagles (hon. member)

The Eighty Club (committee member)

The Einstein Club

The English Branch of the League for the Preservation of the
    Beauty of Switzerland (chairman)

The Eugenics Society

The Guild of University Extensionists (vice president)

The Hakluyt Society (council member)

The Hellenic Society

The Himalayan Club (founder member)

The Imperial Liberal Council (treasurer)

The Imperial War Museum (director general and trustee)

The International Education Society (committee member)

The Kensington Library Committee

The Kent Archaeological Society (president)

The Kinsmen (chairman)

The Liberal Central Association

The Liberal League (vice president)

The Liverpool Art Club (committee member)

The Liverpool Art Workers' Guild

London University Summer Art School for American Students
    (chairman)

Maidstone Grammar School (governor)

The Medico-Psychological Clinic (treasurer)

The National Art Collections Fund (committee member)

The National Association for the Advancement of Art (hon. secre-
    tary)

The National Portrait Gallery (trustee)

The Optimists' Club (chairman)
The Piccadilly Club
The Public Schools Alpine Sports Club
The Royal Archaeological Institute (council member)
The Royal Commission on Museums
The Royal Geographical Society (vice president)
The Royal Institute of British Architects (hon. fellow)
The Royal Society Club
St. Stephen's Club
The Savile Club
The Social and Political Education League (president)
The Society of Antiquaries (committee member)
The Society of Arts
The Sunday Tramps
The US Club
The Victoria and Albert Museum (committee member)
The Wallace Collection (trustee)

Day after day, Conway's London diaries record meetings, lunches and dinners with friends and acquaintances. He was sociable by nature, and Victorian society offered far fewer solitary distractions. Today, technology provides any number of alternatives to the oldest form of human entertainment, and this has had an atomising effect on society. Even in public, people increasingly avoid social interaction, plugging their ears with private entertainment, and most people probably look forward to spending a day at home 'doing nothing', whereas Conway, I suspect, hated it. And he hated travelling alone even more: 'I have seldom had the bad luck to be obliged to wander alone abroad',[252] he noted in his memoirs.

Conway went to Zermatt because he was lonely and bored, and craved the company of fellow Englishmen. He also went because a letter from Marble advised him that 'your book will be worth twice as much in money to your publisher, and to you, if you include the ascent...of the Matterhorn and the Monte Rosa...To the general [public] it will be absurd to talk about "the Alps from End to End" and only cross one of those lumps [Mont Blanc] known as big and hard.'

Conway travelled by coach to Visp, and took the new railway to Zermatt, the preparations for which he had witnessed in 1887: 'Fancy they are surveying to make a railroad up to Zermatt from Visp...but I don't know whether they will get the money to make it. I can't imagine how it could be made to pay. They reckon to bring 40,000 people to Zermatt every year.' Despite his normal objections to the vulgarisation of the Alps, he approved of the new railway: 'Before the Zermatt railway was made, 30,000 people annually visited the place. They had to walk or ride from Visp to S. Niklaus by the single mule-path, and their baggage had to be taken by pack-animals. The foul condition into which the road was brought by the end of August can scarcely be conceived and will never be forgotten by those who experienced it.'[253] However, when the railway inevitably attracted even more visitors to Zermatt his attitude became more ambivalent: 'The crowds that flood Switzerland in the best season of the year only become endurable to mountain lovers when they are dammed into channels and controlled. They consist for the most part of glorified trippers – good folk of their sort, but not beautiful *en masse*.' Today, Zermatt receives an astonishing 2 million visitors each year.

In his book, Conway tries to convey the impression that he travelled to Zermatt, climbed the Nordend (4,609 m), the second highest peak of the Monte Rosa massif, and then resumed his journey. His diary presents a somewhat different picture. When he arrived he checked into the Monte Rosa Hotel, the spiritual home of the Alpine Club in Switzerland. The next day, he walked up to the Riffelalp for tea. He did the same thing the following day and stayed at the Riffel Inn overnight. On the fourth day he climbed the Nordend and returned to the Riffel Inn. On the fifth he returned to Zermatt, where he was joined by Fitzgerald, fresh from his business in Florence. In accordance with Marble's instructions, Conway intended to climb the Matterhorn as well as Monte Rosa, but the mountain was out of condition so he gave up the attempt and instead spent two further days in Zermatt and Visp before resuming his walk.

By 1911, when he was asked to contribute a piece on mountaineering to *The Encyclopaedia of Sport*, Conway had clearly forgotten his momentary lapse in Leukerbad: 'Take a long piece of mountain range, cross pass after pass, and climb peak after peak...changing your sleeping place from day to day...[Y]ou will meet with varied adventures, and you will avoid the fatuous stupidity to be found in large hotels. The man who once acquires a taste for mountain travel will never be likely to slide back into a *flâneur* about centres.'[254] The use of the word *flâneur*, so beloved by 'psycho-geographers', is particularly apt. For a *flâneur* − an uninvolved, bourgeois dilettante, strolling through the streets − is an emphatically urban creature, and Zermatt, even in Conway's day, was a little piece of urban life grafted onto a Swiss mountainside. The Monte Rosa Hotel was about as close to London as you could get without leaving Switzerland.

John Muir maintained that 'only by going alone in silence, without baggage, can one truly get into the heart of the wilderness. All other travel is mere dust and hotels and baggage and chatter.'[255] Conway certainly enjoyed the wilderness, but he also enjoyed hotels and baggage, and especially chatter. Nearly all walkers and climbers are prone to romantic exaggeration about their love of solitude. In his famous essay on walking, Henry David Thoreau started by saying: 'If you are ready to leave father and mother, and brother and sister, and wife and child and friends, and never see them again − if you have paid your debts, and made your will, and settled all your affairs, and are a free man − then you are ready for a walk',[256] but within a few pages he had discovered that 'there is in fact a sort of harmony discoverable between the capabilities of landscape within a circle of ten miles' radius, or the limits of an afternoon walk, and the three score years and ten of human life'.

I visited Zermatt before starting my journey through the Alps and returned there when it was complete. It seemed like the best place to begin and end my quest to understand how Conway saw the Alps. Conway's first visit to Zermatt was in 1872 when he was 16 years old and his last was in 1935 at the age of 79. On each occasion he stayed at the Monte Rosa Hotel, and so did I. For 17 years prior to his walk through the Alps, Conway had been a regular guest at the hotel; the proprietor even visited him in Cambridge during a visit to England in 1879: 'It is impossible to speak too highly of the uniform kindness and attention which M. and Mme. Seiler have for so many years shown to their guests. Better managed mountain hotels cannot be found in any other place in the Alps.'[257]

Even today, the exterior of the hotel is still recognisable from Edward Whymper's engraving of the Alpine Club at Zermatt in 1864. A plaque beside the front door describes it as 'the mountaineer's true home', a quote from Conway's friend and fellow member of the Alpine Club, Charles Mathews. On the first floor, the dining room still retains something of the atmosphere of bygone days, but today it tends to be filled with Japanese tour groups, whose national tradition of sacred mountains long pre-dates that of the British. The wood-panelled 'Salon Whymper' nearby is lined with old photographs: Clinton Dent who proposed Conway for membership of the Alpine Club in 1877; Douglas Freshfield who introduced him to the Royal Geographical Society; Leslie Stephen who invited him to join the Sunday Tramps; Charles Mathews who arranged for the third and final Arts Congress to be held in Birmingham in 1890; Horace Walker from Liverpool; Arnold Lunn who, together with his father Henry, did so much to popularise winter sports in Switzerland; and Geoffrey Winthrop Young who critiqued Conway's last book in the early 1930s. Conway would doubtless be both surprised and disappointed to find that his own photograph is not included alongside so many of his friends and acquaintances. There is also no photograph of Mattias Zurbriggen amongst the guides, despite the fact that he was born in the neighbouring Saas valley, perhaps because he later moved to Macugnaga and was adopted as a national hero by Italy after his conquest of Aconcagua. Fittingly, there is a memorial to Zurbriggen on the summit of the Monte Moro Pass between Saas Fee and Macugnaga on the border between Switzerland and Italy, a route that he frequently used to smuggle contraband between the two countries.

At the reception of the Monte Rosa Hotel I asked permission to look at the guest books for the period when Conway was a regular visitor, which provided much of the material for the *Zermatt Pocket Book*. The manageress, who was obviously well practised in dealing with bores from the Alpine Club, put me in touch with the Public Relations manager who kindly sent me facsimile copies of the pages from the book containing Conway's familiar handwriting, boasting of his achievements.

When Conway climbed the Nordend, the Monte Rosa hut (as distinct from the hotel) was still under construction, so they started from the Riffel Inn just after midnight. Unlike today, almost the entire route from the Gornergletscher onwards was on snow. As they climbed, the wind picked up and it became extremely cold. Slowed down by the need to cut steps in the ice, Amar Sing got mild frostbite in his toes. When they reached the summit 'clouds were sweeping down towards us in massed battalions, and wreaths of snow were whirling about in tiny cyclones'.[258] On the way back, when they reached the site of the new hut, Conway discovered that 'the bitter cold had wrought an internal mischief in me'.[259] His diary is less cryptic: 'frightful "piles" came on during day'. They reached the Riffel Inn 18 hours after their departure. Despite all this, Conway enjoyed the experience, at least in retrospect: 'Such struggles with nature produce a moral invigoration of enduring value. They wash the mind free of sentimental cobwebs and foolish imagining. They bring a man in contact with cold stony reality and call forth all that is best in his nature. They act as moral tonics.'[260] Conway may have rejected much of the religious dogma of his childhood but, just like his father, he still believed in the moral value of hard work and of suffering.

As with Mont Blanc, Fiona and I climbed Monte Rosa out of sequence. We decided to climb the Dufourspitze (called the Hochspitze in Conway's day, but since named after General Dufour) which is the highest point in the Monte Rosa group at 4,634 m and the highest mountain in Switzerland. Conway chose the slightly lower Nordend (4,609 m) because he had already climbed the Dufourspitze eight times but had failed to reach the summit of the Nordend on his single attempt in 1878. Unlike Mont Blanc, where the summit day is short, both the Nordend and the Dufourspitze involve many hours of glacier plodding. The first time I climbed the mountain, over 25 years ago, the hut that Conway saw being constructed was still in use. Today, it has been replaced by a gleaming metal tower with an asymmetric ribbon of smoked glass providing panoramic views from an interior 'cascading staircase'. The sparse, light wood interior of the hut apparently retains 90% of the heat generated in the building, but feels strangely remote from the exterior world of rock and ice, unlike the draughty old hut.

With a reasonable forecast and a reservation at the hut, we walked up to the Riffelalp and contoured round the mountainside past the Riffelsee. Across the valley, the solitary Matterhorn and the great ridge of mountains from the Breithorn to Monte Rosa appeared from time to time through broken clouds. We crossed the flat expanse of the Gornergletscher and climbed a ridge of lateral moraine and slabby rocks beside the Grenz glacier to reach the hut. Like everyone else, we paced around the terrace, willing the clouds to clear, before turning in for an early night.

Next morning we set off at 03:00 beneath a starless sky, following a party of three Frenchmen up the rocky slopes behind the hut to reach the Monte Rosa glacier. After several hours of steady climbing, following a clear trail that wove its way between crevasses, dawn broke and the clouds that surrounded us gradually got brighter. The French turned back towards the hut but we carried on, trying to convince ourselves that the sky above was brightening, but there was little wind to bring a change in the weather. A steeper slope of hard snow finally led to a col and we turned left, climbing snow and scratched rocks to a final ridge and rocky scramble to the summit. There was no view, but the air was calm and surprisingly mild, and the scene had a certain airy silent beauty. After a rest, we started the long descent through increasingly soggy snow, passing several parties on their way to the summit. After stopping at the hut for tea, we continued across the Gornergletscher and caught the Gornergrat railway back to Zermatt at the end of a long day.

Peaks, Passes and Glaciers

Meanwhile, back in Leukerbad, I decided to carry on to the Lötschental, as Conway had originally intended, but first I had a rest day, starting with a leisurely breakfast at a civilised hour. A miniature plastic rubbish bin was provided on each breakfast table to accommodate the sundry butter wrappers, jam pots, cheese rinds and sachets of chocolate that inevitably accumulate during a proper Swiss breakfast. I suddenly realised that this crucial item –perhaps the greatest Swiss contribution to the culinary arts – had been missing during my walk through the French-speaking part of the country. Was this small plastic rubbish bin the first tangible proof that I had crossed from French- to German-speaking lands?

After breakfast I wandered around Leukerbad, replenishing my stock of cheese and salami, drinking coffee, catching up with my diary, watching people splash around in the baths, and generally being a bit of a *flâneur*. Murray's 1892 *Handbook for Travellers* described the bathers in Leukerbad as 'a motley company, of all ages, both sexes, and various ranks, delicate young ladies, burly friars, invalid officers, and ancient dames...ranged around the sides on benches, below the water, all clad in woollen mantles'. The guide noted that 'it is not a little amusing' to observe the spectacle.[261] On the day that I was there, the 'burly friars' were not in evidence, but a noticeably high proportion of visitors to Leukerbad were orthodox Jews.

I was joined in Leukerbad by Fiona, recently released from a conference in Basle, for the first long section of the walk that we had planned to do together. In British travel writing, husband and wife teams are exceedingly rare. Adventurous women wisely avoid the company of men, because to travel in their company inevitably reduces their own adventurousness in the prejudiced minds of both male and female readers. Likewise, the presence of a woman calls into question the heroic credentials of the intrepid male. It is, of course, inconceivable that Conway would have invited Katrina to join him on his walk through the Alps, and even more inconceivable that she would have agreed to go. In an interview with the *Daily Chronicle* in 1893, Conway was asked whether women were ever likely to take up mountaineering. 'Hardly, I should think', he replied. 'I'm rather afraid that mountaineering is not well suited to women, or they to it. A woman lacks staying power.'[262]

Throughout Conway's life, women played a small and narrowly defined role. From the age of 10, when he was separated from his two sisters and sent to an all-male boarding school, almost his entire professional and social life revolved around institutions that were actually, or effectively, all-male. Except when he needed money or a babysitter, he rarely visited his mother or his two sisters and, after their initial courtship, his relationship with Katrina appears to have been emotionally distant, despite the sentiment-laden letters that they exchanged during his long absences from home. In later life, Conway had at least two mistresses and clearly enjoyed the company of his daughter, Agnes, but only after she had learned to share his enthusiasms, and to subordinate her will to his. To Conway, the inequality of the sexes and the 'two spheres' in which they led their separate lives were unquestioned facts. While (English) men were bold and courageous, women suffered from a 'constitutional and proper timidity'.[263] It simply would not have occurred to Conway that a woman might consider herself his equal.

In 1924, during a debate in parliament on 'the flapper vote' – a proposal to reduce the voting age for women from 30 years – Conway supported a reduction to 25, but not to 21, because, as he pointed out in his speech, the years from 21 to 25 are a woman's 'flowering time': 'The older I get the more wonderful, the more beautiful, and the more admirable to me is that glorious flowering time of the young woman between the ages of 21 and 25...At that time of life they possess great and peculiar privileges, a tremendous opportunity, enormous power, and a halo of glory which the vote will not perhaps much dim, but which, at all events, it will not illuminate...[A] young woman of that age ought to be paying attention to other matters than voting. She ought to have her eye upon the glory of life at the threshold of which she stands and upon the prospects of family, of man's devotion and all that area of activity and command which is open to a woman.'[264] It was, perhaps, not entirely coincidence that the 68-year-old Conway was at this time having an affair with a 24-year-old woman called Monica Hadow.

While Conway continued his ruggedly all-male expedition, by hiring a horse and riding up the Lötschental, Fiona and I caught the cable car to the Rinderhütte. Rain lashed against the windows of the cabin and clouds obscured the view as we gained 1,000 warm, dry and effortless metres. At the top, we huddled in the cable car station and put on extra clothes before venturing out into the driving rain. On a clear day, the path to the Lötschental must be beautiful. It contours round the Torrenthorn, climbs over the desolate Restipass and then drops gradually down to Restialp. Near Kummenalp we disturbed a flock of mountain choughs that took off as one and scattered into the grey wind. The cloud began to break up as the day progressed, giving glimpses into the forested and rocky depths, but the mountain tops remained hidden and the hanging glaciers on the far side of the narrow valley seemed to fall out of the clouds.

Beneath Kummenalp, the Lötschenberg railway tunnel burrows through the mountainside, while above lies the old Lötschen Pass. Despite the presence of a glacier, battles between Bernese and Valaisan troops took place on the summit of the pass in 1384, 1419 and 1656. During the seventeenth century, the Bernese built a paved mule track on their side of the pass, but the Valaisans refused to pave their side, fearing that increased traffic would spread the influence of Protestantism. Today, the map of religious beliefs in Switzerland is a patchwork quilt of Catholicism and Protestantism, but the border between the Bernese Oberland and the Valais still marks a sharp divide between the two faiths. Catholicism held on in the remote mountains and valleys to the south of the Lötschen Pass, and so too did much older mysteries, such as the goblins and ghosts that still live in the dark forests and haunt the icy wastes.

We stayed at Fafleralp, in an old wooden hotel mellowed by time and use. The owner told us that it was built in 1908 and suffered a number of hard years during the First World War, but then 'the bankers from Geneva discovered it' and it has done well ever since. After a hot bath we crawled under crisp white duvets. This is how I remember holidays in Switzerland as a child. On rainy days, my parents would declare a 'Federbett day' and retreat to their room to read or sleep, while I impatiently paced about the hotel.

The next morning was clear. We rose early and followed the path upwards through pine forests that thinned out as we gained height, until there were just a few solitary trees stooped against the glacier winds. We climbed a boulder slope to the Anenhütte, a private refuge built in severe modernist style after the previous hut was swept away by an avalanche. After climbing ice-planed rocks and moraine on the true right of the glacier for a few hundred metres, we dropped onto the ice and roped up. I had crossed several glaciers during my solitary walk to this point, but they were all either relatively flat (and therefore unlikely to be heavily crevassed) or on mountains that were unlikely to have much snow cover, which makes solo glacier walking lower risk because you can see the crevasses. Over the next three days we were going to be almost continuously on ice, much of it probably covered with snow, and it felt good to have the security of a rope.

Conway recorded that the glacier had retreated about one kilometre up the Lötschental since the time his map was made. It has retreated at least another kilometre since. Above, we could see a centipede of a dozen or more 'climbers', led by a guide, descending the glacier in single file. Personally I cannot imagine anything worse than being part of such a large group, but at least they left a good trace through the fresh snow. Climbing steadily upwards we reached the Lötschenlücke (3,178 m) and gazed down upon the greatest glacier basin in the Alps on a perfect day. The sky was clear blue. To the right the black rocky ribs and dazzling white seracs of the Aletschhorn reached down to the flat expanse of the glacier. To the left a line of snowy peaks led eastwards towards the still-hidden Jungfrau, and in the distance stood the massive buttresses, snowfields, ridges and peaks of the Fiescherhorn, the Grünhorn and the Finsteraarhorn. Below, in the valley, a shimmering opalescent pool of mist hovered above the glacial crossroad of Konkordia. During a long walk you are often almost unaware of your surroundings. The body coasts along more or less rhythmically while the mind rambles through a hinterland of memory and hope. And then you see a view such as this, and it is a physical shock to see something so beautiful. The feeling lasts less than an instant, and then you get on with the business of drinking water, eating cheese, taking photographs. But an instant like that is more precious than a month of normal life.

The plod down the glacier to Konkordia was an anticlimax, and it was a hot struggle to get off the heavily crevassed glacier and up piles of loose moraine to the steps leading up to the hut. Looking down from the Lötschenlücke you might think that here, at least, is a truly wild scene that has changed very little since Conway's time. The steps to the hut show how wrong you would be. When the hut was built in 1877, the ice lay just 40 m below. The pioneers left that margin because they did not know whether the glacier would advance or retreat. During the intervening 140 years it has done both, but the overall trend has been a dramatic retreat. Today 60 m vertical height of ice has simply melted away, leaving the hut suspended some 100 m above the glacier on an ice-polished rocky plinth up which a remarkable metal staircase has been constructed. Konkordia has one of the most dramatic hut views in the Alps. To the north stand the Jungfrau and the Mönch. Directly below, four great glaciers meet and meld into one at the Konkordiaplatz (named after the Place de la Concorde in Paris – the same name given by Conway to a similar glacier crossroads in the Karakoram). To the south the Aletsch glacier, the longest in the Alps, sweeps majestically on towards the Valais with two distinctive black bands of medial moraine. Inside the hut there is a photograph of the glacier taken in 1890, just four years before Conway's visit, and exactly the same view taken today. The change is dramatic. As a result of higher temperatures, lower precipitation, or a combination of the two, this great river of ice is melting away and it is easy to imagine that it will disappear completely within a few generations if the present trend continues. However, alpine glaciers have advanced and retreated repeatedly in the relatively recent past, and not obviously because of human activity. In the Middle Ages several passes that are now covered by glaciers were free of ice and formed important trade routes. During the 'Little Ice Age', from about 1600 to 1850, the glaciers advanced and there were extremely cold periods around 1600, 1640, 1820 and 1850. The glaciers retreated again from 1850 to 1950 and then there was another short period of cooling. In *The Passage of the Alps*,[265] written in 1984, the main concern was that a future ice age might block existing transportation routes; but since the 1980s the alpine glaciers have retreated dramatically.

Conway's original plan was to climb the Finsteraarhorn, the highest peak in the Bernese Oberland. However, 'Fitzgerald's fortnight in hot Italy had put him out of condition...and he felt the need of repose.'[266] As a consequence, while Fitzgerald slept, Conway sent Carrel and Amar Sing down to Eggishorn for provisions, while he set off with Aymonod and Karbir to climb the Jungfrau (4,158 m). Not for the first time, I decided to deviate from Conway's route, but on this occasion I knew that I would have had Conway's full support for doing so. Even in Conway's day the Jungfrau was a relatively popular mountain. Today it is one of the most crowded 4,000 m peaks in the Alps. In 1896, two years after Conway's journey, engineers started tunnelling from the

Kleine Scheidegg near Grindelwald upwards through the Eiger to the Jungfraujoch (3,471 m), creating the highest railway in Europe. The railway finally opened in 1912, nine years behind schedule. Originally the engineers planned to continue to the summit of the Jungfrau, but the First World War intervened. In 1907 a planning application was also lodged to build a funicular railway up the Matterhorn, and the following year the Jungfraujoch railway company applied for permission to build a cable car to the summit of the Eiger.

The reaction to these developments in England was a scream of horror. In the 1880s Mark Twain estimated that 'half of the summer horde in Switzerland is made up of English people'.[267] By the 1900s, English tourists had been joined by large numbers of Germans, Americans, Russians and other nationalities, but they remained an influential force in the Swiss tourist industry. After writing a letter to *The Times*, Conway was elected President of the English branch of the League for the Preservation of Swiss Scenery in 1907. In its Second Annual Report, the League celebrated its success in opposing the Matterhorn railway, noting that 'English opinion is constantly appealed to in order to impress respect for unspoiled mountain scenery.'[268] Amongst its many activities, the English branch also successfully petitioned the council of Grindelwald to outlaw advertising placards in the town, campaigned against a proposed railway from Grindelwald over the Grosse Scheidegg to Meiringen and another from the summit of the Grosse Scheidegg, via the Faulhorn, to the Schynige Platte, as well as a 'sledge-train railway' down the Aletsch glacier from the Jungfraujoch station, across Konkordiaplatz, to Bel Alp in the Valais. The League was unashamedly elitist and puritanical in its outlook. It opposed both 'the vulgarisation of the Alps' and 'luxurious excitements of...bands, balls, parades and casinos'. The Bishop of Bristol stated that 'it was not merely the beauty, but the mystery of the beauty, that appealed to men...[W]hen the mystery, or the veil that hides the details, could be lifted only by a very few persons, then the beauty was at its very highest.'[269] Conway described the experience of seeing the view from the Jungfraujoch after climbing there, as opposed to travelling up on the railway, as 'the difference between a war medal and a five shilling piece'.[270]

Today, half a million tourists visit the Jungfraujoch each year. You can have lunch, send a postcard (marked with a special postmark) or make a call on your mobile to tell a friend where you are. At £100 for a second class ticket, the Jungfraujoch railway is deliberately packaged as a high-end tourist experience. The walls of the station are plastered with advertisements for Swiss watches and other expensive trinkets. There is also a huge photograph of the view, in case clouds mask the real thing. Large groups of Japanese tourists happily take photographs of each other against this photographic background.

Since we arrived at the Konkordia hut on a Friday in August, Fiona and I preferred to follow Conway's original plan of climbing the more remote Finsteraarhorn (4,274 m), rather than joining crowds of weekend climbers on the Jungfrau. The next day we set off late, climbed easily over the Grünhornlücke, and descended to the Finsteraarhorn hut which sits just above the Fiescher glacier at 3,048 m. The following morning we got up at 03:30 and were away by 04:00. My head torch refused to work and Fiona's faded alarmingly after a few minutes, so we stumbled up the rock and moraine slope behind the hut in semi-darkness. An angry dawn broke as we reached the ice, with black clouds towering over a fiery red horizon. As we climbed up the glacier towards a rocky ridge the wind grew stronger and the air was filled with biting particles of ice. At the Hugisattel, named after a geologist who reached this point in 1828, we huddled in the lee of a rocky outcrop and put on more clothes. A Swiss guide with two clients shouted out: 'In Scotland you would call this a sunny day.' The route to the summit is up an easy angled but exposed ridge of granite and ice. On a calm sunny day it must be a delight, but battered by snow-laden gusts of wind, we looked rather apprehensively up at the narrow rocky arête as it twisted into the clouds. After climbing for about an hour we reached a highpoint on the ridge and decided to call it a day. Did we reach the top? No; but it was good enough. We headed back down, reversing a steep section of mangled ice with some difficulty, and were soon racing back down the glacier to the hut.

Conway had even worse luck. Waking at 02:00 the weather was so bad that they abandoned all idea of climbing the Finsteraarhorn and instead headed over the Oberaarjoch to the Grimsel Pass. We followed in their footsteps the next day, dropping down onto the Fiescher glacier in time to witness a perfect dawn. Gazing across the rippled grey surface of the glacier we watched as the low-slanting sun slowly illuminated the peaks from top to bottom, turning the dark rocks of the Grosses Wannenhorn a rich chestnut brown. No matter how many alpine dawns you may have seen each one is still astonishing, as the sun over-compensates for hours of darkness with a blaze of glorious colour, before resuming normal daylight service.

After a few kilometres we turned left and climbed up the broken Galmi and Stude glaciers towards the Oberaarjoch. The sky was crystal clear and as we gained height the view that we should have seen from the Finsteraarhorn started to reveal itself: the Weisshorn, Matterhorn and Mischabel group floated on a sea of valley mist, glinting in the sun. It was turning into a hot day. Two long lines of climbers descending the broad glacier below the Oberaarjoch passed us like caravans in a desert. By the time we reached the col, the sky was bleached with light and the boulders of silvery-gold mica schist pulsated with heat. The Oberaar glacier stretched eastwards, seemingly for miles, before disappearing into a distant shimmering mirage. According to Emerson, 'the health of the eye seems to demand a horizon. We are never tired, so long as we can see far enough',[271] but it is a hot and weary vision to see a far distant horizon, and to know that it is your destination. We stumbled down through wet snow and rotting ice, reaching the terminal moraine just above the lake, and joined a good path running along its northern shore. A marmot whistled as we finally left the sterile world of rock and ice. After three days above the snowline we felt like pit ponies unleashed as we walked into the all-enveloping aroma of a warm alpine meadow.

Conway skirted the end of the Unteraar glacier and followed a path beside the infant River Aar at the start of its long journey through the lakes of Brienz and Thun to the capital city of Bern. The track he followed now lies deep beneath the waters of the Grimselsee. By coincidence, Coolidge followed the same route a few days after Conway. 'We saw your tracks on the Oberaarjoch, 5 days after you crossed', he wrote from the hotel at Grimsel. 'They are still full of the Gurkhas here – I was so sorry to miss them and you.'

We followed a road, and then an old mule track, above the south side of the new lake before dropping down to the Grimselpass road and crossing the dam to the Hospice. As we descended into the valley, the wind carried the unmistakable sound of an alpenhorn. The solitary player, presumably banished by family and neighbours, was accompanied by a haunting echo from the mountain walls.

Uri and Glarus

The Grimsel Hospice marked the midpoint of my journey through the Alps. After a long grey winter in London, Fiona and I returned to Switzerland in July the following year to resume the walk. The Grimselpass also marked a more subtle point of transition for Conway. By the time he arrived here he had been travelling for 50 days and, having climbed Mont Blanc and the Jungfrau, and made his side-trip to Zermatt to climb Monte Rosa, he had completed his journey through the highest and best known peaks of the Western Alps. Most members of the Alpine Club regarded the lesser peaks of the Eastern Alps as barely worthy of attention and one senses that Conway was beginning to lose momentum. Increasingly he adopted a 'rush and rest' approach, with three or four very long mountain days, followed by one or more rest days to recover. In his book, he gave detailed routes and times for each peak; and by this stage in his journey he was certainly very fit and moving fast. But perhaps he was getting bored and every mountain day, no matter how short, was becoming an effort. Conway's companion in the Karakoram, Charlie Bruce, was responsible for the controversial decision to equip the British army in India with shorts in 1897, but Conway always climbed in tweeds, as tradition dictated. With no water-proof clothing, his only protection against the wind and rain was a thick layer of dense wool; so as the days got hotter, he regularly complained about the suffocating heat in the valleys. He also complained about being footsore, which is hardly surprising given the distances he covered each day in heavy nailed boots. Modern clothing makes mountain travel comfortable in all but the most extreme conditions and this encourages the walker to linger. I suspect that part of the reason Conway hurried was because he was nearly always uncomfortable.

Conway's designated rest day at the Grimsel Hospice extended into

two, but the weather on the second day was so good that he felt guilty
and decided to set off after supper and climb through the night. Starting
just before midnight, they walked up the Nägelisgrätli to the Rhône
glacier and climbed the Galenstock (3,586 m). Two lantern slides in the
RGS Archives show dawn breaking from the arête of the Galenstock
and the Rhône glacier below, covered in deep snow. They descended all
the way to Göschenen, via the Tiefen and Damma glaciers, arriving late
in the afternoon. Following this lengthy outing, the Gurkhas rebelled
and demanded another rest day.

After nearly nine months without doing any serious mountaineering, Fiona and I decided that a 25 km walk with a height gain
and loss of well over 2,000 m and a high point of 3,586 m was probably not the best way to ease ourselves into the second leg of the journey.
As Conway observed: 'Before I was thirty years of age, I could go from
England to the Alps and climb the first day; it takes me now longer
every year to get into climbing condition.'[272] Instead, we decided to
divide the walk into two. From the Grimsel Hospice we walked up to
the pass, following in the footsteps of the French troops who in 1799
defeated the Austrians, who had taken up a defensive position on the
Grimselpass in an attempt to block the French advance into the Rhône
valley. After the battle, the dead were thrown into the 'Totensee', or Lake
of the Dead, on the summit of the pass. In Conway's day, a carriage road
was slowly being blasted through the rocky landscape; and today the
Totensee still retains its sombre atmosphere despite the busy road that
passes along its northern shore.

The weather was dull when we set out, but the warm sun soon
burned off the morning mist. Climbing slowly up the granite staircase
of the Nägelisgrätli, views began to open up back towards the snowy
Finsteraarhorn and Oberaarhorn. Rather than heading up the Rhône
glacier to the Galenstock, as Conway had done, we crossed the ice to
the moraine slopes above Belvedere and contoured round the hillside
to the Furka Pass. During the last Ice Age, the Rhône glacier was the
longest in the Alps. Fed by numerous tributaries from the Bernese and
Pennine Alps, it filled the Valais with ice. At Lake Geneva it divided into
two: the northern limb scoured its way across the plains to Bern, while
the southern limb reached the outskirts of Lyon. At the beginning of the

nineteenth century the glacier still stretched as far as the village of Gletsch, and in Conway's day it terminated in a spectacular icefall into the upper Valais, remnants of which I remember seeing as a child. Today all that remains is a waterfall. Even the famous ice grotto above the fall is melting away, despite being swaddled in white plastic in a vain attempt to deflect the sun's destructive rays.

From the Furka Pass we walked to the Sidelenhütte, which was full of weekend visitors drawn to the rock climbing on the granite spires that surround the Galenstock. Many of them were clearly regulars. When the guardian announced the dinner menu each course got a cheer, but the biggest roar was reserved for the chocolate mousse. Next morning we followed the 'Nepali Highway', skirting steep cliffs to the snout of the Tiefen glacier, where ice has scooped the valley floor into rounded troughs and domes of granite, some almost as smooth as a kitchen worktop. The path climbed steeply upwards to the Lochberglücke (2,815 m) with fine views back to the Galenstock and the more distant Weisshorn and Dom. The path was more *Berg* than *Weg*, but eventually we reached the high meadows of the Göscheneralp, where a herd of goats with hair the colour of a freshly opened conker formed a strong attachment to us and pursued us almost to the lake shore.

The town of Göschenen stands at the point where the St. Gotthard railway and motorway plunge underground to reappear on the southern slopes of the Alps at Airolo in the Ticino. The valley of the Reuss is a good example of geological determinism: at a stretch, you could almost argue that Switzerland itself is the product of the St. Gotthard Pass. Opened up in the thirteenth century, the pass was initially nothing more than a narrow path with a few bridges suitable for pack animals or porters, but the St. Gotthard provided the most direct and the lowest (at just 2,106 m) route between northern and southern Europe in the central Alps. The wealth of Lucerne, and the three cantons of Schwyz, Uri and Unterwalden that formed the nucleus of the Swiss Confederation, was largely built on the trade that flowed over the St. Gotthard between Flanders and Milan. During the eighteenth century the spectacular 'Devil's Bridge' over the River Reuss became a famous stopping-off point on the Grand Tour, inspiring numerous artists, including Turner, and helping to establish Switzerland as a tourist destination in its own right. A carriage road was built in 1822 and the railway was completed 60 years later, at a cost of more than 200 lives, including the chief engineer who died of a heart attack in the tunnel.

Conway took the train down the valley from Göschenen to Amsteg, and it is true that the appeal of walking between these two towns is not immediately obvious from the map. The valley of the Reuss seems barely wide enough to accommodate a river, a road, a motorway and a railway. However, the footpath that starts at Göschenen station and advertises itself, rather unpromisingly, as the Gotthardbahnweg proved to be of interest even to non-train spotters. Passing through woods, orchards and scattered chalets, with wild strawberries growing beside the path, it provided a remarkably peaceful route through the valley, while railways and roads bored through the mountainside or soared overhead on concrete stilts. At roughly the midpoint lies the village of Wassen, where the railway passes through two huge corkscrew tunnels to gain height. Conway and his fellow climbers used to amuse themselves by watching their compass needles revolve as the train steamed through the darkness. The railway briefly turned Wassen into an unlikely industrial centre. Granite quarried near the village was used to build the harbour of Valletta in Malta as well as the fine baronial-style turbine hall at Amsteg, where hydroelectricity was generated to power increasingly heavy trains up the steep incline when the railway was electrified in 1920.

A series of interpretative boards along the path extol these feats of Swiss engineering and the strategic significance of the St. Gotthard railway as the main transportation link between Germany and Italy. One board explained that during the Second World War the pass was vital to the Germans as they sought to extend the war in Italy after the collapse of Mussolini's government in 1943. As one board proudly explained, allowing the German army free access to the railway for the transportation of men and arms to Italy 'probably enabled Switzerland to preserve its neutrality'.

In Amsteg, Conway stayed at 'the old Hôtel Stern' where 'the kindly host...made us comfortable for the night, and we slept so well that it was nine o'clock next morning before we were on the road'.[273]

We too stayed at the Hotel Stern, attracted by the sweet smell of linden trees growing in the garden. The hotel has been extended over the years but the original inn has been preserved and is now a protected building. The dining room and the *Gaststube* both have low wood-beamed ceilings and panelled walls, with huge sideboards and a wood-burning stove dating from 1788, fed via a hatch door in the hall. The racks above the stove must have dried the clothes of generations of travellers passing up and down the St. Gotthard Pass before the railway was built. Goethe stayed here three times. So too, no doubt, did many famous Englishmen, but they were of less interest to the Tresch family that ran the hotel for over 200 years until it was sold just a few years ago. Even in Conway's day, the Hotel Stern was a quiet backwater, left behind by the modern technology of steam.

Conway continued his rather slow progress the next day by wandering up the Maderanertal for a few hours before spending the night at the Swiss Alpine Club hotel. Showing slightly more resolve, we walked up the valley, had a coffee at the hotel, which has changed little since Conway's time, and continued to the Hüfihütte. The lower part of the Maderanertal is a pretty, wooded valley famous for its quartz crystals. The hut sits at the head of the valley, on a grassy shoulder overlooking the final icefall of the Hüfi glacier with the craggy peaks of the Gross Windgallen and the Schärhorn standing behind. We were the only people staying at the hut and the guardian, who spoke splendidly guttural and completely incomprehensible *Schwyzerdütsch*, seemed slightly surprised to see us. Nevertheless, he provided a fine dinner rounded off with a huge bowl of banana custard – evidently the house speciality since there was a great pile of empty Fyffes boxes in the cellar.

The next day Conway walked up the valley, past the hut, and continued up the ice, climbing a low ridge on the south side of the Hüfi glacier to a col, which he named Gurkha Pass. He and Fitzgerald then climbed the two rocky peaklets either side of the col, claiming two first ascents. Conway conceded that there appeared to be a cairn on the top of his peak, but he always maintained that a first ascent only counted if it was recorded. From the col, they descended to the Russien Alp and intended to climb the Tödi the following day, via the Porta da Spescha, which celebrates an attempt by the Benedictine monk Placidus a

Spescha to climb the mountain in 1824. However, bad weather forced them to give up the attempt and instead they climbed back over the Sand Pass and descended towards Linthal.

We left the Hüfi hut in thick mist with a warm wind blowing from the south. Through breaks in the clouds the high rocky pyramid of the Windgallen appeared from time to time, apparently suspended in mid-air. Roping up, and taking a compass bearing, we picked our way easily enough through the lower crevasses but, as we gained height, soft slushy snow covered the surface of the glacier sufficiently deeply to obscure the crevasses, but not deeply enough to support our weight. About half way up, the inevitable happened and I fell into a crevasse and spent a breathless few minutes trying to fight my way out. Near the col the glacier steepened slightly and visibility deteriorated further. We followed an encouraging line of stakes near the summit (3,007 m) and started to descend the Clariden glacier before realising our mistake and turning back. There are few things as tiring as climbing back up a steep slope that you have just descended as a result of a navigational error, but vigorous swearing helps to alleviate the toil. Finally, the Planura hut loomed out of the mists, perched on a rocky stump, and we joined a well-marked path for the 2,200 m descent into the Linthal, over snow and dark shaley scree. To our left, cascades of melt water from the Clariden glacier tumbled over limestone cliffs. Ahead, the rocky buttresses of the Tödi rose up and disappeared into the clouds. After about 800 m of descent, moss and a few flowers began to appear amongst the rocky rubble. At Ober Sandalp a thin but fairly continuous carpet of grass sprinkled with asters covered the gravelly soil. Cows appeared, and a few summer chalets. Unexpectedly, the river we had been following suddenly ran dry, its waters diverted into a man-made sink hole. We descended a steep cow path carved into the mountainside to Hinter Sand, where an amphitheatre of rocky peaks almost enclosed a flat expanse of sleek grass. High above, a powerful waterfall burst over boulders and ledges and then simply disappeared, leaving the riverbed in the valley below completely dry. By now the cow path had become a track and at Vord Sand scattered birch and spruce appeared. The diversity of species multiplied as we descended until we were walking through mixed woodland with a dense undergrowth of shrubs. The gritty grey soil of the high meadows was replaced by rich, brown loam, and garish green moss clung to every boulder. As Conway observed: 'Never do low levels look so beautiful, so incredibly rich, as when one descends upon them after several days spent in the heights.'[274]

We were in limestone country, and the rivers have carved deep sinuous channels through the rock, resembling caves more than valleys. At a narrowing in one gorge the track crossed the Pantenbrücke, an ancient stone bridge thrown across a gap less than 10 m wide but perhaps 50 m deep. The Pantenbrücke is now a double-storeyed bridge consisting of a lower footbridge, which Conway must have used, originally constructed in the fifteenth century and most recently repaired in 1854; and a narrow road bridge dating from 1902. Continuing down the valley we finally arrived in Tierfehd (805 m) and found the explanation for the disappearing rivers. The valley floor was entirely occupied by a vast construction site where contractors were building a reservoir, a pumping station and a series of tunnels to gather the waters of the surrounding valleys into the Limmersee dam, 1,000 m above Tierfehd. It was an unpleasant surprise to discover that the hotel where Conway stayed, and where we had also hoped to spend the night, was at the very centre of the site and now served as a construction camp for the people who worked there. After another weary hour of walking we gratefully arrived at the Obbort Gasthaus on a grassy platform some 200 m above the valley floor, with a bird's-eye view of the construction activity below.

At Tierfehd, Fitzgerald had discovered that he was suffering from toothache and decided to go directly to Bad Ragaz by the valley route with Aymonod. Conway was also dreaming of 'the flesh-pots of Ragatz' and 'a day or two's rest, in the company of friends and baggage';[275] but whereas Fitzgerald had a private income of £5,000 a year and probably didn't give a damn what people thought, Conway had a living to earn and a reputation to make. Next day he set off, with Carrel and the Gurkhas, to climb the Hausstock, and Fiona and I dutifully followed in his footsteps.

The route to the Muttseehütte follows a series of grassy alps interspersed with cliffs, and then climbs over a col to a desolate rocky hollow. Conway described the hut, which was built in 1887, as 'the perfection of an Alpine refuge...warmly built of wood, sufficiently furnished and excellently situated', and declared the area 'essentially "wild"'.[276] He would not recognise the scene that awaited us. A white modular construction camp had been assembled beside the inky waters of the Muttsee, served by an aerial cable way. Surrounded by a bleak landscape of dark shattered cliffs and slatey rubble, it looked like a science fiction mining camp on some remote and barren planet. The Muttsee hut was overheated and boasted a flat screen TV for the entertainment of the construction workers who are paid to stay there. Climbers, who pay for the pleasure of staying in cold mountain huts, instinctively reject such comforts.

Next morning we left the hut just before dawn and contoured above what remained of the lake on a wet slippery slope of rocky debris. Men and machines were already at work in the fenced and floodlit construction site and a persistent, penetrating drizzle fell upon the dismal scene. The Ruchi (3,107 m) is a mountain that is well advanced in the process of disintegrating into mud. In level places, the saturated rock had a curious bouncy feel, like springy turf. On the steep rubbly slopes it was a bitter struggle to make upward progress. Stand still for a moment to recover your breath and you gently slide back into the valley. Eventually we got off the rotting west face and climbed the ridge to the summit in dense cloud. Retracing our steps and dropping down slightly, we followed the north-east ridge for a short distance before it narrowed to a sharp arête of crumbling slate and dropped steeply to a notch. On the far side the ridge broadened, purple boulders of slate glistened in the sleety rain, and a short scramble led to the summit of the Hausstock (3,158 m). Zero visibility, sleet and a brisk wind did not encourage us to linger, and we soon set off down a snowfield leading, we hoped, to the Glacier de Mer. The slope was just a bit too steep and icy to allow a descent facing out and so necessitated laborious kicking facing into the slope. When we finally reached the glacier we dropped beneath the cloud base and crossed a crevasse zone just above the terminal moraine. Following a small river down towards the Panixerpass, we walked through a desert of broken rock. Eventually a few solitary flowers appeared amongst the rubble. By the time we reached the pass we were walking through a gorgeous alpine meadow. An old mule track led over the pass and down a steep-sided limestone valley with two steps over which waterfalls gushed and spumed. Joining the road at Unter Stafel, we descended into a verdant valley of emerald fields and dripping trees. Behind us, the Hausstock was still shrouded in cloud, but ahead the sun shone on the village of Elm with its dark wooden chalets, bright red geraniums and comfortable well-fed cats.

During our descent from the Panixerpass to Elm we had unwittingly reversed the route followed by the great Russian general Alexander Suvorov during his 1799-1800 campaign against the French in Italy and Switzerland. Suvorov was 70 years old and the veteran of no fewer than 63 battles against Prussians, Poles and Turks when he set out to fight Napoleon. After defeating the French army near Milan he triumphantly entered Turin and was made a Prince of the House of Savoy by King Charles Emmanuel of Piedmont-Sardinia. Continuing his advance towards Genoa, he chased the French back to the Riviera, but Russia's Austrian and British allies switched the main focus of the campaign to the Low Countries and Suvorov never achieved his ambition of meeting Napoleon on the battlefield. Diverted north to Switzerland, he was confronted by a vastly superior French force of 80,000 men and, on 6 October 1799, he and his 18,000 regulars and 5,000 Cossacks were forced to make a tactical retreat over the Panixerpass. He safely reached Chur in the Rhine valley with the bulk of his army intact, but lost many of his cannons; and some 200 men froze to death crossing the pass in deep snow. Suvorov was one of the very few military leaders in history who never lost a battle – a distinction he shares with Alexander the Great and Genghis Khan – and was rewarded with the highest Russian military title of Generalissimo. There is a plaque on the chalet where he stayed in Elm and a statue of the great man in the main street.

Elm is also famous for a huge landslip that occurred in 1881, just a few years before Conway's visit. Conway devoted a whole chapter of his book to the disaster, which I suspect he had written before he left London and simply posted to the *Pall Mall Gazette* from Elm as an easy way of meeting his obligation to submit ten articles. Nevertheless, it is an interesting tale. The slopes above Elm contain valuable deposits of slate that were worked by the villagers over several decades in an increasingly chaotic manner. Cracks and minor landslips began to occur near the quarries, but the warning signs were ignored until a series of huge mud and rock slides destroyed the village on 11 September 1881. As the dust settled, it revealed a scene of utter devastation. The rock avalanche buried an area of 900,000 square metres to a depth of between 10 and 20 metres, and 115 villagers lost their lives. When Conway visited Elm, the villagers still recalled the day with 'tears in their eyes and white horror upon their faces'.[277] Today the tongue of rubble is covered with trees, but a memorial in the churchyard records the names of the dead.

High above the village there is a remarkable natural arch called the Martinsloch, through which the rising sun illuminates the church tower in Elm twice each year, at around the time of the equinox. Feeling lazy after a long day on the Hausstock, we took the cable car to the Tschingelalp and walked slowly up to the Segnaspass hut on the ridge just to the north of the Martinsloch. Conway set off early from Elm, determined to reach Bad Ragaz. He climbed up to the Martinsloch, ascended the Piz Segnas, and walked down the Calfeisenthal to Vättis arriving late in the afternoon. Having secured lodgings for Carrel and the Gurkhas in the village, he hired a coach for himself and set off for Bad Ragaz, urging the coachman to drive as fast as possible to avoid a rainstorm that was coming down the valley. They finally arrived 'at the door of the Quellenhof, whose well-dressed inhabitants, just emerging from dinner, regarded, and were justified in so doing, as some wild apparition dropped upon them from another world'.[278]

We followed at a more measured pace, enjoying the dawn views from the ex-army observation post overlooking the Sardona 'tectonic arena' of folds and thrusts (a world heritage site), before dropping down to flattish moraine at the foot of Piz Segnas. After climbing a small snowfield to mid height, we zigzagged up unconsolidated rubble to the east ridge and the summit (3,099 m). To the south, the early morning sun illuminated the rippled surface of a cloud sea over Flims. To the west, there were fine views of the Hausstock and the icy Glarner-Vorab-Bündner, with the Tödi in the distance and the fertile valley of Elm below. Conway must be one of the very few people who has climbed Piz Segnas and not continued to the summit of Piz Sardona (3,056 m).

Just 2 kilometres apart, the ridge connecting the two peaks barely drops below 3,000 m and provides easy walking with grand views in both directions. Returning to a small col beneath the second peak, we headed east down the Sardona glacier to a line of cliffs with a steep scrambling descent to the lower glacier and a good path down a moraine ridge to the Sardona hut.

By the time Conway arrived in the Calfeisenthal he was footsore, weary and in a foul mood. He cursed the lumpiness of the ground, the vileness of the path and the fecklessness of the drunken peasants. Conway frequently remarked upon the propensity of the Swiss to lie drunk in their fields with wooden spirit-flasks held to their mouths. Such displays of public inebriation are not an image that one instantly associates with Switzerland today, but is there a deeply repressed Dionysian streak lying dormant within the modern Swiss? Perhaps one catches a glimpse of it in the guilty pleasure they obviously take in drinking a glass of strong lager first thing in the morning.

Our walk down the beautiful Calfeisenthal was more enjoyable than Conway's. Seen from above, the valley looks as if someone has taken a crumpled sheet of green baize and poked tiny pine trees into it to produce the perfect combination of forest and meadow. There is a good track along the valley floor, passing through tunnels beside the long, dark Gigerwaldsee in its narrow gorge. We arrived in Vättis to find the village plagued by flies. Our evening meal, on a sunny terrace beneath the rocky spires of Calanda, was punctuated by regular thwacks as a Swiss woman at the next table administered a fly-swat, neatly piling up the corpses in an ashtray.

Next day we strolled down to Bad Ragaz on a clear sunny morning, passing through cool woods with patches of mist hanging over the river, and grassy meadows where the farmers were making hay. At Valens we descended steeply through forest to the romantic River Tamina and reached Bad Pfäfers, a baroque bathhouse with a long vaulted hall running the length of the building and tiled baths in the dank cellars. A pathway led from the baths into a deep and spectacular gorge, broad at the base but narrowing to a tiny slit near the top. Shafts of sunlight entered the gloomy depths like golden spotlights. It must have been a truly sublime experience for early visitors to the baths, who were blindfolded for their peace of mind and then lowered into the gorge on the end of a rope.

Standing close to the banks of the Rhine, Bad Ragaz has the feel of a prosperous and rather dull provincial town in southern Germany. Lowland architecture has crept up the valley to the edge of the Alps and ice axes look distinctly out of place here. I wondered why Conway had made such a long detour to get here until I read Murray's 1892 *Handbook for Travellers in Switzerland*, which states that Bad Ragaz 'thrives chiefly on visitors attracted by its excellent hotels'. The *Handbook* described Conway's chosen rest halt, the Quellenhof, as 'a palace in extent and architecture'. Naturally, it boasted an Anglican church. The Quellenhof still stands amidst formal gardens, with the hot baths, a golf course, a casino and the church all close at hand. The modern visitor also benefits from one further amenity. Across the river, near Maienfeld, stands Heididorf – a re-creation of the village invented by Switzerland's best-known author, Johanna Spyri. Here visitors can meet Heidi and Peter the goatherd, and presumably take it in turns to push Klara's wheelchair over a cliff. Heididorf is said to be extremely popular, particularly with Japanese tourists. Unfortunately, our schedule did not allow us time to visit it.

While Conway and Fitzgerald enjoyed themselves 'upstairs' at the Quellenhof, the guides were having an equally good time in the servants' quarters. Reflecting the diversity of the guests staying at the hotel, there were maids and manservants from England, France, Germany, Austria, Holland, Russia, Turkey and Egypt. Carrel was particularly taken by a young maid from Constantinople who sat next to him at the servants' table, while Aymonod praised the excellence of the food and declared that Bad Ragaz was the finest place he had ever visited. After three days of indulgence, Conway finally managed to drag himself away from the Quellenhof, taking the train to Grüsch and walking up to the Schamella hut (now called the Schesaplana hut).

Following a stormy night, staying at a comfortable but more modest hotel in Bad Ragaz, Fiona departed for London, while I pressed on to Austria. Walking across the rich agricultural valley of the Rhine, the cool morning air smelt pleasantly of wet earth and cow manure. On the lower slopes of the mountains on the far side of the valley I passed through vineyards with bunches of unripe grapes the size of peas. Above, the path climbed into the cloud forest. At Enderline the trees came to an end and the path went up a series of narrow grassy ramps between steep limestone cliffs to the Fläscher Fürggli. I had intended to climb the Falknis, which stands just above the pass, in order to step briefly into Liechtenstein, but in the end I couldn't be bothered. Sliding down a muddy cow track, I walked past a string of small lakes in the Fläscher valley before contouring and climbing to the Schesaplana hut, which was packed with weekend walkers and mountain bikers.

The next morning, cloud was dammed up in the valley, but the sky directly overhead was brighter and I had hopes of breaking through into sunshine as I climbed. Seen from directly below, the south face of the Schesaplana, the highest peak of the Raetikon Alps, looks steep and rocky; but as you climb up, the angle relents and breaks appear between the outcrops. Conway stated that a clever pony might be taken up it, which is probably an exaggeration, but a good path laces its way between the difficulties to emerge on the shoulder of the mountain just below the summit which, on this occasion, was just above the clouds. In the distance a few other snow-capped peaks poked out above the surface of the clouds, but the plains of northern Europe lay beneath a thick layer of cumulus. Like Aconcagua, which fails to reach the arbitrary, but magical, height of 7,000 m by just 40 m, the Schesaplana fails to reach 3,000 m by a similar margin. Nevertheless, Conway appears to have counted this as one of his 'peaks', justifying its inclusion on the grounds that 'of all the mountains in the Alps, this is perhaps the one which, in the case of English climbers, has attracted the very élite. On its summit have stood almost all the men of a former climbing generation, who gave to mountaineering its peculiar *éclat*.'[279] On a Saturday morning in late July, the summit was crowded with walkers, happy to stand on this sunny northern outpost of the Alps, before returning to the workaday plains beneath the clouds. Descending its rocky eastern slopes, I entered Austria.

Chapter Six
Lord Conway 1918–37

The Best Club in the World

Manton Marble left a legacy that was far smaller than Conway had hoped for and imagined. Like any wise and wealthy man, Marble had given freely while he was still alive to enjoy his own generosity – 'given as though you weren't giving at all, but as it were dealing out some common fund', as Conway approvingly remarked following their visit to Egypt in 1889. The heavy demands placed upon his benevolence by his stepdaughter and her husband, combined with the losses that he sustained by co-investing with them, steadily depleted even Marble's considerable fortune, and by the time he died there was relatively little left. As a result, Conway's long-term financial position remained precarious. Nevertheless, he embarked upon a new phase of building at Allington, creating a formal garden, a gatehouse and restoring Solomon's Tower in the south-west corner of the castle. Much of the planning was carried out by Philip Tilden, an impoverished but brilliant young architect whom Agnes had met during the war. Tilden later worked on Chartwell in Kent for Winston Churchill and designed Bron-y-de in Surrey for David Lloyd George. A further phase of work was carried out at Allington some years later with the restoration of the north-east wing, including the 'reconstruction' of the Great Hall, based on the hall at Berkeley Castle near Bristol, which Conway visited in 1927. The Great Hall was completed, but never heated, while the north-east wing was still work in progress at the time of Conway's death.

Dame Joan Evans, who wrote a history of the Conway family in 1966, first appears in Conway's diary in 1918, when she visited Agnes at Allington Castle. Later a respected medievalist and art historian, Evans described Agnes' rooms in Solomon's Tower as being the most beautiful in all the castle 'in their simplicity and appropriateness to a medieval setting',[280] suggesting that she did not entirely approve of Conway's collection of Egyptian artefacts, Greek and Roman busts, medieval statues, Italian Renaissance paintings, Elizabethan furniture, ceramics, Turkish and Kashmiri carpets, Hindu temple friezes, Chinese silks and walrus heads. She later described Conway as a man of 'interesting but fallible taste'.

The constituency of the Combined English Universities, for which Conway was now one of two members of parliament, was created in 1918 to represent the graduates of the eight English universities that then existed in addition to Oxford, Cambridge and London, which already returned members of parliament. In order to have a *pied à terre* close to Westminster, Conway purchased 47 Romney Street, within the division bell district and just a few hundred metres from his childhood home in Dean's Yard. He described it as being a small Westminster slum. The same house is now 'a spacious elegant end of terrace house with five bedrooms' and was on the market in 2010 for £2 million.

During the 12 years that he served as a member of parliament, Conway fought and won five general elections, steadily increasing his majority almost regardless of the national swing. He had resigned his membership of the Liberal Eighty Club and withdrawn his subscription from the Liberal Central Association in the 1900s, long before he became a Conservative member of parliament, but Conway still found David Lloyd George and Ramsay MacDonald, the Liberal and Labour leaders respectively, more congenial than the leaders of his own party, Bonar Law and later Stanley Baldwin. Conway reconciled the apparent contradiction of joining a party with which he had little political sympathy by convincing himself that the university constituencies were, in some way, above party politics. 'Fortunately for me a University Member is not supposed to be a strong party man, so I was able as such to fulfil my function without distress',[281] he noted.

With his puckish manner, Conway allowed himself gently to chide members of his own party, as well as Liberal and Labour, in speeches that were variously described as 'original' or 'vigorous and picturesque'.[282] He used his first major speech in the House (in relation to a housing bill intended to expedite the construction of 'homes fit for heroes') to express his astonishment at finding that 'in the minds of the bulk of Hon. Members the good things of this world consisted in higher wages and shorter hours of labour'. As Conway pointed out: 'Neither higher wages nor shorter hours of labour in themselves are a good thing...Money is no good unless you know how to spend it, and time is no good except to those who know how to use it.'[283] He also opposed unemployment insurance: 'It is so easy, under the enthusiasm of sympathy...to vote the money of other people for the alleviation of distress. Anyone can do that and go away home feeling as though he has performed a virtuous action, when, in fact, he has quite vicariously satisfied an emotion by charity which involves no sacrifice whatever on his part.'[284] On education, he advocated that greater trust be placed in teachers, who should be freed from the tyranny of fixed curricula and inspections: 'I am sorry to observe a considerable diminution in the number of boys who run away to sea...it seems to be a practice which is falling into desuetude. I am sorry to hear it...The diminution in the number of boys running away to sea rather tends to show that there is a diminution of adventurousness in our boys. What is the cause of that? I am sorry to say the answer is a simple one. It is our system of education. We educate every boy who comes to school in a manner which makes him a clerk in an office.'[285]

Occasionally Conway's lack of strong party affiliation enabled him to be disarmingly honest about the realities of democratic government. The parliament that was elected in 1918 had to cope with a massive deficit after the war, just as today we face the consequences of the financial meltdown in 2008. Then, as now, politicians chose to ignore economic realities as they sought election: 'I do not think many candidates at the last General Election went before their constituencies and said, "We have passed through a war, we have come out from it victoriously, but we have lost all our savings in the process. We are going now to have to work harder than ever before. We are going to have to live on a lower standard of life than before. We have got to save, we have a vast debt to pay, we have got to knuckle down to it and work as we never worked in our lives before." That would have been a reasonable thing to say, but how many candidates at the last General Election said anything at all comparable to that? The result was that the House of Commons was elected, charged, or at all events inspired, by the country to give everybody a good time.'[286] But speeches of this kind were the exception rather than the rule.

During his early years as an MP, Conway harboured ambitions of holding high office. When he entered parliament the Conservatives formed part of a coalition led by the Liberal prime minister Lloyd George – 'the man who won the war' – but the coalition became increasingly fractious with the advent of peace. Winston Churchill, at this point in his career a member of the Liberal party, but invariably ambitious, started to take soundings from Conway and other back-benchers about whether he should challenge Lloyd George for the leadership. Conway's diary for 20 April 1921 reads: 'Savile, dinner of 14 with Winston Churchill for guest. Revelled at [Lord] Winborne['s] House till 1:30...Supposed to be part of propaganda for Winston to be next PM.' The Conservatives ultimately withdrew from the coalition, forcing a general election in November 1922 in which Bonar Law became the new Conservative prime minister. Conway was re-elected with an increased majority but remained a backbencher, much to his disappointment.

Law resigned due to ill health and was succeeded as prime minister by Stanley Baldwin, who called another election in 1923, which resulted in a hung parliament. Baldwin was forced to resign after losing a vote of no confidence in 1924, and Ramsay MacDonald became the first Labour prime minister. Two days after his defeat, Conway recorded in his diary that he had a 'long talk with Stanley Baldwin. Found him very simple, attractive and entirely composed...Has done his best under circumstances over which his control was of the slightest.' Two weeks later Conway 'met Ramsay MacDonald on the steps of the US Club and lunched there with him. Long and intimate talk. Asked me to propose him for the Athenaeum which I did.' Later that month, at MacDonald's request, Conway intervened in the 'Luxor excavation squabble' following Howard Carter's spectacular discovery of Tutankhamen's tomb, although it is not entirely clear what the squabble was about or what his intervention consisted of. On 4 March, Conway successfully shepherded MacDonald's election through the Athenaeum membership committee. The following day the prime minister dined with him at the club.

Having established good relations with the Conservative and

Labour prime ministers who would hold office for the remainder of his political career, Conway turned his attention back to Churchill, who clearly fascinated him. In the 1922 election the electorate of Dundee were presented with a clear choice between Winston Churchill and a socialist prohibitionist. They chose the latter. Churchill contested the 1923 election as a Liberal standing in Leicester, and lost again. By 1924 his political allegiance was gradually shifting back towards the Conservative party, but he contested the by-election in the Abbey division of Westminster as an 'Independent Anti-Socialist'. Conway 'dined at Lady Astor's…went on to Winston Churchill's and there met some 20 MP who stopped in and discussed [Churchill's] policy as candidate for Westminster…Home very late.' The Westminster constituency was home to at least a hundred MPs, including Conway, and the by-election generated considerable interest. Despite standing against the official Conservative party candidate, Churchill succeeded in enlisting nine sitting Conservative MPs, including Conway, to preside over the ward committees. Conway chaired a large and rowdy election meeting in Drury Lane on 11 March and the next day called on Lord Beaverbrook, the press baron, to drum up media support for Churchill's campaign. Meanwhile, Churchill drove around the West End in a coach and four with a trumpeter on the box. Churchill described it as 'incomparably the most exciting, stirring, sensational election I have ever fought',[287] but he was defeated by 43 votes, much to his and Conway's disgust. Nevertheless, Conway enjoyed the lunch arranged by the Duke of Marlborough for Churchill and his closest supporters. Later that year, Conway played a minor role in persuading Baldwin to put down the motion that removed Ramsay MacDonald from office and returned Baldwin as prime minister. 'It has been most exciting', he wrote to Katrina, but Baldwin did not offer him a ministerial post, and Conway began to lose interest in politics.

During one of his Slade lectures at Cambridge, Conway observed that 'the safe alternatives for an art critic are praise and silence'.[288] Increasingly he adopted a similar approach to politics, devoting himself less to causes than to courting popularity: 'From the very beginning I devoted myself to the Smoking Room, and there I made friends with men of all parties',[289] he recalled in his memoirs. Conway regarded the

House of Commons as the best club in the world and set about becoming the best-liked clubman within it. A 'Political Sketch' in *The Graphic*, published on 1 August 1925, probably gives a fair idea of Conway's public image as a politician: 'Of course he is frightfully clever, as the Slade Professor of Fine Arts at Cambridge is bound to be. He knows most of what there is to know about art, literature and many other matters, but I can imagine a hostess telling expectant guests that he is clever in such a "nice" way...He became, perhaps, the most famous of English mountaineers...He has explored great tracts of unknown territory, discovered gold-fields and rich rubber-producing areas, has scores of times been within an ace of various forms of sudden and violent death...He has, I believe, very clear cut political views, but he seldom puts them forward...[He is] a very companionable man.'

During the course of his life Conway perfected the art of making useful friends (and marriages) and he used his new status as a member of parliament to seek fresh rewards and recognition. Despite his speech on the need for fiscal restraint, he vigorously defended universities, art galleries and museums against budget cuts and was duly rewarded with honorary doctorates from Durham and Manchester University, a trusteeship of the National Portrait Gallery and membership of the Advisory Committee of the Victoria and Albert Museum. After conducting a successful campaign on behalf of gramophone manufacturers to change the copyright laws relating to dramatic and musical performances, Conway 'went to Oxford Street gramophone depot to choose a machine which they are giving to me in memory of my getting their bill passed last session of parliament'. Conway's concern with border security sounds remarkably modern: 'Honest citizens are met with every kind of difficulty, but your revolutionary of the lowest order has very little difficulty indeed in dodging all the impediments put in his way, and I should think it was far preferable to let in an occasional undesirable in order to save the time, worry, nerve, temper and efficiency of the vast mass of our own people travelling abroad.'[290] But his vigorous campaign against the imposition of visas and passport controls was inspired not by 'honest citizens' but by the tourist industry, led by his good friend Sir Henry Lunn, who saw to it that Conway enjoyed a vast amount of free travel.

During the latter part of his parliamentary career the issues with which he concerned himself were essentially non-political, and largely concerned with the preservation of things or places that he regarded as beautiful. He rarely spoke in the House, but when he did it was generally as spokesman for the arts: seeking to exclude fine works of art from death duties (to abate the flood of art treasures across the Atlantic) or campaigning for the preservation of ancient monuments, particularly City churches. He also started a public campaign against littering in public parks and pleasure gardens and opposed uncontrolled ribbon development along major roads – the 'horrible outburst of bungaloid encrustments'[291] – that threatened the beauty of the English countryside. Reflecting the breadth of his interests, he was also a founder member of the Einstein Society, a group of MPs who persuaded Stanley Baldwin to attend a dinner in the House of Commons addressed by Professor Eddington of Cambridge University on the theory of relativity: 'I don't remember a word of it, but it was excellent entertainment while it lasted, and it lasted very late.'[292] An article in *The Times* dated 25 November 1928, towards the end of his political career, carried the headline 'Sir Martin Asks'. It noted that 'Sir Martin Conway is the least inquisitive of men. He seldom asks a question in the house. When he does it is a sure sign that some outpost of our intellectual life is being grievously assaulted and equally sure that nothing will be done about it.'

Periodically, Conway also gave vent in parliament to his increasing interest in mysticism. In 1927, a majority of the House rejected a proposed revision of the Book of Common Prayer because it was too 'papistical'. Conway also opposed the changes, but not on orthodox Anglican grounds. Presaging some of the themes that were to emerge in his final book, his speech expressed the view that 'we are waiting for someone who will not overthrow the old revelation, who will not disestablish the old faith, but who will carry us into a wider field and will give us a new vision of the world that is beyond, a new vision of the unknown, of the eternal, toward which we ordinary folk can but blindly grope. My criticism of the new Prayer Book, the reason why I cannot vote for this Measure, is that it does nothing whatever to express that widely-spread aspiration towards the divine.'[293]

His parliamentary duties being generally light, Conway found ample time to pursue his other interests. He was appointed a Vice President of the Royal Geographical Society in 1919, even though he had done no serious geographical work for over 25 years. He became interested in psychoanalysis, read the English translations of Freud's work published by Leslie Stephen's daughter Virginia and her husband Leonard Woolf, and became treasurer of the Medico-Psychological Clinic, which offered the first training programme in psychoanalysis in Britain, as well as providing therapy to shell-shocked soldiers. In 1920 he published *Mountain Memories: A Pilgrimage of Romance*. It was Conway's favourite book, according to Arnold Lunn,[294] combining memories of youthful adventures with more mature reflections on the importance of mountains in his life. It completed the gradual evolution of his vision of the mountains from the dramatic backdrop to the heroic adventures of his youth, through the scientific exploration and aesthetic appreciation of his middle years, to the mysticism of his old age. Remembering his walk down the Biafo valley nearly 30 years earlier he wrote: 'Romance almost became a reality. The gods were very near at hand. We touched, as it were, the skirts of their garments. Yet even at the culminating moments of these strenuous dream-days there still lingered the sense of incompleteness, of something lacking. The secret was almost disclosed, but never quite, the veil never entirely withdrawn.'[295] *Mountain Memories* was also a defence of what Roland Barthes later called the 'Helvetico-Protestant' world view that equates morality with solitude and effort. As he settled into comfortable old age, Conway became increasingly convinced that hardship was a means of discovering beauty: 'It is not Nature that illuminates the mind, but the mind that glorifies Nature. The beauty that we behold must first arise in ourselves. It is born for the most part in suffering.'[296]

In the early years of the twentieth century numerous travel writers and explorers felt drawn into the realms of Eastern mysticism, including Conway's old friend Sir Francis Younghusband. Younghusband published a series of increasingly bizarre books, including *The Heart of Nature; or The Quest for Natural Beauty* (1921), which combined roman-tic descriptions of the Himalayas with obscure philosophical ramblings. While certainly slightly batty, Younghusband's beliefs were unquestionably heartfelt. Exactly how sincere Conway's new-found mysticism really was is harder to judge. Always an intellectual magpie, Conway may simply have embellished his youthful adventures with mystical overtones in order to sell the book. In his diaries and letters at the time of his Himalayan expedition he was clearly far more concerned with money than with mysticism. In a letter sent to Abigail Marble from India in 1892 he wrote: 'I wish MM were here to tell me how to turn the present situation to profit.' Some 30 years later, even without Manton Marble's help, he succeeded: *Mountain Memories* sold well.

By the early 1920s, Conway's life had settled back into a reasonably stable pattern after the interruption of the war. During the week he stayed in London, partly, one suspects, to avoid Katrina who remained physically frail and deeply depressed. He typically got to his Imperial War Museum office at about 10.30, but rarely worked on museum business. He lunched at the Athenaeum or at someone else's club. He occasionally went to the House of Commons or the House of Lords for lunch or to listen to a speech, and he voted when asked to do so by the Whips. In the evening he dined with friends and acquaintances and attended events at the Alpine Club, the Royal Geographical Society, the Burlington Fine Arts Club or some other society. On Friday afternoon he was driven to Allington, where he and Katrina usually had weekend guests.

During parliamentary recesses he travelled constantly and almost invariably at someone else's expense. In 1921 he spent January in St. Moritz as the guest of Sir Henry Lunn. In August, Lunn invited both Conway and Katrina to stay at the Palace Hotel des Alpes in Mürren, 'travelling free and having free hotel for as long as we want'. Katrina felt too ill to travel, so Conway took Agnes instead. Conway paid for their keep by giving an illustrated talk to the other guests on the prospects for the first Everest expedition, which was vigorously championed by Sir Francis Younghusband, now President of the Royal Geographical Society.

At the age of 65, after the long gap of the First World War, Conway was overjoyed to return to the Alps in summer, and discovered that his love of the mountains had fundamentally changed. He no longer felt the climber's need to possess them by collecting summits, but 'gazed aloft on the Jungfrau and beheld her with the eyes of a boy – a vision of pure beauty, robed in mystery as of yore'.[297] As Conway entered the seventh age of man, he no longer looked upon the mountains 'with the cultivated vision of an artist, but with the simple joy of a child. I felt like clapping my hands with delight.'[298] Despite his vocal opposition before the war, he gleefully took the railway to the Jungfraujoch and declared it 'unvulgarizable'. 'Close at hand were the slopes I had climbed in 1894 and tracks up them which might have been those we left...it was a costly journey – at least £4 – but worth it...for its revival of memories.' A few days later he failed to reach the summit of the Schilthorn (2,970 m) from Mürren, but it was still 'about the splendidest day I ever remember in the Alps'.

The following year he visited the French Riviera with Agnes (and wrote two articles for *Country Life*) before returning to the Palace Hotel des Alpes in Mürren. A newspaper cartoon showed Sir Martin in the hotel with 'a bad hand' at bridge. He also paid his last visit to Coolidge in Grindelwald: 'He is ill, has been very ill. I fear he won't last much longer, tho' he has been much cheered by the death of [Sir Edward] Davidson (of the AC) who was his arch-enemy!' Towards the end of the year, Conway travelled to Pontresina, staying as a guest of Sir Henry Lunn at the Schlosshotel Enderlin, and joyfully revisited the mountains he had climbed during his first full alpine season in 1876.

Travel and Treasure

The nearest that Conway came to courting controversy during the latter part of his parliamentary career was his support for Zionism and the creation of a Jewish state. Despite his unshakable belief in the superiority of the Anglo-Saxon race, Conway had more Jewish friends than most other members of the establishment at the time because of his frequent dealings with Jewish art dealers, financiers and businessmen. He even went so far as to suggest that 'the English Jew' can be 'just as much an Englishman as the purest descendent of Anglian forebears'.[299] He was on particularly friendly terms with Sir Alfred Mond, later Lord Melchett, who as First Commissioner of Works in Lloyd George's wartime administration had recommended that Conway be appointed as director general of the War Museum. After the war, Mond merged three companies into the family firm of Brunner Mond to form Imperial Chemical Industries, at that time one of the greatest industrial corporations in the world. The relationship between the two men was so close that Mond even guaranteed one of Conway's overdraft facilities at the bank. When Mond died in 1930, Conway was terrified that the bank would call in the loan, but then he realised that if they did Alfred Mond's estate would pay.

It was a strange relationship. In 1928, Aldous Huxley imagined 'the Ascent of Man' where 'a very small monkey was succeeded by a very slightly larger pithecanthropus, which was succeeded in its turn by a slightly larger Neanderthal man. Palaeolithic man, neolithic man, bronze-age Egyptian and Babylonian man, iron-age Greek and Roman man – the figures slowly increased in size. By the time Galileo and Newton had appeared on the scene, humanity had grown to quite respectable dimensions. The crescendo continued uninterrupted through Watt and Stephenson, Faraday and Darwin, Bessemer and Edison...to come to a contemporary consummation in the figure...of Sir Alfred Mond.'[300] However, this industrial colossus was not a particularly likeable man. Blunt, direct, blustering and frequently ill-mannered, the 1937 edition of the *Dictionary of National Biography* described him as 'a typical Jew in appearance, with...none of the suave Hebrew adroitness that often disarms opposition'. Even Conway conceded that 'his manner was not exactly ingratiating', but maintained that 'the first impact was the worst'.[301] Why did two such different men as Mond and Conway become friends? They shared a love of art collecting and, as always, Conway was doubtless a charming and entertaining guest. But perhaps there was more: despite their apparent success, both men still thought of themselves as rebels, adventurers, outsiders. Mond was probably amused and flattered by Conway's irreverent attitude to the English establishment, while Conway had once again succeeded in befriending a difficult man, who guaranteed his overdraft. As he noted approvingly in his memoirs: 'Beside being large-hearted [Mond] was inventively generous.'[302]

Mond was an active figure in the campaign to support Jewish settlement in Palestine, so Conway was soon enlisted to the cause. In 1923 he travelled with Mond to Morocco and to Palestine, dining with Baron Eduard de Rothschild in Paris en route, and published his impressions in a book which he dedicated to Mond's wife Violet, 'who lent me the best of travelling companions'. Conway's book was broadly supportive of the Jewish cause: 'Civilization, in the form of highly-civilised men, bringing science and capital with them, comes to Palestine from the West by sea. Mere population drifts into it from the East by land. These two so different streams of humanity here meet and must learn to live together...It is surely obvious...the more highly-endowed race will rule.'[303] However, he privately described his visit to Palestine as 'not sight-seeing but people-seeing – all kinds of Jews and Arabs and their mutual quarrels'. His book also favourably compared French colonialism in Morocco to British colonialism in Egypt and Palestine, mainly on the grounds that he preferred Franco-Moroccan architecture to British colonial architecture and the fact that the French had made no attempt to introduce Western education or democracy to Morocco: 'The likes of "Young Turks" and Indian or Egyptian nationalists will not be created in Morocco if the French can help it. The [ruling class] will remain Moroccan aristocrats. They will expect to command, not to vote or to be elected.'[304]

A year after his visit to Palestine, Conway was invited to America to lecture on Zionism. Lacking anything original to say on the subject, he decided to visit Russia first, to investigate the treatment of Jews following the revolution. The Russians correctly judged that Conway was essentially apolitical, and so granted him a visa. They then skilfully transformed the purpose of his visit from investigating the treatment of Jews to investigating the art treasures of Russia.

Conway was impressed by Moscow. 'Everything we are told in England...about Russia is lies', he wrote to Katrina. 'All talk of dirt is false. The people I have seen look particularly clean – the children much cleaner than the brats of Westminster...Moscow is wonderful!' The only disadvantage was the cost because, for once, Conway was paying for himself. He was horrified when dinner, bed and breakfast at a Moscow hotel cost him over £5 a day (compared to 6/- (30p) in one of the best hotels in Lisbon, which he had passed through the previous year on his way to Morocco), so he took up residence at the British Consulate to reduce his outgoings. During his visit he was given unfettered access to works of art that no Englishman had seen before. In the Kremlin 'they took me to an inner chamber and set me down in a comfortable chair...I was encouraged to light my pipe...[A neat wooden box] was taken out...unlocked, and the contents placed in my hands. It was the Crown of all the Russias – I suppose, the most splendid piece of jewellery existing in the world.'[305] He found the riches spread before him dazzling, but ultimately depressing. 'After an hour or two, I had seen enough. Gold and precious stones impress by their rarity...When such a multitude are...passed in review before one's eyes...the sense of rarity vanishes, and one begins to think of jewels as common things.'[306]

He travelled to Petrograd (St. Petersburg) where he spent several days in the Hermitage 'absolutely alone – the whole place empty, silent, and me like the last survivor left in an empty world. I go where I please, smoke my pipe, look at pictures, write notes till I can no more.' It was an extraordinary experience: 'Hour after hour I wandered alone...sitting at will now before a gem-like Raphael, now inspecting the magic mystery of the great Rembrandts, now passing into the Winter Palace and lingering in absolute solitude in the very chamber where Catherine II died.'[307] Amidst all this history and splendour, the plight of the Russian Jews was completely forgotten. Even when two professors, whom he was due to meet for dinner, were arrested that same afternoon and one of them committed suicide, Conway remained convinced that 'the Soviet Government is really trying to do its best by the folk, but it lives in terror just as the Czars did and strikes blindly not knowing who will presently strike it'. Conway's visit to post-revolutionary Russia added considerably to his prestige in England, providing material for numerous newspaper articles and a book entitled *The Art Treasures of Soviet Russia* (1925).

Despite rather losing sight of his mission in Russia in 1924, Conway continued to support the Zionist cause in England. He addressed a large Jewish gathering at the Kingsway Hall on 25 April 1925 to celebrate the foundation of the University of Jerusalem, and his friendship with the Mond family extended to the next generation. At the request of Alfred's son, Henry, he became president of the 'English Maccabees', a Jewish youth organisation named after a rebel

Jewish army that seized control of Judea 100 years before Christ. Conway rather innocently referred to the movement as 'a sort of Jew boy scouts'. In 1935 he proposed Henry (who had been an MP and a director of Barclays Bank before he inherited his father's title of Lord Melchett and took over as chairman of ICI) for membership of the Athenaeum. Conway campaigned hard on his behalf, writing 50 letters to members of the club in support of his candidature. Mond's ballot papers were signed by over 100 supporters, including Sir Edwin Lutyens and Lord Rutherford, but 35 members blackballed him and he was not elected. The 1935 membership list of the Athenaeum includes a number of Jewish names, so his rejection was probably not on religious grounds. Instead, it appears that members of the Athenaeum were shocked by his scandalous lifestyle. Henry Mond, his wife Gwen, and the writer Gilbert Cannon, a close friend of D. H. Lawrence, lived for a time in a *ménage à trois*. Moreover, they celebrated their unconventional lifestyle by commissioning a splendid work of art entitled 'Scandal', now in the Victoria and Albert Museum, which shows Henry and Gwen dancing naked before a group of outraged middle-aged onlookers. True to his rebellious spirit, Conway probably rather enjoyed the scandal, but he was profoundly annoyed about the time he had wasted trying to get Henry Mond elected to the Athenaeum.

1925 was a vintage year for free travel. It began with a trip to the south of France with Agnes, before going to the Engadine in Switzerland as the guest of Sir Henry Lunn. Conway's winter holidays now followed a fixed pattern with a leisurely breakfast, followed by a short walk, lunch, afternoon tea (or chocolate), then dinner, followed by bridge, a lecture or some other entertainment, such as a fancy dress ball. Much to his satisfaction, he was constantly surrounded by interesting new acquaintances. Conversation was now his greatest joy in life. In one of his Slade lectures, entitled 'The Art of Living', he described 'the delights of human intercourse, of the contact of man with man, culminating in that most widely enjoyable of human pleasures – conversation...delights that cost nothing and are within the reach of every intelligent and cultivated person'.[308] In the spring he travelled to Italy, going first to Venice and then to Pavia, as an invited guest at the celebrations to mark the eleventh centenary of the university. In Venice he took a motor launch along the Grand Canal to the Hotel Monaco. 'St. Mark's...seemed to me more wonderful than ever...My motor boat collided with a gondola on reaching the hotel and smashed the plate glass cabin windows...An expensive day!'

During his visit to Italy he convinced himself that he had identified the landscapes in his 'Giorgione' paintings and publicised this remarkable discovery in *Giorgione as a Landscape Painter* (1929). By coincidence, the following year he decided to sell the paintings in New York, but even Joseph Duveen had difficulty persuading potential buyers of their authenticity. In his book, Conway claimed to have identified a tower and a farmhouse depicted in some acknowledged Giorgione paintings, and from them identified the landscape in 'The Finding of Paris' as the Lower Brenta valley, and that in 'Paris Given to Nurse' as the fortified town of Marostica, both near Castelfranco, where Giorgione was born. The book included 22 plates of Giorgione paintings, including the two attributed by Conway, but for some reason he did not include photographs of the actual tower, the farmhouse or the landscapes that he had discovered, in order to allow a comparison to be made. As Conway's obituarist in *The Times* noted, *Giorgione as a Landscape Painter* 'reveals most engagingly his mixture of common sense and romantic fancy, and his tendency to ride a hobby horse into regions of speculation'.[309] The paintings were finally sold at auction after Agnes' death in 1951. The Sotheby's catalogue described them as 'Giorgione (attributed to)'.[310]

Continuing his travels in 1925, Conway set off in May for an excursion to the Isle of Skye, as the guest of the Ministry of Agriculture. Ramsey MacDonald and his daughter Isabel spent the weekend at Allington Castle in June, and in July Conway spent the weekend with David Lloyd George and his daughter Megan (who became the first female MP for Wales in 1929) at Bron-y-de in Surrey. The following month, Conway was rewarded for a favourable mention he had given in *Palestine and Morocco* (1923) with an invitation to join a Mediterranean cruise as the guest of the Messageries Maritimes. In October, he and Katrina went to Algeria as guests of the Algerian tourist office, in order to publicise the attractions of the country as a holiday destination. Finally, in December, Conway travelled to Rome and

Naples with Lloyd George and his private secretary, mistress and future wife, Frances Stevenson. Conway thoroughly enjoyed travelling with the former prime minister and revelled in the Fascist receptions that were laid on to welcome them: 'Red carpet, royal waiting room, flowers, hats off. LG's attempt at incognito is a failure.'

Conway first met Lloyd George in July 1917 at a house party at Melchet Court, Alfred Mond's country house. He spent a long time speaking to Lloyd George's loyal and long-suffering first wife, Margaret, recording in his diary that 'she is a bit socialistical. I spoke to her...about LG, about his need for personal support, about my politics etc. She has no frills and no foolishness – a real dear I call her.' During their visit to Rome, Lloyd George had no time for monuments, churches or museums, but he enjoyed walking the streets, extolling the virtues of 'the common people'. Conway soon wearied of this constant enthusiasm and later claimed that he challenged Lloyd George by declaring: 'You promote education; you want access to the University for all your fellow citizens; you strive to raise the general standard of living. In so far as you succeed you do away with the very class you call "the common people". If they are so lovely why not let them be?'[311] However, since Lloyd George's response is not recorded we may assume that this 'conversation' took place in Conway's imagination. Despite their political differences, Conway remained on friendly terms, visiting Lloyd George at his home in Criccieth and attending an Eisteddfod near Holyhead in August 1927. He last visited Lloyd George in 1932, after which he wrote to Agnes telling her that he 'had lots of fun and helped polish up epigrams for LG's next speech'. Once again, it is hard to imagine why a Liberal ex prime minister should have socialised with a Tory back-bencher such as Conway but, as Roy Hattersley observed, Lloyd George was 'the Great Outsider', and so too, in his way, was Conway.

Conway celebrated his 70th birthday at Allington on 'the most beautiful cloudless spring day I ever remember'. He also renewed his business connections with Bolivia after one of his old mining concessions unexpectedly burst back into life and even appeared, briefly, to contain an economic gold deposit. Conway was instantly swept up by a wave of optimism, informing Katrina that 'I will make not less than £150,000 out of the gold syndicate and that...is CERTAIN and will come soon!!' Four years later the company established to exploit the deposit was liquidated and a disgruntled shareholder brought an action against Conway in 1930 for misrepresentation. Initially Conway tried to avoid giving evidence on the grounds of ill health, but in the end he was subjected to more than 10 hours of intense cross-examination by 'a nasty young Jew barrister'. The case was eventually dismissed, but then Conway was summonsed by the Board of Trade for failing to file accounts and hold a statutory meeting.

Did Conway deliberately deceive his investors? Read by today's standards, the disclosure of investment risks in the prospectuses he drafted is minimal. However, Conway probably deceived himself as much as his investors and the junior mining sector is still home to stock promoters who share their dreams of untold wealth with prospective investors who willingly place bets in the full knowledge that there is a casino element to all early stage exploration. Conway invested his step-father-in-law's money (which, in due course, he presumably expected to inherit) in all of his speculative ventures and appears to have earned a good return on the money he invested in paintings. He lost money on his mining ventures because he knew much less about business than he did about art. Professional investors frequently asked Conway to get independent valuations of the properties that he promoted, but he pre-ferred to back the judgement of men he knew and liked, most of whom were adventurers and opportunists like himself, spurred on by lots of optimism and, in some cases, an eye for a quick buck – not so very dif-ferent from junior mining companies today.

In 1926, Britain was gripped by a general strike and for nine days it seemed possible that parliamentary democracy might be overthrown. The strike prevented Conway from travelling to Grindelwald to attend Coolidge's funeral, but shortly afterwards he was invited to Spain by Lowenstein, 'a financier with a touch of genius',[312] who arranged for him to take a flight over the Pyrenees in 'the newest and most up-to-date monoplane'.[313] It was his first experience of flying and he was entranced, describing the experience in a lengthy article in the *Alpine Journal*. Lowenstein had the misfortune to fall out of a similar aeroplane shortly afterwards while it was flying across the English Channel.

Most of the money that Katrina had inherited was still invested in the United States. In 1926, Conway estimated their income from dividends and interest at £5,000, but it was probably far less since he added 'at all events I can make it amount to that without taking any risk', which must have worried Katrina. During a visit to New York, Conway happened to meet Henry Goldman, son of the founder of Goldman, Sachs and Company, whom he had previously met in Berlin on his way to Moscow. At the time, Goldman Sachs was one of the most reputable investment banking and brokerage houses on Wall Street; but they were later drawn into the collective madness of the stock market bubble, setting up a number of highly leveraged investment trusts that went spectacularly bust in the Great Crash of 1929. Goldman invited Conway to lunch to see his art collection and gave Conway some free investment advice, which was probably highly rewarding for the next three years, but which perhaps contributed to Conway's later financial embarrassment. Even in 1926, he was constantly short of money and invariably wrote newspaper articles during his travels to cover part of the cost.

By this time, Katrina and Conway had more or less abandoned entertainment at Allington during the winter, because of the prohibitive cost of heating the vast castle. However, in the summer months they continued to hold weekend house parties at which Conway's political and business contacts mingled with artists and architects, including Sir Edwin Lutyens, Augustus John and Roger Fry. Lutyens had recently completed work on the imperial capital of India in New Delhi and was now designing the Roman Catholic cathedral in Liverpool. He joked about the Archbishop and the cathedral (which would have been the second largest church in Christendom had construction not been abandoned in 1941) and then turned to Agnes and said: 'My dear, you don't mind my being frivolous, do you? You *don't* think I oughtn't to build a cathedral?' Agnes found Lutyens 'fatiguing, in spite of his brilliance'.[314]

Agnes and her Cambridge friends were frequent guests at the Allington weekend parties, but Katrina was an increasingly unreliable hostess. Joan Evans recalled that she 'might not appear at all, or [would] lie like Ilaria di Caretto on a draped couch, only able to speak to one person at a time, and that in an exhausted whisper pointed by the minuscule gestures of a skeletal hand'.[315] Meanwhile, Agnes continued to work for the Imperial War Museum until 1926, organising the women's section and writing a history of women's work during the war for *Encyclopaedia Britannica*. She also organised the campaign by Newnham graduates to be admitted to full membership of Cambridge University. She was awarded an MA by London University in 1926 for a study of Henry VII's relations with Scotland and Ireland, and was subsequently awarded a Litt.D. by Trinity College Dublin for a book on the same subject. In 1927 she travelled to the Middle East, visiting Cairo, Jerusalem, Petra, Damascus, Baghdad and Tehran. Two years later she returned with George Horsfield, a family friend who was Director of Antiquities in Transjordan, to undertake the first excavation of Petra, financed by a grant from Henry Mond. At the end of their first season of digging on the site they reported their findings to Emir Abdullah Ibn Hussein, who criticised T. E. Lawrence and insisted that his recently published book, *The Seven Pillars of Wisdom*, was written purely for his own aggrandisement.

After returning to England, and working on their discoveries at Cambridge, Agnes travelled to New York to stay with her American relatives and gave a lecture on Petra at the Cosmopolitan Club. The lecture was attended by Joseph Duveen who immediately sent a telegram to Conway: 'The most wonderful and absorbing lecture I have ever listened to... Your daughter is a wonder never realized she was so talented.' The success gave Agnes the confidence to lecture at universities and museums across the continent, including Columbia, Yale, Washington, Ohio and Toronto. In June 1930 she read a paper on Petra at the Royal Geographical Society, which was published in the *Geographical Journal*.[316] Conway was delighted. Ever since their holiday together in Italy, when she was 16, his admiration for his daughter and the way that she had coped with her injury had grown. In a letter to Katrina he wrote: 'Almost every woman would have been slain by it, but she has gone on and on, so bravely adding to her good looks by developing her mind and heart... Every year as she goes on writing her character in her face she will become more and more good-looking. She is a wonder.' Agnes was equally devoted to her father; blossoming under his attention and apparently impervious to his neglect. Throughout her life, she regarded

Conway utterly uncritically, as an omniscient scholar and gallant adventurer.

The Flowering Age

In 1924, when Conway was 68, another young woman entered his life. Monica Hadow, a 24-year-old secretary and driver, came to work for him at the Imperial War Museum office. For the next six years, Conway and Monica had a relationship that left both of them deeply dissatisfied and unhappy.

During the war, Monica had been a driver, often working close to the front line in France, and had an affair with a soldier who proved to be already married. After several other unhappy relationships she married a pilot in the Royal Flying Corps whose nerves had been shattered by the war and who was frequently drunk and violent towards her. She eventually divorced him for cruelty. No doubt Conway felt sorry for her and perhaps, having lost her innocence during the war, she deliberately set out 'to bring him to her feet', as Conway later believed. Certainly, Conway fell an easy victim to her youthful charms. In a draft of an unpublished semi-autobiographical 'confession', entitled *An Old Man's Last Idyll*, written in about 1930 when the relationship had come to an end, Conway wrote and then partially crossed out: 'I had only known two women before her and loved but one, and they were simple souls; but she was learned in novel arts that took me by surprise and galvanised me into servitude.'[317] Initially Conway felt his youth renewed by her unconventional behaviour and carefree joy of sex. He even found her envious socialism exciting. But gradually, as she became more demanding and possessive, he began to find her amorality offensive, observing that 'sexuality seemed to her as unimportant as the satisfaction of hunger'.

Both Katrina and Agnes seem to have known about the relationship from a fairly early stage. Agnes, in particular, often attended social events in London where both Conway and Monica were present. Henry and Gwen Mond certainly knew about the affair but, given their own domestic arrangements, were hardly likely to condemn it. Joan Evans, Agnes' friend and biographer, also met Monica, describing her as 'unfastidious, ignorant and indiscreet',[318] but in accordance with the conventions of the time, she did not mention Monica by name in her history of the family.

In mid 1929, Monica demanded that Conway leave Katrina and go away with her. He refused, but later regretted the refusal. In September she informed him that she had met someone else and that she intended to marry him. At first Conway was unconcerned, believing that he had more to offer her than mere bourgeois security, but by November she was engaged and in December she married. Conway watched the ceremony from a dark corner of the church. Afterwards, he turned to Katrina for sympathy: 'Sad reminiscent talk with K much of the night about M.H.' Monica moved into a small terraced house in Belfast with her new husband, but in January she met Conway in Liverpool and they travelled to Allington Castle together. 'K talked to Monica for more than 2 hrs last night', he recorded in his diary, followed (in a later hand) by: 'and laid the foundation for infinite troubles'. Conway even sought the sympathy of his daughter: 'I am just back from seeing Mrs Hadow [sic] off to her beastly husband in Belfast', he wrote. 'Your father is the victim of a ghastly tragedy.'

One of the characters in Conway's semi-autobiographical 'confession', *An Old Man's Last Idyll*, is an elderly mountaineer who describes himself as 'the last of three men slain by women in the same way. One was a Prime Minister of a great European nation…One was a general whose name was in all men's mouths. The third am I.' The manuscript goes on to extol the virtues of female private secretaries: 'Each of us had a private secretary, most capable and devoted, who became the main-spring of our lives…Each of us three was wonderfully served. The slightest tendency to stoop from high ideals was instantly repressed, for a fine woman feels, and never fails to feel, the slightest slipping away from what is highest in her man's emotion. By such means she obtains a control over both heart and mind in him and acting thus she best acts out herself.'

The 'Prime Minister of a great European nation' was almost certainly David Lloyd George, who had a long affair with his private secretary, Frances Stevenson, finally marrying her after the death of his first wife, Margaret. It is not clear which particular general Conway had in mind. The manuscript of *An Old Man's Last Idyll* was presumably typed by Monica's successor as Conway's private secretary, Miss Hood, which must have provided an interesting introduction to her new boss. Conway even suggested at one point that Agnes should read the manuscript, but better sense prevailed and he later forbade her to do so.

For a time in early 1930 Conway thought that Monica had agreed to return as his secretary, or that she might accompany him on a trip abroad, but neither transpired. Katrina threatened to leave Conway if he went abroad with Monica, but Conway told Agnes that he could not help himself: 'My life is intolerable and Mother won't change one jot.' He was in the middle of defending the legal action brought against his Bolivian gold mine at this time, which probably added to his depression. In April, with the court case finally dismissed, he met Monica once again in London and they dined on lobster at Overton's. They spent the night at a friend's house but 'it became clear to me that M. is only thinking of herself and does not really care for me a bit. So I gave her £5 for express back to Belfast, which she took as she takes anything I give her, but will give nothing in return; so I said goodbye and went to dine at Athenaeum and then to pack.'

'Am very very lonely and fathomlessly sad', he wrote in his diary the next day. As always, he sought refuge in the mountains. He went first to Switzerland and then to Chamonix, where he stayed at Couttet's and walked up to Flégère, as he had during his long walk through the Alps in 1894. Immediately he felt 'greatly improved in health, spirits and strength'. He returned to Switzerland and walked over the Simplon Pass into Italy, following the same route he had taken as a young man in 1882, and then travelled to Venice, where he walked around St. Mark's and bathed at the lido. He was slowly recovering from his depression when a telegram arrived from Monica saying that she intended to join him in Italy. Conway was initially optimistic that they might resume their relationship, but a few days after her arrival 'M knocked the bottom out of my dreams forever, and everything will hence-forward be entirely different. I feel an old old man, with no future and no hope.' His diary contains a photograph of Monica. She looks very young and very thin, with a fashionably flat chest and a mass of dark curly hair.

Once again Conway set out for the mountains. He travelled to

Zermatt, stayed at the Monte Rosa Hotel and walked up to the Riffelalp ('2 hrs up and 50 mins down'). 'I have come to seek once more "the deep authentic mountain thrill"', he wrote in his diary. In early August, Agnes joined him (following her lecture tour in America and another painful operation on her face). Soon afterwards Charlie Bruce, now a brigadier general, arrived to chair the annual dinner of the English Society of Members of the Swiss Alpine Club: 'Afterwards he and I told stories etc and we had lots of fun.' With his spirits revived, Conway travelled to Venice to stay with Henry Mond and Randolph Churchill, Winston's son. By September he was back in Allington and the affair with Monica was effectively at an end.

This period saw the onset of the Great Depression, when industrial production in Britain fell by over 25% and unemployment reached nearly 70% in some northern industrial towns and cities. Despite being a member of parliament, almost the only allusion to these events in Conway's diary is a private dinner at the Athenaeum with Ramsay MacDonald, Lloyd George and Winston Churchill: 'Wonderful talk till midnight about getting all parties together to overcome danger to country.' Despite his love of talk, Conway had lost interest in politics and decided not to stand again for parliament. After suffering from pneumonia in the autumn he and Katrina spent part of the winter at Glion in Switzerland. Presumably thinking of Monica Hadow (rather than the Great Depression) his diary entry for 31 December 1930 reads: 'Thus ends the most unhappy year of my life.'

As his career as an MP drew to a close, Conway lobbied vigorously to be made a peer. He wrote to Lloyd George and Ramsay MacDonald and approached all the members of the upper house that he knew well enough to signal his ambition. In January 1931 he travelled to Rome with Henry Mond (now Lord Melchett, after the death of his father) where they met Mussolini and had an audience with Pope Pius XI. Conway instantly recognised Mussolini as a 'great man' during a discussion in which Il Duce dismissed democracy as an anti-modern conception and read from a book of statistics that demonstrated how much better off Italy was under a Fascist dictatorship. After their 'long and stimulating talk' Conway felt 'refreshed and aroused as though we had been drinking draughts of champagne'.[319]

The Pope had been an accomplished mountaineer in his younger days, pioneering the route that Conway had taken to the summit of Mont Blanc during his walk through the Alps: 'He is a dear old man. We talked about mountains, Coolidge, religious education, Liverpool, the new RC cathedral, its archbishop etc all very charming and simple...The Pope has edelweiss on his desk.' In a letter to Agnes, he observed that the Pope was dressed all in white – 'apparently a woollen stuff rather soiled, as tho' it were washed weekly and the washing day was near at hand'.

On 23 September 1931, two days after Britain abandoned the gold standard and just a few days before parliament was dissolved, Conway attended a meeting addressed by Mahatma Gandhi: 'He is not impressive at all. The word "freedom" seems to have hypnotised him.' The following day he had dinner with Charlie Chaplin in the House of Commons, who was far more congenial. On 8 October, at the age of 75, Conway ceased to be a member of parliament. He also decided that he could no longer keep pace with his ever-expanding collection of photographs, which now numbered between 200,000 and 300,000 items, and offered the entire collection to the Courtauld Institute. Initially he asked for £2,000 and two assistants to put the collection in good order, but he subsequently dropped the demand.

The Institute was founded by Samuel Courtauld, who had inherited a fortune from the textile business founded by his great uncle, and acquired an outstanding collection of French Impressionist and post-Impressionist paintings under the guidance of Roger Fry. Lord Lee of Fareham, a diplomat and art collector who bequeathed Chequers to the nation in 1921, and Sir Robert Witt, the art historian who shared Conway's passion for collecting art photographs, were co-founders. Sir Joseph Duveen, recently knighted and shortly to become a peer, was actively involved in the background. The Institute was founded for the teaching of art history in recognition of the fact that the tradition of amateur connoisseurship was fast disappearing and the great private collections were being broken up and sold. The purpose of the Courtauld, announced in a letter to *The Times*, was reminiscent of Conway's National Association for the Advancement of Art, almost half a century earlier. Lord Lee noted that 'there is, we know, a rooted, and to some extent a healthy, distrust in this country of anything which can be called "high-brow." When an Englishman declares – probably quite inaccurately – that he "knows what he likes" in art, he is apt to think that the last word has been said.'[320] Conway's only stipulation was that the filing system of his collection should remain chronological, a fundamental principle that he had applied since its inception: 'It makes little matter whether they were painters or gem engravers; the point is they were contemporaries one of another, expressing in different forms the ideas of one time.'

On 19 October 1931, at the age of 47, Agnes announced her engagement to George Horsfield. An illustrated article in *The Sketch* shows Agnes and George 'breakfasting on the "dig"'. The photograph looks like a still from an Agatha Christie film, with George and Agnes wearing Arab headdresses, sitting on deckchairs at a table laid for breakfast, in what appears to be a tomb or cave. The article described Conway as 'the distinguished Professor and authority on art and archaeology' but conceded that 'Miss Conway is herself interested in archaeology'.[321] At a party in Cambridge to celebrate the couple's engagement, Conway took the opportunity to read aloud some extracts from his forthcoming book of reminiscences entitled *Episodes in a Varied Life*, for which he had been paid an advance of £1,000 by *Country Life*. The book was published in 1932 and was well received. It is an entertaining, discursive book, not unnecessarily weighed down by details or factual accuracy. As a kindly reviewer for *The Times* observed, it looked back over a career 'that seems fantastically eventful'.

The Climber's Last Quest

On 18 November 1931 'came a letter from Prime Minister in the afternoon saying that I am to be made a Baron!' The next line in his diary reads: 'Home to K, Agnes being away at Cambridge.' His first thought on achieving this culminating ambition had been of his daughter, not Katrina.

Two days later Conway travelled to Cambridge to tell Agnes the good news, and took the opportunity to attend a Cambridge University Mountaineering Club dinner with Charlie Bruce, Geoffrey Winthrop

Young, Gino Watkins 'and other good company'. After returning to London, Conway 'called on Garter at the College of Arms about my name etc. Then to House of Lords to the Crown Office where they floored me by demanding £350 in fees.' Conway was so incensed at being charged for the privilege of becoming a peer that he wrote to the prime minister, but for once he failed to get something for nothing. It was not just pride that made him resent the payment: Conway was heavily in debt and struggled to find £350.

His coat of arms comprised a shield with an ice axe in the centre and a crest consisting of a castle gate-house. The shield is supported by a Himalayan ibex and an Astor Markhor (a species of wild goat native to Kashmir). His motto, '*Donec in te*', appears to be taken from St. Augustine's *Confessions*: 'You have made us for yourself, and our heart is restless until it rests in thee.' In his diary there is a copy of a *Punch* cartoon depicting the 1st Baron Conway of Allington. The somewhat ambiguous caption reads: 'The Climber'.

Conway was not an active member of the House of Lords. His maiden speech in the upper house opposed the construction of Waterloo Bridge and he subsequently made occasional short speeches deploring the destruction of historic buildings and monuments. His final speech, in January 1935, related to the loan of paintings to and from the National Gallery. 'The H. of Lords is a dreadfully DULL place,' he wrote to Agnes, 'far worse than I expected.' He preferred the Smoking Room in the House of Commons and continued to spend much of his time there. 'I'm always afraid that someone may make a fuss, saying "it's all right for a peer to look in now and again...but this man lives in it"...[but] thus far everyone welcomes me.'

Agnes and George Horsfield were married in St. George's Cathedral in Jerusalem on 28 January 1932 and moved into their new home at Jerash, in Jordan. Neither Conway nor Katrina was present. The volume of correspondence between Conway and his daughter increased after her marriage, suggesting that Conway missed their regular meetings in London and weekends at Allington. A few weeks after the wedding Katrina took an overdose of morphine, probably accidentally. She recovered sufficiently to go with Conway on a winter cruise through the Adriatic from Venice to Greece. The following winter

Conway visited Egypt and Palestine as a guest of Henry Mond and went to Jerash to stay with Agnes and George. Katrina was not well enough to go with him, but she did feel able to contemplate the long journey at the end of 1933. Her depression and ill health had long been an accepted fact within the family, and yet when Katrina arrived in Palestine Agnes was struck by how very old and frail her mother now appeared. Katrina, Agnes and George visited Baalbek, Palmyra and Damascus before travelling to Jerash, where Katrina fell ill with dysentery. Agnes took her to Jerusalem where she was immediately admitted to hospital. Katrina died on 22 November 1933, at the age of 76, and was buried on a bluff overlooking the mountains of Moab.

Agnes sailed for England to help Conway sort out Katrina's affairs. The castle and its contents were all in Katrina's name, partly to avoid British inheritance tax and partly because Marble had paid for most of it. Nevertheless, it came as a shock to both Conway and Agnes to discover that Katrina had left her entire estate to Agnes. The family finances were under considerable strain following the stock market crash and Agnes did what she could during her short visit to get both Allington and Romney Street into a state that might allow them to be let.

Conway had spent his younger years living off his mother, his middle years living off his wife's family, and now his old age living off his daughter. He sent all his bills to Agnes for payment and continued to behave as if the castle was his, occasionally trying to sell a painting or an ornament to meet current expenses, apparently not realising, or not caring, that they were not his to sell. Eventually Agnes had to instruct the servants at Allington not to allow Conway to remove any valuable items from the building. 'Thank goodness my book is in the hands of the printers', Conway wrote to her in disgust. 'Do you claim that as yours?' Eventually Agnes was obliged to raise a mortgage on the castle to provide Conway with pocket money.

On 17 November 1934, less than a year after Katrina's death, Conway married Iva, widow of Reginald Lawson, of Saltwood Castle, Kent. Iva was a Texan, and the Conways and Lawsons had become friends during the 1920s through their common interest in restoring old castles. Iva and Reginald Lawson had already restored Hurstmonceux Castle near Eastbourne and had started work on Saltwood Castle near

Hythe when Reginald accidentally shot himself in 1930. At the time of his engagement, Conway owed £40,000 and had negligible assets. He probably saw the marriage as a feudal alliance, uniting his title with her money. His friends hoped that their common interests would make the marriage a happy one, but Conway had finally met his match: Iva was delighted to become a baroness, but she refused to give Conway any money. 'She is very sweet to me and very attractive', Conway informed Agnes after five months of married life, 'but she is hard to touch for money.' After numerous difficult discussions, Conway finally conceded defeat in his diary for 27 July 1935: 'I definitely learn that Iva will never give me any money – so that's that...Had a very sleepless and unhappy night.' As a result, Conway spent occasional weekends at his wife's castle, but never made it his home. Instead, his daughter continued to meet his expenses and to worry about money on his behalf.

Karl Pearson had been the first friend to meet Conway and Katrina after they were married, and Conway wrote to him again soon after his second marriage to Iva. The letter, written on House of Lords notepaper, hinted that Conway hoped to arrange an honour for Pearson: 'I feel so ashamed that so much recognition has come to me', he wrote. Pearson was delighted to hear from Conway after so many years, but dismissive of honours and, by implication, of the path that Conway had chosen to follow, rather than pursuing his early promise as a scholar: 'I think all honours should be given to young men...they encourage them when they begin to doubt whether their work is of value...But as the distribution of medals and honours as a rule lies in the hands of the aged, and they have no energy to appraise the doings of the young, they award such things to the aged, who...growing senile delight in them as toys.'

As Conway grew older he increasingly suffered from a febrile restlessness. After opening a camping exhibition at the Imperial Institute ('a jolly show of tents and caravans and gadgets') he decided that he wanted to live in a caravan. The whim passed, but he nevertheless travelled constantly, and increasingly alone. Even in London, he rarely stayed in one place for very long. His diary for 28 February 1935 reads: 'Miss Hood [his private secretary] came with a typescript of *Pilgrimage*. Lunch at Athenaeum. Went to Lunn's about an April cruise. To the Alpine Club.

To Ed Duveen. To Sotheby's. To Burlington Fine Arts Club for tea. To Athenaeum to write to Iva and so home for dinner.' Conway was bored and lonely: 'Reading in Athenaeum alone. No one wants to take me anywhere.' Despite neglecting her for most of her lifetime, he missed Katrina: 'Very sad day – wanting K. Have no longer any desire to live.' But despite his self-pity, he was still capable of self-deprecating humour: 'Drove to the foot of Beachboro' Hill and climbed it to the little temple...fine views, strong wind – rather a tough job but I got up all right by traversing and climbing...The hill...is 526 ft high.' His restless wandering took him to Palestine, to lay flowers on Katrina's grave, and to Zermatt, to gaze once more upon the mountains of his youth. He met Frank Smythe, recently returned from Everest, in the Monte Rosa Hotel.

Conway's health was deteriorating. He suffered from sleeplessness and occasional fits, and his handwriting, normally bold and perfectly legible, became increasingly erratic, with spelling errors and half finished sentences. Just before his final illness, in September 1936, he paid his last visit to the Alps, making a nostalgic journey to some of the places he had visited during his walk through *The Alps from End to End*. Starting at Salzburg, he drove to the foot of the Grossglockner and revisited Sterzing, where he had stayed as a member of a Cambridge reading party in 1875. He passed Christmas with the Monds and was planning a winter visit to Rome and Athens, but on 15 January 1937 he fell seriously ill and was admitted to hospital. Agnes was living in Athens by this time. She caught the Orient Express and arrived in London on 19 January. For a time Conway seemed to recover, but he fell ill again in April and died in the early hours of 19 April 1937. He was 81. A memorial service was held for him at his father's old church of St. Margaret's, Westminster two days later.

In 1900, when Conway was 43 years old, he was asked to write a short autobiographical piece. He started the article with the words: 'I am not going "to wear my heart upon my sleeve", or take the public into the confidence of my soul.'[322] Towards the end of his life, he changed his mind. His last book, *A Pilgrim's Quest for the Divine*, published in 1936 when he was 80, is a semi-autobiographical novel that draws on themes from many of his earlier books and lectures, and endeavours to set out his philosophy of life. It is a brave book, but an unsatisfactory one, and Conway knew it. 'I trust that it will be sympathetically regarded by all those into whose ken it may come', he wrote. 'I have expressed my faith as well as I could.'[323] By the time that he completed the final draft, he had difficulty in writing even a short letter to his daughter.

In *A Pilgrim's Quest*, Conway reasserted his belief that the emotional response to great works of art or natural landscapes defies rational explanation and that 'beauty' appeals directly to the soul. He recognised that beauty exists only in the imagination of the beholder and that perceptions of beauty are culturally dependent, but he believed that each successive generation strives to catch a revelatory glimpse of 'the eternal and the divine', in art and in nature, and that 'the search for beauty is the search for truth'. He rejected the idea of life everlasting, envisaging instead an eternal life of the soul where the entirety of a person's physical life on earth, both good and evil, would be experienced in an everlasting 'now'. He denied the possibility of repentance and redemption for 'what we do in time is eternal. It admits of no forgiveness, it awaits neither Judgment nor Resurrection for all that ever was still is.' He found consolation in the thought that, after death, 'at all events [a man] will not be alone...All the contacts he has had in life with his fellows still remain.'

In a strange echo of the words written to him by his father when he was a boy, Conway concluded that 'the tremendous importance of life lies in this, that during every hour of it a man is making or marring his eternal soul'. He regarded the physical universe as 'the raw material out of which we have to build our eternal life' and believed that the object of a good life should be 'to fashion this raw material into beauty – beauty of form, beauty of action, beauty of thought, beauty of faith'. He concluded with the belief that 'if we determine to live in an atmosphere of beauty and goodness we shall find the divine gifts quietly awaiting our acceptance'.

A Pilgrim's Quest was the second time that Conway had used the idea of a pilgrimage – a journey with a sacred destination – as an allegory for life. His 1920 autobiography *Mountain Memories* was subtitled *A Pilgrimage of Romance*, and as he grew older he increasingly saw his life as a quest for beauty, love and truth. In the Preface to the published version, Conway wrote that he had started work on *A Pilgrim's Quest* in 1878 and had completely rewritten it four times. Several of the ideas contained in the book echo a paper that Conway read to the 'Bachelor's Society' of Trinity College, Cambridge, in May 1880, in which he stated his conviction that beauty is 'the flickering of a shadow of a vaster and eternal reality dimly perceived now by us as it crosses our path but hereafter to be seen in nobler reality, in adamantine permanence'. He expanded his ideas into a paper entitled 'Eternity – The Product of Time and Space', written in 1881, which drew on Karl Pearson's speculations about relativity. It was 'the maelstrom of misery that engulfed millions of human beings during the Great War' that impelled Conway to take up the work once more. A typed and bound manuscript of the draft that preceded the published version survives in the Cambridge University Library. Entitled *The Pilgrimage of the Soul*, it is written in the third person but is, in some respects, a more autobiographical book than the final version. Conway asked Geoffrey Winthrop Young to read it, and at his suggestion he switched from the third person to the first to make it more personal, but then deleted several passages that he clearly found too embarrassing for publication in the first person.

In a letter to Agnes, he described the unpublished *Pilgrimage of the Soul* as 'a novel' in which 'the characters I've brought in are taking charge themselves and doing quite unexpected things!' Unlike the chaste published version, it contains two love affairs. The first is with a selfish young woman called Clare, who seduces the hero despite his best endeavours to keep his mind on spiritual matters. He finally succumbs to temptation in a flowery alpine meadow above Stalden, near Zermatt, where 'the male awoke in him and he returned her fire'. Later she rejects him in favour of a dashing young army officer who rescues her from almost certain death during a storm on the Matterhorn. At first the hero is distraught, but soon he realises that what he felt for Clare was merely physical passion, while what he sought was divine passion, which the love of a woman can be, but only if she is worthy.

The second love affair is with Mary, the widow of a Cambridge friend killed during the First World War. Through his platonic relationship with her, the hero realises that human love provides a more direct sense of beauty and goodness than all the works of poets, philosophers, prophets or saints. In the final scene she sets out in a gondola across the Venice lagoon on a moonlit night to the Island of San Francesco del Deserto, where the hero is camping in solitary contemplation. She arrives just as dawn is breaking and they clasp each other in a divine embrace.

The character of Clare is clearly based on Monica Hadow, though Conway has somewhat upgraded the social standing and heroic status of the man who stole her away from him. But who is Mary? At first I thought she must be Katrina, but many of the scenes and events in which Mary appears in the manuscript – an open air opera in the Piazza of St. Marks in Venice, a visit to Rome, the island near Venice where St. Francis of Assisi prayed – occurred in real life, but not with Katrina. In each case, Conway was with Henry Mond and his young wife Gwen. It appears that while he was writing the penultimate version of his final book, after his relationship with Monica Hadow had come to an end, but before Katrina's death and his marriage to Iva, Conway thought that he had finally found the beauty of true love, and the object of his affections was Gwen Mond.

Conway spent a great deal of time with Henry and Gwen Mond, and dedicated his 1929 book *Giorgione as a Landscape Painter* to the young couple. Gwen also seems to have been fond of Conway. She threw a 'black and white' cocktail party for his 77th birthday that went on until dawn, and another, slightly more subdued, party for his 80th birthday. She planned a third fancy dress party, with 'everyone dressed "according to Freud" – whatever that means', but it never happened. She also commissioned a wonderful portrait of Conway by Augustus John, painter of beautiful women, adventurous men and wild mountains. The painting, showing off his irregularly long grey hair, was exhibited at the Royal Academy and was 'warmly approved for the most part by folk of the younger taste', according to Conway's diary.

Gwen was a 'show stopping beauty'[324] whose uninhibited behaviour scandalised London society. After a particularly lively argument with her husband she put an announcement in *The Times* that read: 'Lady Melchett and Lord Conway will leave shortly for Palestine and South Africa and will be away for some months. No correspondence will be forwarded.' Although they had vaguely talked of a trip to Cape

Town (where Gwen's father lived) the announcement came as a complete surprise to Conway. He attended a meeting at the Royal Geographical Society the day the notice appeared and his fellow council members 'asked me if it is true that I'm going to elope with Gwen'. However, Gwen was unreliable as well as unconventional. She frequently changed her mind, cancelled visits at short notice, or simply failed to turn up 'as seems to be the habit of [her] generation', and the relationship between Conway and Gwen, whatever it had once been, began to cool.

Arnold Lunn observed of Conway that 'few men had a larger circle of friends and few...felt less need for the more intimate and enduring forms of friendship'.[325] While Conway was writing the penultimate, unpublished version of his final book, he apparently thought that he had finally reached the destination of his long pilgrimage in search of love and beauty. By the time that he came to write the final version, he had resumed his lonely lifelong quest.

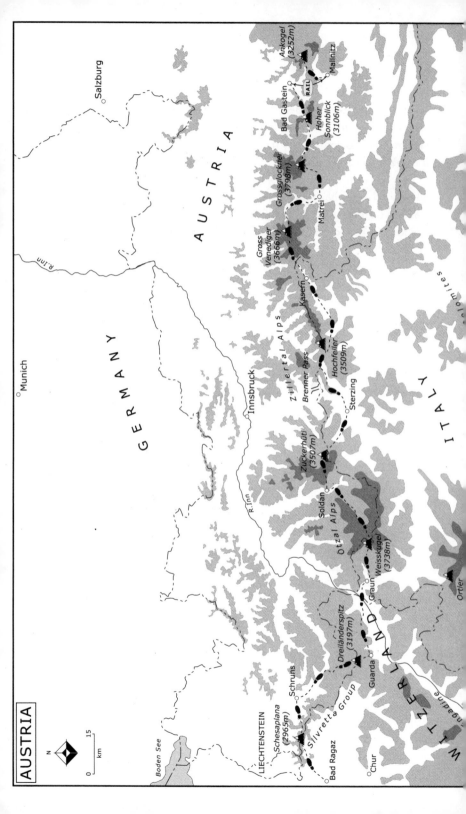

Chapter Seven
To Austria

The Vorarlberg

Both Conway and I entered the westernmost Austrian province of
Vorarlberg just below the summit of the Schesaplana and descended
the rocky path to the cloud-shrouded shores of the Lünersee, once the
largest natural mountain lake in the Eastern Alps, before it was dammed
and enlarged in 1958. The definition of a mountain lake (as opposed to
a valley lake?) is clearly open to interpretation, but the number of high
lakes in the Alps that now exceed the size of the Lünersee underlines
just how many of them are artificial. Purists would argue that all dams
are a bad thing, and no doubt some beautiful valleys have been flooded;
but in other cases these man-made lakes have enhanced the landscape,
their smooth horizontal expanses of water both reflecting and contrasting with the craggy verticality of the surrounding peaks.

From the lake shore, I climbed over two low cols in light rain and
picked my way through muddy cow pastures beneath a huge wall of
deformed limestone. Slabs of rock like toppled tombstones were interspersed with great whorls and flourishes of folded strata, picked out by
ten thousand years of wind and rain. A deep notch in the ridge called
the Schweizertor ('Swiss gate') gave misty views south, over rolling
green country to the valley of the River Landquart. I spent my first
night in Austria in the Lindauer hut, where a friendly waitress advised
me that the rather unexciting *demi-pension* set meal was about to run out
and that if I waited I could get a *Wiener schnitzel* instead. It was sound
advice and my patience was amply rewarded.

After several wet and cloudy days the sun shone brightly in the
morning and the whole world, including me, blossomed in its warmth.
Walking down through alpine meadows to Schruns, a summer breeze
rippled the long grass, freshly opened flowers bobbed and bowed to
passing bees, crickets chirruped, and beneath every rock pale nameless

things wriggled purposefully in the damp, warm earth. Conway was fed up with the Swiss. He probably agreed with Coolidge's assertion that 'the Swiss with whom the ordinary traveller comes into contact, especially the German portion of them, are either polyglot waiters, grasping landlords, or slow-witted and churlish peasants'.[326] Conway had now entered the Austro-Hungarian Empire which, while in no way comparable to England, was nevertheless a great European power, and he expected better things. He immediately commended the people of Schruns as 'evidently of a different race from the surly people south of Ragatz'[327] and praised them for their industriousness. Schruns remains a neat and pleasant town, clustered around a large Catholic church with an onion-topped bell tower and a painting of St. Francis sitting under a pine tree outside his chalet, surrounded by forest animals.

In prehistoric times, Austria was occupied by Celtic and Raetic tribes who were progressively conquered by the Romans.[328] Five centuries of Roman rule ended with a series of invasions from the north by Goths and Huns. Theodoric incorporated the region into his Ostrogothic empire in AD 493, but mass migrations from the north and east continued as Frankish, Bavarian and Slavic tribes competed for control. Charlemagne eventually established Frankish rule over much of the region, but mounted Magyar invaders continued to threaten from the east until King Otto I decisively defeated them in AD 955.

Despite these invasions, traces of Roman language (Romansh) and culture clung on, particularly in the mountains. Christianity was reintroduced, partly by Irish and English clerics, during the seventh and eighth centuries, but German progressively replaced the Latin-based languages. During the twelfth century, the Counts of Tyrol established control over a feudal patchwork of small lordships from their stronghold in Merano (south of the main alpine chain in present-day Italy), while the Babenbergs ruled large parts of the remainder of present-day Austria. When the last Babenberg died in battle in 1246 without leaving a male heir, the region was plunged into a crisis from which the Habsburgs eventually emerged as rulers. They remained so until 1918, two decades after Conway's journey through the Alps.

The Habsburgs came from Aargau in present-day Switzerland, where the Habichtsburg ('Hawk's fortress') was situated, but they were pushed out of their original homeland by the Swiss Confederacy. They acquired the Tyrol in 1363, thereby establishing control over the main trade route between Venice and Germany, while Vienna became a major entrepôt for the land trade between Europe and Constantinople, bringing considerable wealth to the kingdom. Over the ensuing four centuries the Habsburgs built a vast empire through an astute combination of war and marriage, becoming Kings of Germany and Holy Roman Emperors. In 1452 Frederick III created the acronym AEIOU – *Austriae est imperare omni universo* – 'it is for Austria to rule the whole world', an ambition that the family almost achieved in the sixteenth and seventeenth centuries. Frederick's son, Maximilian, moved his capital to Innsbruck, at the northern foot of the Brenner Pass, midway between Austria and his new possessions, acquired through marriage, in Burgundy and the Netherlands. There he built a magnificent chapel dedicated to the royal ancestors claimed by the Habsburg family, including Arthur, King of the Britons. Maximilian arranged marriage alliances with Castile which ultimately led to the Habsburgs claiming the Spanish throne. When Cortez invaded Mexico in 1519 and Pizarro conquered Peru in 1532, the New World was added to the family possessions, leading to vast inflows of bullion. However, the 'Holy Roman Empire' was hopelessly dispersed geographically, and poorly administered internally, compared to emerging nation states such as France and England.

Threatened by Ottoman invaders from the south and the spread of Protestantism from the north, the Austrian branch of the family was constantly forced to compromise with one or the other, while seeking to further their ambition to unite all of Christendom under one Holy (Catholic) sceptre. The Turks laid siege to Vienna in 1529 and again in 1682, while the Thirty Years War (1618-48) between Protestants and the newly resurgent Catholic counter-Reformation devastated large parts of Germany and Silesia. However, for a time it appeared that even England might fall under Habsburg rule, when Philip II from the Spanish branch of the family married Queen Mary, daughter of Henry VIII. After Mary died without children, Philip made overtures to Queen Elizabeth I in 1559 but was rebuffed. The issue was finally settled with the destruction of the Spanish Armada in 1588.

The male Habsburg line in Spain died out, leading to the War of the Spanish Succession of 1700-1714. Bourbon France established control over Spain but the Austrian branch of the Habsburgs retained control of large parts of Italy and the Netherlands, thanks in part to an alliance with England. After the revolution in 1789, France continued to pose a military threat, as well as representing an ideological challenge to the Habsburgs, whose authority was founded upon the three pillars of the monarchy, the aristocracy and the Catholic Church. Allied to Russia, Prussia and England, the Austrians eventually prevailed over France and the conference to decide the post-Napoleonic shape of Europe was held in Vienna in 1815. Despite negotiating from a position of weakness, the Habsburgs did well out of the settlement, swapping Belgium and Swabia for Venice, Salzburg (until then an independent archbishopric), Brixen and Trent, thereby turning the empire into a contiguous geographical block for the first time. However, for many of their citizens the Habsburgs represented the conservative and repressive enemy of liberalism and nationalism.

The revolutions of 1848 failed to depose the monarchy, partly because the aspirations of the revolutionaries within the vast supranational empire were so divided and contradictory, but the final collapse was merely deferred. In 1859 Austria lost control of Lombardy to Piedmont, at the start of the unification of Italy. In 1866 the Austrian army was crushed by the Prussians and the Habsburgs were forced to cede control of Venetia to the new Kingdom of Italy. When Conway travelled through Austria in 1894, the empire was in a state of political crisis, almost paralysed by rivalries between German, Magyar, Czech, Polish, Serb, Croat, Romanian and Slovene nationalists. But *fin de siècle* Austria, especially Vienna, was also a hotbed of intellectual activity where Freud, Wittgenstein, Schoenberg and others 'invented the twentieth century'.

Karl Kraus described Austria-Hungary as the 'proving ground for the world's destruction'.[329] When Austria declared war on Serbia on 28 July 1914, just twenty years after Conway's visit, it plunged the whole of Europe into war and over six centuries of Habsburg rule was swept away, together with the Ottoman Empire to the south and the Russian Tsars to the east. In the economic chaos that followed the dismemberment of the empire, the Vorarlberg held a plebiscite in which over 80%

of the population voted in favour of becoming a canton of Switzerland, but their wishes were rejected both by Austria and by the French- and Italian-speaking cantons of Switzerland. The remainder of Austria overwhelmingly supported a union with Germany, but this was vetoed by France. Cut off from its former empire, Austria's economy collapsed and society polarised into modern, mainly socialist, Vienna and the conservative, Catholic provinces. At the turn of the century, Jews had dominated the intellectual and commercial life of Vienna, but during the 1920s and 30s anti-Semitism increased dramatically. And while Conway made his journey across Austria in 1894, the 5-year-old Adolf Hitler was growing up in Braunau am Inn, just 100 miles to the north.

Conway's route through the Vorarlberg took him up the Montafon valley to Partenen and over the Vermunt Pass into the Lower Engadine. Despite his *excentrist* belief that the ideal climber 'must alternate between high and low, difficult and easy, between ice and woodland, meadow and rock, snowfield, valley and lake',[330] Conway, as usual, chose not to walk in the valley, but instead hired an *Einspänner* (a one-horse carriage). It probably never even occurred to Conway to walk. The world was sufficiently untravelled and unknown to present a challenge without adding unnecessary difficulties, and as the first person to attempt a journey through the Alps from end to end, he took transport whenever it was available. I suspect that Conway would have found the artificial obstacles invented by today's 'explorers' in their quest to do something original, completely incomprehensible. However, had I adopted the same approach as Conway, I would have spent much of my journey sitting in a car; so while Conway trotted along in his *Einspänner*, I walked beside the River Ill enjoying the smell of freshly mown hay.

Conway devised a high level route through most of the Western Alps. The Eastern Alps are lower and more spread out, so his journey necessarily involved more days in the valleys. Inevitably the lowlands have changed much more than the mountains, especially in relatively populous regions like the Montafon. Presumably a fairly high proportion of the new buildings that have sprung up in the valley are holiday homes, but there is also a sizeable permanent population engaged in summer and winter tourism, hydroelectricity, agriculture, local government and other services. For a climber, the main surprise walking through a long valley like the Montafon is the number of cyclists. In normal circumstances, climbers and cyclists inhabit completely separate worlds in the Alps, and I was astonished to discover just how popular the sport has become.

The road from Partenen leads up the Untervermunt valley to the saddle of the Bielerhöhe before dropping eastwards through the Klein Vermunt to the ski resorts of Galtür and Ischgl. The roadless valley to the south of the col has been flooded, but in the Middle Ages this was a major trade route to the Engadine valley in present-day Switzerland. A mule track used to lead over the Vermunt Pass, but the southern portion was deliberately destroyed in 1622 as a defence against possible invasion from the north. Soon afterwards the climate cooled, a glacier formed on the northern slope, and the route was largely forgotten until it was rediscovered by mountaineers in the nineteenth century. The Bielerhöhe also marks the watershed between the Rhine and the Danube. To the east, the rivers are tributaries of the Inn, a powerful mountain river with a greater flow-rate than the Danube at the point where the two join. After passing through the old Habsburg capital of Innsbruck, the waters from these alpine streams flow through Vienna, Bratislava, Budapest and Belgrade on their way to the Black Sea. If the Po belongs to Italy, the Rhône to southern France and the Rhine to Germany, then the Danube surely still belongs to the Austro-Hungarian Empire.

After two warm and cloudless days, the clouds gathered as I walked up to the Wiesbadener hut beneath the Vermunt Pass. Pausing beside the Silvretta-Staussee, I watched the Great Britain rowing team training for the London Olympics on the large artificial lake (which lies above 2,000 m) until a flurry of hailstones and a few flashes of lightning hurried me along. A light drizzle continued until I reached the hut, with the Silvrettahorn and the Piz Buin occasionally appearing through tears in the cloud, coated with a dusting of fresh snow. Conway also had bad weather, and the maps of Austria were less accurate than General Dufour's maps of Switzerland. He got lost at the head of the valley and unintentionally climbed partway up the north-eastern slopes of the Dreiländerspitze before crossing a col to the east of the Vermunt Pass. With a better map, I planned to climb to the summit of the Dreiländerspitze (3,197 m) before contouring round to the pass.

Heavy rain fell throughout the afternoon and evening. By morning it had stopped, but a dark ceiling of cloud hung low over the hut and everyone lingered over breakfast, wondering whether it was going to clear. In the end I got bored and set off, following a good path over moraine and snow on the true right of the Vermunt glacier and then up a steeper section to the west ridge of the Dreiländerspitze. The final climb over snow-covered rocks was dramatic: the summit cross is connected to the main bulk of the mountain by a narrow blade of rock with steep drops into the cloudy depths on either side. Mountain memories are often distorted by the photographic record. I have stood on the summit of every mountain over 3,000 ft in Scotland, but I doubt if I have seen the view from more than half of them. Yet when I look at all the photographs I have taken, I see a world of sunny mountains, sparkling lochs, cloudless skies and dramatic sunsets. My cloudy ascent of the Dreiländerspitze was a fine climb. I had the whole mountain to myself and the drifting mists added to the lonely beauty of this normally popular peak, but in the absence of photographs I wonder whether it will linger in my memory as long as sunnier summits.

Retracing my steps to the glacier, I passed two other parties making their way up, and then headed west, contouring round to the Vermunt Pass. Like Conway, I had some difficulty locating the pass in the cloud, but eventually I found the small hut near the summit and stepped back over the border into Switzerland. The Dreiländerspitze really does stand on the border of three lands: the Vorarlberg, the Tyrol and the canton of Graubünden (Grison) in Switzerland. The three glaciers that fall from its three faces reflect this diversity: the western one is a '*Gletscher*' (German), the eastern one a '*Ferner*' (Tyrolean and Bayern German), while the southern one is a '*Vadret*' (Romansh). A good path led down the far side of the pass, across a small snowfield and past a grey moraine lake, to the Engadine.

The Engadine and Öztal Alps

When they destroyed the mule track over the Vermunt Pass in 1622, the residents of the Lower Engadine succeeded in isolating the valley from foreign influences to the north. Even today, there is a dramatic cultural change as you go over this relatively low pass (2,798 m). To the north, the Vorarlberg is German-speaking and the houses are traditional stone and wood-built chalets. To the south, the Engadine is mainly Romansh-speaking and the older houses are massive stone-built mansions, often housing two or more families, with stone ramps leading up to large arched doorways. The houses are rendered and painted with limewash, and on many the wash has been delicately scraped away to reveal the grey render beneath, creating beautiful floral and scrolled designs around the windows and doors – a technique called *sgraffito*. In Guarda, the first village on the southern side of the Vermunt Pass, several of the houses also have family coats of arms, and the dates of building or restoration work. Conway, who was in a hurry, did not comment on this dramatic change in architecture, perhaps because the houses in the Engadine were more run down then and the decoration less obvious. Several of the larger houses in Guarda were restored in 1943, reflecting the economic boom enjoyed by the region during the Second World War.

The Engadine is one of the few remaining strongholds of Romansh. Derived from vulgar Latin, anyone with a knowledge of French or Latin can have a reasonable stab at understanding the written form, but it is almost impossible to understand the spoken word. 'Engadine' translates as the Garden of the River Inn (En, in Romansh), a 100 km long valley through which the river flows from its source near St. Moritz to the border with the Tyrol. The continental mountain climate of this high valley, with its rarefied air, clear skies and intense sunshine, first attracted visitors to the region in search of a cure for tuberculosis, and I too decided to have a rest day before walking on to the Tyrol.

I checked into an '*hôtel de charme et calme*' in Guarda. It enforced its reputation for *calme* by requiring that residents not take baths between 22.00 and 07.00, and its reputation for *charme* by casting disapproving looks at inappropriate dress in its restaurant. It is hard to maintain one's sartorial elegance on a long walking holiday. Manufacturers of outdoor kit charge huge premiums for clothes that purport to look good while remaining reasonably serviceable in the mountains. But no matter how much you pay, after two or three weeks in a rucksack they all mulch down into a uniform crumpled mess.

On my rest day I strolled up the valley to the village of Lavin, which is less attractive than Guarda but boasts a splendid bakery where I bought a spinach quiche and a huge apple tart. During my entire journey through the Alps to this point I had met just one American, in a deserted campsite in the Maritime Alps. To my amazement, I found the bakery in Lavin packed full of Americans. Furthermore, there were at least two separate groups, and they seemed to be at least as surprised as I was: 'You're from San Diego? No! I'm from Los Angeles. Trust two Californians to meet in a cake shop!'

The following morning I continued my journey along broad terraces on the south-facing side of the Engadine, passing through sunny hay meadows and hamlets. Conway walked as far as Schuls, and then decided to take the diligence to Nauders in the Tyrol, while the rest of his party continued on foot. He remarked on a new spa development near the castle at Tarasp, but confessed that he dozed in the warm sun during most of the journey. I suspect that the Engadine, more than most major valleys, has changed relatively little since Conway's time. Much of the land to the south, stretching to the Italian border, is a national park and was presumably always sparsely inhabited. Schuls is now a major town lying in the bottom of the valley and there is a prominent line of pylons running along the valley floor, but the smaller villages on the terraces above the valley floor have changed relatively little. I spent the night at Sent, a small town full of grand old houses with wood-panelled rooms and finely decorated gables.

The following morning it started to rain as I set out to walk through three countries – Switzerland, Austria and Italy – and it continued all day. Crossing the River Inn, I followed a muddy track through a dank dripping fir forest to S. Niclà and climbed over the wooded shoulder of the Piz Land into Austria. Ducks paddled happily in the Schwarzersee, but the far bank of this local beauty spot was invisible in the mist and driving rain. From the lake shore I followed a path – half track, half river – down to the Reschenpass, crossed the main road and walked along the Via Claudia Augusta, an ancient Roman road that once ran from the Po valley to southern Germany. Crossing the border into Italy, I splashed along the path beside the Reschensee in sheeting rain, trying to imagine the famous view of the Ortler range to the south.

The boundary between France and Italy has changed slightly since Conway's time, but the boundary between Austria and Italy has been completely redrawn. After leaving Italy near the summit of Mont Blanc, Conway did not re-enter the country on his walk, whereas I, following exactly the same route, spent a further 10 days walking through Italy. The 1919 Treaty of St. Germain (the Austro-Hungarian equivalent of the Treaty of Versailles dealing with Germany) rewarded the Allied victors in the First World War and punished their enemies. In compensation for the losses they had suffered, the Italians made substantial territorial claims in Austria and the Balkans; but the French and the British, led by Lloyd George, were not impressed, judging the demands to be out of all proportion to Italy's contribution to the Allied victory. As the British ambassador in Rome observed: 'The signal for the armistice was the signal for Italy to begin to fight.'[331] At one point Orlando, the chief Italian negotiator at the peace conference, made an impassioned speech and left the table in tears, while the French prime minister, Clemenceau, looked on impassively and the British incredulously. Sir Maurice Hankey, the conference secretary, remarked that he would have spanked his son for such a disgraceful show of emotion.[332] Nevertheless, a large part of the German-speaking Tyrol was sliced off Austria and handed over to Italy, where it remains like a foreign body to this day.

Despite the best efforts of Mussolini's Fascist government, which banned the use of German in education and the public sector and encouraged inward migration by Italian-speakers, the 'Süd Tirol' has remained stoically Germanic. In 1943, when Mussolini's government collapsed, Germany occupied the region and effectively annexed it. It was restored to Italy in 1945 on condition that it was granted a high degree of independence by the Italian state. Today the region is semi-autonomous, with wide-ranging legislative powers and the right to retain some 90% of taxes levied. It has become one of the richest regions in Italy. I happened to be climbing in the Ortler range in the South Tyrol during the 2006 World Cup and watched the final, between Italy and France, in a bar in the 'Italian' village of Suldan. Nobody seemed very interested, even when Italy beat France 5:3 on penalties. Possibly they were still recovering from their celebration of Germany's victory over Portugal to take third place.

True to the 'Süd Tirol' tradition, my *pension* in Graun was thoroughly Germanic. After getting out of my soaking clothes and warming up in a hot bath, I went down to the bar, where my request for a glass of Pinot Grigio met with a slightly frosty reception. Glancing round, I became conscious that I was standing in a room full of out-of-work extras from a Herzog movie – stubbly jaws, long thinning blond hair, bulging eyes and worryingly prominent thyroid glands. The young barmaid was friendly enough but apparently incapable of smiling, as if struggling to come to terms with some terrible tragedy in her life. Perhaps someone had just told her that she was Italian.

Conway described the Langtauferer valley as 'very normal'. I thought it was a bit better than that, despite the persistent rain that continued to fall. Fiona rejoined me in Graun for a high level walk through the Öztal and Stubai Alps, and we set off together up a pleasant, though rather wet, track through pine forests on the north-facing slope of the valley, with views down onto chalets and meadows on the south-facing slope. From Melager Alm a zigzag path led steeply up to the Weisskugelhütte, situated in a shallow rocky hollow above the Zunge glacier. A photograph showed the old hut that Conway fulsomely praised in his book: 'The fittings of the place are excellent; chairs, tables, beds, and a hayloft for the guides. It is only in Tirol that such luxuries are to be found.'[333] Inside the hut we discussed our proposed route over the Weisskugel to Vent with three Austrian climbers who all agreed that we were mad: 'Nobody does that route any more,' one of them declared. 'It is too long.' Fortified with pork cooked with ham and cheese, rosemary potatoes and fruit custard, we resolved to try anyway.

It rained heavily overnight and a coating of fresh snow lay around the hut as we set off before dawn the next morning. Dropping down onto the glacier, we climbed up a band of medial moraine before turning right onto the Langtauferer Ferner and up snow slopes to the Weisskugeljoch and the border with Austria. When dawn broke, the day looked quite promising, but as we climbed higher the sky started to cloud over and the summits disappeared from view. On the far side of the col, the icy expanse of the upper Hintereis glacier was interrupted by a few rocky islands, against which the dark clouds seemed to break like ocean waves. A long traverse and a short climb led to the broad snowy shoulder of the Weisskugel which we walked up, with a short scramble along a rocky ridge to the summit cross (3,738 m). Conway was blessed with a clear day and claimed that he saw 'a purple ocean, within whose depths peaks were submerged like coral reefs and soft clouds floated like fair creatures of the sea'.[334] He probably also saw the Öztal Alps, close at hand, and in the distance, the Silvretta and Ortler ranges. Conway frequently gave long descriptions of clouds, partly in imitation of Ruskin, but also because, before the invention of aircraft, only mountaineers saw clouds from above. When he described looking *down* upon clouds, he was describing something that most of his readers had never seen and probably had difficulty imagining. As they stood upon the summit they also saw another unusual sight: an unguided (Conway thought 'misguided') man and his wife 'toilsomely ascending the final rocks of the southern arête'[335] to reach the summit cross.

Retracing our steps to the beginning of the traverse, Fiona led the way on the long descent to Vent. As the Austrians at the hut had predicted, the route had an old-fashioned feel to it with over 7 kilometres of glacier-plodding, first on the right and then straight down the centre of the Hintereisferner. About halfway down, Fiona broke the monotony by disappearing up to her waist into a well-disguised crevasse. Despite the apparent loneliness of our surroundings, as we struggled to pull her out of the hole we became conscious that our efforts were being observed by a group of people standing near a cable car station on a distant ridge high above the glacier. Throughout the day there were occasional showers of hail and it was very cold, for which we were grateful. If it had been hot we would certainly have fried, and possibly fallen into a bigger crevasse. The snout of the Hintereisferner consisted of a dramatic ice cave, out of which the milky waters of the Rofenache emerged from the smooth blue innards of the glacier.

A rough path on the left bank led to the Hochjochhospiz, a fine granite-built hut with baronial turrets, where Conway stopped for a late lunch and we had a hot chocolate. In order to reach the hut, Conway had to cross the snout of the Hochjoch glacier. Today the same glacier has retreated some 4 kilometres up a side valley. A lithograph produced in 1869, showing the panorama from the nearby summit of the Kreuzspitze, records just how heavily glaciated the Öztal Alps were in the mid nineteenth century. Glaciers that have now all but disappeared used to snake their way far down into the valleys. Continuing over the rubble they have left behind, we walked through the Rofenache gorge where the river has carved a steep canyon through rusty rocks, dotted with dwarf pine trees. A notice board informed us that the Tyrol Water Company intends to build a 170 m high dam here. Beyond the gorge, the path became a track and descended to the highest permanently inhabited village in Austria at Rofen. We crossed the river on a new suspension bridge, and walked down through an alpine garden to Vent.

Conway had a rest day in Vent, but he did not enjoy it much. Even as they approached the village he had misgivings about the climbers that they passed: 'They were all Germans and of a different class from the normal travellers in Switzerland. Most carried their own packs.'[336] To his horror, the inn had been 'invaded by a horde of tourists, for the most part drawn from the very much lower-middle classes of small south-German towns...The fact is, parts of the Tirol, though practically free from the herd of English Cook's tourists, are over-run by an even less lovely crowd...an undesirable multitude, who love closed windows, bad air, and strong coarse food...The activities of the German and Austrian Alpine Club have no doubt opened the mountains to a number of persons who otherwise would never have visited them, and who profit greatly by the exercise, the fine air, the noble views, that Nature provides for all alike; but in so doing, it has made parts of the country unpleasant to travel in.'

The English may have 'made' the Western Alps,[337] but the development of the tourist industry in the Eastern Alps was overwhelmingly driven by the Germans. The Austrian and German Alpine Clubs merged into one in 1874, by which time they already had over 18,000 members. At the same time the (English) Alpine Club had just 450 members. While the Alpine Club was deliberately kept small and socially exclusive, the continental alpine clubs were national associations, set up to provide cheap accommodation for their membership, which included large numbers of mountain walkers as well as climbers. Given its size, the

German and Austrian Alpine Club divided itself into local sections for administrative purposes, and each section competed with the others to increase membership and to raise money for hut building in the Alps. The approach vastly increased the number of alpinists emerging from Germany and Austria in the late nineteenth century and, as a result, they caught up and progressively overtook the British at the forefront of mountaineering, particularly after the First World War.

After another wet night in Vent, Fiona and I woke to an autumnal scene, with snow almost down to the valley floor. We followed the road down the narrow Ventertal to Bodenegg and then a path to the village of Zwieselstein at the junction with the Gurgler Tal, which contains the highest parish in Austria at Obergurgl (1,907 m). The path beyond Zwieselstein ran through a steep wooded gorge, where the fast-flowing River Öz was almost choked with huge fallen boulders. Leaving the beautiful gorge behind, we abruptly arrived in the tourist conurbation of Sölden, and a high density development of back-to-back chalets.

The once tiny hamlet of Sölden is now a popular ski resort which has expanded and engulfed the surrounding villages filling the wide valley of the Öz. The river front in the centre of town resembles a garish seaside resort with advertising hoardings proclaiming the virtues of 'Bier Himmel' and 'The Lucky Shag' (an Irish bar). As the *Michelin Guide to Austria* observes: 'Holidaymakers in Sölden can continue partying at full steam until well into the night.' An old photograph in the hotel where we stayed showed just how much the town has expanded, but equally striking was the amount of reforestation that has taken place above the village, perhaps because of a warmer climate, or deliberate planning to reduce the risk of avalanches and landslides.

In Sölden, as in many other villages in Switzerland and Austria, the town planners have made some attempt to preserve the 'alpine' character of the village. Many of the modern houses and apartment blocks consist of a white concrete box to which a pitched roof, rough stone cladding and wooden balconies have been added in a more or less successful pastiche of a chalet. From a distance the effect is not too bad, but the layout of the town is still incongruous. In traditional villages, people adapted their buildings to nature, using raw materials that were readily available and positioning the chalets to make best use of the land.

Contours were used to give direct access to various floors of the building. Sites were chosen to avoid avalanche paths and flooding, to provide easy access to running water or hay meadows, or simply to catch the morning sun. Seen in plan, the arrangement of the houses looks random, but each site was chosen for a purpose. In contrast, the chalet suburbs of Sölden, and many other expanding villages, have been designed by architects and planners from the distant plains, who expect nature to adapt to the needs of people. More than anything else, it is the straight lines of houses that destroy the natural harmony of the scene.

The Stubai Alps

After a rest day in Sölden, we took the path up the wooded valley of the Windache, in company with many other walkers who greeted us and each other as we slowly zigzagged up the hillside. In Switzerland the most common greeting in the mountains is '*Gruetzi*'. In Austria the older generation say '*Grüss Gott*', while the young seem to prefer the more secular and international '*Allo*'. Higher up the valley, the crowds and the forest gradually thinned out until there were just the two of us and a few stunted and wind-battered trees, tugging at the thin soil. When we stopped for lunch, two weasels with golden brown backs and bright white bellies ran around the rocks in front of us, apparently unconcerned by our presence. Continuing up the mountainside we reached the Hildesheimer Hütte, built by the Hildesheim section of the German and Austrian Alpine Club, which stands on the edge of the Stubai Alps with grand views back towards the Weisskugel and other Öztal peaks. In the hut there was a bank holiday atmosphere, with several large groups of walkers and climbers drinking beer and telling tales. The demographics were striking: the youngest members of the larger groups appeared to be in their late 40s and the eldest were certainly in their late 60s. After dinner the singing started, accompanied by schnapps and a guitar. Breakfast at 05.00 the following morning was a subdued affair, with several people clearly nursing massive hangovers.

Leaving the hut, we dropped down to a small lake and climbed up a boulder slope to join the Pfaffen glacier which led easily to the Pfaffenjoch. The early morning sun lit up a few high, broken clouds, and the distant glaciers of the Öztal Alps sparkled on the horizon. On the far side of the pass a clear path led through deep snow to the saddle below the Zuckerhütl (3,507 m). The sun had melted the top of the sugar loaf, once a perfect white cone, leaving a rocky brown scramble to the top. As we climbed, a small wisp of cloud inconveniently settled on the summit and obscured the view. A sticker attached to the summit cross declared (in German) that 'the South Tyrol is not Italian'.

Returning to the snowy saddle, we collected our sacks and climbed a slope of loose scree to the Wilder Pfaff (3,456 m). The summit stands at the junction of four rocky ridges separated by four glaciers and gives a wide panorama over a pristine landscape of ice, rock, clouds and sky. When a journalist asked T. E. Lawrence what it was that attracted him to the desert he is reputed to have replied: 'It's clean.' No doubt there was a moral dimension to his answer, following in the long literary tradition contrasting the purity of the wilderness with the corruption, greed and vanity of cities; but perhaps there was also a purely physical side to his answer. At the beginning of the twentieth century, heavy industry, coal fires, inadequate sanitation and horse manure created an atmosphere in many British cities more akin to an overcrowded slum in today's developing world than to a modern European city. Conway's diary for 24 July 1904 contains a newspaper cutting reporting the extraordinary weather conditions that had occurred the previous day, when a strong wind temporarily blew away the thick pall of smoke that habitually hung over the city of London: 'People armed with telescopes and field glasses had gathered...to enjoy the rare spectacle of their city lying before them unveiled, from Hampstead to Woolwich, from Epping to Dulwich...across the river the twin towers and rounded block of the Crystal Palace stood up on the ridge.' Perhaps part of the appeal of mountains and deserts really was that they were *clean.*

From the summit of the Wilder Pfaff, we climbed down the narrow eastern arête on the frontier between Austria and Italy. Conway would have disapproved of the cables that were attached to the steeper sections: 'The Tirol is cursed with wire-ropes. Wherever a good scramble was offered by nature, it has been ruined in this fashion by man, with the result that any lumpkin can get conveyed almost anywhere in this mountain area.'[338] We arrived at the Müllerhütte (just below the ridge on the Italian side) at midday, dropped off our sacks, had a bowl of pea and sausage soup, and set off to climb the Wilder Freiger (3,418 m). Crossing the glacier, we scrambled up to the Signalgipfel, walked along the summit ridge and descended the south-west arête. The Stubai Alps consist of high glaciers and low mountains, so it is easy to traverse two or three peaks on a good day. Conway, however, was caught in fog and rain, which turned to snow as he climbed: 'In such weather peak-climbing could not be thought of. To cross a pass of 3,327 metres was already enough to tax our energies to the utmost.'[339]

We went to bed early, but the August bank holiday celebrations continued well into the night in the Müllerhütte, where an accordion player accompanied enthusiastic singing, stomping and yodelling. The following morning we were amongst the few to watch the sun rise over Italy. Along the distant horizon, the jagged towers of the Dolomites were silhouetted against a rose pink sky. In the middle distance, ridge upon ridge rose out of the soft mist in the Ridnauntal, and in the foreground the snow and ice of the Botzer reflected the glowing dawn above the icy grey wastes of the Eben glacier. We crossed the glacier towards the Beckerhaus, which was under construction when Conway passed this way. He described it as a 'veritable hotel, built in two stories with many rooms, and inhabited by servants all the summer'.[340] Like Conway, we followed the rough stone staircase constructed for the porters who carried up the materials for the building from the valley nearly 2,000 m below. After crossing a second snowfield we dropped down to the Übertalsee, mesmerised by the ever-changing cloud effects in the valley as the low-angled sun cut through a semi-transparent veil of mist. A well-engineered path led past the Teplitz hut to the Grohmann hut, which Conway described as being near the glacier foot, but which today sits in a grassy hollow far below the snowline. The path continued down through the Fernerbach valley to a beautiful tree-lined gorge filled with flowers and ferns where the river tumbled round innumerable mossy boulders and bubbled over rocky ledges. Below, a fertile U-shaped valley stretched out before us, with the church of St. Magdalena standing on a wooded knoll.

When he reached the valley floor Conway described 'a frightful disfigurement – the whole paraphernalia of a mining establishment on a large scale, with smoking chimney, hideous buildings, and a brown dust and scum over everything, bringing death to all neighbouring trees'.[341] Vegetation has covered the waste dumps and tailings, while the old buildings now house a mining museum. The valley processing plant was once connected by tramway to the Schneeberg silver mines, high above the valley, where mining has taken place for almost 800 years. We followed the old miners' track down through the Ridnaun valley to the riverside village of Mareit, sheltered below the baronial-style Wolfsthurn Castle, now a museum of hunting and fishing.

Conway spent the night at Mareit, where a 'domestic fiend' put his boots too near to the kitchen fire and burnt the side of one to a cinder. Next day he drove to Sterzing in search of a cobbler. We went directly to Sterzing, following a cycle track through a small industrial estate and across a motorway, to reach the old town. Conway first visited Sterzing in 1875 as part of a Cambridge reading party. In 1894 he returned to the Krone Inn where he had lodged as a student and found the son of the old proprietor in charge and his room unaltered. We arrived, hot, tired and dehydrated, to find the Ferragosto holiday celebrations in full swing. Rows of tables and benches were laid out in the main square, filled with people eating sausages and drinking beer while a brass band belted out Tyrolean tunes. The old town (confusingly called the New Town after it was rebuilt following a fire in 1443) is essentially a single street through which much of the trade between Venice and southern Germany once flowed on its way up and down the Brenner Pass. In the middle of the town are a tall stone tower and gateway, built in 1472, decorated with the double-headed eagle of the Habsburgs, representing the twin authority of church and state. Most of the houses on the street were constructed in the fifteenth and sixteenth centuries in late Gothic style, with crenellated roofs, stone arcades, bow windows and decorative wrought-iron signs. A lantern slide in the RGS Archives shows the same street in 1894: the road is unpaved, and has a shallow drainage ditch in the middle, but the houses are unchanged. The building that once housed the Krone Inn still exists. The first floor is now occupied by a firm of lawyers, while the cavernous basement has been converted into a mall of small boutiques and renamed Elvis Presley Boulevard. Only the Kronen Keller maintains the building's 700-year tradition of religious and then secular hospitality. Goethe appears to be the alpine equivalent of Mary Queen of Scots – almost every old hostelry claims that he stayed at least once, and the Krone is no exception. Archduke Franz Ferdinand was also a guest, in the dying days of the Austro-Hungarian Empire.

In the post office at Sterzing, Fitzgerald discovered that he had been summoned to London on urgent business, and departed for home. Deprived of his company, and his contribution to expedition expenses, Conway dismissed Aymonod and Carrel and completed the rest of the journey with the two Gurkhas. In the absence of Fitzgerald's manservant he also had to send his luggage on by post. I too was summoned to business meetings, in London, Sweden and the USA, but unlike Fitzgerald I returned to Sterzing, determined to complete the journey before the first snows of autumn. During the meeting in the USA we approved a major investment in a gold mine in Peru, so I felt that Conway would have sympathised with the reasons for my temporary absence.

The Zillertal and Venediger Groups

I arrived back in Sterzing on a cool but clear evening in the first week of September. The brass band had packed up and gone home, and so had most of the crowds. Sitting in the main street drinking a glass of wine, it was easy to imagine the essentially medieval way of life that Conway described in his diary for 1875. The following day I set off on a drizzly morning to walk up the Pfitscher Tal. Conway took the train to Brennerbad, waved goodbye to Fitzgerald, and walked over a low col to reach the same valley at Kematen. I followed the valley, passing a small seventeenth-century chapel dedicated to Our Lady of Mercy, which was built shortly after the region had been ravaged by 30 years of religious wars and devastated by the Great Plague. Higher up, the Zillertal Alps came into view to the east with the jagged saw-tooth ridge of the Hochferner to the south. I spent the night in a simple but friendly *Gasthof* in Stein and continued my damp walk the following morning along a good forest track. An indistinct path tempted me to gamble on a shortcut to a long zigzag in the track and I was soon fighting through fallen trees and clawing my way up blank, moss-covered walls of rock. Wet, cut and bruised, I eventually staggered out of the undergrowth and back onto the track, having demonstrated, yet again, that there is rarely time for a shortcut on a mountain walk.

The path climbed steadily up, with the Gilder and Weisskar glaciers periodically visible through clouds at the head of a wild and desolate valley. Some of the boulders of silvery mica schist lying beside the path were studded with ruby red garnets. I dropped off most of my kit at the Hochfeilerhütte and continued up the Hochfeiler (3,509 m). The rain turned to snow as I climbed, but a good path led almost to the summit cross, the final part up a snow-covered ridge with dramatic views through mist and falling snow to glaciers on either side. From the summit the icy north face dropped precipitously into the clouds. There were no footprints in the snow and the muffling silence of falling flakes added to the sense of isolation and wildness of the peak. Humans are gregarious animals and even in the mountains the presence of other people gives a sense of comfort. But several fatalities in the high Himalaya appear to have been caused, at least in part, by the presence of large numbers of climbers, lulling each other into a false sense of security. Alone, you know that you have no one else to rely on and it pays periodically to ask the 'Joe Simpson question': If I broke my leg here, how long would it take to crawl to safety?

We are all accustomed to topographical maps where the distance between two objects on the map is proportional to their horizontal separation in reality. On the plains this gives a reasonable measure of isolation, but not in the mountains. A plain-dweller might describe a place as 5 miles distant, but in the mountains distance is measured in hours not miles. A *topological* map showing how long it takes to walk from one place to another would be broadly similar to a topographical map in flat country, but in a hilly region the peaks would expand, while the valleys would contract. In the mountains, you are often within sight of a town or village, but it may take many hours, even days, of effort to get there. Measure isolation by time, not space, and vast regions of wilderness open up in the mountains.

By this stage in his walk, Conway was thoroughly fed up with isolation and rapidly falling out of love with the Alps. After travelling for

75 days and finding himself deprived, once again, of English company, he discovered that 'nothing is nastier than a stony path. Loose stuff slips under the foot, whilst fixed lumps trip you up...How annoying a small discomfort may become if it continues long enough!'[342] Beset by snow and high winds, he gave up his attempt on the Hochfeiler: 'The Hochfeiler may be the easiest mountain in the Alps, but that day it would have killed us',[343] he wrote. Nevertheless, he appears to have included it in his tally of peaks; and just a short time later he described seeing the distant Dolomites under a clear blue sky.

At the Hochfeiler hut I asked for breakfast at 06.00 the following morning. There were only three other people staying at the hut and the guardian suggested 07.00 instead. I showed him on the map where I intended to walk the next day and he informed me that the path was *kaput*. We compromised on 06.30. Dawn broke as I set off, to reveal a clear sky and fresh powdery snow around the hut. I crossed the Gilder glacier, over a flat section of ice runnelled with meltwater channels, and arrived on the far side to find a short rock wall with a steel ladder suspended in space several metres above the glacier. Fortunately there was a perfectly easy way up the rocks just round the corner. I climbed up to the Weisszint Pass (2,974 m) and followed a good path on the far side, looking down onto the Eisbruggsee in its shadowy hollow, with the Marmolada glinting in the distance. Ignoring the guardian's warnings, I followed the Höhenweg through an alpine garden, contouring high above the blue waters of the Neves-Stausee, with fine views of the snowy Gross Möseler. Almost directly beneath the summit of the Möseler, the path was indeed *kaput*, in so far as it had been washed away by a river, but anybody incapable of fording the river and climbing the steep bank on the far side should not have been there in the first place. When hut guardians give stern warnings of this kind, I worry that I must look like a bit of a wimp.

Conway stayed at the Nevesjoch hut and enlivened his account of the night by claiming that the hut was haunted (by mice). I carried on down a good path to Weissenbach (or Rio Bianco) where two rivers, one perfectly clear, the other loaded with white sediment, join in the middle of the village. A steep track led down, past the 14 stations of the cross, to the small town of Luttach in the main valley. As I checked into a quiet hotel, I imagined that I would have the place to myself, but as I hung out my washing on the balcony two coachloads of old-age pensioners arrived just in time for dinner, and they were clearly very hungry. After soup and pasta I was feeling pleasantly full, but the old boys and girls continued to tuck in with a vengeance. Elbowed aside at the salad bar, I caught the eye of one of the coach drivers, who had been practically wrestled to the ground by the wrinkled hordes. He gave a resigned shrug and raised his eyes to heaven. The following morning the pensioners laid siege to the breakfast buffet, stuffing their handbags with food for the long coach trip to the next meal.

Conway hired an *Einspänner* for the 15-mile journey through the Ahrntal to Kasern, describing the valley as 'not above the average'.[344] The fact is, Conway was running out of things to say, a problem that afflicts all travel writers as they reach the end of a long journey. Even Ruskin admitted to the difficulty: 'I determined that the events and sentiments of this journey should be described in a poetic diary...Two cantos of this work were indeed finished – carrying me across France to Chamouni – where I broke down, finding that I had exhausted on the Jura all the descriptive terms at my disposal, and that none were left for the Alps.'[345] However, the Ahrntal, like so many alpine valleys, was isolated for so long that it developed a distinctive character, still discernible today. Along the valley floor, the paths are dotted with crucifixes and some of the older houses have wall paintings, faded but still preserved, of the Madonna or St. George. There was also a painting of a poor man begging a mounted knight for mercy or for alms. Several of the older wooden chalets have partially boarded-up balconies, with just a horizontal slot to let in the light, making them look a bit like a gun emplacement. Above the valley floor, a dense network of paths, many not shown on the 1:50,000 map, connects chalets, hay barns and meadows, providing a peaceful highway through the valley, while above the forests to the north a few small glaciers creep down the valley side from the spiny ridge of the Zillertal Alps.

You know that you are reasonably fit when a 15-mile walk carrying a heavy rucksack, with a height gain of about 2,000 ft, feels like a rest day. It was pleasantly warm in the valley, with a silky wind, so I lay on a flowery bank and watched the farmers bringing in the hay. Lazily rolling over, I took a closer look at the crop that has underpinned the alpine economy for generations. An 'intelligent designer' would surely have carpeted the hillside with one or two perfectly designed species of plant. Only a messy, random process like evolution could have produced such a profusion of species: up to 50 different, slightly imperfect and extraordinarily varied solutions to the unique problem of survival, on one square metre of alp.

There is still some light industry in the valley, but the Ahrntal is probably less industrialised now than it was in the nineteenth century. Beside the fast-running rivers stand numerous abandoned watermills, and museums at Steinhaus and Kasern record the valley's rich mining history. Copper was mined here from the fifteenth century until 1893 – just one year before Conway's visit – when the metal price dropped in response to rich discoveries in the New World. Just below Kasern are the ruins of a copper smelter that must once have filled the valley with the acrid stench of sulphur dioxide. Presumably the forests were much reduced too, as timber was harvested for fuel and pit props.

I arrived at the *Gasthof* in Kasern in the early afternoon. The owner was enjoying an afternoon snooze, but the cook banged on his bedroom door and woke him up. 'This is the proprietor', she explained, as he greeted me in his underpants. Next morning I walked into the Naturpark Riserferner Ahrn, which was crowded with visitors even though the scenery was not markedly different from the deserted paths just outside the park. A path ran up the valley floor, through birch trees just beginning to turn to autumn gold. From the Birnlücke hut there were good views back along the almost straight Ahrntal to the mountains above Luttach, over 20 miles away. Based on recent precedent I expected the hut to be empty, but a large group of walkers was having lunch. After the meal was cleared away they began to sing, in close harmony, a series of drinking songs and sad ballads. It was hard to tell whether this was a group of singers who had gone for a walk or a group of walkers who just happened to be very good singers. After a final glass of schnapps, and a song for the guardian, they departed for the valley.

Next morning I climbed up to the Birnlücke and re-entered Austria (where Conway had been all along). The summit of the rocky pass looked out over the broad Krimmler glacier, pouring slowly down the side of the great mountain bowl like blue-tinged porridge. Conway had to cross the glacier to reach the Warnsdorfer hut. Today it has retreated into the cirque and the path passes over ridges of terminal moraine, marking successive phases of melting. Conway was impressed by the Warnsdorfer hut, so I stopped for tea to inspect it: 'This was the first specimen I saw of the modern elaborate German and Austrian Club-huts. Its like does not exist outside the Tirol...It has a dining-room, kitchen and various bedrooms. A clean little woman lives in it all summer and does cooking and service. The traveller can procure a hot meal of fresh meat and the like at any time. He can have a fire in his bedroom! He can buy wine and liqueurs...There are tables and table cloths, beds with sheets, books, clocks, barometer, a post-box, maps, a guitar, looking-glasses, and all conceivable fittings...Such is the modern type of hut, which the rivalry of the Sections of the German and Austrian Alpine Club has generated...The wretched Mont Blanc shelter would not be tolerated in Tirol by a third-rate D. u. Oe. A.V. Section.'[346] His description fits perfectly today, and Austrian huts are still vastly superior to French ones.

After tea, I climbed up the mountainside behind the hut, crossed the bleak, rocky Krimmler Törl and got my first proper view of the Grossvenediger range with its four magnificent broken glaciers almost meeting beneath the distant Kürsinger hut, my destination for the night. In Conway's day all four glaciers converged into a huge icefall called the Turkish Camp (because it was chaotic?). Today the glaciers flow into a shallow lake above a waterfall. I walked down the left bank of the Obersulzbach glacier, which was more crevassed than I had anticipated. Geographers define two types of glacier: 'dry' glaciers have no covering of snow and are typically wet with meltwater; whereas 'wet' glaciers are covered with snow and are usually dry. The Obersulzbach is a 'dry' glacier and so relatively safe for solo travel because the crevasses are clearly visible. However, its surface is corrugated with smooth meltwater channels and waterfalls cascade into deep blue sink holes in the ice. I left the glacier about halfway down and scrambled down a rocky ridge to the milky lake beneath the glacier snouts. The map showed a long detour along the base of a line of cliffs, but a magnificent new path, equipped with cables, climbed directly up the mountainside with fine views back onto the ice lake and the glaciers beyond.

The Kürsinger hut can accommodate 150 people, but there seemed to be just five other guests. Conway spent four nights here, trapped by bad weather. The second day of his confinement was the birthday of the Emperor Franz Joseph, who ruled over the Austro-Hungarian Empire for 68 years from 1848 to 1916. An Austrian sailor staying at the hut insisted that Conway should send a porter down to the valley to buy champagne: 'Our Emperor is a good man, and withal a merry. He understands a joke. If he knew that we had drunk his health up here in the snow, he would be pleased, but if he also knew that we had made an Englishman pay, if he knew that Austrians had drunk his health at a foreigner's cost, that would really delight him.'[347] A porter was duly dispatched and a photograph taken of the toast, with the Gurkhas standing proudly to attention. On the morning of the fifth day Conway climbed over the Venedigerscharte, a high col just 250 m below the top of the Grossvenediger, but was driven back from the summit by freezing winds. Nevertheless, he appears to have counted the Grossvenediger as one of his 'peaks', and one wonders whether he would have made it to the top of the Grossvenediger (and the Hochfeiler) if Aymonod and Carrel had still been with him.

Fiona rejoined me at the Kürsinger hut, and we set off before dawn the next day. After several cloudy summits, it was a joy to wake up and find a perfectly clear sky. We climbed a ridge on the right bank of the Obersulzbach glacier, crossed a crevasse zone, and walked up snow to the Venedigerscharte (3,407 m). Leaving our rucksacks near the pass, we continued up a snowy ridge and joined the milling crowds around the huge summit cross of the Grossvenediger. A superb panorama opened up as we climbed. To the east, the gaunt rocky pyramid of the Grossglockner dominated the horizon above the smooth white expanse of the Schlaten glacier. To the south, a succession of hazy ridges led to the Dolomites and a contingent horizon of rocky spires, partially hidden by a line of fluffy cumulus. To the west, the ridges and glaciers of the Venediger group and Zillertal Alps sparkled in the morning light; while to the north, green valleys and hills led to the Zumspitze, the highest peak in Germany.

We walked down the Schlaten glacier, which was rapidly turning to slush in the warm sun, and crossed a boulder field to the Neue Prage hut. After a bowl of soup, we carried on down a good path through high alpine meadows above the long crevassed tongue of the Unterer Keesboden and down a rocky step to the Gschlössbach. A pleasant track led through the wooded valley, passing an improbably clean riverside hamlet. Any cow that had the temerity to leave a pat here would have been instantly banished to a less fastidious herd.

The Grossglockner

We spent the night at Matreier Tauernhaus, which has been managed by the Brunner and Rieper families since the nineteenth century. The Hohe Tauern region is named after these ancient mountain inns, which have provided food and shelter for travellers and traders since Roman times. Next day, we walked gently down the Tauernbach valley through forests and meadows where the hay cut the previous day and left to dry was spangled with morning dew. Only a long line of pylons disfigured the scene. While some hydroelectric dams may enhance the landscape, the same cannot be said of the transmission lines that carry the power to distant consumers. Power lines inevitably have to pass above all obstructions and pylons are deliberately sited on prominent knolls, to reduce the risk of avalanche damage. As a result, they spoil the appearance of many beautiful valleys, but no doubt it would be prohibitively expensive to bury them.

Dropping down to Matrei we entered a fertile agricultural valley protected by a white castle on a rocky mount, surrounded by neat chalets, barns and orchards of plum trees. A large church at the centre of the small town had an airy white interior, a richly decorated altar and large windows giving views of the surrounding peaks. Conway's boots, burnt by the 'domestic fiend' in Mareit, had continued to give him trouble. He had them repaired in Sterzing, St. Jakob just below Kasern, and again at Luttach. My clothing and equipment were also beginning to show some signs of wear and tear. The soles of my boots were worn almost smooth, I was reduced to one trekking pole after the other snapped during a rather hard landing from a leap over a river, and the ankles of my overtrousers were perforated with crampon holes. The latter needed urgent repair, but for some reason Fiona's German O-level vocabulary did not extend to the word for 'gaffer tape'. We went into a small stationer's in Matrei, with no particular expectation of success, only to be confronted with a vast array of *Gewebeband* in assorted widths and colours. Evidently I was not alone in having to conduct some running repairs in Matrei.

After a rest day, we set out on a cloudy morning to walk over the Kals-Matreier-Törl, a grassy col between the two towns that apparently has fine views of both the Grossvenediger and the Grossglockner. Throughout his long walk, Conway had gone at his own pace, relying upon the guides to keep track of the Gurkhas, who no doubt followed rather more slowly with their heavy packs. Now in sole charge of the Gurkhas, but eager to get down to the valley in time for lunch, Conway set off down the grassy slopes of the Kals-Matreier-Törl at a brisk pace, having vaguely pointed out the distant Stüdlhütte on the far side of the valley as their destination. The village of Grossdorf immediately below the pass did not have an inn, so he carried on to Kals. After a leisurely lunch he set out for the Stüdlhütte, despite the fact that the Gurkhas had still not appeared. Upon arrival at the hut, he became increasingly annoyed at the prospect of his ascent of the Grossglockner being delayed if they failed to turn up. Amar Sing and Karbir eventually arrived the following morning, having searched two valleys for Conway and spent the night in a haystack. Bored with waiting for them in the overcrowded Stüdlhütte, Conway immediately insisted that they carry on to the Erzherzog-Johann-Hütte, the highest in Austria.

From Kals, we walked up the Ködnitztal to the Lucknerhaus which was 'named from its peasant owner'[348] according to Conway. Today the Luckners appear to be prosperous hoteliers. The steep valley framed fine views back to the wooded slopes of the Kals-Matreier-Törl and up to the grey pyramid of the Grossglockner. It was a clear day but a cool wind carried a strong hint of autumn as we climbed up to the Berger Törl and contoured round the upper valley of the Leiter to the Salmhütte. The hut is named after the Carinthian Prince-Bishop Franz Xaver Graf von Salm-Reifferscheid, who sponsored the first expedition to climb the Grossglockner in 1799. Six local men reached the top of the Kleinglockner but feared to make the exposed traverse to the higher peak. The Bishop sent an even larger expedition the following year, consisting of 62 people, five of whom succeeded in reaching the Grossglockner and built a cross upon the summit. At the celebrations that followed, 'Champagne, Tokay and Malaga flowed as if they were pressed from the nearby glacier',[349] according to the expedition's chronicler. The mountain is the highest peak in Austria at 3,798 m and has the longest glacier in the Eastern Alps (the Pasterze). It is an imposing mountain, dwarfing the surrounding peaks and dominating the valleys below. It is also very popular. In the main square of Kals, beside the church, there is a sobering memorial to hundreds of climbers that have died on the Grossglockner, the majority of them young men.

The season was definitely drawing to a close, and we were the only people intending to climb the mountain from the Salmhütte next day. We set off before dawn on a good path, passing the site of the old hut, built for the first expedition to the peak. After crossing the rock-covered snout of the Hohenwartkees we climbed steeply up through mist to a small col overlooking the Hofmann glacier. Dawn broke and the low sun periodically burst through gaps in the grey clouds, illuminating patches of rock and ice below. Climbing up the glacier and a rocky ridge above, we reached the Erzherzog-Johann hut, where Conway stayed, and continued up the glacier behind the hut to a muddy couloir. Conway climbed a sharp snow arête to the top of the Kleinglockner. We scrambled up the ridge on perfect rock to the famous Obere Glocknerscharte – 'the theatrical portion of the mountain'[350] – a narrow rocky notch between the Klein and Grossglockner with steep drops to either side. At the elaborate summit cross we found a party of four Poles taking photographs, but no view. Conway climbed the peak on a perfect day and took one photograph looking back to the Grossvenediger and another looking across the Obere Glocknerscharte to the Kleinglockner, showing the narrow gap under at least a metre of snow.

Conway claims that he descended from the summit to the hut in 17 minutes. By now there were no witnesses to question his account. Both Amar Sing and Karbir were illiterate, and only their fellow Gurkhas heard their account of the journey. We returned more slowly to the Salm hut and ate a bowl of pumpkin soup before continuing down the valley to Heiligenblut. Distant rumbles of thunder and inter-mittent marmot whistles accompanied us through high pastures and scattered larch forest, slowly turning to autumn gold. By the time we reached Trogalm, the storm was directly overhead with brilliant flashes of lightning and torrential rain. We jogged down the track to Heiligenblut and sheltered in the church, which contains a remarkable carved and painted altarpiece depicting the Virgin Mary surrounded by saints. The late Gothic church was built with money from the mines that flourished in the Goldberg mountains above Heiligenblut in the fif-teenth and sixteenth centuries, before the glaciers advanced and covered up the workings. The wealth of the gold miners was sufficient to attract sculptors and artists to this remote mountain village, and their work still shines with beauty, centuries after the closure of the mines.

Next morning we set off to climb the Hoher Sonnblick, passing through an old mining district in the Kleinfleisstal, where tourists now pan for gold. The track continued up through forests, over rocky ledges and up the Kleinfleiss glacier to the Zittelhaus, perched on the very top of the Hoher Sonnblick (3,106 m) on the border of the province of Salzburg. Through broken clouds, the peak appeared to command a fine panorama of the Goldberg and Grossglockner groups, but Conway dis-missed the view as 'overpraised' by the 'crowds of visitors who daily throng' to see it.[351] The descent was via a long rocky arête above the Goldbergkees, which led to more mine workings near the snout of the glacier. Waste dumps, a tramway and the ruins of a watermill that must once have crushed the ore are still visible amongst the rock dumps and moraine. We followed an old miners' track down to the Ammerhof, a beautifully preserved mountain inn dating from 1897, where another guest told us that he had stayed there every year for the last 40 years. 'It hasn't changed a bit', he said. 'Only the glaciers have gone.' The terrace overlooked the upper Hottwinkltal with the Zittelhaus clearly visible on the summit of the Sonnblick and small remnant glaciers and waterfalls cascading into the deep wooded valley below.

After two peaks in two days, we decided a rest day was in order and walked gently over the Bockshartscharte to Bockstein. Morning mist clung to the treetops in the Hottwinkltal but the mountain peaks shimmered in the sun. On the far side of the pass, the track dropped down past lakes and scattered workings where miners had chased a vein of ore up the mountainside. A steep drop led to Sportsgastein, a cable car station, busy even at this time of the year, sitting on the flat grassy floor of a rocky cirque. We followed the river down through a steep valley containing numerous relics of past mining activity, including an early-nineteenth-century crushing plant and the remnants of a cable tramway – apparently the first in Europe – that once brought ore down to the valley from the mines high above. In Bockstein, several of the houses bore the miners' mark of two crossed picks.

From Bockstein, Conway walked up to the Hannoverhaus and spent the night before climbing the Ankogel, his final peak. A lantern slide in the RGS collection shows the Gurkhas emerging from the small wooden hut on the last day of their expedition. As we were now well into the second half of September, we telephoned to check that the hut was still open: we were told that it relied upon a nearby cable car station for water, and since the cable car had closed for the season the previous weekend, the hut was obliged to do the same. As a result, we decided to catch the shuttle train from Bockstein through the tunnel to Mallnitz, to climb the Ankogel from there.

I set off at 6 o'clock the following morning from the Alpenrose Gasthof at the foot of the mountain. Initially I followed an old path that zigzagged up the mountain, but soon got bored and climbed directly up the steeper ski runs that have been bulldozed through the forest almost directly beneath the cable car. A light drizzle fell, but the cloud base remained high and I hoped for a view from my final peak. With just a light pack I reached the hut in a little over two hours and headed east, following a good path just below the line of the ridge. The glacier mentioned by Conway on the southern slope has melted away almost to nothing, but the Ankogel remains a 'snowy alp' with a larger glacier on its north-east slope. Wispy clouds began to gather around the summit as I climbed the rocky ridge to the Kleiner Ankogel and walked along the narrow, almost flat, arête beyond. As I climbed up the loose rocky slope to the top, the clouds came down and obscured the view. I had intended to write 'The End of the Alps' in the summit book, but the metal box attached to the cross contained nothing but a soggy lump of paper.

I sat on the summit for about half an hour, partly because I still hoped that the clouds might clear, but mainly because this was the last mountain top on my long walk through the Alps. Conway, I have no doubt, felt an enormous sense of relief. He had done what he set out to do, and now all he wanted was to resume his interrupted social life in London: 'As the seasons go by, it happens that the aesthetic interest, which was at first the climber's main delight, begins to fade...The old glory has vanished from the scene...the effect...is one that many of us have felt, especially towards the close of...[an] extensive journey of exploration. There is one remedy – to quit the mountains for a while and attend to the common business of life.'[352] My thoughts were somewhat different. Perhaps because I had spread the walk over two summers, I still felt 'the climber's main delight' and, like Robert Louis Stevenson, believed that 'to travel hopefully is a better thing than to arrive'.[353] I had been preoccupied with Conway and his walk for more than two years, and now it was done: one more dream fulfilled; one more mystery explained.

The view did not clear, but I was rewarded with a 'glockenspectre' – a huge shadow of myself projected onto the mist hanging above the glacier, surrounded by a rainbow aura. Starting back down the boulder slope, an eagle appeared out of the clouds and circled overhead before wheeling back into the drifting mists. I jogged back down the ski runs and, seven hours after I had set out, I was back at the Alpenrose.

We caught the shuttle train back through the tunnel to Bockstein and set off for Bad Gastein. Gradually, the reason for Conway's selection of the Ankogel as 'the last of the snowy Alps' became clear. As well as being a 'series of peaks and passes',[354] Conway's walk was also a series of resorts offering first-class hotels: Valdieri (where the hotel was unfortunately shut), Courmayeur, Chamonix, Leukerbad, Zermatt, Bad Ragaz and finally Bad Gastein. After descending from the Ankogel, Conway hurried along the Elisabeth-Promenade, 'a well rolled bath-chair path'[355] named after the beloved wife of Emperor Franz Joseph, whose health Conway had toasted in the Kürsinger hut. He failed to notice that the Gurkhas were dragging behind, and when he abruptly turned into his hotel, where luggage and letters awaited him, the Gurkhas carried straight on down the valley. They spent the night somewhere near Hof Gastein and the following day carried on to Lend, more than 20 miles from their starting point. Conway eventually found them two days later 'looking disconsolate enough'.[356]

Bad Gastein was a favourite resort for the upper classes of Vienna at the end of the nineteenth century. Built in a horseshoe shape above a rocky step in the valley, a waterfall plunges through the centre of the town, overlooked by gracious but dilapidated palace hotels. We stayed in Sigmund Freud's villa, where he enlivened the holidays of his rich and neurotic clients with a bit of psychoanalysis. Each of the bedrooms had a padded door, and in the cellar there were a series of rooms providing warm 'radon baths', which may sound carcinogenic but apparently cure all ills.

Suitably cured, we set out to explore the town and discovered that it was the harvest festival. Farmers dressed in breeches, green woollen jackets and Tyrolean hats drove tractors and trailers decorated with hay and pine trees through the town, accompanied by cows, goats, horses and a brass band. A hunters' float was decorated with a neat row of dead marmots. Many of the farmers had a big bottle of beer in their hand and a little bottle of schnapps in their pocket, and even the cold wind and driving rain could not dampen their spirits. After completing the walk, we too were in the mood to celebrate and the festivities continued into the night. At about 10 o'clock we were sitting in a bar when all the lights suddenly went out and an air-raid siren started to wail. The customers in the bar speculated on what the young farmers were up to, but it was generally agreed that it would be unsafe to walk home in the dark, so more drinks were ordered. By this time the rain had turned to snow and the following morning nearly a foot had settled over the town and the surrounding forests. On the very last day of the journey, winter had arrived and we were trapped in Bad Gastein. Resigned to our fate, we decided to have another radon bath.

When Katrina heard that Conway had finished his walk, she rushed to congratulate him: 'I am glad with all my heart that you have added this achievement to your Indian one; but as then so now, my unrest about you has been great and the relief from it an immense comfort. I am immensely proud of what you have undertaken and accomplished.' On the journey home, Conway lost the Gurkhas again. While he slept in his first-class compartment, an officious German ticket inspector ordered the Gurkhas out of their third-class carriage at Aschaffenburg. When they failed to appear at Frankfurt, Conway telegraphed all the stations down the line and eventually tracked them down in Mainz. The remaining journey to London was 'fortunately productive of no further incidents'. On 1 September 1894, Conway 'arrived in Liverpool St via Harwich about 9 a.m. Drove to Robinsons about photos, to Poole's about clothes, Fauerbach's for tobacco, and home, where I found Bruce and handed the Gurkhas over to him'.

Chapter Eight
Arrival

When I decided to retrace Conway's journey through *The Alps from End to End*, I set out to explore both the mountains and the man; to discover how much of the world that Conway described still exists today. I wanted to understand not only the physical changes that have taken place in the landscape but also how the English idea of the Alps has evolved over the past 120 years.

Superficially, the physical landscape has withstood over a century of rapid change and development remarkably well. The major additions to the man-made environment – reservoirs, tourist resorts, roads and other infrastructure – tend to be confined to the valleys; and while some of them are certainly hideous, they are at least relatively local in their impact. Dams have no doubt flooded some beautiful valleys, and power lines disfigure many others, but in some cases these man-made lakes have enhanced the natural landscape. In Switzerland and Austria in particular, local planning legislation has sought to preserve the vernacular architecture of the region and to encourage the use of local materials and designs in new buildings. While many of the resulting 'chalet suburbs' are a crude pastiche of traditional mountain architecture, they are perhaps less intrusive than the alternative. In Conway's day the most prominent man-made structures in the Alps were often forts, and this is one aspect of the built environment where there have been relatively few additions over the past half century, as the region has enjoyed an almost unprecedented period of peace and prosperity. However, the prosperity is increasingly founded upon a single industry: tourism. Forestry and agriculture have diminished in economic significance, and so too have mining and quarrying. Industrial development, apart from power generation, remains scattered and small scale and several of the valleys that I passed through were probably more industrialised in Conway's time than they are today. As a consequence, those parts of the high Alps that have failed to attract tourists have suffered massive depopulation.

Above the valley floor, the biggest change that has taken place in the landscape is the retreat of the glaciers. Even during the 40-odd years that I have visited the Alps, many of the highest peaks have assumed a rockier appearance and glaciers have visibly shrunk, leaving vast areas of moraine that are gradually being colonised by plants. If the current trend continues, it is not hard to imagine that the great glaciers and snowfields of the Alps will eventually disappear, together with much of the characteristic flora and fauna of the region. But despite these changes, most of the mountain scenery that I passed through during my 1,000-mile walk was still instantly recognisable from Conway's 120-year-old descriptions, and for some reason that feels good. It is, of course, precisely this 'unspoilt' character of the landscape that continues to attract tourists from the industrial and post-industrial towns and cities of the plains, and we should, I suppose, celebrate the triumph of capitalism that has allowed so many to enjoy the 'playground of Europe', while transforming picturesque but poverty-stricken peasants into prosperous hoteliers.

The English have, in some respects, fared less well than the Alps since 1894. We have grown richer in absolute terms, but poorer in relative terms: the empire has gone, we no longer rule the waves and we have unquestionably lost both pomp and circumstance in the world. When Conway talked about 'England', he meant the whole of Great Britain (and sometimes Ireland as well), but when he talked about 'the English' what he actually meant was an elite group of men, educated at Oxford and Cambridge, who ruled over an empire covering one quarter of the globe and dictated its moral, ethical and cultural norms. Today, Conway's England is called Britain and the English are struggling to find a new identity in a post-imperial world.

Describing the Gothic Age, Conway wrote: 'It is assuredly not easy to imagine oneself living in such surroundings, acting on such motives, and incorporating such peculiar notions.'[357] Just 103 years separate Conway's birth from mine; but as cultural change has accelerated, even the relatively recent past has become a remote and foreign place. By modern standards, Conway was not a likeable man in many ways: his attitudes to class, race and gender grate upon our twenty-first-century sensibilities. The behaviours that he valued in himself and others combined 'manliness' – courage and romantic chivalry – with ruthless individualism – free speech, free thinking, free markets, free enterprise – and a belief that extreme inequality of both opportunity and outcome is natural and inevitable. Moreover, Conway's belief in free speech and free thinking, and his toleration of other people's views, was founded upon an unshakeable belief that the English way of doing things was the best. He may have rejected the absolute truth of the Bible, but he retained a strong sense of moral and cultural absolutism, and he was highly judgemental: any world view that conflicted with his own was simply wrong. These were the self-confident traits that enabled the English to undertake their long voyage of world conquest and settlement, during the course of which they 'seemed to have conquered and peopled half the world in a fit of absence of mind', as Sir John Seeley observed in 1882.

Today, neither manliness nor unfettered individualism is held in high esteem, and political correctness dictates that the English are rarely, if ever, judgemental (at least in public). Britain is a more equal, democratic place than Conway's England, and its inhabitants are certainly less arrogant and conceited than Conway's English, but they are also less self-assured, and less certain of what they stand for and believe in. Today, the English are taught to espouse a creed of moral and cultural relativism where almost everything is equally right or wrong, and equally good or bad, and we tolerate almost anything except intolerance. As Jolyon Forsyte observed: 'We've lost conviction. How and when self-consciousness was born I never can make out...Never to see yourself as others see you, it's a wonderful preservative.'[358]

Throughout his life, Conway was popular with his peers, underlining the fact that his values and social attitudes were quite normal for his class and generation. In The Crowd in Peace and War, his vigorous defence of individualism against 'crowd-despotism', he wrote: 'The secret of charm is a beautiful spontaneity and unexpectedness, a spontaneity of action, thought and speech, welling forth from the richness of a full and individual nature...regardless of public prejudice and popular judgement.'[359] Conway clearly possessed great personal charm and, in some respects, led a charmed life, with wealth and honours heaped upon him. But it would be a mistake to see his rise to 'greatness' (or at least the House of Lords) as entirely effortless. Conway worked hard, and the fact that he largely relied upon his mother, his wife and then his daughter to pay his bills was no disgrace. In Victorian society, a man who married well was considered a greater success than one who was obliged to work for a living.

Despite his propensity to cheat and exaggerate, it would also be a mistake to underestimate his achievements. He was the first Professor of Art History in Britain, and had no precedent to follow when he wrote his lectures. Several of his books and articles are scholarly and knowledgeable and his systematic use of photography for the study of art was a genuine insight. He was a successful journalist and critic, several of his travel books sold well, and he created a whole new genre of literature with his Climbers' Guides. He initiated and led the first major expedition to the Himalaya, a region almost totally unknown to Europeans at the time, and pioneered the career path of future professional mountaineers with the now ubiquitous newspaper articles, expedition book and lecture tour. He almost certainly did not set a new world record for altitude with his ascent of Pioneer Peak in the Himalayas, but he probably equalled the record when he made the fourth ascent of Aconcagua in the Andes, and all of his major expeditions demanded considerable determination and fortitude. His business career was largely a failure, but reflected his pioneering spirit, while his parliamentary career was notable mainly for the facts that it did not start until he was 63 years old and that he gained almost universal popularity in both Houses. The broad scope of the issues on which he felt qualified to opine – from Architecture to Zionism – is also striking. Conway almost certainly believed that his greatest achievement was to be made a Baron, and in a sense he was right; but as his obituarist in the *Geographical Journal* observed: 'He probably owed his peerage mainly to the universal affection and regard in which he was held by all parties',[360] rather than to any particular achievement. The historian Peter Stansky was less charitable, noting that Conway was 'a man of intelligence, power, charm, and many gifts, none of which he seems to have fully realized, except perhaps his gift for self-advancement'.[361]

Despite his many talents, Conway failed to achieve real distinction in any single field because of his restless curiosity and inability to apply concentrated effort to any subject for a sustained period of time. He also lacked the originality of mind to be a true Renaissance man. Instead, he was an ambitious dilettante: a remarkable weather vane for the intellectual winds blowing through Victorian and Edwardian society. As Geoffrey Winthrop Young observed, he was 'a romantic, a sociologist, an art connoisseur, a wordling, an omniscient lecturer and compiler, a busy public character, and a completely casual will-o'-the-wisp'.[362] The same restless energy characterised his personal relationships. Apart from his two older mentors, Henry Bradshaw and Manton Marble, he made no deep and lasting friendships. Despite his vast, ever-changing circle of acquaintances, Conway was a lonely man.

Unlike many of his Victorian contemporaries, whose personal philosophy and politics ossified in early middle age, Conway continued to pursue his quest for new ideas and experiences until his death. In twenty-first-century Britain, perhaps just a few British Muslims experience a childhood as deeply religious as Conway's: brought up to believe in a simple unambiguous faith, that brooks no questions and requires no proof. As Conway reached maturity, faith was increasingly being replaced by doubt, but he remained essentially religious and spent much of his life seeking a substitute for the simple certainties of his childhood. Conway lived through a period of bewildering cultural change, as the church, scientists, artists, poets, philosophers and politicians battled for authority in the ideological vacuum left by fundamentalist religion. At various points in his life Conway 'believed' in science as an alternative source of authority to God; culture – 'the best that has been known and thought in the world'[363] – to guide society away from amoralism, materialism and anarchy; social Darwinism and eugenics to maintain the purity of the race that upheld high civilisation; nationalism and imperialism to provide a sense of common purpose and identity; psychoanalysis to explain the unhappiness of life; quirky mysticism to provide comfort in death; and 'great men' to lead society forward in the absence of the guiding hand of God. Conway flirted with almost every big idea (except socialism) that emerged in Victorian and Edwardian England, and came to regard his life as a pilgrimage – a sacred quest in search of some ideal – but in the end he was still left with a nagging sense of nostalgia for the simple truths of his childhood: 'Each generation makes of the world more or less the kind of place they dream it should be; and each when its day is done is often in a mood to regret the work of its hands and praise the conditions that obtained when it was young.'[364]

Only one idea remained constant throughout Conway's life: his belief in the redeeming beauty of wild places. Conway was a restless, selfish, ambitious, discontented man. In a letter to Manton Marble in 1895, he wrote: 'I have come to the conclusion that the pursuit of any pure ideal is a chimera. What one accomplishes is the only thing that matters, and all accomplishment is imperfect.' Throughout his long, imperfect life, whenever he was depressed or faced a setback in his febrile pursuit of accomplishment, his first reaction was to seek solace in travel and in the mountains.

Today, nearly all of Conway's Victorian ideas and beliefs have been discredited. Science can prove that a hypothesis is false, but unlike faith it can never provide the comforting certainty of 'the truth'. The Victorian 'canon' of culture and good taste persisted for almost a century. My generation witnessed perhaps its final flowering with the 1969 BBC television programme *Civilisation*, in which Lord Clark (who visited Allington Castle in 1934) tried to teach the masses civilised (i.e. European) values, but by then art historians, like Lord Clark and Lord Conway, were already seen as 'the clerks of the nostalgia of a ruling class in decline'.[365] We no longer believe in the innate superiority of men over women, or whites over blacks. Eugenics has been comprehensively discredited by the horror of the holocaust, and we no longer regard the children of the rich as inherently superior to the children of the poor. The vast majority of British people probably never did care much for the Empire, and today we are inclined to look back at our former imperial greatness with a slightly guilty sense of astonishment. English nationalism has been claimed by racist thugs; few people now expect psychoanalysis to solve the problems of the world; while mysticism is ridiculed. Moreover, as we have got to know our 'great men' (and women) better, often through the mediation of a free and frequently prurient press, we are inclined to regard many of their actions as motivated by sex, greed or self-aggrandisement.

Of Conway's many ideas and beliefs, one of the very few that has survived more or less intact into the twenty-first century is the belief in the redeeming power of natural beauty. For many millions of Britons, a Sunday walk in the country has become the secular equivalent of prayer and hundreds of thousands make an annual pilgrimage to the Alps, in search of an experience that will uplift and revitalise both the body *and* the spirit. After 120 years of bewildering cultural change, when so many Victorian values and beliefs have been tested and found wanting, the strange notion that the Alps are beautiful — an idea that Conway helped to construct and to popularise — has proved to be remarkably resilient. It is now so powerful that the millions of tourists who visit the Alps each year know exactly what they are going to see, and what they are going to *feel*, even before they arrive.

Physically the Alps have changed remarkably little over the past 120 years, while the English have changed a great deal. How strange that one of the few things that Conway and I would agree upon is that these piles of rock and ice are beautiful, and that to climb to their summits is one of the greatest joys that life can offer.

Appendix
Summary of Route

The table below summarises my route through *The Alps from End to End*. As described in the text, the actual sequence followed was different (notably the ascents of Mont Blanc, the Wildhorn and the Monte Rosa) and the table also excludes rest and travel days. The journey involves complex navigation over mountainous terrain, numerous glacier crossings and climbing up to *Peu Difficil* level and should only be considered by experienced parties. Both times and height gains are approximate.

	Major peaks and passes	Destination	Approx. time hrs	Height gain m
		Limone		
1	Passo Ciotto del Mieu (2,274 m)	Trinità	8.00	1,900
2		Rif. Soria Ellena	6.00	1,300
3	Colle di Fenestrelle (2,463 m)/Colle del Chiapous (2,526 m)	Rif. Morelli Buzzi	5.00	1,200
4		Rif. Questa	6.00	1,000
5	Colle di Vascura (2,520 m)/Colle d'Orgials (2,600 m)/Colle della Lombarda (2,476 m)	S. Anna di Vinadio	8.00	1,300
6	Passo di Bravaria (2,550 m)	Sambuco	7.00	1,300
7	Colle del Mulo (2,527 m)	Vernetti	7.00	1,300
8		Elva	7.00	1,200
9	Pelvo d'Elva (3,064 m)	Chiesa	6.00	1,400
10	Passo S. Chiaffredo (2,743 m)	Rif. Q. Sella	7.00	1,400
11		Crissolo	2.00	
12	Colle di Porte (2,264 m)	Torre Pellice	7.00	900
13	Colle Guilian (2,451 m)	Ghigo	9.00	2,000
14		Balsiglia	5.00	500
15	Colle dell'Aberglan (2,713 m)	Usseaux	8.00	1,600
16	Colle dell'Assietta (2,472 m)	Rif. D. Arlaud	5.00	1,000
17		Rif. Levi Molinari	5.00	800
18	Col d'Ambin (2,899 m)	Aussois	10.00	1,100
19		Ref. de l'Arpont	7.00	1,000
20		Ref. de la Leisse	6.00	600

Major peaks and passes	Destination	Approx. time hrs	Height gain m
21 Col de la Leisse (2,700 m)	Tignes	4.00	200
22 Colle della Goletta (3,117 m)/Colle Bassac Déré (3,082 m)	Rif. Mario Bezzi	8.00	1,600
23	Bonne	2.00	
24 Testa del Rutor (3,486 m)	La Thuile	11.00	1,600
25 (Bus Courmayeur-Chamonix)	Chamonix	4.00	
26 (Train/cable car/tram Chamonix- Mont Lachat)	Goûter hut	5.00	1,600
27 Mont Blanc (4,810 m) (Tram/cable car/train Mont Lachat-Chamonix)	Chamonix	10.00	1,000
28	Ref. Pierre à Bérard	5.00	400
29 Buet (3,099 m)	La Gueulaz	8.00	1,500
30 Col de Barberine (2,481 m)/ Col d'Emaney (2,462 m)/ Col du Jorat (2,210 m)	St. Maurice	10.00	1,500
31	Gryon	3.00	600
32	Anzeindaz	3.00	750
33 Les Diableret (3,209 m)	Sanetsch Hotel	8.00	1,400
34 Col des Audannes (2,886 m) Wildhorn (3,247m)/ Rawilpass (2,429 m)	Wildstrubel hut	10.00	1,600
35 Wildstrubel (3,243 m)	Leukerbad	9.00	600
36 (Transport to Zermatt)	Monte Rosa hut	6.00	1,200
37 Monte Rosa (4,634 m) (Train Rotenboden-Zermatt)	Zermatt	13.00	2,200
38 (Cable car Leukerbad- Rinderhutte) Restipass (2,626 m)	Fafleralp	6.00	400
39 Lötschenlücke (3,178 m)	Konkordia hut	8.00	1,600
40 Grünhornlücke (3,280 m)	Finsteraarhorn hut	4.00	400
41 Finsteraarhorn (4,274 m)	Finsteraarhorn hut	8.00	1,300
42 Oberaarjoch (3,256 m)	Grimsel Hospice	8.00	500
43 Furkapass (2,429 m)	Sidelenhütte	7.00	1,000
44 Lochberglücke (2,815 m)	Göschenen	9.00	400
45	Amsteg	5.00	
46	Hüfihütte	7.00	1,800
47 Hüfipass (3,007 m)	Obbort	9.00	1,000
48	Muttsee hut	5.00	1,450
49 Ruchi (3,107 m)/Hausstock (3,158 m)	Elm	11.00	800
50 (Cable car to Tschingelalp) Segnas Pass (2,627 m)	Segnas Pass hut	3.00	1,200
51 P. Segnas (3,099 m)/ P. Sardona (3,056 m)	Vättis	10.00	700

	Major peaks and passes	Destination	Approx. time hrs	Height gain m
52		Bad Ragaz	5.00	
53	Fläscher Fürggli (2,247 m)	Schesaplanahütte	8.00	2,100
54	Schesaplana (2,965 m)/ Verajochl (2,330 m)/ Ofenpass (2,297 m)	Lindauer Hütte	7.00	1,400
55		Schruns	3.00	
56		Partenen	4.00	500
57		Wiesbadener Hütte	6.00	1,400
58	Dreiländerspitze (3,197 m)/ Vermunt Pass (2,798 m)	Guarda	10.00	900
59		Sent	5.00	300
60		Graun	7.00	700
61		Weisskugel Hütte	6.00	1,000
62	Weisskugel (3,738 m)	Vent	11.00	1,300
63		Sölden	4.00	
64		Hildesheimerhütte	5.00	1,600
65	Pfaffenjoch (3,208 m)/ Zuckerhütl (3,507 m)/Wilder Pfaff (3,456 m)/Wilder Freiger (3,418 m)	Müllerhütte	10.00	1,000
66		Sterzing	10.00	
67		Stein	5.00	500
68	Hochfeiler (3,509 m)	Hochfeiler Hütte	7.00	2,100
69	Eisbruggjoch (2,545 m)/Unter Weisszintschart (2,974 m)/ Nevesjoch (2,420 m)	Luttach	8.00	500
70		Kasern	5.00	600
71		Birnlücken Hütte	6.00	800
72	Birnlücke (2,665 m)/Krimmler Törl (2,776 m)	Kürsinger Hütte	7.00	1,300
73	Grossvenediger (3,666 m)	Matreier Tauernhaus	10.00	1,300
74		Matrei	4.00	
75		Kals	6.00	1,250
76	Berger Törl (2,651 m)	Salmhütte	5.00	1,200
77	Grossglockner (3,798 m)	Heiligenblut	11.00	1,200
78	Hoher Sonnblick (3,106 m)	Ammerhof	10.00	1,800
79	Bockhartscharte (2,226 m) (Train Bochstein–Mallnitz)	Mallnitz	5.00	600
80	Ankogel (3,252 m) (Train Mallnitz–Bockstein)	Bad Gastein	8.00	2,100

Notes

Abbreviations

AJ	*Alpine Journal*
CUL	Cambridge University Library
GJ	*Geographical Journal*
IWM	Imperial War Museum
RGS	Royal Geographical Society

1   W. M. Conway, *Aconcagua and Tierra Del Fuego: A Book of Climbing, Travel and Exploration* (London: Cassell, 1902), p.viii

2   J. Evans, *The Conways: A History of Three Generations* (London: Museum Press, 1966), p.8

3   W. M. Conway, *The Alps* (London: Adam and Charles Black, 1904), p.176

4   Letter from the prime minister, Lord Rosebery, to Conway, dated 24 May 1895 (CUL P/244)

5   *The Graphic*, 1 Aug. 1925

6   W. M. Conway, *Climbing and Exploration in the Bolivian Andes* (London: Harper & Brothers, 1901), p.219

7   C. Wilson, 'Obituary of Martin Conway', *AJ* 49 (1937), p.252

8   M. Shelley and P. B. Shelley, *History of a Six Weeks' Tour Through Part of France, Switzerland, Germany and Holland*, 1989 Oxford ed. (1817), p.151

9   W. Wordsworth, 'Tintern Abbey' (1798)

10 W. M. Conway, *The Alps from End to End*, Nelson ed. (London: Constable, 1895), p.9

11 R. Barthes, *Mythologies*, 2009 Vintage ed. (Paris: Editions du Seuil, 1957), p.xix

12 C. Dickens, *The Mystery of Edwin Drood*, 1961 Signet Classic ed. (London: 1870), pp.22-3

13 W. M. Conway, Manuscript notes for an unfinished autobiography, *c.*1928, p.5 (CUL Y/92)

14 W. M. Conway, *Episodes in a Varied Life* (London: *Country Life*, 1932), p.14

15 L. Strachey, *Eminent Victorians*, 2009 Oxford Classics ed. (London: 1918), p.149

16 Conway, *The Alps*, p.2

17 W. M. Conway, *Mountain Memories: A Pilgrimage of Romance* (London: Cassell, 1920), p.21

18 J. Ruskin, *Praeterita and Dilecta*, 2005 Everyman ed. (London: George Allen, 1889), p.101

19 Conway, *Mountain Memories*, p.23

20 Conway, *Episodes in a Varied Life*, p.10

21 W. M. Conway, 'Some Reminiscences and Reflections of an Old Stager', *AJ* 31 (1917), p.147

22 E. V. Lucas, *The Colvins and Their Friends* (London: Methuen & Co., 1928), p.28

23 G. W. Prothero, *A Memoir of Henry Bradshaw* (London: Kegan Paul, Trench & Co., 1888), p.3

24 Conway, *Episodes in a Varied Life*, p.50

25 Lucas, *The Colvins and Their Friends*, p.27

26 Conway, unfinished autobiography, p.4

27 J. Bunyan, *The Pilgrim's Progress*, 2003 Oxford ed. (1678), p.71

28 E. Gosse, *Father and Son*, 2009 Oxford ed. (London: 1907), pp.5 and 185

29 W. M. Conway, *A Pilgrim's Quest for the Divine* (London: Frederick Muller, 1936), p.11

30 A. Lunn, 'The Playground of Europe 1871 to 1971: A Centenary Tribute to Leslie Stephen', *AJ* 77 (1972), p.4

31 L. Stephen, *The Playground of Europe*, 1936 Blackwell ed. (London: Longmans, Green, 1871), p.197

32 See K. E. Higgon, 'Photography and Art History in the Nineteenth Century: Martin Conway and the Origins of the Conway Library' (MA, Courtauld Institute of Art, 2005)

33 E. Waugh, *A Handful of Dust*, Penguin 2000 ed. (London: Chapman & Hall, 1934), p.217

34 Conway, 'Some Reminiscences and Reflections of an Old Stager', p.152

35 Ibid., p.151

36 From a report sent to a potential publisher [Kegan Paul?] by an anonymous reader [Bentley?], dated Nov. 1882 (CUL P/47)

37 W. M. Conway, *The Literary Remains of Albrecht Dürer* (Cambridge University Press, 1889), p.8

38 W. M. Conway, *The Artistic Development of Reynolds and Gainsborough* (London: Seeley & Co., 1886), p.2

39 W. Benjamin, *One-Way Street*, 2009 Penguin ed. (London: 1928), p.84

40 Conway, *The Alps from End to End*, p.153

41 *Once a Week*, 1 June 1861, quoted in S. Sontag, *On Photography*, 2008 Penguin ed. (London: Allen Lane, 1978), p.184

42 Ibid., p.85

43 J. Bordy, *Cézanne à Aix: L'Art Vivant* (1926), quoted in M. Andrews, *Landscape and Western Art* (Oxford University Press, 1999), p.149

44 *The Times*, 21 April 1937

45 A. P. Harper, 'Fifty Years Ago', *AJ* 53 (1914), p.93

46 *The World*, Nov. 1886

47 W. Morris, *News From Nowhere*, 2009 Oxford ed. (London: 1890), p.69

48 W. M. Conway, *The Sport of Collecting* (London: T. Fisher Unwin, 1914), p.17

49 Benjamin, *One-Way Street*, p.171

50 Conway, 'Some Reminiscences and Reflections of an Old Stager', p.154

51 C. P. Snow, *The Two Cultures*, 2009 ed. (Cambridge University Press, 1959)

52 K. Clark, *Civilisation* (London: John Murray, 1969), p.346

53 From an 1880 lecture on 'The Beauty of Life' quoted in S. Calloway and L. F. Orr, eds., *The Cult of Beauty: The Aesthetic Movement 1860-1900* (London: V&A

Publishing, 2011), p.30
54   Undated newspaper cutting, probably *The Times*
55   *The Scots Observer*, 14 June 1890 (CUL Y/74)
56   W. A. B. Coolidge, *The Alps in Nature and History* (London: Methuen, 1908), p.397
57   Quoted in R. W. Clark, *An Eccentric in the Alps: The Story of W. A. B. Coolidge, the Great Victorian Mountaineer* (London: Museum Press, 1959), p.197
58   Quoted in W. Unsworth, *Hold the Heights: The Foundations of Mountaineering* (London: Hodder & Stoughton, 1993), p.97
59   L. G. Wickham Legg, ed., *Dictionary of National Biography* (Oxford University Press, 1949), p.192
60   Quoted in Clark, *An Eccentric in the Alps*, p.139
61   'A Gallery of English Art', *The Times*, 11 April 1890
62   See F. Driver, *Geography Militant: Cultures of Exploration and Empire* (Oxford: Blackwell, 2001), p.69
63   J. Conrad, *Heart of Darkness*, 1973 Penguin ed. (London: J. M. Dent, 1902), p.7
64   W. M. Conway, 'Exploration in the Mustagh Mountains', *GJ* II (1893), p.299
65   From a resolution passed at meeting of the Raleigh Travellers' Club in 1830, which effectively marked the foundation of the RGS. See Driver, *Geography Militant*, p.27
66   D. W. Freshfield and W. L. J. Wharton, eds., *Hints for Travellers Scientific and General*, 7th ed. (London: RGS, 1893).
67   W. M. Conway, 'Centrists and Excentrists', *AJ* 15 (1891), p.397
68   Wilson, 'Obituary of Martin Conway', p.250
69   Letter from Conway to D. Freshfield, address 'Baltoro Glacier', dated 30 Aug. 1892 (RGS Archives)
70   A. Crowley, *The Confessions of Aleister Crowley* (London: Mandrake Press, 1929), p.310
71   Conway, *Mountain Memories*, p.127
72   G. W. Young, G. Sutton and W. Noyce, *Snowdon Biography* (London: J. M. Dent, 1957), p.31
73   K. Mason, *Abode of Snow: A History of Himalayan Exploration and Mountaineering* (London: Rupert Hart-Davis, 1955), p.105
74   M. Zurbriggen, *From the Alps to the Andes*, British Library ed. (London: T. Fisher Unwin, 1899), p.50
75   Freshfield and Wharton, eds., *Hints for Travellers*, p.16
76   Conway, *Mountain Memories*, p.131
77   Ibid., p.140
78   'Description of Two Skulls brought by Mr. Conway from Nagyr' in W. M. Conway et al., *Climbing in the Himalayas: Maps and Scientific Reports* (London: T. Fisher Unwin, 1894), p.97
79   Crowley, *The Confessions of Aleister Crowley*, p.150
80   W. M. Conway, *Climbing and Exploration in the Karakoram-Himalayas* (London: T. Fisher Unwin, 1894), p.414
81   W. M. Conway, 'Alpine Climbing as a Sport', *Pall Mall Gazette*, 6 Dec. 1893
82   Conway, *The Sport of Collecting*, p.83

83   T. G. Bonney, 'Review of "Climbing and Exploration in the Karakoram-Himalayas" by W. M. Conway', *AJ* 17 (1894), p.213

84   Conway, *Climbing and Exploration in the Karakoram-Himalayas*, p.ix

85   Harper, 'Fifty Years Ago', p.94

86   Crowley, *The Confessions of Aleister Crowley*, p.311

87   C. G. Bruce, *Himalayan Wanderer* (London: Alexander Maclehose & Co., 1934), p.82

88   Zurbriggen, *From the Alps to the Andes*

89   In a 'Publisher's Note', T. Fisher Unwin (who was also Conway's publisher) noted that '[Zurbriggen's] absence in India has prevented him from...correcting his proofs'. Since the book was 'the work of one more used to the ice-axe than the pen', TFU felt free 'to avail himself of the generous assistance of those who could speak with authority on matters-of-fact' by asking them to check and correct the proofs. Top of the list is Sir Martin Conway.

90   Conway, *Episodes in a Varied Life*, p.40

91   Matthew 26, 11

92   W. M. Conway, *Early Tuscan Art from the 12th to the 15th Centuries* (London: Hurst and Blackett, 1902), p.48

93   Conway, *The Alps from End to End*, p.9

94   Ibid., p.11

95   Ibid., p.22

96   Ibid., p.334

97   Ibid., p.28

98   Ibid., p.13

99   See Coolidge, *The Alps in Nature and History*, p.83

100   H. W. Tilman, *Two Mountains and a River*, 1997 Diadem ed. (Cambridge University Press, 1949), p.536

101   Bunyan, *The Pilgrim's Progress*, p.16

102   See C. Duggan, *The Force of Destiny: A History of Italy Since 1796*, 2008 Penguin ed. (London: Allen Lane, 2007), p.193

103   Conway, *The Alps*, p.88

104   G. W. Young, 'Mountain Prophets', *AJ* 54 (1942), p.112

105   R. L. G. Irving, *The Alps*, 1947 ed. (London: B. T. Batsford, 1939), p.19

106   R. Deakin, *Waterlog*, 2000 Vintage ed. (London: Chatto & Windus, 1999), p.4

107   Conway, *The Alps from End to End*, p.264

108   Ibid., p.36

109   Ibid., p.38

110   Conway, *The Alps*, p.179

111   Wilson, 'Obituary of Martin Conway', p.250

112   Conway, *The Alps from End to End*, p.106

113   W. M. Conway, *A Guide Book to the Pennine Alps, From the Simplon to Arolla Intended for the Use of Mountaineers* (London: Edward Stanford, 1881), p.134

114   Conway, *The Alps*, p.216

115   Conway, *The Alps from End to End*, p.13

116   Ibid., p.8

117   W. M. Conway, 'The Alps from End to End', *Pall Mall Gazette*, 21 June 1894

118   W. A. B. Coolidge, ed., *A Handbook for Travellers in Switzerland: Part II - The Alps of Savoy and Piedmont, the Italian Lakes and part of the Dauphiné*, 18th ed. (London: John Murray, 1892), p.662

119   Conway, *The Alps from End to End*, p.59

120   See S. Butler, *Alps and Sanctuaries of Piedmont and the Canton Ticino*, 2009 ACN ed. (London: 1881).

121   Coolidge, ed., *A Handbook for Travellers*, p.428

122   See W. A. B. Coolidge, 'The Pelvo D'Elva', *AJ* 15 (1891)

123   W. A. B. Coolidge, ed., *A Handbook for Travellers in Switzerland: Part I - Switzerland without the Pennine Alps.*, 18th ed. (London: John Murray, 1892), p.24

124   Conway, *The Alps from End to End*, p.59

125   W. Unsworth, *Encyclopedia of Mountaineering*, 1977 Penguin ed. (London: Robert Hale, 1975), p.139

126   B. Russell, *Autobiography*, 1998 Routledge ed. (London: George Allen & Unwin, 1967), p.38

127   W. M. Conway, 'Edward Fitzgerald 1871-1931', *AJ* 43 (1931), p.163

128   Conway, *The Alps from End to End*, p.67

129   W. A. B. Coolidge, 'Review of "The Alps from End to End" by W. M. Conway', *AJ* 17 (1894), p.533

130   Conway, *The Alps from End to End*, p.68

131   See *Le Chien de Protection sur Troupeau Ovin* (Montana: Pascal Wick, 1992)

132   Conway, *The Alps from End to End*, p.74

133   W. M. Conway, 'Winter Sports in the Alps', *Pall Mall Magazine* (1910), p.195

134   See J. Starobinski, 'The Idea of Nostalgia', *Diogenes* 54 (1966)

135   Quoted in J. Wylie, *Landscape* (Abingdon: Routledge, 2007), p.51

136   Conway, *The Alps*, p. 273

137   Conway, *The Alps from End to End*, p.77

138   Ibid., p.78

139   W. M. Conway, 'A Letter to a Friend', *Harper's Weekly*, 31 Dec. 1900

140   W. M. Conway, *The Dawn of Art in the Ancient World: An Archaeological Sketch* (London: Percival & Co., 1891), p.122

141   Conway, *The Alps from End to End*, p.93

142   Coolidge, ed., *A Handbook for Travellers*, p.684

143   D. Roberts, 'Hanging Around', *Mountain Gazette* 19 (1974), in J. Perrin, ed., *Mirrors in the Cliffs* (London: Diadem, 1983), p.643

144   A. Lunn, *The Alps* (London: William Norgate, 1914), p.135

145   See J. Harris, *Private Lives, Public Spirit: A Social History of Britain 1870-1914*, 1994 Penguin ed. (Oxford University Press, 1993), p.209

146   V. Woolf, *Mrs. Dalloway*, 2009 Oxford ed. (London: Hogarth Press, 1925), p.61

147   Conway, *The Alps from End to End*, p.111

148   Ibid., p.111

149   Coolidge, ed., *A Handbook for Travellers*, p.681

150   W. M. Conway, 'The Alps from End to End', *Pall Mall Gazette*, 21 July 1894

151   W. M. Conway, 'A Flight Over the Pyrenees', *AJ* 40 (1928), p.325

152 Review of 'The Alps from End to End', *GJ* VI (1895), p.478

153 *Scottish Mountaineering Club Journal*, vol. 3, no.6, 1895

154 Letter from W. Coolidge to P. Farrar dated 8 July 1918, quoted in B. Imeson, *Playing the Man: A Biography of the Mountaineer Captain John Percy Farrar DSO* (Loose Scree, 2010), p.132

155 Conway, *Episodes in a Varied Life*, p. 41

156 G. R. Searle, *A New England? Peace and War 1886-1918* (Oxford University Press, 2004), p.135

157 'Sir W. Martin Conway in Bath: His Political Campaign', from a local Bath newspaper, dated on or about 28 May 1895 (CUL Y/74)

158 Bath United Liberal Association report, 'Bath Liberals at Guildhall: Enthusiastic Demonstration. Speeches by Lord Tweedmouth, Mr W M Conway, Mr J E Barlow, M.P., Mr G P Fuller, M.P. and others', 9 May 1895

159 Conway, *Episodes in a Varied Life*, p.39

160 *The Times*, 11 Nov. 1896

161 *Travel*, April 1897

162 Conway variously spelt Spitsbergen with a 'z' and an 's' before deciding that 'the common spelling "Spitzbergen" is an ignorant blunder' in W. M. Conway, *With Ski and Sledge Over Arctic Glaciers* (London: J. M. Dent, 1898), p.vi

163 Conway, *Episodes in a Varied Life*, p.204

164 Conway, *With Ski and Sledge Over Arctic Glaciers*, p.17

165 Quoted in G. Rowell, *In the Throne Room of the Mountain Gods* (San Francisco: Sierra Club, 1977), p.38

166 Crowley, *The Confessions of Aleister Crowley*, p.16

167 *Dictionary of National Biography, Second Supplement*, vol. I (London: Smith, Elder & Co., 1912), p.131

168 Conway, *The Bolivian Andes*, p.5

169 Ibid., p.7

170 Ibid., p.8

171 Ibid., pp.10–11

172 T. G. Bonney, 'Review of "The Bolivian Andes" by Sir Martin Conway', *AJ* 20 (1901), p.553

173 W. M. Conway, 'The Ascent of Yllimani', *Daily Chronicle*, 30 Sept. 1898

174 W. M. Conway, 'Climbs in the Andes in 1898', *AJ* 19 (1899), p.514

175 'A Great Climb', *Daily Chronicle*, 15 Sept. 1898

176 'A Great Climber and Explorer: A Chat with Sir Martin Conway', *St. James's Gazette*, 14 Feb. 1899

177 Conway, *The Bolivian Andes*, p.273

178 Conway, *Episodes in a Varied Life*, p.88

179 Conway, 'Climbs in the Andes in 1898', p.520

180 E. A. Fitzgerald, *The Highest Andes* (London: Methuen & Co., 1899)

181 Conway, *Mountain Memories*, p.260

182 Conway, *Aconcagua and Tierra del Fuego*, p.165

183 Ibid., p.227

184 Ibid., pp.149 and 191

[185] Conway, 'Some Reminiscences and Reflections of an Old Stager', p.156
[186] Conway, *The Bolivian Andes*, p.219
[187] Ibid., p.221
[188] B. Chatwin, *What Am I Doing Here?* 2005 Vintage ed. (London: Jonathan Cape, 1989), p.273
[189] Conway, *Aconcagua and Tierra del Fuego*, p.viii
[190] *Evening Post*, 13 June 1907
[191] *The Times*, 18 Aug. 1900
[192] Conway, *Mountain Memories*, p.92
[193] J. Galsworthy, *The Forsyte Saga*, 2001 Penguin ed., vol. I (London: William Heinemann, 1920), p. 604. The fictional character Soames Forsyte was born in 1855, one year before Conway.
[194] Conway was less explicit in his letters, diaries and other papers about the nature of his relationship with Mrs Kemp-Welch than he was about his later relationship with Miss Monica Hadow. The explanation for the relationship ending is from Joan Evans' book. I assume that Agnes was the source.
[195] W. M. Conway, 'In the Days of my Youth', *M.A.P.*, 13 Jan. 1900
[196] See Conway, *Episodes in a Varied Life*, p.106
[197] L. Grant, 'Time and the Conways: The Beginnings of Art History and the Collecting of Photographs in Britain', *Visual Resources* XIII (1998), p.302
[198] W. M. Conway, *The Domain of Art*, 2010 BiblioBazaar ed. (London: John Murray, 1901), p.1
[199] Ibid., p.10
[200] Conway, *Episodes in a Varied Life*, p.90
[201] Ibid., p.37
[202] Evans, *The Conways*, p.208
[203] Conway, *The Alps*, p.17
[204] W. M. Conway, 'The Destruction of the Beauty of the Alps', *The Times*, 12 Aug. 1905
[205] Conway, *The Sport of Collecting*, p.107
[206] Conway, *Episodes in a Varied Life*, p.93
[207] Ibid., p.156
[208] A. V. L. Guise, *Six Years in Bolivia: The Adventures of a Mining Engineer* (New York: E. P. Dutton, 1922), p.231
[209] W. M. Conway, 'The Derby and Old-Age Pensions', *The Times*, 26 May 1909
[210] *The Times*, 3 April 1921
[211] *Burlington Magazine*, Jan. 1915, p.143
[212] W. M. Conway, 'The Joy of Winter Sports', *Country Life* 1914, p.116
[213] W. M. Conway, 'An Immortality of Shame', *Country Life* 1914, p.433
[214] W. M. Conway, *The Crowd in Peace and War* (London: Longmans, Green and Co., 1915), p.307
[215] Ibid., p.200
[216] Ibid., p.292
[217] Ibid., p.170
[218] Dr. Max Friedlander quoted in 'Conway, W. M.' www.dictionaryofarthistorians.org

retrieved 8 March 2011. Conway met Friedlander at the exhibition in Bruges in 1902.

219 *The Times*, undated press cutting, probably *c.*1924

220 W. M. Conway, 'Notes on a Visit to the War-Area in France, September 1-11, 1918', IWM Archives, pp.16, 6 and 26

221 W. M. Conway, 'Diary of a Visit to the Front in France, July 1917', IWM Archives, p.9

222 Conway, 'Notes on a Visit to France 1918', pp.24 and 16

223 Conway, *A Pilgrim's Quest for the Divine*, p.34

224 Conway, 'Some Reminiscences and Reflections of an Old Stager', p.157

225 See J. Steinberg, *Why Switzerland?* (Cambridge University Press, 1976)

226 W. M. Conway, 'The Treasury of S. Maurice D'Agaune', *Burlington Magazine* 1912, p.262

227 Conway, *The Alps from End to End*, p.130

228 Ibid., p.132

229 See P. P. Viazzo, *Upland Communities: Environment, Population and Social Structure in the Alps since the Sixteenth Century* (Cambridge University Press, 1989)

230 Conway, *The Alps*, p.263

231 Conway, *Mountain Memories*, p.88

232 Conway, *The Alps*, p.235

233 Coolidge, ed., *A Handbook for Travellers*, p.256

234 M. de Certeau, *The Practice of Everyday Life* (1984), quoted in M. Coverley, *Psychogeography* (London: Pocket Essentials, 2006), p.105

235 Conway, *The Alps from End to End*, p.141

236 Chateaubriand, quoted in Steinberg, *Why Switzerland?* p.6

237 See ibid., p.68

238 Conway, *The Alps from End to End*, p.143

239 Ibid., p.143

240 Ibid., p.203

241 Ibid., p.203

242 Ibid., p.149

243 R. W. Emerson, *Nature and Selected Essays*, 2003 Penguin ed. (1836), p.39

244 M. Twain, *A Tramp Abroad*, 1997 Penguin ed. (Hartford: American Publishing, 1880), p.252

245 Coolidge, ed., *A Handbook for Travellers*, p.xxiii

246 Quoted in J. Ring, *How the English Made the Alps* (London: John Murray, 2000), p.189

247 W. M. Conway, 'The Gurkhas', *National Observer*, 19 Aug. 1893

248 Conway, *Climbing and Exploration in the Karakoram-Himalayas*, p.474

249 Coolidge, ed., *A Handbook for Travellers*, p.16

250 See A. Beattie, *The Alps: A Cultural History* (Oxford: Signal Books, 2006), p.173

251 L. N. Tolstoy, *War and Peace*, 1978 Penguin ed. (1869), p.757

252 Conway, *Episodes in a Varied Life*, p.130

253 Conway, *The Alps from End to End*, p.156

254 W. M. Conway, 'Mountaineering', in *The Encyclopaedia of Sport* (London:

Heinemann, 1911), p.222
255   From a letter from John Muir to his wife, July 1888
256   H. D. Thoreau, *Walking*, 2007 Arc Manor ed. (1862), p.8
257   Conway, *The Zermatt Pocket-Book*, p.5
258   Conway, *The Alps from End to End*, p.167
259   Ibid., p.168
260   Ibid., p.170
261   Coolidge, ed., *A Handbook for Travellers*, p.241
262   Interview with Martin Conway in the *Daily Chronicle*, 30 Dec. 1893
263   Conway, *The Crowd in Peace and War*, p.27
264   Hansard: http://hansard.millbanksystems.com/people/sir-martin-conway, 29 Feb. 1924
265   E. Pyatt, *The Passage of the Alps* (London: Robert Hale, 1984)
266   Conway, *The Alps from End to End*, p.178
267   Twain, *A Tramp Abroad*, p.161
268   Second Annual Report of the English Branch of the League for the Preservation of Swiss Scenery (1907)
269   Report of the Annual Meeting of the English Branch of the League for the Preservation of Swiss Scenery, 30 Oct. 1907
270   Conway, *The Bolivian Andes*, p.2
271   Emerson, *Nature and Selected Essays*, p.43
272   Conway, *The Alps from End to End*, p.19
273   Ibid., p.203
274   Ibid., p.213
275   Ibid., p.223
276   Ibid., p.219
277   Ibid., p.243
278   Ibid., p.229
279   Conway, *The Alps from End to End*, p.249
280   Evans, *The Conways*, pp.237 and 8
281   Conway, *Episodes in a Varied Life*, p.45
282   Newspaper cutting dated 15 June 1930, probably *The Times*
283   Hansard, 8 July 1919
284   Hansard, 29 March 1923
285   Hansard, 27 April 1923
286   Hansard, 23 June 1921
287   W. Churchill, *Thoughts and Adventures* (1932), quoted in R. Jenkins, *Churchill*, 2002 Pan Books ed. (London: Macmillan, 2001), p.389
288   Conway, *The Domain of Art*, p.68
289   Conway, *Episodes in a Varied Life*, p.148
290   Hansard, 27 March 1922
291   Hansard 17 February 1930
292   Conway, *Episodes in a Varied Life*, p.151
293   Hansard, 15 December 1927
294   Wickham Legg, ed., *Dictionary of National Biography*, p.191

295   Conway, *Mountain Memories*, p.151

296   Ibid., p.3

297   Conway, 'Some Reminiscences and Reflections of an Old Stager', p.148

298   Conway, *A Pilgrim's Quest for the Divine*, p.46

299   Conway, *The Crowd in Peace and War*, p.261

300   A. Huxley, *Point Counter Point*, 2004 Vintage ed. (London: Chatto & Windus, 1928), p.274

301   Conway, *Episodes in a Varied Life*, p.132

302   Ibid., p.133

303   W. M. Conway, *Palestine and Morocco: Lands of the Overlap* (London: Edward Arnold & Co., 1923), p.11

304   Ibid., p.74

305   W. M. Conway, *Art Treasures in Soviet Russia* (London: Edward Arnold & Co., 1925), p.62

306   Ibid., p.67

307   Ibid., p.23

308   Conway, *The Domain of Art*, p.47

309   *The Times*, 20 April 1937

310   Sotheby & Co. Catalogue, 31 Jan. 1951

311   W. M. Conway, unpublished manuscript entitled 'An Old Man's Last Idyll', dated *c.*1930, p.4 (CUL Y93)

312   Conway, *Episodes in a Varied Life*, p.124

313   Conway, 'A Flight Over the Pyrenees', p.325

314   Quoted in Evans, *The Conways*, p.249

315   Ibid., p.249

316   'Historical and Topographical Notes on Edom with an Account of the First Excavations at Petra', *GJ* LXXVI, no.5, Nov. 1930

317   Conway, 'An Old Man's Last Idyll', pp.35 and 47 (CUL Y/93)

318   Evans, *The Conways*, p.252

319   Conway, *Episodes in a Varied Life*, p.194

320   'Art and the Expert' by Lord Lee of Fareham, *The Times*, 27 Oct. 1930

321   *The Sketch*, 4 Nov. 1931

322   W. M. Conway, 'In The Days Of My Youth', *M.A.P.*, 13 Jan. 1900

323   Conway, *A Pilgrim's Quest for the Divine*, pp.8, 244, 251, 227, 253 and 255

324   'The Sculpture that Revealed an Aristocrat's Guilty Secret', *The Independent*, 18 April 2009

325   Wickham Legg, ed., *Dictionary of National Biography*, p.192

326   Coolidge, ed., *A Handbook for Travellers*, p.73

327   Conway, *The Alps from End to End*, p.253

328   See S. Beller, *A Concise History of Austria* (Cambridge University Press, 2006)

329   Quoted in Beller, *A Concise History of Austria*, p.142

330   Conway, 'Centrists and Excentrists', p.397

331   M. Macmillan, *Peacemakers. The Paris Conference of 1919 and its Attempt to End War* (London, 2002), p.289, quoted in Duggan, *The Force of Destiny*, p.613

332   Ibid., p.288

333   Conway, *The Alps from End to End*, p.265

334   Ibid., p.267

335   Ibid., p.367

336   Ibid., pp.270 and 271

337   See Ring, *How the English Made the Alps*

338   Conway, *The Alps from End to End*, p.267

339   Ibid., p.276

340   Ibid., p.278

341   Ibid., p.282

342   Ibid., p.288

343   Ibid., p.293

344   Ibid., p.298

345   Ruskin, *Praeterita and Dilecta*, p.136

346   Conway, *The Alps from End to End*, p.301

347   Ibid., p.308

348   Ibid., p.317

349   http://www.grossglockner.at/en/grossglockner/erstbesteigung-grossglockner.htm, accessed 30 Sept. 2011

350   Conway, *The Alps from End to End*, p.323

351   Ibid., p.330

352   Conway, *The Alps*, p.16

353   From Robert Louis Stevenson's essay 'El Dorado'

354   Conway, *The Alps from End to End*, p.9

355   Ibid., p.339

356   Ibid., p.340

357   W. M. Conway, *The Van Eycks and Their Followers* (London: John Murray, 1921), p.2

358   Galsworthy, *The Forsyte Saga*, p.421. The fictional character 'Young' Jolyon Forsyte was born in 1847 and died in 1920.

359   Conway, *The Crowd in Peace and War*, p.212

360   Obituary of Martin Conway, *GJ* XC, no. 1 (1937), p.94

361   P Stansky, *Victorian Studies* XIX, no. 4 (1976), p.467

362   Young, 'Mountain Prophets', p.112

363   M. Arnold, *Culture and Anarchy: An Essay in Political and Social Criticism*, 2009 Oxford ed. (London: 1869), p.viii

364   Quoted in R. W. Clark, *The Victorian Mountaineers* (London: B. T. Batsford, 1953), p.40

365   J. Berger, *Ways of Seeing*, 2008 Penguin ed. (London: BBC and Penguin Books, 1972), p.25

Bibliography

Archives

Alpine Club, Conway Correspondence
Cambridge University Library, Conway Papers
Courtauld Institute, Conway Correspondence
Imperial War Museum, Conway War Diaries
Royal Geographical Society, Conway Collection

Books by Martin Conway

W. M. Conway, *A Guide Book to the Pennine Alps from the Simplon to Arolla intended for the use of Mountaineers* (London: Edward Stanford, 1881)

W. M. Conway, *The Woodcutters of the Netherlands in the Fifteenth Century* (Cambridge University Press, 1884)

W. M. Conway, *The Artistic Development of Reynolds and Gainsborough* (London: Seeley & Co., 1886)

W. M. Conway, *Early Flemish Artists and Their Predecessors on the Lower Rhine* (London: Seeley & Co., 1887)

W. M. Conway, *The Literary Remains of Albrecht Dürer* (Cambridge University Press, 1889)

W. M. Conway, *The Dawn of Art in the Ancient World: An Archaeological Sketch* (London: Percival & Co., 1891)

C. T. Dent, W. M. Conway et al., *The Badminton Library of Sports and Pastimes: Mountaineering*, 2nd ed. (London: Longmans, Green, 1892)

W. M. Conway, *Climbing and Exploration in the Karakoram-Himalayas* (London: T. Fisher Unwin, 1894)

W. M. Conway et al., *Climbing in the Himalayas: Maps and Scientific Reports* (London: T. Fisher Unwin, 1894)

W. M. Conway, *The Alps From End to End*, Nelson ed. (London: Constable, 1895)

W. M. Conway, *The First Crossing of Spitsbergen* (London: J. M. Dent, 1897)

W. M. Conway, *With Ski and Sledge over Arctic Glaciers* (London: J. M. Dent, 1898)

W. M. Conway, *Climbing and Exploration in the Bolivian Andes* (London: Harper & Brothers, 1901)

W. M. Conway, *The Domain of Art*, 2010 BiblioBazaar ed. (London: John Murray, 1901)

W. M. Conway, *Early Tuscan Art from the 12th to the 15th Centuries* (London: Hurst and Blackett, 1902)

W. M. Conway, *Aconcagua and Tierra del Fuego: A Book of Climbing, Travel and Exploration* (London: Cassell, 1902)

W. M. Conway, *The Alps* (London: Adam and Charles Black, 1904)

W. M. Conway, *Great Masters 1400-1800: Reproductions in Photogravure from the Works of the Most Famous Painters* (London: Heinemann, 1904)

W. M. Conway, ed., *Early Dutch and English Voyages to Spitsbergen in the Seventeenth Century* (Hakluyt Society, 1904)

W. M. Conway, *No Man's Land: A History of Spitsbergen from its Discovery in 1596 to the Beginning of the Scientific Exploration of the Country* (Cambridge University Press, 1906)

W. M. Conway, 'Mountaineering', in *The Encyclopaedia of Sport* (London: Heinemann, 1911).

W. M. Conway, *The Sport of Collecting* (London: T. Fisher Unwin, 1914)

W. M. Conway, *The Crowd in Peace and War* (London: Longmans, Green and Co., 1915)

W. M. Conway, *Mountain Memories: A Pilgrimage of Romance* (London: Cassell, 1920)

W. M. Conway, *The Van Eycks and Their Followers* (London: John Murray, 1921)

W. M. Conway, *Palestine and Morocco: Lands of the Overlap* (London: Edward Arnold & Co., 1923)

W. M. Conway, *Art Treasures in Soviet Russia* (London: Edward Arnold & Co., 1925)

W. M. Conway, *Giorgione: A New Study of his Art as a Landscape Painter* (London: Ernest Benn, 1929)

W. M. Conway, *Episodes in a Varied Life* (London: Country Life, 1932)

W. M. Conway, *A Pilgrim's Quest for the Divine* (London: Frederick Muller, 1936)

Selected Articles by Martin Conway

W. M. Conway, 'Centrists and Excentrists', *Alpine Journal* 15 (1891)

W. M. Conway, 'Tyndall as a Mountaineer', *Westminster Gazette* (1893)

W. M. Conway, 'Climbing in the Karakorams', *Alpine Journal* 16 (1893)

W. M. Conway, 'The Crossing of the Hispar Pass', *Geographical Journal* I (1893)

W. M. Conway, 'Exploration in the Mustagh Mountains', *Geographical Journal* II (1893)

W. M. Conway, 'The Climbing of High Mountains', *Alpine Journal* 16 (1893)

W. M. Conway, 'MacCormick's Sketches in Kashmir and the Karakoram-Himalayas', *Alpine Journal* 17 (1894)

W. M. Conway, 'An Alpine Journal', *Contemporary Review* (1894)

W. M. Conway, 'Mountain-Falls', *Contemporary Review* (1894)

W. M. Conway, 'Spitzbergen', *Alpine Journal* 17 (1894)

W. M. Conway, 'The First Crossing of Spitsbergen', *Geographical Journal* IX, no. 4 (1897)

W. M. Conway, 'High Altitudes', *Alpine Journal* 19 (1898)

W. M. Conway, 'The Ascent of Yllimani', *Daily Chronicle*, 30 Sept. 1898

W. M. Conway, 'Explorations in the Bolivian Andes', *Geographical Journal*, no. 6 (1899)

W. M. Conway, 'Climbs in the Andes in 1898', *Alpine Journal* 19 (1899)

W. M. Conway, 'Climbs and Explorations in the Andes' (Paper presented at the Royal Institution of Great Britain, Weekly Meeting, 26 May 1899, London)

W. M. Conway, 'Aconcagua and the Volcanic Andes', *Harper's Magazine* (1899)

W. M. Conway, 'The Ascent of Illimani', *Harper's Magazine* (1899)

W. M. Conway, 'Climbing Mount Sorata', *Harper's Magazine* (1899)

W. M. Conway, 'The Southern Andes: An Orographical Sketch', *Alpine Journal* 20 (1900)

W. M. Conway, 'Mount Sarmiento', *Harper's Magazine* (1900)

W. M. Conway, 'Some of the Undeveloped Resources of Bolivia', *Journal of the Society of Arts* XLVIII, no. 2,463 (1900)

W. M. Conway and D. W. Freshfield, 'The Future of the Alpine Club', *Alpine Journal* 20 (1900)

W. M. Conway, 'The Romance of Mountaineering', *Strand Magazine* (1907)

Report of the Annual Meeting of the English Branch of the League for the Preservation of Swiss Scenery (1907)

Second Annual Report of the English Branch of the League for the Preservation of Swiss Scenery (1907)

W. M. Conway, 'Winter Sports in the Alps', *Pall Mall Magazine* (1910)

W. M. Conway, 'The Treasury of S. Maurice D'Agaune', *Burlington Magazine* (1912)

W. M. Conway, 'Tragedies and Heroisms among the Mountains', *The Quiver* (1914)

W. M. Conway, 'The Treasure Cities of Belgium', *Country Life* (1914)

W. M. Conway, 'The Joy of Winter Sports', *Country Life* (1914)

W. M. Conway, 'An Immortality of Shame', *Country Life* (1914)

W. M. Conway, 'The Abbey of St. Denis and its Ancient Treasures', *Archaeologia* 66 (1915)

W. M. Conway, 'Some Reminiscences and Reflections of an Old Stager', *Alpine Journal* 31 (1917)

W. M. Conway, 'A New Age', *Edinburgh Review*, April 1924

W. M. Conway, 'A Flight Over the Pyrenees', *Alpine Journal* 40 (1928)

W. M. Conway, 'Edward Fitzgerald 1871-1931', *Alpine Journal* 43 (1931)

Obituaries

C. G. Bruce, 'Obituary of Martin Conway', *Alpine Journal* 49 (1937)

C. Wilson, 'Obituary of Martin Conway', *Alpine Journal* 49 (1937)

F. Younghusband, 'Obituary of Lord Conway', *Nature*, 29 May (1937)

Bollettina della R. Societa Geografica LXXIV, no. VII (1937)

Geographical Journal XC, no. 1 (1937)

The Times, 21 April 1937

Biographies and Articles about Conway

J. Evans, *The Conways: A History of Three Generations* (London: Museum Press, 1966)

L. Grant, 'Time and the Conways: The Beginnings of Art History and the Collecting of Photographs in Britain', *Visual Resources* XIII (1998)

A. P. Harper, 'Fifty Years Ago', *Alpine Journal* 53 (1914)

K. E. Higgon, 'Persistence of Antiquity' (Paper presented at the Research Forum/Conway Library Project, 2005)

K. E. Higgon, 'Photography and Art History in the Nineteenth Century: Martin Conway and the Origins of the Conway Library' (MA, Courtauld Institute of Art, 2005)

P. Stansky, 'Art, Industry, and the Aspirations of William Martin Conway', *Victorian Studies* XIX, no. 4 (1976)

G. W. Young, 'Mountain Prophets', *Alpine Journal* 54 (1942)

Selected General References

M. Andrews, *Landscape and Western Art* (Oxford University Press, 1999)

A. Beattie, *The Alps: A Cultural History* (Oxford: Signal Books, 2006)

S. Beller, *A Concise History of Austria* (Cambridge University Press, 2006)

C. G. Bruce, *Himalayan Wanderer* (London: Alexander Maclehose & Co., 1934)

S. Calloway and L. F. Orr, eds., *The Cult of Beauty: The Aesthetic Movement 1860-1900* (London: V&A Publishing, 2011)

K. Clark, *Landscape Into Art* (London: John Murray, 1949)

R. W. Clark, *The Victorian Mountaineers* (London: B. T. Batsford, 1953)

R. W. Clark, *An Eccentric in the Alps: The Story of W. A. B. Coolidge, the Great Victorian Mountaineer* (London: Museum Press, 1959)

P. Coates, *Nature: Western Attitudes since Ancient Times* (Cambridge: Polity Press, 1998)

R. Colls and P. Dodd, eds., *Englishness: Politics and Culture 1880-1920* (Beckenham: Croom Helm, 1986)

W. A. B. Coolidge, 'The Pelvo D'Elva', *Alpine Journal* 15 (1891)

W. A. B. Coolidge, ed., *A Handbook for Travellers in Switzerland: Part I - Switzerland without the Pennine Alps*, 18th ed. (London: John Murray, 1892)

W. A. B. Coolidge, ed., *A Handbook for Travellers in Switzerland: Part II - The Alps of Savoy and Piedmont, the Italian Lakes and part of the Dauphine*, 18th ed. (London: John Murray, 1892)

W. A. B. Coolidge, *The Alps in Nature and History* (London: Methuen, 1908)

A. Crowley, *The Confessions of Aleister Crowley* (London: Mandrake Press, 1929)

F. Driver, *Geography Militant: Cultures of Exploration and Empire* (Oxford: Blackwell, 2001)

C. Duggan, *The Force of Destiny: A History of Italy Since 1796*, 2008 Penguin ed. (London: Allen Lane, 2007)

J. Duncan and D. Gregory, eds., *Writes of Passage: Reading Travel Writing* (London: Routledge, 1999)

O. Eckenstein, *The Karakorams and Kashmir: An Account of a Journey* (London: Fisher Unwin, 1896)

R. Ellis, *Vertical Margins: Mountaineering and the Landscapes of Neoimperialism* (Wisconsin: University of Wisconsin, 2001)

J. Elsner and J.-P. Rubies, eds., *Voyages and Visions: Towards a Cultural History of Travel* (London: Reaktion Books, 1999)

E. A. Fitzgerald, *The Highest Andes* (London: Methuen & Co., 1899)

J. D. Forbes, *Travels Through the Alps of Savoy*, 2nd ed. (Edinburgh: Adam and Charles Black, 1845)

P. French, *Younghusband: The Last Great Imperial Adventurer*, 1995 Flamingo ed. (London: Harper Collins, 1994)

D. W. Freshfield and W. L. J. Wharton, eds., *Hints for Travellers Scientific and General*, 7th ed.

Bibliography

(London: Royal Geographical Society, 1893)

E. Gosse, *Father and Son*, 2009 Oxford ed. (London: 1907)

A.V. L. Guise, *Six Years in Bolivia: The Adventures of a Mining Engineer* (New York: E. P. Dutton, 1922)

P. H. Hansen, 'British Mountaineering 1850-1914' (PhD, Harvard, 1991)

J. Harris, *Private Lives, Public Spirit: A Social History of Britain 1870-1914*, 1994 Penguin ed. (Oxford University Press, 1993)

R. Hattersley, *David Lloyd George: The Great Outsider* (London: Little, Brown, 2010)

K. T. Hoppen, *The Mid Victorian Generation: 1846-1886* (Oxford University Press, 1998)

R. Jenkins, *Churchill*, 2002 Pan Books ed. (London: Macmillan, 2001)

M. Isserman and S. Weaver, *Fallen Giants: A History of Himalayan Mountaineering from the Age of Empire to the Age of Extremes* (New Haven: Yale University Press, 2008)

M. Johnson, *Ideas of Landscape* (Oxford: Blackwell, 2007)

E.V. Lucas, *The Colvins and Their Friends* (London: Methuen & Co., 1928)

A. Lunn, *The Alps* (London: William Norgate, 1914)

A. Lunn, *Switzerland and the English* (London: Eyre & Spottiswoode, 1944)

A. Lunn, *A Century of Mountaineering 1857-1957* (London: George Allen & Unwin, 1957)

C. R. Markham, 'The Present Standpoint of Geography', *Geographical Journal* 2 (1893)

K. Mason, *Abode of Snow: A History of Himalayan Exploration and Mountaineering* (London: Rupert Hart-Davis, 1955)

K. Morgan, *Ramsay MacDonald* (London: Haus Publishing, 2006)

A. F. Mummery, *My Climbs in the Alps and Caucasus*, 2004 Ripping Yarns ed. (London: Fisher Unwin, 1895)

R. Overy, *The Morbid Age*, 2010 Penguin ed. (London: Allen Lane, 2009)

A. Perkins, *Baldwin* (London: Haus, 2006)

G. W. Prothero, *A Memoir of Henry Bradshaw* (London: Kegan Paul, Trench & Co., 1888)

M. Pugh, *We Danced All Night: A Social History of Britain between the Wars* (London: Vintage, 2008)

J. Ramsden, *A History of the Conservative Party: The Age of Balfour and Baldwin 1902-1940* (London: Longman, 1978)

J. Ring, *How the English Made the Alps* (London: John Murray, 2000)

J. Ruskin, *Praeterita and Dilecta*, 2005 Everyman ed. (London: George Allen, 1889)

S. Schama, *Landscape and Memory* (New York: Alfred A. Knopf, 1995)

G. R. Searle, *A New England? Peace and War 1886-1918* (Oxford University Press, 2004)

J. Steinberg, *Why Switzerland?* (Cambridge University Press, 1976)

L. Stephen, *The Playground of Europe*, 1936 Blackwell ed. (London: Longmans, Green, 1871)

L. Stephen, *Men, Books and Mountains: A Collection of Essays* (University of Minnesota Press, 1956)

S. Thompson, *Unjustifiable Risk? The Story of British Climbing* (Cumbria: Cicerone, 2010)

M. Twain, *A Tramp Abroad*, 1997 Penguin ed. (Hartford: American Publishing, 1880)

W. Unsworth, *Encyclopedia of Mountaineering*, 1977 Penguin ed. (London: Robert Hale, 1975)

W. Unsworth, *Hold the Heights: The Foundations of Mountaineering* (London: Hodder & Stoughton, 1993)

305

P. P. Viazzo, *Upland Communities: Environment, Population and Social Structure in the Alps Since the Sixteenth Century* (Cambridge University Press, 1989)

A. D. Wallace, *Walking, Literature, and English Culture* (Oxford University Press, 1993)

J. R. H. Weaver, ed., *Dictionary of National Biography*, vol. 1922-1930 (Oxford University Press, 1937)

L. G. Wickham Legg, ed., *Dictionary of National Biography* (Oxford University Press, 1949)

A. N. Wilson, *The Victorians* (London: Hutchinson, 2002)

J. Wylie, *Landscape* (Abingdon: Routledge, 2007)

M. Zurbriggen, *From the Alps to the Andes*, British Library ed. (London: T. Fisher Unwin, 1899)

Index

Index

Index

Index